# Trauma and Human ~~~~~~~

"Awareness of the political implications of trauma perpetration has grown so obscured among academics that in many quarters it has almost entirely faded from view. This volume is a sorely needed corrective, examining trauma through the lens of power and oppression. *Trauma and Human Rights* reveals that at its core interpersonal assault is not only a source of enduring psychological damage, but a violation of basic freedom and dignity as well."

—Steven N. Gold, *Ph.D., Director of Trauma Resolution & Integration Program and Professor at Center for Psychological Studies, Nova Southeastern University, USA*

"This important volume enhances readers' understanding of the forces and impact of human suffering by integrating the human rights framework and the trauma framework. An early chapter written by the editors is such a rich discussion of trauma and human rights and their intersection that it should be required reading for all social service and mental health professionals. As a whole, the book is an impressive addition to the literature and will encourage more effective practice across the micro-macro spectrum."

—Lynne M. Healy, *Ph.D., Board of Trustees Distinguished Professor Emerita, University of Connecticut, USA*

"The global movement to advance human rights is one of the great social hallmarks of the late twentieth and early twenty first Centuries. Despite egregious setbacks this remains the most important legal framework to advance human welfare and protection. Over the same period scientific understanding of the health impacts of exposure to catastrophic trauma has changed forever the understanding of human adversity. The authors have provided a seminal work that integrates these two frameworks in a masterful series of contributions that bring greater depth to the understanding of both. This should be essential reading for anyone interested in better understanding human rights and trauma."

—Zachary Steel, *Ph.D., St John of God Chair in Trauma and Mental Health, School of Psychiatry, University of New South Wales, Australia*

Lisa D. Butler · Filomena M. Critelli ·
Janice Carello
Editors

# Trauma and Human Rights

Integrating Approaches to Address Human
Suffering

Editors
Lisa D. Butler
School of Social Work
University at Buffalo
Buffalo, NY, USA

Filomena M. Critelli
School of Social Work
University at Buffalo
Buffalo, NY, USA

Janice Carello
Department of Social Work
Edinboro University
Edinboro, PA, USA

ISBN 978-3-030-16397-6     ISBN 978-3-030-16395-2   (eBook)
https://doi.org/10.1007/978-3-030-16395-2

This Palgrave Macmillan imprint is published by the registered company Springer Nature
Switzerland AG
The registered company address is: Gewerbestrasse 11, 6330 Cham, Switzerland

*We dedicate this book to the victims and survivors of traumatic events and human rights violations and to all those everywhere—students, instructors, researchers, human rights advocates, helping and human service professionals, health care providers, counselors, lawyers, ministers—whose efforts make such a difference.*

# Foreword

## (Re)Contextualizing Trauma-Informed and Human Rights Frameworks

Anyone who has worked in the field of trauma for a number of years is familiar with the cycle of contextualizing, decontextualizing, and then recontextualizing key ideas. For example, the concept of trauma itself has been understood in multiple contexts, ranging from those focused on its being "out of the ordinary range of human experience" to those emphasizing its nearly normative quality. *Decontextualizing* refers to the frequently reductive ways in which each of these understandings comes to be seen as standing on its own, regardless of the real-life contexts that attend traumatic events. De-contextualizing (literally) subtracts context. The challenge, then, comes with the task of *recontextualizing* traumatic experiences, putting them back into some kind of meaningful context that makes sense of them in a new way. For example, adding the idea of *potentially traumatic experience* to that of trauma itself adds a key understanding that offers a different context for trauma. It offers a reframing of trauma that shifts the very definition to a subjective one in which the trauma survivor is the expert with respect to their own experiences and is able to say when a potentially traumatic experience becomes an actual trauma as well.

Human rights frameworks have similar patterns, I am sure, though I am not as familiar with that field of study, so I don't know them as well. The editors and chapter authors of the current volume, though, have certainly made an impressive case for the intersection and, ultimately, the integration of trauma-informed and human rights-based approaches. I will argue in this foreword that the extent to which these two frameworks become integrated depends to a significant degree on the similarity and compatibility of their *cultures*. Similarity in culture in turn depends on the core values and principles of trauma-informed and human rights-based approaches.

When Maxine Harris and I first made the distinction between trauma-informed and trauma-specific levels of intervention, we had in mind a particular kind of relationship between these two types of models: that being *trauma-informed* would create a *context* for the effective implementation of *trauma-specific* services. As we developed these ideas further, we began to label our approach *creating cultures of trauma-informed care* (Fallot & Harris, 2009, 2011). Much of this work focused on the need for organizational transformation planted firmly on the core values of safety, trustworthiness, choice, collaboration, and empowerment (Fallot & Harris, 2008). Our earliest conceptualizations, though, were found wanting on a number of levels. First, we had clearly focused too much attention on the needs of individual trauma survivors. We referred to this as the "Basic Lesson" we learned from this first phase of our consultations.

> Staff members—*all* staff members—can create a setting of, and offer relationships characterized by, safety, trustworthiness, choice, collaboration, and empowerment *only* when they experience these same factors in the program as a whole. It is unrealistic to expect it to be otherwise. (Fallot, 2011, n.p.)

In other words, we had discovered that creating an organizational culture meant that this culture affected everyone in the organization, not just those people who receive services there. In this way, we learned that safety, trustworthiness, choice, collaboration, and empowerment need to characterize the relationships staff members have with each other and with the administration of the organization, as well as with clients.

The second part of our *recontextualizing* the idea of trauma-informed care was recognizing that culture could not, should not, be restricted or limited to a single organization. Not long after the publication of *Using Trauma Theory to Design Service Systems* (Harris & Fallot, 2001) we began to hear about other sites that were adopting *trauma-informed* approaches to their work. They ranged enormously in size and complexity, from school systems in Massachusetts and Washington State, to coalitions of mental health and/or substance abuse service providing organizations in Connecticut and South Carolina, to communities like Tarpon Springs, Florida, and parts of St. Louis, Missouri, to major cities like San Francisco and Philadelphia, to states like Oregon, Vermont, and Wisconsin. It is not surprising to many of us that such a range of places would decide to create a shared culture of trauma-informed care.

The third part of recontextualizing trauma-informed care is reaffirming the five core values that describe its culture. Safety, trustworthiness, choice, collaboration, and empowerment have proven themselves to be feasible and effective in a wide number of settings and with a wide range of participants. We have come to see these core values as virtually universal in all of the environments we have experienced. When the Federal Substance Abuse and Mental Health Services Administration (SAMHSA) decided to create its own trauma-informed care model it adapted these five core values (SAMHSA, 2014).

The core values are based on numerous interviews, informal group discussions, and one-on-one conversations with survivors of trauma and the staff members who work with them. Safety is the first value because it is the most fundamental to establishing a sense of security and protection. Avoiding retraumatization and traumatic memory triggers are key to developing a safe context. All five core values apply equally to client and staff. Trauma-informed care requires a transformation of culture: safety is as important to staff as it is to clients. Staff may experience, for instance, not only vicarious or secondary traumatization but may bring their own trauma histories to the workplace. Trustworthiness, as the second core value, requires the creation of a context and relationships that do not replicate prior experiences of betrayal. Transparency and honesty are corollaries of trustworthiness. They provide another antidote to the toxic effects of betrayal trauma. Choice, the next core value, is important because all trauma is forced on people; no one would choose it. Given choices, though, survivors and staff often come to recognize the centrality to well-being of freedom and control. Collaboration involves the leveling of hierarchy in relationships. This means people work *together* rather than one person or group doing something for or to another. Finally, for people who have experienced themselves as without power, empowerment is a top priority. When people have been exposed to disempowering relationships, either in childhood or adulthood, they often look to power to remedy this deficit. Acknowledging people's strengths and affirming their value as human beings are ways a trauma-informed culture embodies the importance of empowerment.

Human rights-based approaches claim a similar universality of core values, whether these core values are based on the documents themselves, such as the *United Nations Universal Declaration of Human Rights* or its subsequent expressions and covenants, or a distillation of these values as in the work of David K. Androff (2016; Chapter 12, this volume). Androff divides two main values, human dignity and nondiscrimination, into five principles. These are (1) human dignity and (re)humanization; (2) nondiscrimination and the historically and socially excluded; (3) participation and engagement; (4) transparency and truth-seeking, (5) accountability and human rights culture. Similarly, Kim, Berthold, and Critelli (Chapter 10, this volume) take Androff's five values of a human rights-based social work practice and lay them out in tandem with the five core values of trauma-informed care. Clearly, these represent attempts to integrate the two frameworks, a goal that seems at the heart of what the editors of this volume (Butler & Critelli, Chapter 2, this volume; Carello, Butler, & Critelli, Chapter 1, this volume) want to accomplish. This integrative task, though, rightly relies on the extent to which the two frameworks represent similar and compatible cultures, that is, the degree to which their core values are similar and compatible. A not unrelated issue is whether and how much the idea of trauma and the idea of human rights violation overlap.

Let us begin with this second issue first, i.e., the degree to which the idea of trauma in trauma-informed care is similar to that of human rights violations in rights-based approaches. Many of the authors of this current volume assume that these two ideas are very similar, in fact using them almost interchangeably. However, it is worth questioning this assumption a bit more rigorously, before assuming its truth. Trauma, as it is currently understood, involves a subjective state of feeling overwhelmed by a particular circumstance or set of circumstances. This is the distinction between a *potentially traumatic experience* and an actual trauma that I mentioned earlier. Further, and perhaps more importantly, though, is the fact that the two frameworks draw on such different bases of traumatic experiences. The human rights movement, based in the aftermath of the Holocaust and the United Nations' response to this event, sees trauma as emanating especially from large-scale intergroup or international conflicts including especially wars and civil conflicts. Trauma-informed care has, in contrast, relied more heavily on familial and community violence and abuse rather than the large-scale impact of wars. Trauma-informed care can certainly learn from the trauma associated with war to take into account such large-scale events, drawing on the human rights-based approach and expanding its own purview in relation to it. Similarly, perhaps it is possible for the human rights-based approach to take more seriously the traumatic impact of familial and community violence. Of course, it is essential not to overstate these differences. Many of the movements in the basic human rights framework—e.g., the women's movement (Critelli & McPherson, Chapter 7, this volume); the lesbian, gay, bisexual, transgender, questioning/queer, intersex, and two-spirit group (LGBTQI2S; Elze, Chapter 8, this volume), the indigenous people in this country (Weaver, Chapter 4, this volume); and the Black population in the United States (St. Vil & St. Vil, Chapter 5, this volume)—all have inflated rates of abuse in childhood in the family and community settings. So, in many of these *human rights violations*, there are indications of trauma as it is understood in the trauma-informed care approach. Conversely, there are indicators of trauma like adverse childhood experiences that amount to human rights violations (e.g., of degrading treatment or of treatment that makes it impossible for an individual to achieve their maximum well-being) in the rights-based world. For example, children around the world are frequently subjected to such violations (Wolf, Prabhu, & Carello, Chapter 6, this volume). Older people, as well, especially those near the end of life, are vulnerable to retraumatization when their rights are violated (McGinley & Waldrop, Chapter 11, this volume).

As we have done with the definitions of trauma, so can we do with the sources of trauma, though the sources are largely different in the two frameworks, with the trauma model focusing more on the realms of the family and community while the human rights model emphasizes the larger stage of international conflict. In addition, the requirement that the human rights violation be caused by humans is also a narrow construction of the joint field's reality. Most major natural disasters that affect humans are not caused by humans. Tsunamis, hurricanes, tornadoes, mud slides, droughts are just a few of these. But they are clearly potentially traumatic events for the people who experience them (see also Butler & Critelli, Chapter 2, this volume). As with our findings about the definitions of trauma, though, we summarize by pointing out the large areas of overlap in the midst of this diversity. Overlapping sources of trauma and human rights violations include the full range of childhood and adulthood abuses and exposure to violence (whether experienced individually or as a member of a group).

In conclusion, then, we return to the opening ideas about context, and we are left to wonder whether trauma-informed care and human rights-based approaches might serve as a mutual context for each other. Trauma-informed care could benefit from having a dialogic partner that largely shares its most central values and yet carries enough differences to be distinctive in its approach. Human rights-based workers could also benefit from having a partner that, while similar in core values, is more focused on the "hows" of their shared commitments. Though the two frameworks draw on somewhat distinct understandings of trauma, they have a large enough overlap to sustain a dialogue and, similarly, there is enough overlap in the presumed sources of trauma to contribute to a meaningful conversation.

Further, one could posit a level of mutuality that extends to the central value of a human rights-based culture: accountability. By creating cultures of *mutual accountability*, the two models offer a unique perspective, one that draws on both the mutuality of trauma-informed care and the accountability of the human rights-based system. In leveling the hierarchy in this way, the two approaches become more like partners in the initiatives on which they might share perspectives. Rather than one group holding the other "accountable" (an approach that gives one group more power and authority than the other), this approach assigns equal authority to the two groups and expects each of them to hold themselves and the other group accountable for meeting the goals of the project, goals which were themselves set mutually.

The idea for this context of mutual accountability lies in its origins in the works of those who have advocated for trauma-informed care and for a human rights-based approach. It calls for a new generation of workers who are dedicated to these two frameworks and who are willing to be advocates for both of them simultaneously.

North Haven, Connecticut                    Roger D. Fallot, Ph.D.
January 2019

## REFERENCES

Androff, D. K. (2016). *Practicing rights: Human rights-based approaches to social work practice*. New York, NY: Routledge.

Fallot, R. D. (2011). Trauma-informed care: A values-based context for psychosocial empowerment. *Community Connections*. Retrieved from http://www.nationalacademies.org/hmd/~/media/405DC4EE98E946B692A-7391DE7FC106B.ashx.

Fallot, R. D., & Harris, M. (2008). Trauma-informed services. In G. Reyes, J. D. Elhai, & J. D. Ford (Eds.), *The encyclopedia of psychological trauma* (pp. 660–662). Hoboken, NJ: John Wiley.

Fallot, R. D., & Harris, M. (2009). Creating cultures of trauma-informed care (CCTIC): A self-assessment and planning protocol. *Community Connections*. Retrieved from https://www.theannainstitute.org/CCTICSELFASSPP.pdf.

Fallot, R. D., & Harris, M. (2011). Creating cultures of trauma-informed care (CCTIC): A self-assessment and planning protocol. *Community Connections*. Retrieved from https://www.researchgate.net/publication/242476080_Creating_Cultures_of_Trauma-Informed_Care_CCTIC_A_Self-Assessment_and_Planning_Protocol_Community_Connections_Washington_DC.

Harris, M., & Fallot, R. D. (Eds.). (2001). *Using trauma theory to design service systems*. San Francisco, CA: Jossey-Bass.

Substance Abuse and Mental Health Services Administration. (2014). *SAMHSA's concept of trauma and guidance for a trauma-informed approach*. Rockville, MD: Author. Retrieved from https://store.samhsa.gov/system/files/sma14-4884.pdf.

**Roger D. Fallot, Ph.D.** former Director of Research and Evaluation, Community Connections; Clinical Faculty, Department of Psychiatry, Yale University. Dr. Fallot co-edited (with Maxine Harris, Ph.D.) the seminal volume on trauma-informed care and currently works as a consultant on trauma and trauma-informed care.

# CONTENTS

# NOTES ON CONTRIBUTORS

**David K. Androff, MSW, Ph.D.** is Associate Professor in the School of Social Work at Arizona State University in Phoenix, AZ, USA. He has published widely on human rights and Truth and Reconciliation Commissions.

**S. Megan Berthold, Ph.D., LCSW** is Associate Professor and Director of Field Education at University of Connecticut School of Social Work in Hartford, CT, USA. Since the mid-1980s she has provided clinical and forensic services and conducted research with diverse refugee and asylum seeking trauma survivors. She has published widely on her work, including from a human rights perspective.

**Sandra L. Bloom, M.D.** is a Board-Certified psychiatrist, graduate of Temple University School of Medicine, Past-President of the International Society for Traumatic Stress Studies, and currently Associate Professor, Health Management and Policy at the Dornsife School of Public Health, Drexel University in Philadelphia, PA, USA, and Co-Chair of the Campaign for Trauma-Informed Policy and Practice.

**Elizabeth A. Bowen, Ph.D.** is Assistant Professor in the School of Social Work at the University at Buffalo, in Buffalo, New York, USA. She earned her Ph.D. from the University of Illinois at Chicago Jane Addams College of Social Work. Her work addresses the intersection of homelessness, health issues, and social policy.

**Amanda Brylinski-Jackson** is a MSW candidate in the School of Social Work at the University at Buffalo, in Buffalo, NY, USA, with a specific focus on trauma-informed practice and human rights perspective. She obtained her B.A. in Sociology at Nazareth College of Rochester, NY and works as a direct service professional at a local not-for-profit.

**Lisa D. Butler, Ph.D.** is Associate Professor in the School of Social Work at the University at Buffalo, in Buffalo, NY, USA. She is a psychologist and has published widely on aspects of psychological trauma and most recently on trauma-informed care with respect to mental health, trauma-informed educational practice, and self-care.

**Janice Carello, LMSW, Ph.D.** is Assistant Professor in the Department of Social Work at Edinboro University, in Edinboro, PA, USA. Her research and advocacy focus on retraumatization in educational settings and on bringing a trauma-informed approach to higher education.

**Filomena M. Critelli, Ph.D.** is Associate Professor and the Co-Director of the Institute for Sustainable Global Engagement in the School of Social Work at the University at Buffalo, in Buffalo, NY, USA. Her research focuses on human rights, gender-based violence, and issues related to global migration.

**Diane E. Elze, Ph.D.** is Associate Professor and Director of the MSW Program at the University at Buffalo School of Social Work in Buffalo, NY, USA. Her research focuses on health risk behaviors, and risk and protective factors, among LGBTQ youth and queer-affirmative service delivery.

**Shirley Gatenio Gabel, Ph.D.** is Professor at Fordham University's Graduate School of Social Service in New York City, NY, USA. Her research focuses on human rights and social policies, particularly those affecting children. She is Co-Editor of the *Journal on Human Rights and Social Work* and represents the International Association of Schools of Social Work at the United Nations.

**Isok Kim, Ph.D., LCSW** is Associate Professor in the School of Social Work at the University at Buffalo, in Buffalo, NY, USA. His current research focuses on implementing cultural humility practice within inter-professional health education settings, with special emphasis of trauma and mental health among immigrant and refugee clients.

**Jacqueline McGinley, LMSW, Ph.D.** recently completed the doctoral program in the School of Social Work at the University at Buffalo, in Buffalo, NY, USA. Her research focuses on policies and practices for vulnerable populations, including people with disabilities, who are nearing life's end.

**Jane McPherson, Ph.D., LCSW** is Director of Global Engagement and Assistant Professor at the University of Georgia's School of Social Work in Athens, GA, USA. Her scholarship views social work through a human rights lens, and she has developed measures to investigate and promote rights-based social work practice that have been translated into Chinese, Spanish, Portuguese, Albanian, and others.

**Nadine Shaanta Murshid, Ph.D.** is Assistant Professor in the School of Social Work at the University at Buffalo, in Buffalo, NY, USA. She completed her Ph.D. in Social Work from Rutgers University and Masters in Public Policy from Australian National University. Her research interests and include institutions, structural sources of violence, social policy, health disparities, microfinance participation among women in Bangladesh, and mobile financial services for migrant workers.

**Shraddha Prabhu, Ph.D.** is Assistant Professor in the Department of Social Work at Edinboro University, in Edinboro, PA, USA. Her research, scholarship and practice focuses on issues related to child protection and trauma and resilience among at-risk youth.

**Christopher St. Vil, Ph.D., MSW** is Assistant Professor at the University at Buffalo School of Social Work in Buffalo, NY, USA. Dr. St. Vil's current research focuses on trauma and the experiences of male victims of violent injury as well as cross-age peer mentoring.

**Noelle M. St. Vil, Ph.D.** is Assistant Professor in the School of Social Work at the University at Buffalo, in Buffalo, NY, USA. Her research focuses on black male-female relationships, including the impact of structural racism on these relationships, intimate partner violence, sexually transmitted infections and relationship typologies (monogamous, consensual nonmonogamy and nonconsensual nonmonogamy).

**Éva Szeli, Ph.D., JD** is Senior Lecturer in Psychology at Arizona State University, in Tempe AZ, USA. She has also taught courses in mental disability law, co-authored the first casebook in international human rights and mental disability law, and worked with non-governmental organizations on mental disability rights in post-Soviet Central and Eastern Europe.

**Deborah Waldrop, Ph.D., LMSW** is Professor and Associate Dean for Faculty Development in the School of Social Work at the University at Buffalo, in Buffalo, NY, USA. Her research focuses on aging, end-of-life care and decision-making about goals and preferences in serious illness.

**Hilary N. Weaver, DSW (Lakota)** is Professor and Associate Dean for Academic Affairs in the School of Social Work at the University at Buffalo, in Buffalo, NY, USA. Her work focuses on cultural issues in the helping process with an emphasis on Indigenous populations. Dr. Weaver has presented her work regionally, nationally, and internationally including presenting at the Permanent Forum on Indigenous Issues at the United Nations in 2005–2008 and 2013–2018.

**Molly R. Wolf, LMSW, Ph.D.** is Associate Professor in the Department of Social Work at Edinboro University, in Edinboro, PA, USA. Her research and social work practice focuses on survivors of child sexual abuse, trauma, and trauma-informed care.

# LIST OF TABLES

# CHAPTER 1

# Introduction to *Trauma and Human Rights*: Context and Content

*Janice Carello, Lisa D. Butler, and Filomena M. Critelli*

The impulse to save the world is both grandiose and mundane. Odds are, as a person reading this book, you are someone who strives to make a positive difference in the world and to do what you can to help alleviate human suffering. It is obviously unrealistic to believe that we, as individuals, possess the power to save the world, but it is fatalistic—for ourselves and our species—to believe that we, as individuals, are powerless. Needless to say, humans are capable of committing atrocities. This book will not disconfirm that fact. Hopefully, though, it will reaffirm what is also true but seems hard to discern sometimes: that humans are capable of great compassion and that they can and do accomplish remarkable things when they work collaboratively.

J. Carello (✉)
Department of Social Work, Edinboro University, Edinboro, PA, USA
e-mail: jcarello@edinboro.edu

L. D. Butler · F. M. Critelli
School of Social Work, University at Buffalo, Buffalo, NY, USA
e-mail: ldbutler@buffalo.edu

F. M. Critelli
e-mail: fmc8@buffalo.edu

© The Author(s) 2019
L. D. Butler et al. (eds.), *Trauma and Human Rights*,
https://doi.org/10.1007/978-3-030-16395-2_1

In her seminal text, *Trauma and Recovery*, Judith Herman (1997) observed:

> Psychological trauma is an affliction of the powerless. At the moment of trauma, the victim is rendered helpless by overwhelming force. When the force is that of nature, we speak of disasters. When the force is that of other human beings, we speak of atrocities. Traumatic events overwhelm the ordinary systems of care that give people a sense of control, connection, and meaning. (p. 33)

In many ways, the wellspring of the twentieth-century movements to delineate and affirm universal human rights and to grasp and remedy the lingering effects of traumatic experience has been the compassion of those deeply unsettled by the suffering they saw throughout much of that and previous centuries. Emergent understandings of the causes and consequences of warfare, colonial expansion, tribalism, bigotry, and oppressive social conditions—and of the suffering they create—amplified these traditions into separate frameworks: the *human rights framework* and the *trauma framework*. As described in Chapter 2 (Butler & Critelli, this volume), the human rights framework codifies the conditions necessary to promote and ensure dignity, fairness, respect, diversity, and equality among humans, while the trauma framework offers a vocabulary and methodology for describing aspects of human suffering and approaches to intervene in that suffering. More recent observations by those intervening with victims of trauma have prompted a paradigm shift in the general approach to treatment of trauma-related conditions, that being: *trauma-informed care* (TIC; Harris & Fallot, 2001) and principles to guide its implementation (Fallot & Harris, 2009). This volume seeks to weave these three conceptual strands into a fabric of understanding that can help to illuminate and inform professional approaches with a variety of populations and across multiple settings and levels of practice.

In the first sections of the present chapter, we introduce the concepts of the trauma and human rights (THR) frameworks and then trace the origins of TIC for readers who may be unfamiliar with the concept or the movement toward integration of trauma-informed approaches in behavioral health, child welfare, and educational settings. Following that, we describe the book's origins as background for the chapters that follow by introducing the context in which the book was conceived. These sections are followed by a description of how the book is organized and the book's goals.

## TRAUMA-INFORMED CARE:
## AT THE INTERSECTION OF TRAUMA AND HUMAN RIGHTS

As Becker-Blease (2017) points out, "the term *trauma-informed* is trending" (p. 131). A quick Google search will produce millions of results. Despite the growing popularity of the term, however, many people—including trauma educators, researchers, and therapists—have not developed a clear understanding of what it means to be trauma-informed and often conflate TIC with trauma-specific services. To be *trauma-informed* in any context means to understand the ways in which violence, victimization, and other forms of trauma have affected individuals, families, and communities, and also to *use that understanding* to implement practices and policies that seek to prevent further harm and to promote healing and recovery (Harris & Fallot, 2001). In other words, TIC means accommodating individual trauma through changes in approach at both the client and the system levels.

It is important to remember that *TIC* differs from *trauma-specific services* in that the former refers to direct service and an organizational change process built on a set of principles (Bowen & Murshid, 2016), while the latter refers to individual and group interventions designed to directly treat symptoms and syndromes resulting from trauma exposure (Harris & Fallot, 2001). Examples of trauma-specific services include trauma-focused cognitive behavioral therapy (TF-CBT; Cohen, Mannarino, & Deblinger, 2006), cognitive processing therapy (CPT; APA, 2017), eye-movement desensitization reprocessing (EMDR; Shapiro, 1995), Progressive Counting (Greenwald, 2013), and Seeking Safety (Najavits, 2002). An organization can, therefore, be trauma-informed without providing trauma-specific services; likewise, an organization can provide trauma-specific services without being trauma-informed.

It is also important to remember that trauma-informed approaches were developed as an alternative to coercive medical models of service provision (Harris & Fallot, 2001); Lewis, Kusmaul, Elze, & Butler, 2016). These alternative models began to emerge in the late 1990s in response to the growing awareness of the prevalence and impact of trauma among consumers of behavioral health services. Sandra Bloom's (1997) *Creating Sanctuary: Toward the Evolution of Sane Societies* explored the intergenerational effects of trauma on individuals and institutions and compelled us to start thinking about trauma as a public health issue. Maxine Harris and Roger Fallot's (2001) seminal text,

*Using Trauma Theory to Design Service Systems*, provided an argument for and concrete examples of how to integrate trauma theory into assessment and treatment policies and practices in order to avoid unintentional reproduction of abusive relationship dynamics that often bring individuals into treatment in the first place.

Around the same time that Harris and Fallot coined the term *trauma-informed* and Bloom began building the Sanctuary Model, the first findings of the groundbreaking Adverse Childhood Experiences (ACE) Study were published (Felitti et al., 1998), establishing links between childhood trauma and long-term social, emotional, and health problems in adulthood. The ACE Study also provided evidence that adverse experiences in childhood are not uncommon, as was widely believed. Another influential study from around the same time was the Women, Co-Occurring Disorders and Violence Study and Children's Subset Study, which was sponsored by the Substance Abuse and Mental Health Services Administration (SAMHSA, 2007). The study implemented and evaluated numerous programs designed to help women and their children recover from mental health and substance-use disorders.

Findings from studies such as these, combined with advocacy efforts by individuals such as Ann Jennings (http://www.theannainstitute.org/), helped spark federal- and state-level trauma-informed policy and practice initiatives in child welfare systems and K-12 schools, such as the National Center for Trauma and Trauma-Informed Care (NCTIC), the Trauma and Learning Policy Initiative (https://traumasensitiveschools.org/), and Trauma-Informed Oregon (https://traumainformedoregon.org/). Networks such as The National Child Traumatic Stress Network (https://www.nctsn.org/) and ACEs Connection (https://www.aces-connection.com/) were also created to link service providers, parents, educators, researchers, and individuals to one another and to information and resources related to trauma and TIC.

## About This Book

### *Origins*

In response to the developing understanding of the impact of trauma, Courtois and Gold (2009) called for the inclusion of trauma in clinical training programs. Under the leadership of Dean Nancy J. Smyth, the

University at Buffalo School of Social Work (UBSSW) faculty began infusing a trauma-informed, human rights-based (TI-HR) perspective throughout the Master of Social Work (MSW) program in 2009. As articulated on the UBSSW website (http://socialwork.buffalo.edu/about/trauma-informed-human-rights-perspective.html), this perspective embodies social work values in its commitment to training students to understand the widespread prevalence and impact of trauma on individuals, families, and communities and to use that understanding to promote social and economic justice at the micro-, mezzo-, and macro-levels. The UBSSW was ideally positioned for this innovation given its longstanding educational training focus on trauma, including the creation of a trauma counseling certificate program in 2000 and the development of the inSocialWork Podcast Series (http://www.insocialwork.org) in 2008, which features an entire series on trauma and TIC as well as a number of podcasts addressing human rights issues.

The TI-HR transformation began with several years of discussions among stakeholders and culminated in an application to the school's national accrediting body, the Council on Social Work Education (CSWE), to approve this alternative curriculum. In addition to the project proposal, the alternative reaffirmation project involved updating all course syllabi and content to reflect the refined focus; integrating a new required advanced year course: *Perspectives on Trauma and Human Rights: Contemporary Theory, Research, Practice, and Policy*; enhancing collaborations with field settings; and launching an online "Self-Care Starter Kit" (https://socialwork.buffalo.edu/resources/self-care-starter-kit.html; Butler & McClain-Meeder, 2015).

Research and assessments were also conducted as part of the transformation effort. These have been used for programmatic improvement and have also resulted in several publications and presentations, including those examining the implementation of a TI-HR perspective in course and field curriculum (e.g., Lewis et al., 2016; Richards-Desai, Critelli, Logan-Greene, Borngraber, & Heagle, 2018; Wilson & Nochajski, 2016) and applications to other settings (e.g., Butler, Critelli, & Rinfrette, 2011; Butler & Wolf, 2009; Carello & Butler, 2014, 2015); those exploring TIC among our community agency partners (Wolf, Green, Nochajski, Mendel, & Kusmaul, 2013); those investigating stress, trauma, and self-care among students in clinical training (e.g., Butler, Carello, & Maguin, 2017; Butler, Maguin, & Carello, 2018; Butler, Mercer, McClain-Meeder, Horne, & Dudley, 2019), and others.

Another significant and concurrent development was the creation of the Institute on Trauma and Trauma-Informed Care (ITTIC; http://www.socialwork.buffalo.edu/research/ittic/), which is affiliated with and directed by two UBSSW faculty members. The institute provides research and training for community organizations concerning trauma and TIC, and it offers evaluation, trauma-specific treatment interventions, training, technical assistance, and consultation.

We, the book's co-editors, met through our connection with the UBSSW. Lisa D. Butler joined the faculty at the beginning of the reaccreditation process in 2009 and became a member of both the TI-HR project team and the ITTIC advisory board. As part of that effort, she spearheaded the development of the school's self-care webpages and has since been conducting research on self-care and trauma exposure in clinical training and other trauma-related topics. Filomena Critelli has been a faculty member of the UBSSW since 2005. She is also co-director of the Institute for Sustainable Global Engagement. Her research and advocacy focus on the rights of women and children, including immigrants and refugees, in both domestic and international contexts. Janice Carello was a student in the UBSSW MSW program as the school began to implement this new curriculum. Her innovative application of TI principles to educational practice in an assignment in the THR class inspired her to become a researcher and to develop an investigative focus on retraumatization in educational settings and to advocate for trauma-informed approaches in higher education. All three of us currently teach a section of the THR course, and we have worked together on prior trauma-related research projects and publications. This book represents the outgrowth of our collaboration.

### Organization

Following this introductory chapter, we present the conceptual foundation for the book: Chapter 2 (Butler & Critelli) provides a brief history of the THR frameworks individually and then elucidates the ways in which, when considered together, they enhance our understanding of individual and collective human suffering and the means to alleviate them. Chapter 3 (Bowen, Murshid, Gatenio-Gabel, & Brylinski-Jackson) illustrates the application of a trauma-informed and human rights framework to policy practice. Chapters 4 through 11 explore the occurrence and intersection of traumatic events and human rights violations among specific populations, including Native Americans (Weaver, Chapter 4); African-Americans (St. Vil & St. Vil, Chapter 5); children (Wolf, Prabhu,

& Carello, Chapter 6); women (Critelli & McPherson, Chapter 7); lesbian, gay, bisexual, and transgender individuals (Elze, Chapter 8); individuals with mental disabilities (Szeli, Chapter 9); refugees and asylum seekers (Kim, Berthold, & Critelli, Chapter 10); and older adults (McGinley & Waldrop, Chapter 11). The book concludes with exploration of the use of truth and reconciliation commissions in helping communities recover from THR abuses (Androff, Chapter 12), and thoughtful, historical and personal reflections on the progress made (and still needed) in conceptions of THR (Bloom, Chapter 13, Afterword).

To help ensure consistency in these chapters and attention to the overarching framework for the book, we invited authors to consider the following questions in relation to the issue or population they were addressing in their chapters: What are the specific human rights issues involved? What are the potential trauma issues or adverse life experiences for your population? What would a trauma-informed approach to working with this population look like? How do these frameworks intersect/relate to each other within the issue or population you are discussing? And: What are the resilience factors that should be supported or strengthened in working with these groups or communities? Authors approached their chapters and addressed these questions in a variety of ways: some focused more on trauma, some more on human rights, some more on TIC, and some balanced all three.

As we expected, several significant, crosscutting themes surface in most or all of these chapters: the pervasiveness of historical population-level traumatic episodes and eras and of state-sanctioned violence and human rights violations; the necessity for evolving conceptions of traumatic experience, human rights, and TIC as refined and defined within specific populations; the tensions between those who seek to enlarge the purview of these constructs and those committed to limit or diminish them; the value for professionals of employing the THR frameworks *together*; the importance of civil and political movements to secure human rights and redress individual and collective trauma; and the urgency to continue in these efforts.

## Goals

One of the challenges educators face when teaching THR is that many students are micro-oriented and have trouble understanding how philosophical discussions about THR pertain to their work with clients. It is our hope that each chapter provides sufficient information and examples to help readers better understand the relationship between individuals and systems and better apply the concepts and principles being presented to their own practice experiences.

Another challenge we have each faced as educators in the THR course is that students can feel overwhelmed and powerless in the face of learning about so much suffering in the world. This is a normal response, especially for new practitioners. In the course, we integrate readings and assignments on self-care, vicarious traumatization, secondary traumatic stress, and burnout to help educate students and to mitigate these responses. Additionally, we assign a professional education development project to help students understand that their actions do make a difference and to channel their energy into developing educational materials they can share with others to encourage them to take that one next step toward becoming more THR informed (see, e.g., Virag & Taylor, 2016 and Walkowski, 2017).

Lastly, it is difficult to find scholarship that integrates both THR perspectives for the various populations with which students-in-training and professionals practice. So one of our main hopes for this book is to provide a resource to help students, educators, helping professionals, activists, researchers, and others take that one next step toward developing and implementing a more trauma-informed and human rights perspective in their work.

Herman (1997) observed that, when terrified, individuals call out to others, hoping to be comforted and protected, and if their cries for help go unanswered, they feel abandoned and disconnected from systems of care that keep them alive and give their lives meaning. As we conclude this introduction, we would like to extend our deepest gratitude to you, our readers, and also to our many collaborators—including chapter authors, colleagues, friends, and family members—for all that you do to heed these calls and to help restore hope and connection to others who feel alienated or alone. Your work—our work together—truly does make a difference.

## REFERENCES

American Psychological Association. (2017). *Clinical practice guideline for the treatment of PTSD*. Washington, DC: American Psychological Association. Retrieved from https://www.apa.org/ptsd-guideline/treatments/cognitive-processing-therapy.

Becker-Blease, K. A. (2017). As the world becomes trauma-informed, work to do. *Journal of Trauma & Dissociation, 18*(2), 131–138.

Bloom, S. L. (1997). *Creating sanctuary: Toward the evolution of sane societies.* New York, NY: Routledge.

Bowen, E. A., & Murshid, N. S. (2016). Trauma-informed social policy: A conceptual framework for policy analysis and advocacy. *Perspectives from the Social Sciences, 106*(2), 223–229.

Butler, L. D., Carello, J., & Maguin, E. (2017). Trauma, stress, and self-care in clinical training: Predictors of burnout, decline in health status, secondary traumatic stress symptoms, and compassion satisfaction. *Psychological Trauma: Theory, Research, Practice, and Policy, 9*(4), 416–424.

Butler, L. D., Critelli, F. M., & Rinfrette, E. S. (2011). Trauma-informed care and mental health. *Directions in Psychiatry, 31,* 197–210.

Butler, L. D., Maguin, E., & Carello, J. (2018). Retraumatization mediates the effect of adverse childhood experiences on clinical training-related secondary traumatic stress symptoms. *Journal of Trauma & Dissociation, 19*(1), 25–38.

Butler, L. D., & McClain-Meeder, K. (2015). *Self-care starter kit.* Retrieved from https://socialwork.buffalo.edu/resources/self-care-starter-kit.html.

Butler, L. D., Mercer, K. A., McClain-Meeder, K., Horne, D. M., & Dudley, M. (2019). Six domains of self-care: Attending to the whole person. *Human Behavior in the Social Environment, 29*(1), 107–124.

Butler, L. D., & Wolf, M. R. (2009). Trauma-informed care: Trauma as an organizing principle in the provision of mental health and social services. *Trauma Psychology Newsletter, 4*(3), 7–8.

Carello, J., & Butler, L. D. (2014). Potentially perilous pedagogies: Teaching trauma is not the same as trauma-informed teaching. *Journal of Trauma & Dissociation, 15*(2), 153–168.

Carello, J., & Butler, L. D. (2015). Practicing what we teach: Trauma-informed educational practice. *Journal of Teaching in Social Work, 35*(3), 262–278.

Cohen, J. A., Mannarino, A. P., & Deblinger, E. (2006). *Treating trauma and traumatic grief in children and adolescents.* New York, NY: Guilford Press.

Courtois, C. A., & Gold, S. N. (2009). The need for inclusion of psychological trauma in the professional curriculum: A call to action. *Psychological Trauma: Theory, Research, Practice and Policy, 1*(1), 3–23.

Fallot, R. D., & Harris, M. (2009). *Creating cultures of trauma-informed care (CCTIC): A self-assessment and planning protocol.* Washington, DC: Community Connections. Retrieved from https://traumainformedoregon.org/wp-content/uploads/2014/10/CCTIC-A-Self-Assessment-and-Planning-Protocol.pdf.

Felitti, V. J., Anda, R. F., Norenberg, D., Williamson, D. F. Spitz, A. M., Edwards, V., ... Marks, J. S. (1998). Relationship of childhood abuse and household dysfunction to many of the leading causes of death in adults: The Adverse Childhood Experiences (ACE) study. *American Journal of Preventative Medicine, 14*(4), 245–258.

Greenwald, R. (2013). *Progressive counting within a phase model of trauma-informed treatment.* New York, NY: Routledge.

Harris, M., & Fallot, R. D. (Eds.). (2001). *Using trauma theory to design service systems.* San Francisco, CA: Jossey-Bass.

Herman, J. L. (1997). *Trauma and recovery: The aftermath of violence—From domestic abuse to political terror.* New York, NY: Basic Books.

Lewis, L. A., Kusmaul, N., Elze, D., & Butler, L. D. (2016). The role of field education in a university–community partnership aimed at curriculum transformation. *Journal of Social Work Education, 52*(2), 186–197.

Najavits, L. M. (2002). *Seeking safety: A treatment manual for PTSD and substance abuse.* New York, NY: Guilford.

Richards-Desai, S., Critelli, F., Logan-Greene, P., Borngraber, E., & Heagle, E. (2018). Creating a human rights culture in a master's in social work program. *Journal of Human Rights and Social Work.* Advance Online Publication. https://link.springer.com/article/10.1007%2Fs41134-018-0059-2.

Shapiro, F. (1995). *Eye movement desensitization and reprocessing: Basic principles, protocols and procedures.* New York, NY: Guilford Press.

Substance Abuse and Mental Health Services Administration (SAMHSA). (2007). *The women, co-occurring disorders and violence study and children's subset study: Program summary.* Rockville, MD: Substance Abuse and Mental Health Services Administration.

Virag, N., & Taylor, R. (2016, December 6). *Trauma PSA.* Retrieved from https://www.youtube.com/watch?v=fHdWWFkRE-Y.

Walkowski, D. (2017, July 15). *10 for TIC: Preserving human dignity @ a homeless shelter.* Retrieved from https://www.youtube.com/watch?v=sdUQEO-A88F0&feature=youtu.be.

Wilson, B., & Nochajski, T. H. (2016). Evaluating the impact of trauma-informed care (TIC) perspective in social work curriculum. *Social Work Education, 35*(5), 589–602.

Wolf, M. R., Green, S. A., Nochajski, T. H., Mendel, W. E., & Kusmaul, N. S. (2013). 'We're civil servants': The status of trauma-informed care in the community. *Journal of Social Service Research, 40*(1), 111–120.

# CHAPTER 2

# Traumatic Experience, Human Rights Violations, and Their Intersection

*Lisa D. Butler and Filomena M. Critelli*

The world is rife, these days, with reports of human rights (HRs) abuses and traumatic events, often comingled in victims' experiences. Almost daily we hear national and international accounts of natural disaster, political violence and displacement, personal violence and retribution, and persecution. Many of these reports involve significant violations of basic HRs, yet they are rarely framed in those terms in the American media. Indeed, in the USA, catastrophic events tend to be described (and understood) from the individual-focused referential frame inherent in the trauma model (which includes the diagnostic category of post-traumatic stress disorder [PTSD; American Psychological Association [APA], 2013]) that is the primary basis of trauma work in psychiatry, psychology, social work, and the sub-discipline of traumatology (or trauma psychology).

L. D. Butler (✉) · F. M. Critelli
School of Social Work, University at Buffalo, Buffalo, NY, USA
e-mail: ldbutler@buffalo.edu

F. M. Critelli
e-mail: fmc8@buffalo.edu

© The Author(s) 2019
L. D. Butler et al. (eds.), *Trauma and Human Rights*,
https://doi.org/10.1007/978-3-030-16395-2_2

Although "[t]he study of psychological trauma is an inherently political enterprise because it calls attention to the experience of oppressed people" (Herman, 1997, p. 237), the trauma and human rights frameworks are rarely deployed together, and until recently, there have been minimal efforts to integrate them. However, in some circumstances, one framework has been used to sustain or substantiate claims of the other. For example, Herman (1997), in her seminal exposition *Trauma and Recovery*, describes the episodic cultural and professional amnesia that has long hindered progress in the understanding and treatment of trauma (see also, van der Kolk, Herron, & Hostetler, 1994). She notes that after periods of intense intellectual interest and scholarly study, the subject matter would be abandoned as too controversial, even anathema, only to be rediscovered and revived decades later. Herman concludes, "only an ongoing connection with a global political movement for human rights [can] sustain our ability to speak about unspeakable things" (p. 237).

Some commentators have noted the importance of medical and psychiatric formulations, specifically the diagnoses that pertain to psychological trauma, in substantiating the psychosocial impacts of severe human rights violations (HRVs), such as torture and political conflict. Steel, Bateman Steel, and Silove (2009) describe how, in the 1970s and 1980s, the international focus on extreme state-sponsored HRs abuses became allied with mental health professionals whose work was steeped in the trauma model because these professionals could provide care for and rehabilitation to populations who had suffered HRVs, as well as document their suffering. Goldfield et al. (1988; quoted in Bracken, Giller, & Summerfield, 1995) have argued that: "The medical verification of injuries caused by torture can provide powerful testimony to its occurrence.... [and] will contribute to the international recognition and eradication of this inhumane practice." In short, this association between HR advocates and mental health professionals (both practitioners and researchers) enhanced efforts to document and treat those exposed to political violence, torture, ethnic warfare, and other HRVs (e.g., McDonnell, Robjant, & Katona, 2012; Momartin, Silove, Manicavasagar, & Steel, 2003; Nelson, Price, & Zubrzycki, 2014; Nickerson et al., 2015; Silove, 1999) and thereby contributed to the protection of civil and political rights (Steel et al., 2009). Despite these important benefits of collaboration, Steel et al. (2009) caution that there is a "risk of 'medicalization' of the rights movement by making it excessively reliant on medical outcomes as the criterion to gauge the extent or even the claim to validity of reported HR abuses" (p. 358). Indeed, they warn that the trauma model and its features could "supplant core HRs principles in deciding whether a violation has occurred or not" (p. 363).

This concern is both understandable and sensible if one assumes that one framework must prevail. But is that necessary? We will argue, instead, that each framework contributes invaluable and complementary insights, and the trajectories in conceptual growth of each suggest that their integration, to the extent possible, would help us better appreciate and address adverse human experience.

In this chapter, we describe the two overarching frameworks—as they are currently conceived—that comprise the scaffolding for this volume: *trauma (and PTSD)* and *HRs (and their violations)*, their historical and conceptual origins, some of their strengths, limitations, and criticisms, and where traumatic experiences (TEs) and HRs abuses intersect in the manufacture of terrible human suffering. Finally, we argue that for a more complete understanding of individual and collective suffering an approach that integrates both is necessary.

## THE TRAUMA FRAMEWORK, TRAUMATIC EXPERIENCE, AND THE PTSD DIAGNOSIS

Traumatic events have been the subject matter of historical, literary, and religious texts for millennia, but largely absent in Western (extant) medical or psychological writings until the nineteenth century (Ben-Ezra, 2011). Rarer still are historical autobiographical accounts, such as that of seventeenth-century English diarist, Samuel Pepys, who recorded his emotional reactions following the Great Fire of London in 1666 (Daly, 1983). Academic scholarship appears to have begun in the latter half of nineteenth century with the forensic writings of Tardieu (van der Kolk et al., 1994) and the clinical observations of Janet (van der Kolk & van der Hart, 1991), Briquet, Breuer, and Freud (van der Kolk et al., 1994) concerning the long-term effects of child sexual maltreatment and sexual abuse. In the first half of the twentieth century, in the context of two world wars, scholarship turned to description of the impact of military combat, including works by Freud (1919, as cited in van der Kolk & van der Hart, 1991) and Kardiner (1941), among others.

As the century progressed, additional traumatic events were cataloged (e.g., catastrophic fire; Lindemann, 1944), and distinct trauma-related syndromes began to be described (e.g., survivor [concentration camp] syndrome, Niederland, 1981; rape trauma syndrome, Burgess & Holstrum, 1974; battered women's syndrome, Walker, 1984). Yet, these efforts were without the benefit of a common vocabulary and unifying conceptual framework or nosology.

## Development and Refinement of the PTSD Diagnosis

Formal classification of the impact of TE as a more general phenomenon did not appear in American psychology and psychiatry until the mid-twentieth century with the inclusion of *gross stress reaction* in the first edition of the *Diagnostic and Statistical Manual of Mental Disorders* (DSM) in 1952. This classification encompassed individual exposure to "severe physical demands or extreme emotional stress such as in combat or in civilian catastrophe" (Spitzer, First, & Wakefield, 2007, p. 234). However, the second edition of the DSM (in 1968) dropped the category (for reasons unknown; Spitzer et al., 2007), but did include a category for *transient situational disturbance* that covered all manner of acute reactions to stressful experiences, which were presumed to be temporary (Jones & Wesseley, 2006).

The third edition of the DSM (in 1980) reinstated a category specific to severe trauma and persistent symptomatology in response to the swell of pressure from survivors, most particularly struggling Vietnam combat veterans and their advocates (Scott, 1990), one of whom, psychiatrist advocate and war trauma scholar, Robert Jay Lifton, drafted the initial definition (Jones & Wesseley, 2006). This renewed category included specific diagnostic criteria for a new syndrome: *posttraumatic stress disorder* (PTSD; APA, 1980) that comprised three categories of symptoms: intrusions, avoidance or numbing, and hyperarousal. As Jones and Wesseley (2006) observe, "PTSD entered the psychiatric canon obliquely—not as a result of careful epidemiological or nosological research but more as a result of politically motivated lobbying" (p. 219). Nonetheless, symptom descriptions were grounded primarily in scholarship and clinical observation of trauma survivors, amassed over more than a half-century of wars.

> Only after 1980, when efforts of combat veterans had legitimated the concept of post-traumatic stress disorder, did it become clear that the psychological syndrome seen in survivors of rape, domestic battery, and incest was essentially the same as the syndrome seen in survivors of war. (Herman, 1997, p. 32)

In short, a basic *trauma theory* had arrived which stipulated universal processes of adaptation to traumatic experience that produced predictable psychopathological presentations (i.e., PTSD) among victims.

The third edition of the DSM, and its subsequent revision (DSM-III-R), endeavored to define the necessary conditions for the development of PTSD and included both symptom descriptions and a more specific *exposure criterion* delineating the necessary qualities of TEs. *Traumatic events* were defined as events "outside the range usual human experience and that would be markedly distressing to almost everyone" (Kessler, Sonnega, Bromet, & Hughes, 1995, p. 1057). Yet each part of this definition—that such events were both highly unusual and broadly distressing—was quickly recognized to be problematic. The notion that such events were rare was reflected in contemporary authoritative psychiatric texts that asserted that incest occurred in only about *one in a million* families (e.g., Henderson, 1975)—a claim revealed to be demonstrably false once incest prevalence estimates began to be reported. For example, in a national survey, Finkelhor, Hotaling, Lewis, and Smith (1990) found that 8% of women and 2% of men had experienced sexual victimization by a family member. Likewise, as other disturbing events were examined for their possible traumatogenic potential, it became clear that many people, perhaps the majority, had been exposed at some point in their lives, yet interestingly only a minority of those exposed developed symptoms. In a national stratified probability sample conducted in 1995, Kessler and colleagues found that a majority of those assessed (51.2% of women, 60.7% of men) reported *traumatic event exposure*, but only an estimated 7.8% of the overall sample met criteria for lifetime PTSD, and these estimates varied considerably by gender (10.4% for women vs. 5.0% for men). Consequently, the *exposure criterion* was further specified in DSM-IV (APA, 1994) to accommodate the building research consensus that TEs were much more common than previously understood; did not necessarily result in PTSD for those exposed; had effects that could vary depending on event type and population (Kessler et al., 1995; Spitzer et al., 2007); and typically involved threat to life, limb, or loved one.

The most recent exposure criterion for PTSD (DSM-5; APA, 2013) now requires the experience of serious physical injury or threatened death or sexual violence. Potential traumatic events range from natural (e.g., disaster) to human-caused (e.g., terrorist attack), from intentional (e.g., physical or sexual assault; state-sponsored violence) to accidental (e.g., car accident) or incidental (e.g., witnessing violence), and, by definition, all have the potential to result in the development of post-traumatic stress symptoms. In addition, *exposure* to a traumatic event is distinguished from its prospective impact, being *traumatized,* which is operationalized, in this construction, by DSM-defined posttraumatic stress symptoms. The latest DSM also acknowledges that circumstances prior to, during, or following a trauma (risk and protective factors) can determine, or significantly contribute to, the level of psychosocial distur-bance following trauma exposure (APA, 2013).

Recent research (Kilpatrick et al., 2013), employing a nationally rep-resentative online US adult sample ($N = 2953$) and based on the new, more stringent exposure criteria, found that lifetime exposure to at least one traumatic event was reported by the vast majority (89.7%) of the sample, but only 8.3% (10.5% of those exposed) met criteria for possi-ble lifetime PTSD. Moreover, and importantly, the modal number of traumatic events reported was 3, which indicated both the commonness of TEs and the likelihood of cumulative effects. This led the authors to observe that, "the field must move beyond a narrow focus on PTSD responses to a single event because it is clear from this and previous stud-ies that exposure to multiple events is the norm and that the probability of PTSD increases with greater event exposure" (p. 545).

A recent international report underscores some of these findings. A summary of mental health surveys (using DSM criteria) conducted in 24 countries around the world (Benjet et al., 2016; Koenen et al., 2017) indicates lifetime exposure of 70.4% (with 30.5% exposed to 4 or more events) and a prevalence of lifetime PTSD across countries of 3.9% (5.6% of those trauma-exposed). Interestingly, high-income coun-tries had twice the proportion of PTSD than lower-income countries. Factor analyses (Benjet et al., 2016) determined that traumatic events clustered on 5 main factors: exposure to collective violence; causing or witnessing serious harm to others; exposure to interpersonal violence; exposure to intimate partner or sexual violence; and accidents and inju-ries. (Space does not permit discussion of the parallel development in the World Health Organization's [WHO] International Classification of Diseases [ICD] of *trauma exposure* and *diagnostic criteria* for posttrau-matic conditions and how they compare and contrast with the DSM; we refer interested readers to Hyland, Shevlin, Fyvie, & Karatzias, 2018; Stein et al., 2014.)

## Advances in Understandings of Trauma

Even as the TE definition and PTSD diagnosis narrowed, investigations began to establish that a wider conceptual lens was required to capture the regularity, variety, and collective underpinnings of trauma for many people. In the wider literature on human suffering, documentation and conceptualization of trauma responses have continued to evolve and expand, and many of these innovations are relevant to discussions of the effects of HRVs. Some pick up the conceptual slack of earlier DSM event criteria by elucidating the effects of severe, repetitive, and collective TEs within populations and across generational and developmental temporal periods. Of particular relevance to the overlap between TEs and HRVs are conceptualizations of trauma responses that do not map neatly onto narrow, individualistic constructions or that enlarge our understanding of systemic or psychological circumstances that can act as precipitants or context. Among these conceptualizations are the constructs of historical trauma, transgenerational trauma, complex PTSD, the assumptive world, moral injury, and institutional betrayal.

The term *historical trauma* was coined to capture the effects of colonization, cultural suppression, forced assimilation, and historical oppression of North American indigenous people (Kirmayer, Gone, & Moses, 2014) and has been described by Brave Heart (2003) as "cumulative emotional and psychological wounding over the lifespan and across generations, emanating from massive group trauma experiences" (p. 7). Kirmayer et al. (2014) portray several hypothesized means by which historical trauma may be transmitted from one generation to the next, including pathways at interpersonal, family, community, and nation levels, but also emphasize that ongoing structural violence remains one of the primary reasons for the persisting challenges faced by indigenous peoples.

A related construct, *multi-* or *transgenerational trauma* (Danieli, 1998), refers to how the effects of a profound traumatic event in the experience of one generation can be conveyed to subsequent generations, such as in the case of survivors of the Holocaust (Danieli, 1998) or Indian Boarding Schools (Brave Heart & Debruyn, 1998) and their offspring. Transmission of trauma and its effects is posited to flow through a variety of mechanisms, such as parental behaviors affected by PTSD (including parenting) and related symptomatology, as well as via epigenetic alterations of the stress response system (Kellerman, 2001). Notably,

Bloom (2006) has argued that one of the central (yet unappreciated) determinants of human experience has been "the presence throughout human history of exposure to overwhelming, repetitive, multigenerational traumatic experiences and the potentially negative impact of those experiences on individual, group, and political processes" (p. 17).

*Complex PTSD* (Herman, 1992; known as *Disorders of Extreme Stress Not Otherwise Specified* in the DSM-IV field trials, Friedman, 2013) describes psychological adaptations to prolonged and severe interpersonal trauma, such as chronic childhood maltreatment, concentration camp captivity, and domestic battery. This syndrome is more complicated and persistent than simple PTSD because it involves extensive disturbances in affect regulation, cognition, soma, self-concept, interpersonal relations, and systems of meaning. Some have argued (e.g., McDonnell et al., 2012) that the impact of protracted state-sponsored violence corresponds more closely to the construct of Complex PTSD than to simple PTSD.

Several theoretical models have established the role of violations of deeply held assumptions or values in survivors' experiences of trauma. Almost three decades ago, Janoff-Bulman (1992) observed that TEs often challenge, and sometimes devastate, the unexamined assumptions that people hold about the benevolence and meaningfulness of the world and the worthiness of self, and this *shattering of the assumptive world* may be particularly psychologically injurious. For example, following the first terrorist attack on the World Trade Center in 1993, patients reported that the damage done to their fundamental beliefs about the world, others, and themselves was even more distressing than their PTSD symptoms (Difede, Apfeldorf, Cloitre, Spielmen, & Perry, 1997).

Trauma can also comprise violations of one's private ethical views and values. The construct of *moral injury* refers to the "soul wound" (Shay, 2012, p. 58) suffered by some military personnel involved in "perpetrating, failing to prevent, or bearing witness to events that transgress deeply held moral beliefs and expectations" (Litz et al., 2009, p. 700). These transgressions can issue from acts of commission (actions taken) or omission (failures to act) by the self or others, but they may also involve witnessing terrible suffering or war's grotesque aftermath (Maguen & Litz, 2012). A differing but complementary version of moral injury (Shay, 2012) situates the moral violation in the powerholder or institution that required the action (or inaction) rather than the individual who acted (or failed to act). In Shay's view, which echoes institutional betrayal (described next), moral injury involves "betrayal of what's right...by someone who holds legitimate authority...in a high stakes situation" (p. 59). Nickerson, Bryant, Rosebrock, and Litz (2014) explored the concept of moral injury among traumatized refugees and asylum seekers, finding that the extent to which victims were troubled by acts of others (A. Nickerson, personal communication, July 22, 2018) that transgressed their moral values predicted their mental health status and quality of life, even after controlling for the degree of trauma exposure and post-migration stressors.

Violations of expectations (and of the implicit social contract) are also at the core of *institutional betrayal* (Smith & Freyd, 2014), which refers to instances where "trusted and powerful institutions... [act] in ways that visit harm upon those dependent on them for safety and well-being" (p. 575). System-level betrayal also involves institutional failures to deliver anticipated and depended-upon actions of protection, prevention, and response. Traumas that involve betrayals by individuals or institutions appear to be more toxic for victims than traumas that do not (Smith & Freyd, 2014), and thus, this phenomenon may play a dominant role in the suffering associated with a wide range of state-perpetrated HRVs, such as oppression, persecution, torture, and structural violence.

We have briefly reviewed some major conceptual advances that illuminate further aspects of traumatic responses, as well as a handful of constructs that enlarge the purview of psychological trauma to account for temporal, cumulative, social, and moral aspects. Clearly, traditional PTSD, as defined by DSM criteria, is only one possible expression of response to trauma. Fortunately, the broader trauma framework now catalogs psychological and social mechanisms that speak to the varied phenomenological experiences of survivors. It is worth noting, however, that the aforementioned concepts, while reported in the wider trauma literature, are not included in the current DSM.

### *Limitations and Criticisms of the Trauma Framework and PTSD Diagnosis*

Spitzer et al. (2007) note that, "Since [PTSD's] introduction in 1980, no other DSM diagnosis, with the exception of Dissociative Identity Disorder ... has generated so much controversy in the field as to the boundaries of the disorder, diagnostic criteria, central assumptions, clinical utility, and prevalence in various populations" (p. 233). In fact, the concerns and criticisms are broader still. While one conceptual camp argues that the diagnosis needs greater specificity, another contends that significant questions remain about the reality, core assumptions, and impact of the PTSD construct, and yet another contends that the diagnosis is culturally bound and medicalizes suffering and is consequently inadequate to capture the myriad sources, manifestations, and consequences of trauma in human experience or diverse samples.

*Diagnostic Boundaries, Criteria, and Specificity*
As the preceding outlined, North American psychiatry/psychology over the past four decades has focused much of its attention on endeavoring to carve the PTSD diagnosis at its joints, both by undertaking to demarcate the set of truly traumatic events and, within that framework, the set of common symptomatic features: the syndrome. This nosological focus has been aimed at achieving higher precision in individual diagnosis and treatment, as well as pushing back against efforts to expand what the trauma construct encompasses. Spitzer et al. (2007) have declared: "We believe that a large part of the problem with PTSD concerns the expansion of the PTSD construct of trauma" (p. 234). Those who wish to maintain or narrow the definitional and phenomenological focus have voiced alarm over "conceptual bracket creep" (e.g., Spitzer et al., 2007; McNally, 2009) wherein an expanding list of social ills is anointed with the adjective "traumatic." Their reproach reflects the concern that such definitional expansion could dilute the significance and meaning of PTSD, thereby making the adjective "traumatic" a simple synonym for anything upsetting, uncoupled from its specific conceptual origins. (We note that, as instructors, it is not unusual that we need to clarify for students the distinction between the common colloquial use of the term *traumatic* to connote anything distressing ["I was traumatized that I failed the test!"], and its more deliberative, specific, and circumspect use in the social sciences.) As McNally (2009) has observed, "If everything can count as trauma, the term morphs into a trope for misfortune in contemporary life and loses whatever meaning it originally had" (p. 598).

*Questioning the Reality, Core Assumptions, and Impact*
*of the PTSD Construct*
Some commentators have stepped back to question the reality of PTSD altogether. For example, some argue that PTSD is fundamentally ill-conceived, faddish at best, and in many cases a product of efforts to seek

personal recognition and compensation (e.g., McHugh & Treisman, 2007; McNally, 2009; Summerfield, 2001). This modern view is in keeping with the denial and suspicion that met trauma survivor reports through much of the twentieth century (Herman, 1997; van der Kolk et al., 1994). Others enumerate the numerous construct validity limitations of the PTSD diagnosis (Rosen & Lilienfeld, 2008), but without rejecting the need for understanding and classifying responses to traumatic events. "The question of concern when assessing the validity of PTSD is not the political, economic, or social protection of victims, all of which are profoundly important, but logically separate matters from PTSD's construct validity" (p. 855). Others have suggested that PTSD may be better understood instead as an *idiom of distress* that tacitly communicates "social conflicts and problems that, because of differences in power and access to resources, cannot be fully expressed more directly" (Hautzinger & Scandlyn, 2014, p. 18; see also Summerfield, 2001). We concur, but would add that traditional Western psychiatry's adherence to the narrow focus of their PTSD narrative may reflect an idiom of denial of the full scope of HRVs and TEs that comprise the diagnosis' context.

There have also been important challenges to the core assumption that DSM-defined traumatic event exposure is causative in the PTSD syndrome (reviewed in Rosen & Lilienfeld, 2008). For example, there are reports of the ubiquity of apparent posttraumatic symptoms among non-trauma-exposed psychiatric patients (e.g., Bodkin, Pope, Detke, & Hudson, 2007), suggesting that the syndrome is a nonspecific psychiatric distress response. Additionally, there is a growing body of evidence of cardinal posttraumatic symptomatology in populations experiencing *life stressors* rather than *traumatic stressors* (e.g., Mol et al., 2005); in other words, events that do not involve the immediate and severe (type of) life threat currently required for a PTSD diagnosis. For instance, traumatic stress symptoms have been documented among those who have experienced divorce, bereavement, or illness (reviewed in Larsen & Pacella, 2016), and racial, gender, or sexual orientation *microaggressions* (e.g., Pieterse, Carter, Evans, & Walter, 2010). This enlarged set of trauma symptom-provoking stressors challenges the primary assumption of PTSD: the necessary condition of exposure to severe injury or life threat. Some have viewed these findings with incredulity and even hostility. "Any unit of classification that simultaneously encompasses the experience of surviving Auschwitz and that of being told rude jokes at work must, by any reasonable lay standard, be a nonsense, a patent absurdity" (Shephard, 2004, p. 57). Rosen and Lilienfeld (2008) conclude their extensive review of PTSD validity issues by proposing that: "rather than conceptualizing PTSD as a taxon" [i.e., category in nature], "it may be more fruitful and scientifically supportable to consider PTSD as encompassing a broad range of reactions to adverse events" (p. 858).

*Questions Concerning the Universality and Impact of the PTSD Diagnosis*
Criticisms of the hegemony of the PTSD diagnosis and Western trauma model have come from many quarters. As Westoby (2009) has observed, "the potentially diverse and rich understandings of healing have been overshadowed by a dominant paradigm steeped in therapeutic culture and medical discourse...While this paradigm is useful in specific contexts, it is the *dominance* that is problematic" (italics in the original; quoted in Nelson et al., 2014, p. 572).

Kienzler (2008) has proposed that the range of positions (and corresponding assumptions) regarding the reality of PTSD are anchored by two primarily opposing positions: those who view PTSD as a "universal and cross-culturally valid psychopathological response to traumatic distress which may be cured or ameliorated with (Western) clinical and psychosocial therapeutic measures" (p. 218), and those who view PTSD as a Western medical creation, inextricably bound to its own cultural and moral background, and therefore problematic when applied in other contexts.

In their extensive review of evidence on the validity of PTSD criteria for traumatized members of diverse cultural groups, Hinton and Lewis-Fernández (2011) note that, while there is substantial evidence supporting the cross-cultural validity of trauma and PTSD, there is also strong evidence of significant cultural variability. Specifically, the variability inheres in the salience of particular PTSD symptoms (e.g., avoidance and numbing symptoms), the predominance of other symptom types (e.g., somatic expressions), and the role of interpretation of the trauma in the shaping of symptom presentation—all without adequate discussion in the DSM. These authors also note specific cultural syndromes and idioms of distress related to trauma (Hinton & Lewis-Fernández, 2010). Indeed, some have argued that PTSD symptom criteria are not adequate to embrace the varied range of specific posttraumatic emotional and behavioral responses reported by survivors across different cultural contexts and recorded throughout history (Ben-Ezra, 2011; Hinton & Lewis-Fernández, 2011).

Together these findings suggest that there are many un(der)appreciated ways in which cultural meanings and, perhaps, social and political structures relate to discourses on trauma and PTSD practices. Consequently, although the modern PTSD diagnosis may capture elements of the experience of trauma across a variety of cultural contexts, the strict diagnostic criteria act as Procrustean constraints that limit or distort the posttraumatic presentations that qualify for diagnosis.

A related and highly significant critique of the PTSD paradigm—particularly with respect to HRVs—is that it involves a

> dangerous potential for medicalizing human suffering; that is, for reducing the social and moral implications of traumatizing events, such as war or genocide, to strictly professional, even biological, set of consequences.... [B]y emphasizing the 'reality' of PTSD as a universal biopsychosocial category, research on PTSD may have unintentionally and paradoxically helped decrease social and moral responsiveness to these events. (Hinton & Lewis-Fernández, 2011, p. 784; see also Kienzler, 2008)

In short, medicalizing suffering can obfuscate the wider social and moral implications of these events.

Tension remains between psychological and psychiatric traditions that have focused for the past four decades on more narrowly specifying PTSD and steadfastly defending the dominion of trauma theory against expansion and incursions, and anthropologists, as well as some psychologists, psychiatrists, and others, who have argued for a more critical, nuanced, and inclusive understanding of trauma and its aftermath. As we have described, these critiques stem from observations of the vast range of posttraumatic responses that do not line up neatly with strict PTSD assumptions, criteria, and manifestations, and that encompass the effects of severe, collective TEs within populations and across generational and developmental temporal periods.

## The Human Rights Framework and Human Rights Violations

HRs remain undefinable to many people, yet the basic definition is quite simple: They are rights inherent in all human beings, on the basis of being human, regardless of race, sex, nationality, ethnicity, language, religion, or any other status (United Nations [UN], n.d.). The concept of

HRs rests on philosophical foundations of what it means to be human and the moral nature of "man"; HRs are a *prescriptive* moral account of human possibility (Donnelly, 2013). Over time, HRs have evolved as a moral, political, and legal framework, and as a pathway to achieve a more just world. They have come to epitomize many of our greatest societal aspirations, including global relief of suffering; the protection and restoration of human dignity; the provision of equal economic and social opportunities to all; freedom from discrimination, fear, and torture; world peace and, more recently, protection of the planet and its ecosystems (Moyn, 2010). In the words of one scholar, HRs have become "the moral lingua franca of our age" (Morsink, 2009, p. 1).

## The Roots and Development of the HRs Framework

HRs concepts have evolved gradually through a dynamic process within a long philosophical and political history. Within this process, the idea emerged that people should have certain freedoms; however, the history is controversial and the origins of HRs are contested (Ishay, 2010). A key debate centers on whether HRs are a product of the Western Enlightenment period of the seventeenth and eighteenth centuries (Ife, 2001; Ishay, 2010) or if they originate in earlier religious and philosophical writings that identify concepts comparable to those found in modern HRs instruments (Ife, 2001; Ishay, 2004; James, 2007; Lauren, 2011). For example, HRs notions of equality, social justice, and concern for the poor are found in Islam, Taoist, Confucian, Buddhist, Jewish, and Christian theologies (James, 2007). Lauren (2011), in his inclusive history of HRs, concludes:

> These visions did not evolve from any single society, political system, culture, geographical region, or manner. Some emerged out of religious belief, compassion, or a sense of duty to care for brothers and sisters suffering in distress. Others grew from philosophical discourse about the nature of humankind itself, natural rights, ethical limits on how we should treat one another, the appropriate powers of government, or the rule of law. Some came not from quiet contemplation or careful reflection, but rather from the heat of outrage generated by a passionate sense of individual or collective conscience over an injustice inflicted upon innocent or defenseless victims. Still others arose out of violence and pain from wars, revolutions, upheavals, or brutal atrocities. Over the centuries, these cases have spanned the world, from Asia to Europe, from the Middle East to the Pacific, and

from Africa to the Americas, and have involved exploitation, slavery, racial segregation and apartheid, oppression, gender and class discrimination, persecution of minorities, violence in times of war, torture, conquest, and the mass exterminations of genocide or "ethnic cleansing." (p. 2)

During the Enlightenment, the development of Western philosophical principles unquestionably played an instrumental role in shaping aspects of contemporary thinking about HRs (Ishay, 2005; Hunt, 2007). Among these was the belief in the supremacy of human reason, and the need to question hierarchies and the nature of government and political power and, especially, the need to interrogate the intolerant religious dogmas of their times. Most Enlightenment HRs visionaries imagined that a peaceful world, predicated upon liberal rights, would be realized during a coming era of free economic exchange (Ishay, 2010). The Enlightenment had a practical impact on the American and French revolutions and on the language of rights and constitutional norms and the structures that developed from them (Hunt, 2007; James, 2007). These principles influenced the drafters of the US Constitution and the Bill of Rights, as well as the 1789 Declaration of the Rights of Man and Citizen, a document from the French Revolution, considered a landmark in the history of HRs discussions. However, these philosophies coexisted with radical inequalities, colonialism, racism, sexism, and slavery and the slave trade, the most egregious hypocrisy of the time (James, 2007).

The first half of the twentieth century saw significant gains for HRs ideas, law, and institutions (James, 2007; Lauren, 2011). Issues of race and empire also arose on the international level with the emergence of anti-colonialist movements focused on self-determination, conditions facing indigenous peoples, the struggle against racism, and demands for greater economic and social rights and collective rights. HRs idioms were used by African Americans in the USA, such as W. E. B. Du Bois and Jamaican-born visionary Marcus Garvey, as well as Blacks in South Africa and anti-colonial activists in Asia and Africa (Lauren, 2011). These developments advanced conceptions of HRs beyond the European Enlightenment or Western liberal discourse (Cmiel, 2004; Ishay, 2004; James, 2007; Jensen, 2016).

Nineteenth and twentieth-century socialist movements, along with other collectivist movements, such as the international labor movement and the struggle for universal suffrage, also played an important role in the development of HRs, especially economic and social rights

(Ife, 2001; Ishay, 2005). Socialist ideals influenced many of the principles that were later endorsed by the Universal Declaration of Human Rights (UN, 1948b) and the two 1966 International Covenants (Ishay, 2005). These contributions—to be described in the next section—broadened human perspectives to embrace the full range of rights including social and economic rights as inalienable and indivisible (Ishay, 2005).

### Creation of the Universal Declaration of Human Rights

After the German Nazi (and others') atrocities of World War II, the notion that universal HRs could protect against future attempted genocides and other brutalities took hold (James, 2007). A series of important HRs milestones followed. First, the recognition of the need for a postwar international organization culminated in the Dumbarton Oaks Conference in 1944, with representatives of China, the Soviet Union, the USA, and the UK formulating proposals that became the basis for the UN. The UN Conference on International Organization in June 1945 followed, where a convention of delegates from 50 allied nations met in San Francisco to craft the *United Nations Charter* and the UN officially came into existence on October 24 of that year. Soon after, the newly founded UN began work on two key human rights instruments. The *Human Rights Committee* (HRC) was established in 1947 to draft a comprehensive statement of HRs that countries around the world could agree on. The committee was chaired by Eleanor Roosevelt and comprised global scholars such as the Chinese Confucian philosopher, diplomat, and commission vice-chairman Pen-Chung, Lebanese existentialist philosopher and rapporteur Charles Malik, and the French legal scholar and Nobel Prize laureate Rene Cassin. Their vision for this statement was predicated on a wide range of philosophical and historical texts, and it culminated in the *Universal Declaration of Human Rights* (UDHR; UN, 1948b).

Simultaneously, years of campaigning by the Polish-Jewish lawyer Raphael Lemkin—who coined the term genocide—led to the development of the *Convention on the Prevention and Punishment of the Crime of Genocide (Genocide Convention)* (Sands, 2017). On December 9, 1948, the Genocide Convention became the first human rights instrument adopted by the UN General Assembly (UN, 1948a) and was quickly followed by the adoption of the more well-known instrument, the UDHR on December 10, 1948.

The UDHR (UN, 1948b) represents a broad range of internationally accepted HRs as defined by the UN. As the foundational HRs document, it established HRs standards and norms, gave them political legitimacy, and is widely used as the benchmark of what are considered HRs globally. The UDHR specifies minimum conditions for a dignified life and what is viewed normatively as a life worthy of a human being. The unique contribution of the UDHR is that it brings together HRs principles within the rubric of one comprehensive approach; by enumerating a list of HRs, it says, in effect, "Here's how you treat someone as a human being" (Donnelly, 2013, p. 16). Its drafters envisioned a holistic framework whereby one cluster of rights could not be privileged over another. The principles of universality, inalienability, interdependence, and indivisibility underlie HRs. Rights are universal because all humans are born with and possess the same rights equally. They are inalienable because people's rights can never be taken away, although they may at times be restricted—for example, if a person breaks the law or it is in the interests of national security (Office of the High Commissioner for Human Rights [OHCHR], n.d.). Indivisibility and interdependence denote that all rights are part of a complementary framework and are equal in importance without hierarchy; a particular right is not fully enjoyed without the others.

## The Three Generations of HRs

HRs have been traditionally conceptualized as comprising three overarching types or "generations": civil-political; economic, social, and cultural; and collective or group rights. Karel Vasak, UNESCO's legal advisor and distinguished HRs scholar, introduced this theoretical framework that became part of the standard vocabulary describing HRs (Vasak, 1977).

### First-Generation Rights
First-generation *civil-political* rights deal with liberty and participation in political life and are the most clearly established and widely accepted of the generations of HRs. Civil and political rights have their intellectual origins in the eighteenth-century Enlightenment and development of liberal political philosophy (Bobbio, 1996; Galtung, 1994). They are individually based and concern the fundamental freedoms seen as essential to the effective and fair organization of democracy and civil society.

These rights encompass the state's responsibility to safeguard the dignity and security of the individual against transgressions by the state or by others (Ife, 2001). Civil-political rights are enshrined by Articles 3 to 21 of the UDHR (UN, 1948b) and within the 1966 International Covenant on Civil and Political Rights (ICCPR) (UN, 1966a).

Key rights contained in the ICCPR are *self-determination*, including political status and economic and cultural development; *protection of physical integrity against State actions*, such as the right to life and freedom from torture and from cruel, inhuman, or degrading treatment or punishment; liberty and *freedom from slavery*, including involuntary or forced labor; *the right to liberty and security of person*, including freedom from arbitrary arrest, the right to procedural fairness and reasonable, timely trial and to humane treatment while detained including segregation of juvenile offenders from adults with treatment appropriate to their age and legal status; *equality before the law; freedom of association*, including the right to form and join trade unions; *protection against any form of discrimination*, including on grounds such as race, color, sex, language, religion, political or other opinion, national or social origin, property, birth, or other status; *freedom of belief, thought and speech; freedom of association*, and *the right to political participation*, such as voting. Overall, these rights require governments to refrain from actions that restrain civil or political liberties (Vasak & Alston, 1982). Because of this emphasis on protection, first-generation rights are sometimes also referred to as *negative rights*, in that they are rights that the state must ensure are not threatened or violated (Ife, 2001). Thus, negative rights are not granted, achieved, or realized; rather, they are protected and guaranteed. The traditional way in which first-generation rights have been guaranteed, or at least in which such guarantees have been sought, is through legal mechanisms.

*Second-Generation Rights*
Second-generation rights, otherwise known as *economic, social, and cultural rights*, identify the conditions necessary for meeting the necessities of human life so that human beings can realize their full potential and live in dignity. Economic and social rights are embodied in Articles 22–27 of the UDHR (UN, 1948b) and by the International Covenant on Economic, Social, and Cultural Rights (ICESCR) (UN, 1966b). The ICESCR includes: *the right to social security and social protection, the right to an adequate standard of living*, including access to

food and freedom from hunger, adequate housing, water, and clothing; *rights relating to the workplace*, such as freedom from forced labor, fair wages and equal pay for equal work, leisure and reasonable limitation of working hours, safe and healthy working conditions, joining and forming trade unions, and striking; *the right to health*, including access to healthcare facilities and services, healthy occupational and environmental conditions, sexual and reproductive health, and protection against epidemic diseases; *the right to protection of and assistance to the family*, including marriage by free consent, maternity and paternity protection, and protection of children from economic and social exploitation; *the right to education*; and *the right to participate in cultural life* (OHCHR, 2008).

Second-generation rights are referred to as *positive rights* because they require that governments take specific actions to provide for citizens, implying a more active role for the state (Ife, 2001; Vasak & Alston, 1982). Rather than simply protecting rights, the state is required to take a strong role in ensuring that these rights are realized through various forms of social provision.

Economic and social rights often receive lower priority compared to civil and political rights on HRs agendas (Staub-Bernasconi, 2007). Many people associate HRs with only civil and political rights, and the notion of *HRs violations* (HRVs) or abuses is less often applied to second-generation rights, although this is changing with increased attention to the promotion and protection of these rights by states, judiciaries, and NGOs (OHCHR, 2008). Still, economic and social rights lack legal and political recognition in many countries, including the USA, where adequate income, health care, housing, and other social protections are not guaranteed or even considered rights (Picard, 2010; Staub-Bernasconi, 2007). As the UN emphasizes, economic, social, and cultural rights are not fundamentally different from civil and political rights (OHCHR, 2008); in reality, the fulfillment of any given human right is dependent on fulfillment of the others.

Second-generation rights create the background conditions necessary for the exercise of first-generation rights. For example, it is often harder for individuals who cannot read and write to find work, to take part in political activity, or to exercise their freedom of expression. Similarly, famines are less likely to occur where individuals can exercise political rights, such as the right to vote (OHCHR, 2008).

*Third-Generation Rights*

Third-generation or *solidarity rights* recognize the overlapping nature of global concerns and aspects of life that are collective. This broad spectrum of rights reflects issues of culture and the rights of peoples and groups that go beyond the relationship between the individual and the state. Specific provisions include the right to (collective) self-determination, to economic and social development, to a healthy eco-system, to natural resources, to communication, to participation in activities that promote and maintain cultural heritage, and to intergenerational equity and sustainability (Iyall Smith, 2008). This broad class of rights has been affirmed in international agreements and treaties; however, these rights are more contested than the other types by different countries (Twiss, 2004). Third-generation rights must be guaranteed by international action and are expressed largely in International Conventions and Declarations of the UN such as the 2015 *Paris Climate Accord* and the 2007 *UN Declaration of the Rights of Indigenous Peoples*.

In recent years, the generational framework and dichotomization of positive and negative rights have been critiqued as outdated (Jensen, 2017; Macklem, 2015; UN, 2009). The framework is problematic because it reifies the notion that a chasm exists between civil/political rights and social/economic rights, even though the UDHR makes no distinction between these rights. The distinction was accentuated during Cold War tensions, where first-generation rights were prioritized, and second-generation rights were resisted as socialist notions by Western democracies. This division continues to serve as a political tool of neoliberal economic policies that have gained primacy since the 1980s across many nations and international financial institutions, such as the International Monetary Fund (Jensen, 2017). In the era of economic globalization and policies that promote reductions in public social spending, governments resist making these social investments (Holmes & Sunstein, 1999). Economic, social, and cultural rights, as well as collective rights, may require greater levels of investment to ensure their full realization; moreover, some public expenditure is also required to safeguard civil and political rights, such as functioning court systems, minimum living conditions for prisoners, legal aid, and free and fair elections (OHCHR, 2008).

Rather than a binary framework of positive or negative rights, the UN and others emphasize that it is more appropriate to regard *all* rights as interdependent and indivisible, that *all* may entail a variety of state obligations, and that *all* HRs obligations are characterized by the duty to respect, protect, promote, and fulfill. Moreover, recognition of *all* rights is considered a precondition for achieving social justice. Consequently, in recent decades, HRs treaties have integrated all rights.

*Subsequent HRs Advances*
The 1960s were another critical period in the developing and broadening meaning of universal HRs (Ishay, 2010). Mass movements arose to challenge HRVs in both the developed and developing worlds (Ishay, 2010). In the USA, the civil rights movement organized against institutionalized racism. An array of social movements that advanced grassroots perspectives on justice also flourished, including the labor movement, African Americans, Native Americans, Latinos, women, gay rights, and other national liberation groups.

The composition of UN membership also changed due to decolonization and the admission of newly independent states (e.g., African states, Jamaica). This diverse constellation of states introduced new ideas, methods, and priorities to the HRs agenda. The original goal of the UN HRC was to create binding international HRs law with mechanisms to enforce implementation and practice; however, there was a long-standing deadlock. Among developing nations, the former Soviet Union, the socialist bloc, and the social-democratic Western nations, there was strong support for the recognition of economic, social, cultural, civil, and political rights in a single covenant (James, 2007), but powerful Western nations did not support the inclusion of economic and social rights in a single, comprehensive HRs covenant. Ultimately, these tensions were not resolved; instead, in 1966 two separate covenants were negotiated and adopted: the *International Covenant on Civil and Political Rights* (ICCPR) and the *International Covenant on Economic, Social and Cultural Rights* (ICESCR), each of which stipulated the right to self-determination in its first article (James, 2007; Jensen, 2016). The ICCPR and the ICESCR, together with the UDHR, are known today as *The International Bill of Rights*.

Although HRs and freedoms are based on precepts and values such as dignity, fairness, equality, capabilities, respect, and independence, these concepts must be operationalized and integrated into legal and social practices in order to be realized (Donnelly, 2013). The UDHR, a non-binding declaration, articulates HRs standards and norms and is widely used as the

**Table 2.1**   Nine core international human rights instruments (OHCHR, n.d.-a)

| Instrument | Short name | Date |
|---|---|---|
| International Convention on the Elimination of All Forms of Racial Discrimination | ICERD | December 21, 1965 |
| International Covenant on Civil and Political Rights | ICCPR | December 16, 1966 |
| International Covenant on Economic, Social and Cultural Rights | ICESCR | December 16, 1966 |
| Convention on the Elimination of All Forms of Discrimination against Women | CEDAW | December 18, 1979 |
| Convention against Torture, and Other Cruel, Inhuman and Degrading Treatment or Punishment | CAT | December 10, 1984 |
| Conventions on the Rights of the Child | CRC | November 20, 1989 |
| International Convention on the Protection of the Rights of Migrant Workers and Members of Their Families | CMW | December 18, 1990 |
| Convention on the Rights of Peoples with Disabilities | CRPD | December 13, 2006 |
| International Convention for the Protection of All Persons From Enforced Disappearance | CED | December 20, 2006 |

primary statement of what are considered as HRs today. Since its adoption in 1948, the UDHR has inspired 9 core international HR instruments, including the ICCPR and the ICESCR (see Table 2.1; OHCHR, n.d.-a), among more than 80 international HRs treaties and declarations, as well as a number of regional HRs conventions, domestic HRs bills, and constitutional provisions that codify human rights.

These constitute a legally binding system for the promotion, protection, and fulfilment of HRs (OHCHR, n.d.-b). Because HRs are socially constructed, and our understandings of them are not static, they remain part of an ongoing discourse where "human rights are constructed and reconstructed in a continuing process" (Ife, 2001, p. 8)

Thus, as the needs of certain groups of people are recognized, validated, and defined, or as world events indicate the need for attention to and action on specific HRs issues, international HRs treaties have become more focused and specialized regarding the issues addressed and the social groups identified as requiring protection (UN, n.d.). Only recently have many historically disadvantaged groups—children, women, racial minorities, people with intellectual disabilities, prisoners, immigrants and refugees, and the frail elderly—asserted claims for the HRs previously denied to them (UN, n.d.).

Some of the treaties are supplemented by optional protocols (OPs), which improve or add to the existing treaty or address a substantive area related to the treaty. OPs function as HRs treaties in their own right and are open to signature, accession, or ratification by countries who are party to the main treaty (UN Women, n.d.). International treaties and customary law form the backbone of international HRs law, while other instruments, such as declarations, guidelines, and principles adopted at the international level, contribute to its understanding, implementation, and development. Other instruments, adopted at a regional level, reflect the particular HRs concerns of the region and provide specific mechanisms of protection (OHCHR, n.d.-b).

The feminist movement of the 1960s also advanced a redefinition of HRVs to include the degradation and violation of women because, although such abuses were frequently committed by private citizens, they were often condoned or even sanctioned by states (Bunch, 1990). Historically, the right to respect for family and private life had been interpreted as the duty of state or other bodies "non-interference" in the private and family sphere. This breakdown of the public/private divide within the HRs framework had implications for other oppressed groups, such as children, the disabled, and the elderly.

During the 1970s and through the 1980s, international HRs discourse and activism grew exponentially. HRs emerged as the dominant moral vocabulary in foreign affairs and entered popular parlance, which was attributed to the US foreign policies of President Jimmy Carter and the rapid growth of non-governmental organizations (NGOs) such as Amnesty International and Human Rights Watch, founded in 1961 and 1978, respectively (Cmiel, 2004). These organizations began to operate outside the sphere of the UN and its state-bound machinery, using research and information gathering to combat rights violations around the globe and to influence the media, policymakers, and other third parties. Transnational networks of activists served as a catalyst to further activism (Cmiel, 2004; Moyn, 2010).

The 1980s and 1990s witnessed important markers in HRs history. HRs organizations, both governmental and non-governmental, continued to proliferate, empowered by global information technology

(Hitchcock, 2015). Activism expanded to include health rights, women's rights, economic justice, and indigenous people's rights (Cmiel, 2004). The waning of the Cold War and the collapse of the Communism starting in 1988 gave newfound hope that a unified vision of HRs would emerge, or that the USA, as the hegemonic power would influence decisions in countries around the globe (Ishay, 2004). One commentator noted that with this domination, we had reached "the end of history" (Fukuyama, 1992). In other words, liberal democracy and a globalized free market had triumphed and these would spread freedom, democracy, and HRs. Progressives after the Cold War placed their hopes on the development of a global civil society and global citizenship (Dietrich, 2006).

The years since 1990 have seen incremental progress for HRs, alongside setbacks. The Vienna Declaration and Programme of Action of 1993, the first HRs conference since the end of the Cold War, reaffirmed HRs as relevant universal standards and established the UN's *Office of the High Commissioner for Human Rights.* That same year, the UN expanded the definition of "war crimes" to include systematic rape (Cmiel, 2004). HRs treaties continued to expand and international humanitarian law widened through the creation of the *International Criminal Court (ICC).* Its founding treaty, the Rome Statute, which entered into force on July 1, 2002, created the world's first permanent international criminal court. The court investigates and prosecutes individuals accused of committing crimes such as genocide, war crimes, and crimes against humanity, serving as a court of last resort when states are unable or unwilling to take action. Its international jurisdiction enables it to supersede state sovereignty in order to seek justice and end impunity for egregious crimes that are of concern to the international community. Other progressive developments such as the advance of gay rights took place in some parts of Europe and the Americas (Altman & Symons, 2016).

However, during and since the 1990s, there has been a resurgence of ethnic cleansing, genocide, torture, and terrorism on the international landscape (Cmiel, 2004), and contentions exist regarding the benefits of globalization. Issues concerning cultural differences and socio-economic inequities intensified in both the developed and developing world, with greater fragmentation about definitions of rights. Debates over labor rights in the wake of the globalized free market economy, cultural rights, and the homogenization of world into universal consumerism led to backlashes. Fundamentalist groups, nationalist and right-wing militant movements, and hostility to immigrants were all galvanized. In the aftermath of 9/11, "the War on Terror" and security concerns emerged as paramount, to the detriment of HRs. Moreover, Bush administration violations of provisions in American and international law regarding the treatment of prisoners of war and other detainees during periods of armed conflict undermined the moral authority of the USA (Dietrich, 2006; Fontas, 2010).

During and since the Bush administration, some scholars (Hopgood, 2013; Ignatieff, 2002; Possner, 2014) expressed cynicism that the time of HRs has passed. Others reject such pessimism about HRs laws and institutions and view them instead as enduring (Risse, Ropp, & Sikkink, 2013), while acknowledging that these are indeed hard times for HRs. Divergent views of the future of HRs, particularly in terms of their universal relevance and effectiveness, continue.

## Some Major Critiques/Contemporary Controversies

Since the adoption of the UDHR (UN, 1948b), human rights have come to represent a powerful discourse throughout the world, yet they are not immune to controversy and criticisms.

### Universal Relevance

One of the strongest criticisms has been the question of whether HRs are universally relevant. Cultural relativists and others claim that they privilege Western cultural norms (Ife, 2001), are an essentially Western concept that ignores the diverse cultural, economic, and political realities of the other parts of the world, and may constitute a form of Western imperialism (Hopgood, 2013; Ife, 2001). Those who dispute cultural relativists point out that a closer examination of history (some of which is presented in this chapter) shows that HRs efforts were, from the start, a pluralist project emerging through a multitude of historical processes with a diverse set of actors (Jensen, 2016; Lauren, 2011). Mainstream historical accounts fail to include the important role of the Global South in the emergence of the global HRs regime (Jensen, 2016; Rajagopal, 2003). Although the historical influence of Western legal traditions in the international arena is evident, the rights agreed upon are not exclusively Western moral and political values; they are encountered in every society (Tharoor, 2000/1999; Twiss, 1998).

Furthermore, the notion of "traditional culture," advanced by cultural relativists to justify the nonobservance of HRs, no longer exists in a pure form at the national level anywhere. Culture is not static or monolithic in any society; it is, instead, constantly evolving (Ife, 2001). All cultures change in response to both internal and external influences and circumstances, and there is much in every culture that is naturally outgrown and rejected (Tharoor, 2000/1999). Cultural relativists have been accused of pursuing hidden agendas that privilege certain voices and maintain the status quo (Healy, 2008). Those who affirm the universalism of HRs assert that HRs can be compatible with both liberal and communitarian societies and traditions (Twiss, 1998), and that universality does not require their uniformity (Tharoor, 2000/1999). Glendon (2001) maintains that the UDHR is "flexible enough to allow for differences in emphasis and means of implementation," so that "its fertile principles ... [can] be brought to life in a legitimate variety of ways" within the world's different cultures" (p. 111).

## Effectiveness of HR Law

A second major area of contention concerns effectiveness. That is, whether HRs laws and treaties truly have an impact on HRVs and result in social progress. Over the years since the UDHR, there has been an increased emphasis on measuring and monitoring HRs. A core activity of HRs NGOs, such as Amnesty International and Human Rights Watch, has been to set up monitoring systems to track implementation of international HRs treaties. These NGOs also use data to alert the international community about egregious HRVs, mobilize different constituencies around particular HRs issues, and advocate for additional standard setting in the international law of HRs (Landman, 2013). HRs measures are increasingly employed by social scientists to report on the HRs performance of countries over time. Nonetheless, there have been conceptual and methodological debates about how to measure the impact of HRs and the contribution of international HRs law to social progress (Fariss & Dancy, 2017; for further information about HRs measurement, see Risse et al., 2013).

Activists and scholars disagree about the efficacy of HRs and may use different yardsticks to measure progress. The results to date have been mixed. For example, some studies have found that treaty ratifications are associated with declining repressive violence in countries with active NGO sectors or that are transitioning to democracy

(Powell & Staton, 2009; Simmons, 2009). However, Hathaway (2002) demonstrated that countries that ratify the ICCPR are, counterintuitively, more likely to commit rights violations.

In the current world political climate, it may seem that the field of HRs is fraught, yet activists and scholars remind us that contemporary data may not represent long-term trends in HRs practices (Sikkink, 2011, 2017). The status of HRs around the world is characterized by some retrogression and worsening, such as the situations in Syria, Egypt, Mexico, and the USA, but also by other areas of increasing awareness and improvements, such as greater equality and opportunities for women and sexual minorities. HRs actualization does not follow a linear line of unbroken progress and may never be fully complete (Lauren, 2011). Change can be a slow process that results from struggle and socialization whereby international norms are internalized into the domestic practices (Clark & Sikkink, 2013). Comparing present to past, Sikkink (2011, 2017) demonstrates that genocide and violence against civilians have declined over time, while access to health care and education has increased dramatically. Fukuda-Parr, Lawson-Remer, and Randolph (2015) document strides being made in the Global South regarding social and economic rights that are often overlooked by cynics.

Viewed in the longer term, HRs movements have been vastly effective and have made positive contributions around the world (Sikkink, 2017; Simmons, 2009). Others argue that the increasing reports of HRVs, in some cases, are not an indication of stagnating HRs practices, but reflect a systematic change in the way monitors, such as Amnesty International and the US State Department, encounter and interpret information about HRVs (Clark & Sikkink, 2013; Fariss, 2014).

Over the past several decades, there has been a coalescence of HRs activists and organizations into a truly international HRs movement. Progress has resulted from a long series of HRs struggles, often led by oppressed peoples inspired by HRs ideas that targeted powerful institutions and practices (Sikkink, 2017). Although some states have ceded some of their sovereignty and can now be held accountable to uphold HR standards, in many cases, national sovereignty and interests have continued to trump HRs. Much of the success of the fulfillment of HRs remains in the hands of states, which is one of the great paradoxes of the realization of international HRs. States have been both the most significant abusers and the most significant protectors of rights—"both the cause and the cure" (Lauren, 2011, p. 300). Powerful countries are not always held to the same standards, while the less powerful are held to account, and double standards must be constrained (Forsythe, 2017). For example, the USA has yet to ratify many key international agreements, such as the ICSECR, CEDAW, and the CRC to name a few. The USA is also one of the few countries not to ratify or sign the Rome Statute that established the International Criminal Court. In several cases, the USA also openly disregarded decisions by the International Court of Justice (Dietrich, 2006) and, recently, the USA withdrew from the United Nations Human Rights Council (Piccone, 2018). The right to security has increasingly taken precedence over civil rights, political rights have been elevated over welfare rights, and cultural or religious rights have been emphasized over universal rights (Dietrich, 2006).

*Documenting the Psychological Impact of HRVs*
In addition to documenting the effectiveness of HR legal efforts at societal levels, there have also been efforts to quantify the suffering associated with HRVs. As mentioned previously, some investigators have turned to the trauma framework and PTSD diagnosis to enumerate and substantiate claims concerning the grave impact of some HRVs, but these translation efforts have been met with some concern (e.g., Steel et al., 2009). Nickerson et al. (2014) have noted that "no universally accepted, comprehensive, and unified construct has been developed that adequately encapsulates the wide-ranging effects of exposure to HRVs" (p. 173). This need to acknowledge and encompass the more extensive effects of severe HRVs has led several theorists to propose new frameworks that elucidate the range and possible moderators of effects. Nickerson et al. (2014) have developed a model that explicates three different pathways through which HRVs can result in psychosocial impairment, each moderated by the post-HRV environment: disruptions in interpersonal processes, decreased perceptions of control, and denigration of individual and group identity. Similarly, Silove (1999) has proposed a framework which stipulates that exposure to extreme and traumatic HRVs results in "fundamental challenges to one or more of the major adaptive systems that support a state of psychosocial equilibrium in individuals and their communities" (p. 205). Among these are systems that subsume the functions of personal safety, attachment and bond maintenance, identity and role functioning, justice, and existential meaning.

Such theorizing is necessary because strict PTSD formulations simply do not account for the variety and severity of disturbances survivors of HRVs report. As Momartin et al. (2003) suggest: "it may be that HRs violations pose a more general threat to the survivor's future psychosocial adaptation in areas of functioning that extend beyond the confines of PTSD" (p. 775).

Indeed, additional researchers argue for broader psychosocial or public health frameworks that attend to social, cultural, political dimensions of trauma and better capture the various pathways by which organized violence impacts mental health, especially the role of stressful social and material conditions (de Jong, 2002; Kleber, Figely, & Gersons, 1995; Miller & Rasmussen, 2010). For example, Miller and Rasmussen (2010) found that direct war exposure exerts a significant direct effect on mental health, but daily stressors were also very influential. Stressful social and material conditions significantly increased overall explanatory power within the empirical model and consistently weakened the direct relationship between war exposure and mental health. Similarly, research with refugees consistently indicates that post-migration stressors such as racism, xenophobia, and economic exclusion strongly influence post-resettlement mental health, even after controlling for the effects of previous trauma exposure (Bemak & Chi-Ying Chung, 2017; Nickerson, Bryant, Steel, Silove, & Brooks, 2010; Porter & Haslam, 2005).

Narrow PTSD formulations and conceptions of trauma also fail to denote the complexity of settings characterized by authoritarian repression, war, poverty, and scarce resources (Becker, 1995; de Jong, 2002; Kistener, 2015). For example, the concept of "post" trauma may be inadequate as it suggests that the TE was limited to certain moment in time in the past, when in fact there is an experience of cumulative and continuous trauma (Becker, 1995). Underlying forces of inequality and injustice are contributing factors so that membership in a minority or marginalized group increases the incidence of traumatic events (Duran & Duran, 1998; Neria, Nandi, & Galea, 2008; Vogel & Marshall, 2001). Violence and other potentially traumatic events occur more often in contexts of impoverishment where threats to survival proliferate (Breslau, Wilcox, & Storr, 2003; Carter, 2007). Kistener (2015, p. 2), drawing from an African context, observes: "A traumatic event is never just an event. It is the result of a complex set of interactions between the personal and the collective, between the individual and her social context, and in the end it is always and inevitably a series of events shaped by economic and political imbalances of power." Indeed, no model to date addresses fully the gamut of effects that HRVs have on individuals, families, communities, and overarching systems of meaning.

## EXAMINING THE INTERSECTION OF TRAUMATIC EXPERIENCE AND HUMAN RIGHTS VIOLATIONS

We have outlined the basic history, definitions, and some strengths and limitations of the trauma and HRs frameworks separately because historically they represent two different discourses generated by different disciplines for different purposes. However, importantly, TEs and HRVs often occur together and in some cases are simply different descriptions emphasizing different aspects of the same experience. Most recent scholarship that addresses acute HRVs and trauma together relates to this experiential intersection (e.g., McDonnell et al., 2012; Momartin et al., 2003; Nelson et al., 2014; Nickerson et al., 2014, 2015; Silove, 1999). Individuals or groups at this nexus are subject to the particularly toxic admixture of TEs and HRVs that arise from severe acts of commission (e.g., personal or political violence); indefensible acts of omission (e.g., lack of access to basic goods, service, and protections; lack of respect for essential and inviolable human dignity and autonomy; lack of accountability and judicial redress); and crushing interpersonal or institutional betrayal. Additionally, we propose that such victims may suffer profound dehumanization, an *existential injury*, which can haunt lifetimes and generations.

In addition to the HRV and TE descriptions that represent the same event, there is considerable, although not complete, overlap between many of the other exemplars of these two constructs. The elements that distinguish some TEs and HRVS may be worth noting. First, TEs represent a relatively narrow range of human experiences, currently defined as involving individual exposure to actual or threatened death, serious injury, or sexual violence (APA, 2013), whereas HRVs can occur in virtually every facet of individual and collective human existence. Second, TEs can be *either* natural or human-caused, whereas HRVs are always a product of human action (or lack thereof). Third, HRVs can originate in both acts of commission and acts of omission, whereas human-caused TEs *primarily* derive from acts of commission. Fourth, although previously HRs were understood to be "principally concerned with the individual's relationship to the state" (Steel et al., 2009, p. 359), in the past several decades, HRVs have come to be recognized in transgressions by states, state actors, non-state actors, and even individuals against individuals or groups, just as human-caused TEs can be caused by actions of any individual or group. However, HRs principles place the state in the role of duty-bearer with obligations to protect citizens from violations.

Although these distinctions may be important, in many cases TEs or HRVs can result from, accompany, or result in events of the other type. For example, living through the frightening experience of (and losses wrought by) a natural disaster itself would be a TE, but may not be considered a HRV because there is no human perpetrator. Nonetheless, structural inequalities and institutional neglect may increase vulnerability and contribute to conditions that exacerbate the disaster's impact. Moreover, the catastrophic aftermath may involve multiple HRVs if, for example, there are failures in government/humanitarian provision of disaster relief to provide necessities of life and protections from further victimization during the post-event period, as was the case with the US government's wholly inadequate response following Hurricane Maria's devastation in Puerto Rico in 2017. Thus, consideration of post-disaster adversity is critical to grasping the full impact of a traumatic event because it may involve even more severe and longer-term sequelae, including significant HRVs.

Moreover, while HRVs related primarily to second-generation rights do not typically involve, in and of themselves, *immediate* life threat, they do often occur within populations at significantly higher risk for TEs due to resource scarcity and historical or ongoing persecution and oppression, and lack of medical care access increases the risk of death in many circumstances. Additionally, life stressors, such as violations of second-generation HRs that occur in the wake of a traumatic event, can increase the risk of PTSD (Brewin, Andrews, & Valentine, 2000) among those exposed.

Steel et al. (2009) note that, although mental health professionals are more familiar with abuses to first-generation rights, there is a growing need for attention to second- and third-generation rights "and how these interact with exposure to past trauma relevant to first-generation rights. Recognition that violations can lead to a progressive erosion of rights extending into multiple generations of rights... serves to forewarn trauma professionals of the vulnerabilities of the populations relevant to their work" (p. 363). These observations reinforce the issue of the inextricability of the context in which an event occurs from the full impact of the event itself.

Indeed, we would argue that TEs and HRVs are inseparable because each category can function as the background for, context of, or direct or indirect product of the other. For example, child abuse is at once the threat or actual use of physical violence (a TE) against a minor and a direct contravention of the special care and assistance that the UDHR (UN, 1948b) stipulates for children (Art. 25), as well as the right to life, liberty, and security of person (Art. 3), and the prohibition against cruel, degrading, or inhuman treatment (Art. 5). Similarly, forced displacements can involve coerced movements of individuals to escape repression, persecution, or conflict, which comprise both TEs (e.g., threatened force, violence) and multiple HRVs (e.g., threats to life, liberty, and security of person, protection from torture, arbitrary arrest, detention, or exile, and protections of movement and right to return to one's nation [Arts. 3, 5, 9, 13, respectively]). Experiences such as these appear most amenable to the new, expanded understandings of the varied psychological phenomenology and mechanisms of trauma because the effects of compounded TEs and HRVs often involve collective violence, institutional betrayal, and assaults on victims' worldview and assumptions of a moral universe.

## DISCUSSION

Examining a simple diagnostic snapshot of PTSD symptoms or a list of HRs abuses in isolation is wholly inadequate to the purpose of identifying, understanding, and addressing human suffering. A simple HR formulation can catalog violations and decry abuses, but on its own, it is insufficient to adequately address suffering. It does not entail treatment and therefore does not fully capture the psychological impact, nor specify the remedy, for the individual or community that is *currently* suffering. The broad trauma framework provides a vocabulary for human suffering, whereas the human rights framework articulates a moral order designed to prevent and redress human suffering.

We argue, therefore, that both frameworks, including their limitations and advancements, should be considered in any effort to achieve a comprehensive grasp of the experience of a traumatic event or HRV. In their own way, each contributes to a language of human dignity and security, defining how we should treat each other, and the duties we owe each other as fellow humans. Both delineate boundaries of conduct that, when crossed, cause unacceptable harm and suffering and constitute assaults on humanness. Each framework may also be applied to complement and extend the other. The trauma framework offers terminology for some elements of the experience and its effects, a range of approaches to intervention, and a scientific methodology to elucidate underlying mechanisms and to measure outcomes. In contrast, the HR framework encompasses the wider circumstances that nest traumatic events, identifies essential and inviolable conditions necessary to dignified human existence, and codifies the ethical basis to guide and support efforts at prevention and collective restoration. It establishes standards for a minimum set of goods, services, opportunities, and protections for people and a set of practices to realize them (Donnelly, 2013).

Danieli (2009) has observed that "massive trauma causes such diverse and complex destruction that only a multidimensional, multidisciplinary integrative framework is adequate to describe it" (p. 351). The challenge, then, is to *integrate*, to the extent possible, current and future conceptions of trauma and human rights in how we consider, research, and intervene with survivors of adverse experience, HRVs, or their combination. To do so would provide a more complete understanding of human suffering at both individual and collective levels, its causes and mechanisms, and a much wider range of possible psychological and cultural interventions or sociopolitical resolutions.

The narrow construction of PTSD may be useful for the purposes of medical communication, categorization, and intervention for some who have been traumatized; however, as conceived currently, it fails to encompass the myriad manifestations, psychological mechanisms, and far-ranging and long-term sequelae of trauma. The addition of HR principles helps contextualize the trauma construct, illuminates the conditions of suffering, and recognizes that much suffering stems from broader social problems that require social remedies (de Jong, 2002). Conceptualizing trauma and human rights principles conjointly offers a more holistic framework and language to understand suffering. By incorporating broader historical and sociopolitical dimensions of trauma among individuals and groups, it "re-politicizes" approaches to trauma so that these realities are not obscured (Kistener, 2015). Deployed together, a trauma lens is augmented by such human rights principles as self-determination, equality, anti-discrimination, the right to culture, language and nationality, and the right to the highest attainable standard of physical and mental health. A combined framework assesses trauma from an intersectional standpoint that incorporates class, gender, race, age, ethnicity, nationality, sexual orientation, ability, and other social locations. As Fassin and Rechtman (2009) note:

> Both before and after the tsunami, the survivors in Aceh were already victims of political domination, military repression, and economic marginalization. Both before and after Hurricane Katrina, the people of New Orleans were already victims of poverty and discrimination that reinforced class inequalities through racial distinctions. (p. 281)

The addition of a human rights framework provides an idiom and standards that can speak to the trauma of peoples subjected to the politics of colonialism, past slavery, genocide or refugee camps, the practices of trafficking, torture and sexual violence, as well as victims of institutional negligence and betrayal.

Employing a holistic framework, with a focus on the full range of human rights, also highlights the important relationship between TEs and violations of second-generation economic, social, and cultural rights. Within even the most prosperous economies, poverty and gross inequalities persist and the denial of these rights can have devastating effects and lead to further violations of human rights (Arbour, 2005, as cited in OHCHR, 2008). For example, respect for economic and social rights ensures resources that are necessary to establish a well-functioning mental health system that provides the necessary material, medical, psychological, and social assistance to facilitate treatment and recovery (Jenkins, Baingana, Ahmad, McDaid, & Atun, 2011).

Furthermore, combining the frameworks underscores the social injustice that lies at the root of many TEs and serves as a tool to demand justice. An integrated approach also promotes participation and empowerment, whereby humans are not viewed as passive recipients of services and benefits, but as rights-holders with creative agency and with rights to shape their life (Donnelly, 2013). Human rights instruments codify rights that can be claimed and create participatory and social advocacy roles for helping professionals and victims of HRVs. As rights-bearers, citizens can demand accountability from duty-bearers and pressure institutions, the state, or the international community into action.

The trauma and human rights frameworks continue to be imperfect and contested. Still, their application together can provide a paradigm shift that, without de-emphasizing the importance of specialized treatment, directs itself to the broader social conditions that protect, promote, and restore mental health and human well-being.

## References

Altman, D., & Symons, J. (2016). *Queer wars: The new global polarization over gay rights.* Cambridge, MA: Polity Press.

American Psychiatric Association. (1980). *Diagnostic and statistical manual of mental disorders* (3rd ed.). Washington, DC: Author.

American Psychiatric Association. (1994). *Diagnostic and statistical manual of mental disorders* (4th ed.). Washington, DC: Author.

American Psychiatric Association. (2013). *Diagnostic and statistical manual of mental disorders* (5th ed.). Washington, DC: Author.

Becker, D. (1995). The deficiency of the concept of posttraumatic stress disorder when dealing with victims of human rights violations. In R. Kleber, C. Figley, & B. Gersons (Eds.), *Beyond trauma: Cultural and societal dynamics* (pp. 99–110). New York, NY: Springer Press.

Bemak, F. P., & Chi-Ying Chung, R. (2017). Refugee trauma: Culturally responsive counseling interventions. *Journal of Counseling and Development, 95,* 299–309.

Ben-Ezra, M. (2011). Traumatic reactions from antiquity to the 16th century: Was there a common denominator? *Stress and Health, 27,* 223–240.

Benjet, C., Bromet, E., Karam, E. G., Kessler, R. C., McLaughlin, K. A. Ruscio, A. M., ... Koenen, K. C. (2016). The epidemiology of traumatic event exposure worldwide: Results from the World Mental Health Survey Consortium. *Psychological Medicine, 46,* 327–343.

Bloom, S. L. (2006). Societal trauma: Danger and democracy. In N. Totton (Ed.), *The politics of psychotherapy: New perspectives* (pp. 17–29). London, England: Open University Press.

Bobbio, N. (1996). *The age of rights.* Cambridge, MA: Polity Press.

Bodkin, J. A., Pope, H. G., Detke, M. J., & Hudson, J. I. (2007). Is PTSD caused by traumatic stress? *Journal of Anxiety Disorders, 21,* 176–182.

Bracken, P. J., Giller, J. E., & Summerfield, D. (1995). Psychological responses to war and atrocity: The limitations of current concepts. *Social Science Medicine, 40*(8), 1073–1082.

Brave Heart, M. Y. H. (2003). The historical trauma response among natives and its relationship with substance abuse: A Lakota illustration. *Journal of Psychoactive Drugs, 35*(1), 7–13.

Brave Heart, M. Y. H., & Debruyn, L. M. (1998). The American Indian holocaust: Healing historical unresolved grief. *American Indian and Alaska Native Mental Health Research, 8*(2), 60–82.

Breslau, N., Wilcox, H., & Storr, C. (2003). Trauma exposure and posttraumatic stress disorder: A study of youth in urban America. *Journal of Urban Health, 81,* 530–544.

Brewin, C. R., Andrews, B., & Valentine, J. D. (2000). Meta-analysis of risk factors for posttraumatic stress disorder in trauma-exposed adults. *Journal of Consulting and Clinical Psychology, 68*(5), 748–766.

Bunch, C. (1990). Women's rights as human rights: Toward a re-vision of human rights. *Human Rights Quarterly, 12*(4), 486–498.

Burgess, A. W., & Holstrom, L. L. (1974). Rape trauma syndrome. *American Journal of Psychiatry, 131*(9), 981–986.

Carter, R. T. (2007). Racism and psychological injury: Recognizing and assessing race-based traumatic stress. *The Counselling Psychologist, 35,* 13–105.

Clark, A. M., & Sikkink, K. (2013). Information effects and human rights data: Is the good news about increased human rights information bad news for human rights measures? *Human Rights Quarterly, 35*(3), 539–568.

Cmiel, K. (2004). The recent history of human rights. *The American Historical Review, 109*(1), 117–135.

Daly, R. J. (1983). Samuel Pepys and post-traumatic stress disorder. *British Journal of Psychiatry, 143,* 64–68.

Danieli, Y. (1998). *International handbook of multigenerational legacies of trauma.* New York, NY: Plenum.

Danieli, Y. (2009). Massive trauma and the healing role of reparative justice. *Journal of Traumatic Stress, 22*(5), 351–357.

de Jong, J. (2002). *Trauma, war, and violence: Public mental health in socio-cultural context.* New York, NY: Springer Press.

Dietrich, J. (2006). U.S. human rights policy in the post-cold war era. *Political Science Quarterly, 121*(2), 269–294.

Difede, J., Apfeldorf, W. J., Cloitre, M., Spielmen, L. A., & Perry, S. W. (1997). Acute psychiatric responses to the explosion at the World Trade Center: A case series. *Journal of Nervous and Mental Disease, 185,* 519–522.

Donnelly, J. (2013). *Universal human rights in theory and practice.* Ithaca, NY: Cornell University Press.

Duran, E., & Duran, B. (1998). Healing the American Indian soul. In Y. Danieli (Ed.), *Intergenerational handbook of multigenerational legacies of trauma* (pp. 342–372). New York, NY: Plenum.

Fariss, C. (2014). Respect for human rights has improved over time: Modeling the changing standard of accountability. *American Political Science Review, 108*(2), 297–318.

Fariss, C., & Dancy, G. (2017). Measuring the impact of human rights: Conceptual and methodological debates. *Annual Review of Law Social Science, 13,* 273–279.

Fassin, D., & Rechtman, R. (2009). *The empire of trauma: An inquiry into the condition of victimhood.* Princeton, NJ: Princeton University Press.

Finkelhor, D., Hotaling, G., Lewis, I. A., & Smith, C. (1990). Sexual abuse in a national survey of adult men and women: Prevalence, characteristics, and risk factors. *Child Abuse and Neglect, 14,* 19–28.

Fontas, J. P. (2010). The Bush administration torture policy: Origins and conse-quences. *Inquiries Journal/Student Pulse, 2*(8). Retrieved from http://www.inquiriesjournal.com/a?id=276.

Forsythe, D. (2017). Hard times for human rights. *Journal of Human Rights, 16*(2), 242–253.

Friedman, M. J. (2013). Finalizing PTSD in the DSM-5: Getting here from there and where to go next. *Journal of Traumatic Stress, 26,* 548–556.

Fukuda-Parr, S., Lawson-Remer, T., & Randolph, S. (2015). *Fulfilling social and economic rights.* New York, NY: Oxford University Press.

Fukuyama, F. (1992). *The end of history and the last man.* New York, NY: Free Press.

Galtung, J. (1994). *Human rights in another key.* Cambridge, MA: Polity Press.

Glendon, M. A. (2001). *A world made new: Eleanor Roosevelt and the Universal Declaration of Human Rights.* New York, NY: Random House.

Hathaway, O. (2002). Do human rights treaties make a difference? *The Yale Law Journal, 111*(8), 1935–2042.

Hautzinger, S., & Scandlyn, J. (2014). *Beyond post-traumatic stress: Homefront struggles with the wars on terror.* Walnut Creek, CA: Left Coast Press.

Healy, L. (2008). *International social work: Professional action in an interdepend-ent world.* New York, NY: Oxford University Press.

Henderson, D. (1975). Incest. In A. Freedman, H. Kaplan, & B. Sadock (Eds.), *Comprehensive textbook of psychiatry* (2nd ed., pp. 1530–1539). Baltimore, MD: Williams & Wilkins.

Herman, J. L. (1992). Complex PTSD: A syndrome in survivors of prolonged and repeated trauma. *Journal of Traumatic Stress, 5*(3), 377–391.

Herman, J. L. (1997). *Trauma and recovery: The aftermath of violence—From domestic abuse to political terror.* New York, NY: Basic Books.

Hinton, D. E., & Lewis-Fernández, R. (2010). Idioms of distress among trauma survivors: Subtypes and clinical utility. *Culture, Medicine, and Psychiatry, 34,* 209–218.

Hinton, D. E., & Lewis-Fernández, R. (2011). The cross-cultural validity of posttraumatic stress disorder: Implications for DSM-5. *Depression and Anxiety, 28,* 783–801.

Hitchcock, W. (2015). The rise and fall of human rights? Searching for a narra-tive from the cold war to the 9/11 era. *Human Rights Quarterly, 37,* 80–106.

Holmes, S., & Sunstein, C. (1999). *The cost of rights: Why liberty depends on taxes.* New York, NY: W. W. Norton.

Hopgood, S. (2013). *The endtimes of human rights.* Ithaca, NY: Cornell University Press.

Hunt, L. (2007). *Inventing human rights: A history.* New York, NY: W. W. Norton.

Hyland, P., Shevlin, M., Fyvie, C., & Karatzias, T. (2018). Posttraumatic stress disorder and complex posttraumatic stress disorder in the DSM-5 and ICD-11: Clinical and behavioral correlates. *Journal of Traumatic Stress, 31,* 174–180.

Ife, J. (2001). *Human rights and social work: Toward rights-based practice.* Cambridge, MA: Cambridge University Press.

Ignatieff, M. (2002, February 5). Is the human rights era ending? *The New York Times*, p. A25.

Ishay, M. (2004). *The history of human rights from ancient times to the globalization era.* Berkeley, CA: University of California Press.

Ishay, M. (2005). The socialist contributions to human rights: An overlooked legacy. *International Journal of Human Rights, 9*(2), 225–245.

Ishay, M. (2010). The universal declaration of human rights at 60: A bridge to which future? *Perspectives Development and Technology, 9*(1–2), 11–27.

Iyall Smith, K. E. (2008). Comparing state and international protections of indigenous peoples' human rights. *American Behavioral Scientist, 51,* 1817–1835.

James, S. (2007). *Universal human rights: Origins and development.* New York, NY: LFB Scholarly Publishing LLC.

Janoff-Bulman, R. (1992). *Shattered assumptions: Towards a new psychology of trauma.* New York, NY: Free Press.

Jenkins, R., Baingana, F., Ahmad, R., McDaid, D., & Atun, R. (2011). Social, economic, human rights and political challenges to global mental health. *Mental Health in Family Medicine, 8,* 87–96.

Jensen, S. L. B. (2016). *Decolonization—Not western liberals—Established human rights on the global agenda.* Retrieved from https://www.openglobalrights. org/decolonization-not-western-liberals-established-human-rights-on-g/.

Jensen, S. L. B. (2017). *Putting to rest the Three Generations Theory of human rights.* Retrieved from https://www.openglobalrights.org/putting-to-rest-the-three-generations-theory-of-human-rights/.

Jones, E., & Wesseley, S. (2006). Psychological trauma: A historical perspective. *Psychiatry, 5*(7), 217–220.

Kardiner, A. (1941). *The traumatic neuroses of war.* New York, NY: Hoeber.

Kellerman, N. P. F. (2001). Psychopathology in children of holocaust survivors: A review of the research literature. *Israel Journal of Psychiatry and Related Sciences, 38*(1), 36–46.

Kessler, R. C., Sonnega, A., Bromet, E., & Hughes, M. (1995). Posttraumatic stress disorder in the National Comorbity Survey. *Archives of General Psychiatry, 52*(12), 1048–1060.

Kienzler, H. (2008). Debating war-trauma and post-traumatic stress disorder (PTSD) in an interdisciplinary arena. *Social Science and Medicine, 67,* 218–227.

Kilpatrick, D. G., Resnick, H. S., Milanak, M. E., Miller, M. W., Keyes, K. M., & Friedman, M. J. (2013). National estimates of exposure to traumatic events and PTSD prevalence using DSM-IV and DSM-5 criteria. *Journal of Traumatic Stress, 26,* 537–547.

Kirmayer, L. J., Gone, J. P., & Moses, J. (2014). Rethinking historical trauma. *Transcultural Psychiatry, 51*(3), 299–319.

Kistener, J. (2015). From personal tragedy to global responsibility: Re-politicizing trauma work in an African context. *AIR Thoughts, 1,* 1–6. Retrieved from http://airforafrica.org/wp-content/uploads/2015/05/AIR-thoughts-Issue2-FINAL_WEB1.pdf.

Kleber, R., Figley, C., & Gersons, B. (1995). *Beyond trauma: Cultural and societal dynamics.* New York, NY: Springer.

Koenen, K. C., Ratanatharathorn, A., Ng, L., McLaughlin, K. A., Bromet, E. J., Stein, D. J., ... Kessler, R. C. (2017). Posttraumatic stress disorder in the World Mental Health Surveys. *Psychological Medicine, 47,* 2260–2274.

Landman, T. (2013). Measuring and monitoring human rights. In M. Goodhart (Ed.), *Human rights: Politics and practice* (pp. 363–379). Oxford, England: Oxford University Press.

Larsen, S. E., & Pacella, M. L. (2016). Comparing the effect of DSM-congruent traumas vs. DSM-incongruent stressors on PTSD symptoms: A meta-analytic review. *Journal of Anxiety Disorders, 38,* 37–46.

Lauren, P. G. (2011). *The evolution of international human rights: Visions seen.* Philadelphia, PA: University of Pennsylvania Press.

Lindemann, E. (1944). Symptomatology and management of acute grief. *American Journal of Psychiatry, 151*(6 Suppl.), 155–160.

Litz, B. T., Stein, N., Delaney, E., Lebowitz, L., Nash, W. P., Silva, C., & Maguen, S. (2009). Moral injury and moral repair in war veterans: A preliminary model and intervention strategy. *Clinical Psychology Review, 29,* 695–706.

Macklem, P. (2015). Human rights in international law: Three generations or one? *London Review of International Law, 3*(1), 61–92.

Maguen, S., & Litz, B. T. (2012). Moral injury in veterans of war. *PTSD Research Quarterly, 23*(1), 1–6.

McDonnell, M., Robjant, K., & Katona, C. (2012). Complex posttraumatic stress disorder and survivors of human rights violations. *Current Opinion in Psychiatry, 26,* 1–6.

McHugh, P. R., & Treisman, G. (2007). PTSD: A problematic diagnostic category. *Journal of Anxiety Disorders, 21,* 211–222.

McNally, R. J. (2009). Can we fix PTSD in the DSM-V? *Depression and Anxiety, 26,* 597–600.

Miller, K., & Rasmussen, A. (2010). War exposure, daily stressors, and mental health in conflict and post-conflict settings: Bridging the divide between trauma-focused and psychosocial frameworks. *Social Science and Medicine, 70,* 7–16.

Mol, S. S. L., Arntz, A., Metsemakers, J. F. M., Dinant, G., Vilters-van Montfort, P. A. P., & Knottnerus, J. A. (2005). Symptoms of post-traumatic stress disorder after non-traumatic events: Evidence from an open population study. *British Journal of Psychiatry, 186,* 494–499.

Momartin, S., Silove, D., Manicavasagar, V., & Steel, Z. (2003). Dimensions of trauma associated with posttraumatic stress disorder (PTSD) caseness, severity and functional impairment: A study of Bosnian refugees resettled in Australia. *Social Science and Medicine, 57,* 775–781.

Morsink, J. (2009). *Inherent human rights.* Philadelphia, PA: University of Pennsylvania Press.

Moyn, S. (2010). *The last utopia: Human rights in history.* Cambridge, MA: Harvard University Press.

Nelson, D., Price, E., & Zubrzycki, J. (2014). Integrating human rights and trauma frameworks in social work with people from refugee backgrounds. *Australian Social Work, 67*(4), 567–581.

Neria, Y., Nandi, A., & Galea, S. (2008). Post-traumatic stress disorder following disasters: A systematic review. *Psychological Medicine, 38,* 467–480.

Nickerson, A., Bryant, R. A., Rosebrock, L., & Litz, B. T. (2014). The mechanisms of psychosocial injury following human rights violations, mass trauma, and torture. *Clinical Psychology-Science and Practice, 21,* 172–191.

Nickerson, A., Bryant, R. A., Steel, Z., Silove, D., & Brooks, R. (2010). The impact of fear for family on mental health in a resettled Iraqi refugee community. *Journal of Psychiatric Research, 44*(4), 229–235.

Nickerson, A., Schnyder, U., Bryant, R. A., Schick, M., Mueller, J., & Morina, N. (2015). Moral injury in traumatized refugees. *Psychotherapy and Psychosomatics, 84,* 122–123.

Niederland, W. G. (1981). The survivor syndrome: Further observations and dimensions. *Journal of the American Psychoanalytic Association, 29*(2), 413–425.

Office of the High Commission for Human Rights. (n.d.-a). *The core international human rights documents and their monitoring bodies.* Retrieved from https://www.ohchr.org/en/professionalinterest/pages/coreinstruments.aspx.

Office of the High Commissioner for Human Rights. (n.d.-b). *What are human rights?* Retrieved from https://www.ohchr.org/EN/Issues/Pages/WhatareHumanRights.aspx.

Office of the High Commissioner for Human Rights. (2008). *Frequently asked questions on economic, social and cultural rights: Fact sheet No. 33.* Retrieved from https://www.ohchr.org/Documents/Issues/ESCR/FAQ%20on%20ESCR-en.pdf.

Picard, A. (2010). The United States' failure to ratify the international covenant on economic, social and cultural rights: Must the poor be always with us? *Stetson University College of Law Research Paper No. 2011–04.* Retrieved from https://papers.ssrn.com/sol3/papers.cfm?abstract_id=1794303.

Piccone, T. (2018, June 20). U.S. withdrawal from U.N. Human Rights Council is "America alone." *Brookings.* Retrieved from https://www.brookings.edu/

blog/order-from-chaos/2018/06/20/u-s-withdrawal-from-u-n-human-rights-council-is-america-alone/.

Pieterse, A. L., Carter, R. T., Evans, S. A., & Walter, R. A. (2010). An exploratory examination of the associations among racial and ethnic discrimination, racial climate, and trauma-related symptoms in a college student population. *Journal of Counseling Psychology, 57*(3), 255–263.

Porter, M., & Haslam, N. (2005). Predisplacement and postdisplacement factors associated with mental health of refugees and internally displaced persons: A meta-analysis. *Journal of the American Medical Association, 294,* 602–612.

Powell, E., & Staton, J. (2009). Domestic judicial institutions and human rights treaty violation. *International Studies Quarterly, 53*(1), 149–174.

Rajagopal, B. R. (2003). *International law from below: Development, social movements, and third world resistance.* Cambridge, MA: Cambridge University Press.

Risse, T., Ropp, S. C., & Sikkink, K. (2013). *The persistent power of human rights: From commitment to compliance.* Cambridge, MA: Cambridge University Press.

Rosen, G. M., & Lilienfeld, S. O. (2008). Posttraumatic stress disorder: An empirical evaluation of core assumptions. *Clinical Psychology Review, 28,* 837–868.

Sands, P. (2017). *East west street: On the origins of "genocide" and "crimes against humanity."* New York, NY: Vintage Books.

Scott, W. J. (1990). PTSD in the DSM: A case of politics in diagnosis and disease. *Social Problems, 37*(3), 294–310.

Shay, J. (2012). Moral injury. *Intertexts, 16*(1), 57–77.

Shephard, B. (2004). Risk factors and PTSD: A historian's perspective. In G. M. Rosen (Ed.), *Posttraumatic stress disorder: Issues and controversies* (pp. 39–61). Chichester, England: Wiley.

Sikkink, K. (2011). *The justice cascade: How human rights prosecutions are changing world politics.* New York, NY: W. W. Norton.

Sikkink, K. (2017). *Evidence for hope: Making human rights work in the 21st century.* Princeton, NJ: Princeton University Press.

Silove, D. (1999). The psychosocial effect of torture, mass human rights violations, and refugee trauma: Toward an integrated conceptual framework. *Journal of Nervous & Mental Disease, 187*(4), 200–207.

Simmons, B. (2009). *Mobilizing for human rights: International law in domestic politics.* New York, NY: Cambridge University Press.

Smith, C. P., & Freyd, J. J. (2014). Institutional betrayal. *American Psychologist, 69*(6), 575–587.

Spitzer, R. L., First, M. B., & Wakefield, J. C. (2007). Saving PTSD from itself in the DSM-V. *Journal of Anxiety Disorders, 21,* 233–241.

Staub-Bernasconi, S. (2007). Economic and social rights: The neglected human rights. In E. Reichert (Ed.), *Challenges in human rights* (pp. 138–161). New York, NY: Columbia University Press.

Steel, Z., Bateman Steel, C. R. B., & Silove, D. (2009). Human rights and the trauma model: Genuine partners or uneasy allies? *Journal of Traumatic Stress, 22*(5), 358–365.

Stein, D. J., McLaughlin, K. A., Koenen, K. C., Atwoli, L., Firedman, M. J., Hill, E. D., … Kessler, R. C. (2014). DSM-5 and ICD-11 definitions of post-traumatic stress disorder: Investigating "narrow" and "broad" approaches. *Depression and Anxiety, 31,* 494–505.

Summerfield, D. (2001). The invention of post-traumatic stress disorder and the social usefulness of a psychiatric category. *British Medical Journal, 322,* 95–98.

Tharoor, S. (2000/1999). Are human rights universal? *World Policy Journal, XVI*(4). Retrieved from https://worldpolicy.org/2009/11/11/tharoor-are-human-rights-universal-world-policy-journal-world-policy-institute/.

Twiss, S. (1998). Moral grounds and plural cultures: Interpreting human rights in the international community. *Journal of Religious Ethics, 26*(2), 271–282.

Twiss, S. (2004). History, human rights and globalization. *Journal of Religious Ethics, 32*(1), 39–70.

United Nations. (n.d.). *The foundation of international human rights law.* Retrieved from https://www.un.org/en/sections/universal-declaration/foundation-international-human-rights-law/index.html.

United Nations. (1948a). *Convention on the prevention and punishment of the crime of genocide.* Retrieved from https://treaties.un.org/doc/publication/unts/volume%2078/volume-78-i-1021-english.pdf.

United Nations. (1948b). *Universal declaration of human rights.* Retrieved from https://www.un.org/en/universal-declaration-human-rights/.

United Nations. (1966a). *International covenant on civil and political rights.* Retrieved from https://www.ohchr.org/EN/ProfessionalInterest/Pages/CCPR.aspx.

United Nations. (1966b). *International covenant on economic, social and cultural rights.* Retrieved from https://www.ohchr.org/EN/ProfessionalInterest/Pages/CESCR.aspx.

United Nations. (2007). *United Nations declaration on the rights of indigenous peoples.* Retrieved from https://www.un.org/development/desa/indigenous-peoples/declaration-on-the-rights-of-indigenous-peoples.html.

United Nations. (2009). International human rights law: A short history. *UN Chronicle, XLVI*(1 & 2). Retrieved from https://unchronicle.un.org/article/international-human-rights-law-short-history.

UN Women. (n.d.). *Convention on the elimination of discrimination against women: What is an optional protocol?* Retrieved from https://www.un.org/womenwatch/daw/cedaw/protocol/whatis.htm.

van der Kolk, B. A., Herron, N., & Hostetler, A. (1994). The history of trauma in psychiatry. *Psychiatric Clinics of North America, 17*(3), 583–600.

van der Kolk, B. A., & van der Hart, O. (1991). The intrusive past: The flexibility of memory and the engraving of trauma. *American Imago, 48*(4), 425–454.

Vasak, K. (1977). *A thirty-year struggle: The sustained efforts to give force of law to the Universal Declaration of Human Rights.* Paris, France: United Nations Educational, Scientific, and Cultural Organization.

Vasak, K., & Alston, P. (1982). *The international dimensions of human rights.* Westport, CT: Greenwood Press.

Vogel, L., & Marshall, L. (2001). PTSD symptoms and partner abuse: Low income women at risk. *Journal of Traumatic Stress, 14,* 569–584.

Walker, L. E. (1984). *The battered woman syndrome.* New York, NY: Springer.

# CHAPTER 3

# Moving Toward Trauma-Informed and Human Rights-Based Social Policy: The Role of the Helping Professions

*Elizabeth A. Bowen, Nadine Shaanta Murshid,*
*Amanda Brylinski-Jackson, and Shirley Gatenio Gabel*

Trauma and human rights are both multidimensional concepts. Consequently, preventing and addressing trauma and protecting human rights require a multifaceted response. In this chapter, we focus on the pivotal links between social policy, trauma, and human rights, arguing that the implementation of trauma-informed and human rights-based social policies is essential to advancing social justice for vulnerable and

E. A. Bowen (✉) · N. S. Murshid · A. Brylinski-Jackson
School of Social Work, University at Buffalo, Buffalo, NY, USA
e-mail: eabowen@buffalo.edu

N. S. Murshid
e-mail: nadinemu@buffalo.edu

A. Brylinski-Jackson
e-mail: abrylins@buffalo.edu

S. G. Gabel
Fordham University, New York, NY, USA
e-mail: gateniogabe@forham.edu

© The Author(s) 2019
L. D. Butler et al. (eds.), *Trauma and Human Rights,*
https://doi.org/10.1007/978-3-030-16395-2_3

marginalized populations. We also articulate the unique role that people in the helping professions—such as social work, mental health, nursing, and occupational therapy—can play in advocating for such policies and ensuring that the populations most directly affected by social policies have an active voice in policymaking. Advocacy is rooted in an ability to analyze policies. We offer a simple framework for trauma-informed and human rights-based social policy analysis that helping professionals can use to analyze the policies that affect the populations and communities with whom they work, and provide an example of a policy analysis using the framework. Lastly, we describe how trauma-informed and human rights-based policy analysis can lead to advocacy at various levels.

## DEFINING SOCIAL POLICY

Our working definition of a *social policy* in this chapter is any action proposed or adopted by a government or intergovernmental body at a local (e.g., city or county government), state, federal, or international level. "Policy" is frequently assumed to be synonymous with explicit actions, laws, legislation, regulations, or public programs, as well as nonbinding articles, such as strategy documents or declarations. Social policies can also be implicit, meaning that actions taken in one policy domain can have effects on other populations.

Our primary point with this definition is to distinguish these social policies from the policies of organizations and institutions, such as individual hospitals, schools, or social service agencies. The rich literature on trauma-informed care emphasizes the importance of policy at this organizational level. For example, in their protocol on creating cultures of trauma-informed care, Fallot and Harris (2009) discuss how human services organizations need to implement policies to support touchstones of trauma-informed care, such as self-care for staff and non-retraumatizing de-escalation strategies for clients in crisis. Other authors discuss the role of organizational policies in promoting principles of trauma-informed care such as safety and choice for staff in human services agencies, as well as for clients (Wolf, Green, Nochajski, Mendel, & Kusmaul, 2014).

Although policies at the organizational level are indeed essential for implementing trauma-informed care in health and human services, we argue that discussions of the role of policy in trauma-informed care can and should be expanded to include macro-level social policies as well. Since organizational-level policy change is already well-addressed in the trauma-informed care literature, this chapter will focus specifically on social policies, using examples from a variety of implementation contexts (e.g., city government, US federal policy, United Nations mandates) and issue areas (e.g., intimate partner violence, employment, policing, and drug use).

## LINKING TRAUMA, HUMAN RIGHTS, AND SOCIAL POLICY

The relationships between trauma, human rights, and social policies are not always apparent. Trauma is often conceptualized as an individual event—such as witnessing or experiencing some form of physical, sexual, and/or emotional violence—that a person endures, and then suffers the consequences (McKenzie-Mohr, Coates, & McLeod, 2012). However, trauma can also consist of repeated events that are less pronounced but nonetheless stressful and demoralizing. For example, research indicates that the repeated microaggressions that people face in daily life on the basis of characteristics such as real or perceived race, ethnicity, and sexual orientation can be traumatic and are associated with post-traumatic symptomology (Robinson & Rubin, 2016; Torres & Taknint, 2015). The existence of trauma in all its forms is indicative of human rights not being realized. If human rights were realized, the dignity and worth of individuals would be upheld and individuals would not be subject to experiencing or witnessing abuse, aggression, violence, or abandonment.

The linkage of trauma and human rights violations to social policies in domains including health care, social welfare, and employment may be less clear. Social policies reflect societal goals concerning if and how populations will be helped, or not, and typically guide societal behavioral expectations of populations covered by specific policies. For example, the Temporary Assistance to Needy Families program makes clear that parents seeking assistance are expected to work in order to receive benefits whenever possible, and child welfare policies expect explicit behavioral changes in parenting or children are removed from the home. Many social policies do not consider how trauma may be imposed as a result of policy, or how human rights may be realized or violated. Policies may also not reflect an understanding of how trauma may affect the behaviors of the target population.

We argue that both trauma and violations of human rights are inherently political (Bowen & Murshid, 2016; McKenzie-Mohr et al., 2012).

Although trauma may be experienced by any person of any social standing in any society, some groups are consistently more vulnerable than others. The factors broadly identified as core social determinants of health in a rich and growing literature—poverty and social class; oppression and discrimination on the basis of race, gender identity, sexual orientation, religion, or other identity characteristics; neighborhood-level disadvantage—also function as social determinants of trauma and violations of human rights (Braveman, Egerter, & Williams, 2011; Diez Roux & Mair, 2010; Marmot & Allen, 2014). One example of this is racialized police violence directed at African-Americans in the United States, a phenomenon that has been conceptualized as both traumatic for African-American individuals and community and as violating human rights, including those specified in the UN *International Convention on the Elimination of All Forms of Racial Discrimination* (Levitt, 2015; Staggers-Hakim, 2016; United Nations, 1965). As has been argued in the literature on the social determinants of health, it is not enough to implement programs and services to treat the symptoms of traumatic events or human rights violations after they occur. Rather, it is through social policy that society can move the needle on these social determinants (Braveman et al., 2011; Thornton et al., 2016). We therefore argue from a social justice lens that policy should be shaped in a way that is trauma-informed and promotes human rights.

## ROLE OF HELPING PROFESSIONS

Individuals in helping professions such as social work, counseling psychology, or nursing are likely to see their main role as precisely that: to help individuals who are ill, impaired, or otherwise vulnerable or suffering. Because of their first-hand knowledge of both the hardships that vulnerable populations face and the resilience they demonstrate in their daily lives, we believe that members of the helping professions are essential to advocating for socially just, equitable, and trauma-informed social policies. Although social policies affect all segments of society, vulnerable and marginalized groups—including people with few socioeconomic resources, people of color, sexual and gender minorities, and people with disabilities—may find their lives particularly shaped by the policies that govern civil liberties and access to resources and services. Members of helping professions can advocate alongside or on behalf of the client populations they serve to improve social policies.

While some professions such as social work proudly proclaim policymaking and policy advocacy as part of their history, helping professions have been largely shaped by a medical model (Specht & Courtney, 1994). In this model, professionals are trained and socialized primarily as providers of clinical services, with less attention to activism and advocacy. We believe it is important that the domain of policymaking is not restricted only to elected officials, their staffs, professional lobbyists, and others with technical expertise. Helping professionals should have an active voice in shaping policies (Powell, Garrow, Woodford, & Perron, 2013). It is critical that helping professionals' advocacy efforts are guided by the true needs and desires of their clients or target populations (Mosley, 2013).

From a human rights perspective, those who are affected by social policies should participate in the development of those social policies (Gatenio Gabel, 2016). To ensure this, helping professionals can facilitate clients' direct involvement in policy advocacy. Efforts may range from large-scale grassroots organizing campaigns to simpler, shorter-term efforts, such as chartering a bus to bring clients to meet with legislators in the state capital as part of a statewide lobby day around a particular issue. We discuss different advocacy targets and approaches in greater detail at the end of this chapter.

Including potential recipients in policy development helps to shift policymaking from a needs-based framework to a rights-based one. For centuries, social policies were created by needs-based approaches that stem from the deficit model of practice in which professionals or individuals with greater means diagnose what is "needed" in a situation, and the "treatment" or services required to yield the desired outcome are set by the profession or other persons of advantage. Judgments of need are based on professional research, practice wisdom, and theory steeped in values (Ife, 2012). These values, research, theories, and practices typically reflect the beliefs of the persons pronouncing judgment, not necessarily the values and theories of the person who is being judged. This has the effect of disempowering and diminishing control of those seeking services while privileging professionals (Ife, 2012). In turn, this risks reinforcing passiveness and perpetuating the violation of rights among the marginalized populations that helping professions seek to empower in society (Gatenio Gabel, 2016).

In order for helping professionals to participate in policy advocacy and facilitate vulnerable groups' engagement in advocacy, they must become proficient in basic policy analysis skills. Analyzing a policy involves learning how to identify and understand a policy's component parts, but also inferring the values that the policy reflects (Butterfield, Rocha, & Butterfield, 2010). A number of analytical frameworks exist to help determine the extent to which the components and underlying values of a given policy align with particular criteria shaped by extant theories and models. Examples of these frameworks include strengths-based policy analysis (Rapp, Pettus, & Goscha, 2006) and feminist policy analysis (Pascall, 1997). We believe that the model of trauma-informed care and human rights-based practice is useful for informing social policy analysis, especially for helping professionals.

## TRAUMA-INFORMED AND HUMAN RIGHTS-BASED POLICY ANALYSIS

In a previous article (Bowen & Murshid, 2016), we outlined a model for trauma-informed social policy analysis. The salient features of trauma-informed policy include safety, trustworthiness and transparency, collaboration and peer support, empowerment, choice, and the intersectionality of identity characteristics. By attending to these elements, social policies stand to minimize human rights violations and retraumatization. To illustrate these principles, we use the example of the civil protection order (CPO) or restraining order that individuals experiencing harassment or violence, particularly by intimate partners, can use to mandate distance between themselves and their abusers through domestic relations courts in all 50 US states and the District of Columbia (Keilitz, Hannaford, & Efkeman, 1997).

The right to safety is a basic human right. In our paradigm, *safety* specifically refers to the idea that social policy should have provisions that ensure the safety of vulnerable populations. A CPO is meant to afford direct relief and increase safety for individuals experiencing violence. However, decisions to grant CPOs lie with the judiciary and are often an issue of "he said, she said" (Lucken, Rosky, & Watkins, 2015), which means the policy does not always provide the safety that it is meant to.

*Trustworthiness* is connected to the transparency of intended goals and outcomes of the policy. Consideration of transparency and accountability in social policies reflect a rights-based approach to policy analysis (Gatenio Gabel, 2016). Trust can be hampered by the variations in services that street-level bureaucrats provide, given that much relies on workers' personal discretion, thus producing inconsistent experiences for service users. With regard to CPOs, the fact that judges' discretion plays a role in getting CPOs may create mistrust of the court system, which in turn inhibits eligible individuals from accessing this option for themselves and impedes the realization of an individual's civil and social rights.

*Collaboration* and *peer support* refer to taking into account the experiences of the target population, treating them as partners, and having their voice reflected in policy. The participation of all stakeholders is a basic human rights tenet. In the case of CPOs, this would involve getting input and participation of individuals who have had CPOs—or who have been in need of them—in designing policy guidelines.

*Empowerment* in policymaking is located in the process of policy development as well as the policy objectives, evaluation, and advocacy; it refers to efforts to share power with service users and giving them voice at both individual and policy levels. While some researchers suggest that CPOs can be an empowering tool for survivors of violence, allowing them to leave violent situations and relationships, others suggest that there are disempowering and retraumatizing aspects of obtaining CPOs as well (Goldfarb, 2008; Nichols, 2013). The empowering aspect of CPOs is that individuals can self-initiate the civil process and take responsibility for letting the court know the kinds of relief they require. In effect, individuals need not rely on others, such as an attorney, to obtain CPOs. This is an example of how policy can be empowering in terms of policy objective, but not process, since there is no evidence of collaboration with potential users of CPOs during the drafting of the relevant legislation. On the other hand, the process of obtaining CPOs can have disempowering attributes (McDermott & Garafalo, 2004). As McDermott and Garafalo (2004) suggest, offender accountability conceptualized as harsher punishment for abusive partners may not empower but instead disempower women who want the violence to end without ending the relationship.

*Choice* refers to allowing service users to have control over their options. That individuals can choose the type of relief that they want when they obtain CPOs is an example of how individuals can be given a choice in the type of relief they want from policy. Such choices include, in the case of domestic violence cases for example, mandating child and spousal support, the type of contact they want to have with their abusers, ranging from restricting all types of communication including through third parties to scheduled meetings, or giving up possession of the home or other joint property such as a motor vehicle. The choice in deciding the type of communication is an important one for individuals who may want the abuse to end without ending the relationship (Goldfarb, 2008). However, such choice is often constrained or limited by factors such as knowledge about what service users can and cannot ask for, fear of the legal system (especially in cases where previous contact with the legal system has been contentious), or structural factors such as being homeless or low income.

*Intersectionality* in policy means that policy should recognize and address the needs of different groups of people based on their identity characteristics such as race, gender, and sexual orientation, recognizing the privileges or oppression associated with these characteristics. Intersectionality is consistent with the human rights ideal of non-discrimination (World Health Organization, 2009). Policy should reflect an understanding that policy provisions can affect different communities differentially, in some cases leading to disparities in health and well-being. From a rights-based approach, all social problems must be analyzed to understand the root causes. The root causes manifest themselves in a myriad of ways such as in disparities and inequalities, and until root causes are addressed, social policies will not adequately respond to social problems. In terms of CPOs, intersectional policy would require an understanding of cultural differences in the kind of justice that individuals want for themselves (e.g., restorative or retributive), and providing pathways for individuals and communities to have a say in choosing what they feel is right for them, instead of what is deemed right for them.

## Trauma and Human Rights-Informed Policy Analysis Example

In the following section, we share an example of trauma and human rights-informed policy analysis from a student in a first-year master of social work (MSW) policy class, analyzing New York State's 2016 Fair Wage Act. The assignment asked students to examine a policy of their choice, decipher its intended and consequential impact based on a trauma-informed and human rights perspective, and identify at least one way in which the policy could be changed to be more trauma-informed or better promote human rights. We include this example in order to demonstrate the application of our analysis framework; to show the relevance of trauma and human rights-informed policy analysis for members of the helping professions, including students; and to illuminate how the analysis framework can yield new insights into diverse areas of social policy that may initially seem to have little connection with trauma, such as employment policy.

## New York's Fair Wage Act:
## A Trauma-Informed and Human Rights-Based Analysis

According to the United States Census Bureau (DeNavas-Walt & Proctor, 2015), 14.8% (46.7 million people) in the United States live in poverty. Although there is a federal minimum wage, low-wage employment continues to be a leading factor in the poverty rate, as this baseline does not account for inflation or geographic differences, and has been widely criticized as inadequate to fulfill the minimum needs of a family (DeSilver, 2014). Despite popular belief, a majority of individuals who live in poverty are employed; but with over 40 million jobs in the United States paying $11.11 or less per hour, many individuals are forced to rely on supplemental support from federal and state government in the form of housing and social welfare programs (Coalition for Economic Justice, 2015; Magavern, 2010; Muscavage, 2016).

Since 2007, the country has seen a disappearance of middle-skill-level jobs and an increasing gap between high- and low-skill-level positions, forcing many displaced employees to turn to low-skill jobs because they do not meet the education, training, and skill standards of high-level positions (Considine, 2014). The magnitude of individuals affected by low-wage jobs and the threat to the idealized "American Dream" for hard-working individuals has spurred a movement for a "living wage" that allows a full-time worker with a family of three or four to live at the federal poverty line (Luce, 2012). More than 140 living wage ordinances have been passed in the United States (Luce, 2012). On April 4th, 2016, New York State enacted the Fair Wage Act, which identified a "living wage" compensation for workers of large employers as part of the 2016–2017 budget (New York State, 2016).

### Policy Description
The Fair Wage Act is an amendment to the labor law of New York State and defines a living wage as a minimum hourly rate of $15 for employees. For those employed by businesses included in the policy, such as large employers, transportation businesses, subcontractors, and

corporate retail stores, the Act mandated an incremental rise in minimum hourly wage, following a schedule based on location within the state. Increments are also dependent on the type and size of employer. Workers in New York City (NYC) who are employed by large businesses with at least 11 employees had the minimum wage rise to $11 at the end of 2016, with an increase of $2 each year after until 2018, whereas those in NYC employed by small businesses with 10 employees or less had the minimum wage rise to $10.50 at the end of 2016, with an additional $1.50 each year after until the end of 2019 (New York State, 2016). Workers in other parts of the state have different schedules for the minimum wage increase. Workers in Nassau, Suffolk, and Westchester Counties saw an increase of minimum wage to $10 at the end of 2016, with an additional increase of $1 each year scheduled until the end of 2021. In the rest of the state, workers obtained a minimum wage of $9.70 at the end of 2016, with a rise of $.70 each year after, reaching $12.50 at the end of 2020 (New York State, 2016). The policy also sets an annual increase with the rate of inflation, as measured by the Consumer Price Index.

The State Department of Labor has responsibility to implement and enforce the Fair Wage Act. Employers are mandated to post an announcement about the wage increases in English and Spanish in an accessible part of the workplace and to inform employees of the current living wage and their rights under this article, which assumes the worker's literacy and comprehension of the bulletin. Employers are required to pay their employees at least that wage and retain payroll records of employees for four years, which the employee or designated representative has the right to inspect at any time.

One reason why this policy received opposition from business lobbyists and chambers of commerce is that businesses and employers directly fund this increase in minimum wage. In addition, funding for the enforcement of the policy will be provided through state taxes. Advocates for the policy argue that the increased wage will save taxpayers money in the long term by lifting low-wage employees out of poverty and decreasing the number of individuals who need supportive services (Coalition for Economic Justice, 2015). According to the New York State Web site (2016) and the New York State Department of Labor Web site (2016), it is estimated that more than 2.3 million people will be affected by the increases in the minimum wage. The groups most directly impacted by the policy are those who are disproportionally represented in low-wage work, including members of minority groups typically discriminated against in the workforce and those with less access to higher education; these groups include African-Americans, Hispanics, Native Americans, and women (Bhatia & Katz, 2001; Department of Labor, 2016; Magavern, 2010; Partnership for Working Families, 2015).

The Fair Wage Act excludes a few categories of low-wage workers, including not-for-profit workers, those who work in businesses whose principal industry is manufacturing, employees who customarily receive tips, workers employed by small independent businesses outside of New York City, those who provide services outside of the defined state borders, and workers who are informally compensated. In addition, the Act does not address the need for employee benefits often included in other living wage ordinances (Luce, 2012). Low-wage jobs rarely offer supports and benefits such as health care, paid sick leave, and childcare, and thereby adversely affect single-parent households. Without other benefits or programs in place to assist working parents, the rise in wage helps but still leaves a significant gap for a true living wage.

*Trauma and Human Rights-Informed Policy Analysis*
As the gap between high- and low-wage earners within the United States continues to grow, there is a significant number of individuals employed in low-wage positions who are forced to live in poverty. The prevalence of trauma for individuals living in poverty underlies the need for policies such as the Fair Wage Act to reflect the principles of trauma-informed practice including empowerment, trustworthiness, and choice (Bowen & Murshid, 2016).

**Empowerment**
The process of campaigning to increase the state minimum wage policy was empowering, as low-wage workers played a large role in its success. As Luce (2012) identifies, the continued power and advocacy of low-wage workers are important components to the success of living wage ordinances. With an understanding of the fight, the political process, the possibility of unionizing and having a voice when they were previously silent, low-wage workers are more empowered to stand up for their rights (Coalition for Economic Justice, 2015; Fight for $15, n.d.; Luce, 2012; Tritch, 2015). Although the Fair Wage Act empowers workers to report any injustices in pay to the Department of Labor, it is unclear how this will be implemented. In conflict with human rights, the policy does

not address how employees will be instructed on filing a grievance, and how they will be protected from discipline if they do so. Since many low-wage workers are at a disadvantage in obtaining high-skill or lucrative positions due to their level of education, training, and resources, the loss of their current job is even more detrimental to their well-being when they do not have a savings or checking account to rely on in the interim (Luce, 2012).

## Trustworthiness

The policy relies heavily on the public's trust in the state government to identify, implement, and enforce adequate living wages for employees. Individuals who are members of minority groups and living in poverty may have a decreased level of trust in the government due to the lack of supports available to them as well as structural and historical inequalities experienced by them (Bowen & Murshid, 2016). Those opposing the policy believe that an increase in minimum wage will decrease the number of employees a business can hire, increase automation of the industry, increase the prices of products and goods, or encourage business to outsource jobs, all decreasing the level of employment in the United States (Buss & Romeo, 2006). Although studies of other living wage ordinances have shown no significant impact on the number of jobs in a community or negative effects on the local economy, the policy includes a "safety valve" to determine whether a temporary suspension of the wage increase is needed to prevent negative outcomes (Buss & Romeo, 2006; Luce, 2012; New York State, 2016). This may create further distrust of the power of the government in changing the wages of low-income workers without further input from those impacted by the policy.

## Choice

Since the policy does not mandate any additional skills training or supports in pursuing higher skill-level jobs, low-wage workers are left with limited choice in employment. These individuals are still left in entry-level positions, with minimal opportunities for advancement and without the ability to access the benefits available to individuals in higher-level positions (Considine, 2014). Low-wage workers may be left in a difficult place: unable to access subsidized health care and social services available to individuals living in poverty, and unable to afford these same services on their wages. In addition, employers are left with limited choice in how they can incentivize potential employees. The US economy has largely shifted from manufacturing to service positions (Considine, 2014; Magavern, 2010). Manufacturing businesses are not included in the policy, yet to compete with the service industry, they will need to increase their wages to recruit new workers for what are often loud and dangerous jobs. While other living wage ordinances offer employers different wage floors based on the benefits they offer to their employees, the Fair Wage Act does not provide this incentive for businesses (Luce, 2012). This may decrease the number of benefits that employers offer to their employees in low-income positions to accommodate for the increased wage.

### Human Rights

The Fair Wage Act incorporates several tenets of the Universal Declaration of Human Rights (United Nations, 1948), most directly Articles 23, 24, and 25, which identify components of employment and standards of living. These articles state that "everyone has the right to work, to free choice of employment, to just and favourable conditions of work and protection against unemployment...the right to rest and leisure...and the right to a standard of living adequate for the health and well-being of himself and of his family." The United Nations further defines adequate standard of living to include "food, clothing, housing, medical care, necessary social services, and the right to security."

The principle of living wage ordinances is to provide greater equity for employees within the community, acknowledging that workers in the state are not treated equally (New York State, 2016). The policy does not treat all employees equally, exempting several employment industries as well as setting a minimum wage that varies based on geographic location within the state. Interest groups may view these differences as equitable or unfair based on how they define needs for the employees, employers, and the community (Ife, 2012). For example, to some groups, the type of job a low-wage worker holds may stipulate what wage a person is entitled to, with some eligible for more than others. To other groups, a rise in minimum wage for all individuals is important in helping low-wage workers support themselves and their families. Some employers may dislike the policy, stating that the burden of the minimum wage is not equal among all employers because of the difference in the number of employees. Others argue that the raise in minimum wage is inadequate as a "living wage," due to the absence of further employee benefits and supports that offset the cost of living. Some also argue that the regional difference in minimum wage is equitable because of differences in the cost of living. Since there are such differences within communities and cultures, human rights are purposefully generalized to allow for variability in execution, and it is up to that community to determine exactly what is equitable (Ife, 2012). The Fair Wage Act did not allow for communities to determine variability. Rather, the state determined the rate of wage increase that each community would face and directed these changes.

*Recommendation*
To make the Fair Wage Act more trauma-informed, it would be beneficial to follow the lead of other living wage ordinances and include benefits such as childcare, health care, transportation, paid vacation and sick leave, and retirement benefits (Luce, 2012; Partnership for Working Families, 2015). Incentivizing employers who offer some of these benefits to their low-wage employees by offering two minimum wage rates (one for those who offer benefits and one for those who do not) would help to increase the number of supports available to workers and enhance choice for both the worker and employer. In addition, these benefits would offer some sense of safety to employees and their families for a more stable life. Such additional provisions would help to reduce the inequalities that persist for low-wage workers, including decreased access to adequate childcare and preventative health care, and a sense of security in employment. In fact, the Partnership for Working Families (2015) states that living wage ordinances lead to an "increased efficiency and productivity...decreased employee turnover" and the employment of skilled workers "otherwise...deterred by low wages" (n.p.). These supports would also decrease the amount of money that taxpayers need to provide to supplement low-wage workers' social service benefits.

## Moving from Policy Analysis to Advocacy

Policy analysis need not be an end unto itself; rather, policy analysis can be used as a basis for guiding advocacy efforts. Specifically, trauma-informed policy analysis can direct members of the helping professions and the communities with whom they partner in identifying and subsequently advocating for ways that social policies can be more trauma-informed and human rights-based.

As one example of this, the social work profession has produced some analyses of US drug policies, perhaps most prominently a social justice brief authored by the National Association of Social Workers (2013) titled *A Social Work Perspective on Drug Policy Reform*. The brief discusses the incompatibility of criminalization-focused drug policies with the values and knowledge base of social work and public health. Trauma and human rights-informed policy analysis could extend this critique to highlight the ways in which current policies are not trauma-informed and may violate human rights. It is clear, for instance, that "zero tolerance" drug policies that emphasize jail time even for low-level offenses jeopardize the safety of drug users by removing them from their communities and forcing them into incarceration settings (Moore & Elkavich, 2008). Such policies also ignore the role of previous trauma as an underlying contributing factor for drug use and instead put drug users at high risk for further retraumatization through incarceration (Mate, 2010). Advocacy groups such as the International Network of People Who Use Drugs (2014) have argued that the drug policies of many nations— including the United States—compromise the human rights of drug users, including routinely violating users' bodily integrity, subjecting people who use drugs to arbitrary arrest, and discriminatingly enforcing legal punishments on drug-using people of color.

Analyses that use the language of trauma and human rights to assess the impact of drug policies can guide helping professionals and their clients and constituents in advocacy efforts to make these policies more trauma-informed and protective of human rights. Many helping professionals work closely in clinical roles with individuals and communities impacted by drug use; some may also have personal experience with substance use or be in recovery from addiction. Drawing on these experiences, helping professionals' advocacy to make drug policy more trauma and human rights-informed could take a variety of forms. For example, several US states and cities have recently enacted measures to decriminalize or legalize recreational marijuana use for adults (National Conference of State Legislatures, 2017). Helping professionals could work with marijuana users and those impacted by marijuana-related criminalization to shape decriminalization policies in their cities or states to be as trauma-informed as possible. One illustration of this would be to uphold the principle of choice by removing legal penalties for marijuana use, while also promoting linkages to addiction, mental health, and trauma treatment for those who desire it and ensuring that public treatment systems are adequately funded. Because of the immense stigma and misperceptions surrounding drugs and drug users, advocacy may need to begin with grassroots efforts to empower those most affected and publically challenge stigma and stereotypes, moving toward direct lobbying for legislative policy change (Hardcastle, Powers, & Wenocur, 2011).

Shifting from the local or state level to the federal level, another target of policy change could be to reduce the trauma associated with incarceration and promote human rights and equal treatment under the law by eliminating the racially laden sentencing disparity for possession of powder versus crack cocaine. This disparity was reduced but maintained in the 2010 Fair Sentencing Act (Bjerk, 2017). The highest level of advocacy consists of structural and societal-level systems change (Hardcastle et al., 2011). From a trauma and human rights perspective, this could involve reshaping US drug and healthcare policies from a "War on Drugs" ethos to the "four pillars" model used in parts of Canada and Europe. The four pillars approach emphasizes evidence-based prevention, high-quality treatment on demand for all who want it, harm reduction services including syringe exchange and supervised injection facilities, and sensitive policing and enforcement (City of Vancouver, 2017). Advocacy efforts could ultimately extend beyond the national level to address global drug policies through UN conventions and drug control agreements. Current UN drug policies have been critiqued for their emphasis on criminalization and prohibition and lack of protections for the human rights of those who use drugs and those whose lives are impacted by drug policies in other ways (Glenza, 2016).

## CONCLUSION

Policy change does not typically happen easily or rapidly. Shifting policymaking from a needs-based to a rights-based framework and shaping particular policies to be more trauma-informed and protective of human rights will be a long-term endeavor. Daunting as this may be, we believe this is an endeavor worthy of all helping professionals as well as all concerned global citizens. It is through social policy change that we can strive to prevent much of the suffering incurred by trauma and violations of human rights.

# REFERENCES

Bhatia, R., & Katz, M. (2001). Estimation of health benefits from a living wage ordinance. *American Journal of Public Health, 91*(9), 1398–1402.

Bjerk, D. (2017). Mandatory minimum policy reform and the sentencing of crack cocaine defendants: An analysis of the Fair Sentencing Act. *Journal of Empirical Legal Studies, 14*(2), 370–396. https://doi.org/10.1111/jels.12150.

Bowen, E. A., & Murshid, N. S. (2016). Trauma-informed social policy: A conceptual framework for policy analysis and advocacy. *American Journal of Public Health, 106*(2), 223–229. https://doi.org/10.2105/AJPH.2015.302970.

Braveman, P., Egerter, S., & Williams, D. R. (2011). The social determinants of health: Coming of age. *Annual Review of Public Health, 32*(1), 381–398. https://doi.org/10.1146/annurev-publhealth-031210-101218.

Buss, J. A., & Romeo, A. (2006). The changing employment situation in some cities with living wage ordinances. *Review of Social Economy, 64*(3), 349–367.

Butterfield, A. K., Rocha, C. J., & Butterfield, W. H. (2010). *The dynamics of family policy: Analysis and advocacy.* Chicago, IL: Lyceum Books.

City of Vancouver. (2017). *Four pillars drug strategy.* Retrieved from http://vancouver.ca/people-programs/four-pillars-drug-strategy.aspx.

Coalition for Economic Justice. (2015). *Fight for $15: The year in review.* Retrieved from http://cejbuffalo.org/campaigns/fight-for-15.

Considine, A. (2014). *Employment data for Buffalo.* Partnership for the Public Good. Retrieved from https://ppgbuffalo.org/files/documents/data-demographics-history/demographics_and_data/datademographicshistory-_employment_data_for_buffalo.pdf.

DeNavas-Walt, C., & Proctor, B. D. (2015). *Income and Poverty in the United States: 2014.* Retrieved from https://www.census.gov/library/publications/2015/demo/p60-252.html.

DeSilver, D. (2014). *Minimum wage hasn't been enough to lift most out of poverty for decades.* Pew Research Center. Retrieved from http://www.pewresearch.org/fact-tank/2014/02/18/minimum-wage-hasnt-been-enough-to-lift-most-out-of-poverty-for-decades/.

Diez Roux, A. V., & Mair, C. (2010). Neighborhoods and health. *Annals of the New York Academy of Sciences, 1186*(1), 125–145. https://doi.org/10.1111/j.1749-6632.2009.05333.x.

Fallot, R. D., & Harris, M. (2009). *Creating cultures of trauma-informed care (CCTIC): A self-assessment and planning protocol.* Retrieved from https://traumainformedoregon.org/wp-content/uploads/2014/10/CCTIC-A-Self-Assessment-and-Planning-Protocol.pdf.

Fight for $15. (n.d.). *About us*. Retrieved from http://fightfor15.org/about-us/.

Gatenio Gabel, S. (2016). *A rights-based approach to social policy analysis*. New York, NY: Springer.

Glenza, J. (2016, April 19). UN backs prohibitionist drug policies despite call for more 'humane solution'. *The Guardian*. Retrieved from https://www.theguardian.com/world/2016/apr/19/un-summit-global-war-drugs-agreement-approved.

Goldfarb, S. F. (2008). Reconceiving civil protection orders for domestic violence: Can law help end the abuse without ending the relationship? *Cardozo Law Review, 29*(4), 1487–1552.

Hardcastle, D. A., Powers, P. R., & Wenocur, S. (2011). *Community practice: Theories and skills for social workers* (3rd ed.). New York, NY: Oxford University Press.

Ife, J. (2012). *Human rights and social work: Towards rights-based practice* (3rd ed.). New York, NY: Cambridge University Press.

International Network of People Who Use Drugs. (2014). *Drug user peace initiative: Violations of the human rights of people who use drugs*. Retrieved from https://www.unodc.org/documents/ungass2016/Contributions/Civil/INPUD/DUPI-Violations_of_the_Human_Rights_of_People_Who_Use_Drugs-Web.pdf.

Keilitz, S. L., Hannaford, P., & Efkeman, H. S. (1997). *Civil protection orders: The benefits and limitations for victims of domestic violence*. National Center for State Courts research report. Retrieved from https://www.ncjrs.gov/pdffiles1/pr/172223.pdf.

Levitt, J. I. (2015). "Fuck your breath": Black men and youth, state violence, and human rights in the 21st century. *Washington University Journal of Law and Policy, 49*(1), 87–120.

Luce, S. (2012). Living wage policies and campaigns: Lessons from the United States. *International Journal of Labour Research, 4*(1), 11–26.

Lucken, K., Rosky, J. W., & Watkins, C. (2015). She said, he said, judge said: Analyzing judicial decision making in civil protection order hearings. *Journal of Interpersonal Violence, 30*(12), 2038–2066. https://doi.org/10.1177/0886260514552276.

Magavern, S. (2010). *Who is living in poverty and why?* Partnership for the Public Good. Retrieved from https://ppgbuffalo.org/files/documents/poverty_low_wage_work_income_inequality/truth_commission_report__poverty_in_buffalo_causes__impacts__solutions.pdf.

Marmot, M., & Allen, J. J. (2014). Social determinants of health equity. *American Journal of Public Health, 104*(Suppl. 4), S517–S519. https://doi.org/10.2105/ajph.2014.302200.

Mate, G. (2010). *In the realm of hungry ghosts: Close encounters with addiction*. Berkeley, CA: North Atlantic Books.

McDermott, M. J., & Garofalo, J. (2004). When advocacy for domestic violence victims backfires: Types and sources of victim disempowerment. *Violence Against Women, 10*(11), 1245–1266. https://doi.org/10.1177/1077801204268999.

McKenzie-Mohr, S., Coates, J., & McLeod, H. (2012). Responding to the needs of youth who are homeless: Calling for politicized trauma-informed intervention. *Children and Youth Services Review, 34*(1), 136–143. https://doi.org/10.1016/j.childyouth.2011.09.008.

Moore, L. D., & Elkavich, A. (2008). Who's using and who's doing time. *American Journal of Public Health, 98*(5), 782–786.

Mosley, J. (2013). Recognizing new opportunities: Reconceptualizing policy advocacy in everyday organizational practice. *Social Work, 58*(3), 231–239. https://doi.org/10.1093/sw/swt020.

Muscavage, N. (2016, January 28). *Would a $15 minimum wage get workers off public subsidies?* Retrieved from http://www.lohud.com/story/news/politics/politics-on-the-hudson/2016/01/28/would-15-minimum-wage-get-workers-off-public-subsidies/79460784/.

National Association of Social Workers. (2013). *Social justice brief: A social work perspective on drug policy reform.* Retrieved from https://www.drugpolicy.org/sites/default/files/Drug%20Policy%20Reform%20Brief%20Social%20Justice%20Dept.pdf.

National Conference of State Legislatures. (2017). *Marijuana overview.* Retrieved from http://www.ncsl.org/research/civil-and-criminal-justice/marijuana-overview.aspx.

New York State. (2016, April 4). *Governor Cuomo signs $15 minimum wage plan and 12 week paid family leave policy into law.* Retrieved from https://www.governor.ny.gov/news/governor-cuomo-signs-15-minimum-wage-plan-and-12-week-paid-family-leave-policy-law.

New York State Department of Labor. (2016, February). *Analysis: Raising New York's minimum wage to $15.* Retrieved from https://www.governor.ny.gov/sites/governor.ny.gov/files/atoms/files/Minimum_Wage_Report.pdf.

Nichols, A. J. (2013). Survivor-defined practices to mitigate revictimization of battered women in the protective order process. *Journal of Interpersonal Violence, 28*(7), 1403–1423. https://doi.org/10.1177/0886260512468243.

Partnership for Working Families. (2015). *Policy & tools: Living wage.* Retrieved from http://www.forworkingfamilies.org/resources/policy-tools-living-wage.

Pascall, G. (1997). *Social policy: A new feminist analysis* (2nd ed.). New York, NY: Routledge.

Powell, T. J., Garrow, E., Woodford, M. R., & Perron, B. (2013). Policymaking opportunities for direct practice social workers in mental health and addiction services. *Advances in Social Work, 14*(2), 367–378.

Rapp, C. A., Pettus, C. A., & Goscha, R. J. (2006). Principles of strengths-based policy. *Journal of Policy Practice, 5*(4), 3–18.

Robinson, J. L., & Rubin, L. J. (2016). Homonegative microaggressions and posttraumatic stress symptoms. *Journal of Gay & Lesbian Mental Health, 20*(1), 57–69. https://doi.org/10.1080/19359705.2015.1066729.

Specht, H., & Courtney, M. E. (1994). *Unfaithful angels: How social work has abandoned its mission.* New York, NY: The Free Press.

Staggers-Hakim, R. (2016). The nation's unprotected children and the ghost of Mike Brown, or the impact of national police killings on the health and social development of African American boys. *Journal of Human Behavior in the Social Environment, 26*(3–4), 390–399. https://doi.org/10.1080/1091135 9.2015.1132864.

Thornton, R. L. J., Glover, C. M., Cené, C. W., Glik, D. C., Henderson, J. A., & Williams, D. R. (2016). Evaluating strategies for reducing health disparities by addressing the social determinants of health. *Health Affairs, 35*(8), 1416–1423. https://doi.org/10.1377/hlthaff.2015.1357.

Torres, L., & Taknint, J. T. (2015). Ethnic microaggressions, traumatic stress symptoms, and Latino depression: A moderated mediational model. *Journal of Counseling Psychology, 62*(3), 393–401. https://doi.org/10.1037/cou0000077.

Tritch, T. (2015, November 10). The fight for $15 comes to the Republican debate. *The New York Times.* Retrieved from https://takingnote.blogs.nytimes.com/2015/11/10/the-fight-for-15-comes-to-the-republican-debate/?searchResultPosition=1.

United Nations. (1948). *Universal Declaration of Human Rights.* Retrieved from http://www.un.org/en/universal-declaration-human-rights/index.html.

United Nations. (1965). *International convention on the elimination of all forms of racial discrimination.* Retrieved from http://www.refworld.org/docid/3ae6b3940.html.

Wolf, M. R., Green, S. A., Nochajski, T. H., Mendel, W. E., & Kusmaul, N. S. (2014). 'We're civil servants': The status of trauma-informed care in the community. *Journal of Social Service Research, 40*(1), 111–120. https://doi.org/10.1080/01488376.2013.845131.

World Health Organization. (2009). *Non discrimination.* Retrieved from http://www.who.int/gender-equity-rights/understanding/non-discrimination-definition/en/.

CHAPTER 4

# Enhancing Indigenous Well-Being: Applying Human Rights and Trauma-Informed Perspectives with Native Americans

*Hilary N. Weaver*

Native Americans are diverse Peoples indigenous to the territories that became the United States. This Indigenous status makes them distinct from other groups. They are not simply individuals with a common ancestry, history, and culture. Rather, these Peoples existed prior to the founding of the United States and continue as collective self-governing entities. The United Nations (UN) recognizes the rights of Indigenous individuals and affirms that "indigenous peoples possess collective rights which are indispensable to their existence, well-being and integral development as peoples" (UN, 2007, p. 4). A separate set of laws, policies, and programs apply to Native American nations and individuals, sometimes in addition to and sometimes in place of other laws, policies, and programs.

Each Native American nation establishes criteria for citizenship. Various federal and state programs use their own definitions. The definition used by the US Census Bureau is "a person having origins in any of the original peoples of North and South America (including Central

H. N. Weaver (✉)
School of Social Work, University at Buffalo, Buffalo, NY, USA
e-mail: hweaver@buffalo.edu

© The Author(s) 2019                                                      75
L. D. Butler et al. (eds.), *Trauma and Human Rights*,
https://doi.org/10.1007/978-3-030-16395-2_4

America) and who maintains tribal affiliation or community attachment" (Norris, Vines, & Hoeffel, 2012, p. 2).

The Native American population is young and growing. According to the 2010 Census, there are 5.2 million Native Americans, representing 1.7% of the population (Norris et al., 2012). This is a 39% increase over the 2000 Census. Forty-one percent live in the West with 14% in California, followed by Oklahoma, Arizona, Texas, and New York. Among urban areas, New York City has the largest Native American population at 111,749, followed by Los Angeles at 54,236. The majority of Native Americans (78%) live outside tribal territories (Norris et al., 2012).

As of 2017, there were 567 federally recognized Native nations (Federal Register, 2017). The largest are the Cherokee with a population of 819,105, the Navajo with 332,129, and the Choctaw with 195,764 (Norris et al., 2012). There are also Indigenous Peoples the United States does not acknowledge who are ineligible for federal funding or programming (Tsosie, 2012). Some of these are recognized by states and are eligible for state programming and funding (Salazar, 2016).

There is a distinct relationship between Native American nations (aka tribes) and the federal government established through treaties and affirmed in the US Constitution and subsequent federal legislation (Dunbar-Ortiz, 2014; Venables, 2004). In spite of intrusions on sovereignty leading to exercise of federal authority on reservations (i.e., the Major Crimes Act of 1885), Native American nations maintain self-governance and can operate their own schools, health systems, social services, and law enforcement systems. In most cases, tribal lands do not fall under state jurisdiction, unless tribes delegated authority under a mechanism such as Public Law 280 (Echo-Hawk, 2013).

Extraordinary diversity exists among Native Americans (Dunbar-Ortiz, 2014). While there is a common experience of colonization, Native nations have different languages, customs, forms of social organization, and spiritual traditions. Many federal policies such as allotment and termination were intended to cover all Native Americans, but not all were fully or equally implemented. Likewise, traumatic events that impacted some Native groups were not experienced in the same way or not experienced at all by others.

## Defining and Examining Historical Trauma

Native Americans, like other Indigenous Peoples, typically have some of the lowest indicators of health and social well-being of any population (Browne et al., 2016; Cobb, Espey, & King, 2014). Searching for an explanation, clinicians and researchers proposed that extraordinary events associated with colonization led to trauma that has not been adequately resolved (Brave Heart, Chase, Elkins, & Altshul, 2011; Mohatt, Thompson, Thai, & Tebes, 2014). These include ravages of disease, massacres, forced relocations, and family disruption associated with assimilation policies. Colonization processes also disrupted protective mechanisms and culturally grounded expressions of bereavement, leaving grief unresolved (Brave Heart et al., 2011). This inability to draw resilience from culturally grounded protective mechanisms and expressions of bereavement exacerbates various psychosocial risks and fosters social and health disparities (Brave Heart et al., 2011; Mohatt et al., 2014; Nutton & Fast, 2015).

While *historical trauma* is the most common term used to describe this phenomenon, scholars also use related terms such as *intergenerational trauma* (Myhra, 2011), *colonial trauma response* (Evans-Campbell, 2008), and *historical oppression* (Burnette, 2015; Burnette & Figley, 2017). These terms are sometimes used interchangeably, although proponents of each term have identified distinctions. For purposes of this chapter, the term *historical trauma* is used. Maria Yellow Horse Brave Heart, a Lakota clinician and researcher, is typically credited with early development of historical trauma theory. According to her definition,

> *Historical trauma* (HT) is defined as cumulative emotional and psychological wounding across generations, including the lifespan, which emanates from massive group trauma.... Historical trauma theory frames lifespan trauma in the collective, historical context, which empowers Indigenous survivors of both communal and individual trauma by reducing the sense of stigma and isolation. The *historical trauma response* (HTR) has been conceptualized as a constellation of features associated with a reaction to massive group trauma. *Historical unresolved grief*, a component of this response, is the profound unsettled bereavement resulting from cumulative devastating losses, compounded by the prohibition and interruption of Indigenous burial practices and ceremonies. (Brave Heart et al., 2011, p. 283, emphasis in original)

Historical trauma theory blends theories of psychological trauma and historical oppression. Historical trauma can manifest in individual behavioral health risks (Hartmann & Gone, 2014) and internalized oppression (Durham & Webb, 2014). Historical trauma also affects the well-being of families, communities, and societies (Burnette & Figley, 2017; Evans-Campbell, 2008; SAMHSA, 2014).

Historical trauma theory has advanced our understanding of health disparities and resonates strongly with many Indigenous People and service providers (Hartmann & Gone, 2014). It is important to note, however, that it is not without its critics. Even its proponents note there is a need for empirical validation (Braga, Mello, & Fiks, 2012; Brave Heart et al., 2011; Gone 2009; Walls & Whitbeck, 2012; Whitbeck, Adams, Hoyt, & Chen, 2004). This is not a problem inherent in the theory but rather a call to researchers for further exploration.

A common criticism of historical trauma theory is that it does not adequately address contemporary trauma (Burnette, 2015; Burnette & Figley, 2017; Cavalieri, 2013; Coleman, 2016; Evans-Campbell, 2008; Mohatt et al., 2014). Scholars such as Burnette and Evans-Campbell proposed models that build on historical trauma while being attentive to interactional and cumulative effects of contemporary trauma. It is noteworthy, however, that Brave Heart originally proposed historical trauma theory as a mechanism for understanding the impact of current trauma and reducing stigma associated with health disparities (Brave Heart et al., 2011).

Some scholars believe an emphasis on historical trauma, far from being destigmatizing as intended by Brave Heart, has promoted a deficit focus and has inhibited explorations of resilience (Burnette & Figley, 2017; Evans-Campbell, 2008; Mohatt et al., 2014). Likewise, there is concern the concept has been applied uniformly without attention to intertribal variability.

With the benefit of hindsight, it is possible to examine the tenets of the theory as originally proposed by Brave Heart, how it has been applied by other theorists, clinicians, and researchers, and explore critiques of historical trauma conceptualizations. Indeed, there is consensus that devastating historical events happened to Indigenous Peoples, that there has been intergenerational transmission of trauma, and that historical trauma interacts with contemporary trauma, resulting in ongoing significant health and social disparities (Brave Heart et al., 2011; Coleman, 2016; Durham & Webb, 2014; Hartmann & Gone, 2014).

## Recognizing Human Rights

Beyond its utility as a framework for explaining contemporary health disparities and guiding clinical work, historical trauma theory calls attention to human rights issues that continue to impact Native Americans. Colonization itself is a fundamental human rights issue (Echo-Hawk, 2013). Native Americans have experienced genocide, removal, racism, and forced assimilation (Dunbar-Ortiz, 2014). Denial of human rights and of humanity itself underpins historical trauma and resulting disparities.

There is a global trend to acknowledge human rights and discuss reparations for Indigenous Peoples, yet the United States is blatantly absent from these discussions. Echo-Hawk notes two significant psychological barriers that account for this absence.

> First, the legacy of conquest sorely impugns our self-image, core values, and origin myth; and we cannot face these inner demons without being overcome by paralyzing guilt. Second, our legal system of remedial justice is adept at righting wrongs of victims who present individual claims, but it stops short at reparative justice for collective wrongs committed against groups, especially when the wrongdoer is the American nation. (Echo-Hawk, 2013, p. 17)

Treaties, federal statues, and court cases that articulated or clarified relationships between colonial powers (subsequently the United States) and Native American nations developed into a distinct body of law that governs issues such as jurisdiction, governance, and the role of states on tribal territories. Federal Indian law stands as an anomaly bereft of human rights precepts. This is a departure from the commitment to remedial justice found in other US jurisprudence. US courts, including the Supreme Court of the United States, have consistently ruled that any rights that Native Americans once possessed ended with conquest. Instead of possessing rights, they are now the beneficiaries of charity. Under such logic, "Indian occupancy of ancient tribal homelands developed into simple 'permission from the whites to occupy' the land—a bare entitlement that depends entirely upon the 'compassion' and 'grace' of the American people" (Echo-Hawk, 2013, p. 13). In short, in a conquered land, there are no rights for the original inhabitants.

Framing historical and contemporary circumstances of Native Americans as human rights issues is an important step in understanding and remedying injustice. Restorative justice can lead to transformative social action and restructured relationships as well as remedies that facilitate healing (Echo-Hawk, 2013). International law provides an important foundation for applying a human rights perspective that is lacking within US jurisprudence.

## KEY HUMAN RIGHTS DOCUMENTS

The Universal Declaration of Human Rights (UDHR) is an important articulation of basic rights and entitlements for all human beings. This document was adopted by the UN in 1948 and is the guiding instrument for human rights law. This Declaration constitutes a pledge by UN member states to uphold the equal rights, dignity, and worth of people. The UN subsequently developed a document grounded in these principles focused on the specific circumstances of Indigenous Peoples, the United Nations Declaration on the Rights of Indigenous Peoples (UNDRIP; UN, 2007). The UNDRIP lists states' duties designed to repair lasting harm and continuing damage to Indigenous Peoples within their boundaries. The United States (along with Canada, New Zealand, and Australia) initially opposed UNDRIP but eventually became a signatory.

It is noteworthy that the International Federation of Social Workers (IFSW) proactively developed its own statement on the rights of Indigenous Peoples. The IFSW took their mandate for engagement with Indigenous Peoples from a combination of the UN charter and social work values. They recognized Indigenous Peoples often have no voice and are not viewed as having nation status. Indigenous Peoples experience exploitation and systematic violation of their rights. They are often marginalized and invisible. The IFSW notes that human rights are the cornerstone of the social work profession, thus driving its mandate to serve Indigenous Peoples.

The IFSW policy statement on Indigenous Peoples passed in 2005 (IFSW, 2017), two years prior to the 2007 passage of the UNDRIP (UN, 2007). The IFSW statement borrows heavily from UN draft documents and mirrors the language eventually incorporated in UNDRIP. The IFSW and UN documents affirm the fundamental nature of human rights for Indigenous individuals and collectives. Recognition of collective rights places these documents far ahead of other international human rights documents and scholarship.

Indeed, the concept of collective rights is rarely addressed in human rights discourse (Dahre, 2010). Individualistic conceptualizations of human rights are grounded in the values and beliefs of Western societies who have developed and articulated this stance. "The inadequacy of human rights in relation to indigenous peoples is caused by conceptual blindness.... This is a structural property of the human rights discourse, as it applies to social and political problems with collective dimensions. This is not a coincidence or an unforeseen side-effect. The focus on the individual as a bearer of rights is a structural and systematic property of the human rights discourse itself" (Dahre, 2010, p. 641). Initial opposition to the UNDRIP by the United States, Canada, New Zealand, and Australia was grounded, at least partly in the fact that the document recognized Indigenous populations as *Peoples,* collectivities with rights beyond those possessed by individuals (Tsosie, 2012). The fact that the UNDRIP and IFSW statement on the rights of Indigenous Peoples go beyond individualistic conceptualizations and recognize collective human rights is likely a product of Indigenous input into development of these documents leading to a reflection of Indigenous values, priorities, and worldviews.

In its preamble, UNDRIP affirms that "indigenous peoples are equal to all other peoples, while recognizing the right of all peoples to be different, to consider themselves different, and to be respected as such" (UN, 2007, p. 1). They affirm that "all doctrines, policies and practices based on advocating superiority of peoples or individuals on the basis of national origin or racial, religious, ethnic or cultural differences are racist, scientifically false, legally invalid, morally condemnable and socially unjust" (UN, 2007, p. 2). These provisions condemn the myriad attempts at forced assimilation and denigration of Indigenous cultures and religions around the world.

The UNDRIP was issued in recognition that "Indigenous peoples have suffered from historic injustices as a result of, inter alia, their colonization and dispossession of their lands, territories and resources, thus preventing them from exercising, in particular, their right to development in accordance with their own needs and interests" (UN, 2007, p. 2).

The UN enacted the UNDRIP, "convinced that the recognition of the rights of indigenous peoples in this Declaration will enhance harmonious and cooperative relationships between the State and indigenous peoples, based on principles of justice, democracy, and respect for human rights, non-discrimination and good faith" (UN, 2007, p. 3).

The UN has an important and continuing role in promoting the rights of Indigenous Peoples.

Legal scholar Echo-Hawk (2013) identified UNDRIP as a ground-breaking achievement notable in the history of the world like the Magna Carta, Declaration of Independence, or Brown v. the Board of Education. This landmark document, developed with three decades of Indigenous participation, "makes international law accountable to indigenous peoples. It tells us how recognized human rights should be interpreted and applied in the indigenous context" (Echo-Hawk, 2013, p. 4). The UNDRIP is an authoritative statement drawn from existing international human rights law and thus circumvents the lack of recognition of human rights for Native Americans inherent in US law.

It is noteworthy that the UNDRIP is the written component to the UN's larger commitment to Indigenous Peoples. In 2000, the Permanent Forum on Indigenous Issues was established to provide expert advice and recommendations to the UN Economic and Social Council. Annual forums have been held since 2002. In addition to the Forum, the UN has an Expert Mechanism on the Rights of Indigenous Peoples and a Special Rapporteur on the Rights of Indigenous Peoples to inform their decision-making. Since 2009, the UN has issued regular publications and press releases on the State of the World's Indigenous Peoples (UN, 2018).

While UNDRIP (UN, 2007) provides guidance, these principles must also be written into US law. The Declaration itself does not carry the force of binding law, but some provisions may reflect treaty obligations. Declarations are aspirational statements that provide guidance and moral authority. They can be persuasive and a catalyst for social, cultural, and political transformations that go beyond superficial legal changes (Echo-Hawk, 2013). While the principles outlined in the UNDRIP could have a substantial impact if implemented, more than a decade since its passage, much still remains to be done.

## Trauma and Human Rights in Native American Contexts

The traumatic experiences inherent in colonization were pervasive and cataclysmic. Their lasting impact has been transmitted to subsequent generations and exacerbated by ongoing racism and oppression (Brave Heart et al., 2011; Evans-Campbell, 2008; SAMHSA, 2014).

"Assimilation efforts have been so effective in achieving their aims that generations of individuals who have not directly experienced these policies continue to absorb their effects in the form of historical trauma, historical trauma responses, historical unresolved grief, and colonial trauma responses" (Cavalieri, 2013, p. 30). While an exhaustive list of trauma is beyond the scope of this chapter, this section highlights some of the major traumas experienced by Native Americans.

Extreme population loss was an early source of trauma for Indigenous populations in the Americas. Prior to European contact, Native Americans had thriving societies that included urban areas, cultivated lands, and vast intertribal trading networks. Early Europeans brought diseases never experienced by Indigenous Peoples of the Western Hemisphere. Recent scholarship indicates microbes spread to Indigenous populations with extraordinary speed. By the time colonists arrived, many Indigenous nations were already decimated by disease. Within 130 years of initial contact, approximately 95% of Indigenous Peoples in the Americas had been wiped out (Mann, 2005).

The United States is built upon a foundation of colonization and genocide. The moral philosophy of Manifest Destiny coupled with the legal foundations derived from the Doctrine of Discovery, a Papal Bull that conveyed authority for colonization, left colonists believing they had the right, duty, and obligation to *settle* the land (Dunbar-Ortiz, 2014; Venables, 2004). The ongoing denial of humanity and human rights became another source of trauma. The UDHR Article 7 states that all are equal before the law and deserving of legal protections, but the very act of colonization is predicated on the belief that Indigenous Peoples are not vested with the same rights and protections as colonial powers (UN, 1948).

Understanding genocide is critical to understanding trauma experienced by Native Americans. Beginning with the colonial period and extending to contemporary times, Native Americans have experienced a wide range of traumas including massacres, terror, physical and sexual violence, torture, displacement, and removal of children with little acknowledgment or regret on the part of the United States (Dunbar-Ortiz, 2014).

Legislation in the United States and Canada undermined the equal status of women and traditional gender roles where women often owned houses and were responsible for agriculture while men hunted and fished. "Men were forced into the fields, and women were domesticated, becoming economically and emotionally dependent on their husbands. Men were declared 'head of household' for the purposes of property rights, and women lost their coequal social and political status with men. Thus, European American values congruent with religious ideals, nuclear families, individual wealth accumulation, and individual land ownership were imposed on Native American society" (Turner & Pope, 2009, p. 197). These acts undermined the right to participate in cultural life articulated in Article 27 of UDHR (UN, 1948).

Residential schools were implemented in the United States and Canada as a Social Darwinist policy of assimilation (Turner & Pope, 2009). Children were prohibited from speaking their languages or practicing their religions. They typically had minimal contact with their families or communities as a way to break intergenerational transmission of culture and language. Richard Pratt, credited with founding boarding schools in the United States, coined the motto *Kill the Indian, Save the Man* (Carlisle Indian School Digital Resource Center, 2018). This reflected the intention of using corporal punishment to eradicate Indigenous practices in favor of Christian values. Residential schools were a site of significant physical, emotional, and sexual abuse (Evans-Campbell, 2008). While the UDHR (UN, 1948) does identify a right to education under Article 26, it also notes education is a way to "promote understanding, tolerance, and friendship." It also notes parents should have choices about children's education. These principles, along with Article 18 that supports freedom of thought and religion, were violated by United States, Canadian, and Australian policies that mandated attendance at residential schools and used education as a tool of cultural destruction.

Many Native American Peoples have been forcibly removed from their traditional territories. Most notoriously this includes the forced march of many tribal peoples of the Southeastern United States along the Trail of Tears to Indian Territory (subsequently Oklahoma). Across the United States, tribes were confined to reservations where lands continued to shrink to sizes unable to support their populations. By 1881, Native Americans retained only 156 million acres of land (Dunbar-Ortiz, 2014). The United States expanded its territories by acquiring Alaska and territories in the Pacific. The United States began military control of the Hawaiian Islands in 1874, and in 1898 overthrew the Hawaiian monarchy and annexed the islands as another US territory (Dunbar-Ortiz, 2014).

Demand for land and other resources continued unabated. In 1887, Congress passed the Dawes Act, also known as the allotment policy (Dunbar-Ortiz, 2014; Venables, 2004). Under this law, reservation lands were to be divided and allocated to heads of households rather than held collectively by tribes. Allotment was both an assimilation policy and a method for opening reservation land to non-Native settlement.

Americans viewed communal ownership of land as perpetuating collectivism and interdependence, a right subsequently protected under Article 17 of UNDRIP (UN, 2007). Allotment was promulgated as a way to promote individualism and nuclear families over communities and networks. Once each family's head of household received a parcel of land, the law called for remaining land to be available for non-Native settlement. By the time the Dawes Act was repealed in 1934, Native Americans had lost two-thirds of the land they held prior to its enactment. World War II and various acts of Congress resulted in additional land loss. By 1955, Native Americans retained only 2.3% of their original lands (Dunbar-Ortiz, 2014). Land loss continued in the 1960s including flooding more than half of the Seneca's Allegany Reservation when the US Army Corp of Engineers built Kinzua Dam (Haupton, 2015). Although tribal territories continue to exist, 77% of people living in these areas are not Indigenous (Norris et al., 2012).

In 1971, the Alaska Native Claims Settlement Act (ANCSA) was signed into law. "In one act, the Nixon administration, working with the Congress, extinguished all Native American claims to the state except for 62,500 square miles that would be divided among the Native American peoples" (Venables, 2004, p. 336). The purpose of the act was to dismiss Indigenous Peoples' claims to the land and open up land for development. While Alaskan Natives did receive compensation under ANCSA, their tribal structure was corporatized and they did not retain the same recognition and rights as other Native Americans. Under the ANCSA, Native villages function as corporations managing tribal resources with a business model. They no longer assert their inherent sovereignty over tribal territories, thus losing the jurisdictional capacity maintained by other Native American nations (Tsosie, 2012).

Various laws, policies, and treaty violations compound loss and trauma for Native Americans. These losses are contemporary as well as historical. Violations of the Treaty of Fort Laramie of 1868 led to the sacred Black Hills being overrun by miners and subsequently seized by the United States (Ostler, 2010). Under this same treaty, Lakota Peoples were guaranteed control of land in perpetuity that later became the route of the controversial Dakota Access Pipeline authorized by Presidential Executive Order in 2017 without consent of the Lakota People. This latest example demonstrates that human rights violations continue, even after passage of key human rights instruments. Construction of the Dakota Access Pipeline next to Standing Rock Reservation is frequently cited as a violation of UNDRIP (Braine, 2016; University of Arizona Rogers College of Law, 2018). Article 32, Section 2 states the need to "obtain their free and informed consent prior to the approval of any project affecting their lands or territories and other resources, particularly in connection with the development, utilization or exploitation of mineral, water or other resources" (UN, 2007, p. 12).

Native Americans' ongoing status as wards of the federal government undermines their human rights. Court decisions have designated Native American tribes as *domestic dependent nations* subject to the authority of the United States (Echo-Hawk, 2013). Under these decisions, the federal government owes a trust responsibility to Native Americans. The federal trust responsibility casts Native Americans in a perpetual state of dependency, denying that Native American adults and nations are competent and capable of making their own decisions.

Likewise, a climate of racism and oppression continues to permeate the United States. In this context racial slurs that target Native Americans are protected as freedom of expression (Swoyer, 2017), Native Americans are targeted for hate crimes (Perry, 2009) and suffer microaggressions (Burnette & Figley, 2017; Evans-Campbell, 2008; Klopotek, Lintinger, & Barbry, 2008; Myhra, 2011). Stereotypes flourish, and expressions of religious freedom are still inhibited.

Native Americans exist within a societal context that supports violence (Chenault, 2011; Myhra & Wieling, 2014). Original colonization processes involved warfare and forced removals. Socialization processes, such as the boarding schools, used force to undermine Indigenous cultures, values, and belief systems. Violence is a learned behavior. Colonial powers learned to use violence in their interactions with Indigenous Peoples, and these learned behaviors continue today as illustrated by militaristic force used against Water Protectors near Standing Rock Reservation in 2016.

Native Americans are at greater risk for trauma exposure and posttraumatic stress disorder (PTSD) than other Americans (Beals et al., 2013). Native Americans have the highest rates of intimate partner violence, including rape, stalking, or physical violence, of any group in the United States. Interpersonal violence is experienced by 46% of Native women and 45.3% of Native men (Burnette & Figley, 2017). Domestic violence and sexual abuse are prevalent but often silenced (Amnesty International, 2004; Hedrick, 2016). A study of Native women in New York City found 65% had experienced some form of interpersonal violence. Of these 28% had experienced child abuse, 48% rape, 40% domestic violence, and 40% reported multiple victimizations. They experienced high levels of emotional trauma related to these events. Interpersonal violence is associated with depression, dysphoria, and high-risk sexual behaviors (Evans-Campbell, Lindhorst, Huang, & Walters, 2006). In Canada, Indigenous women age 25–44 are five times more likely to die from violence than other women (Amnesty International, 2004).

Native American children experience PTSD at the same rate as veterans returning from Iraq and Afghanistan. This is triple the rate of the general population (Attorney General's Advisory Committee on American Indian/Alaska Native Children Exposed to Violence [AIANCEV], 2014). Native Americans "could be viewed as ground zero for Adverse Childhood Experiences" (Pember, 2016, p. 9). Contemporary violence is often linked to violence that took place in the boarding schools. In addition to a legacy of physical abuse, boarding schools were regimented institutions where Native Americans were denied parental role models. This contributes to contemporary child abuse, neglect, and removals. It is important, however, not to stigmatize Native Americans but to recognize the impact of historical and contemporary violence and discrimination (Browne et al., 2016)

Many Native American children are exposed to extreme levels of violence and have an exceptional degree of unmet need for services (AIANCEV, 2014). "Today, a vast majority of American Indian and Alaska Native children live in communities with alarmingly high rates of poverty, homelessness, drug abuse, alcoholism, suicide, and victimization. Domestic violence, sexual assault, and child abuse are widespread. Continual exposure to violence has a devastating impact on child development and can have a lasting impact on basic cognitive, emotional, and neurological functions" (AIANCEV, 2014, cover letter).

In spite of enormous resilience, traumatic events have taken a toll on Native American individuals, families, and communities (Evans-Campbell, 2008). Historical trauma is manifested in many ways, including the breakdown of traditional cultures, values, and family systems. Resilience is depleted by substance abuse, violence, internalized oppression, mental health issues, and loss of hope (SAMHSA, 2014). As one Blackfeet activist noted, "Today the anarchic violence that pervades Indian Country is one born of the colonial process and is often a violence of self-hatred that is turned upon family members and members of one's own community, primarily through the use of liquor and drugs, agents which are not part of our traditional cultures" (Kipp, 2004, p. 150).

## TRAUMA-INFORMED APPROACHES
## TO WORKING WITH NATIVE AMERICANS

Being trauma-informed involves recognizing the pervasiveness of trauma and planning interventions and delivery systems accordingly. Trauma-informed practice principles have applicability at both societal and individual levels. The five principles of trauma-informed care are safety, trustworthiness, choice, collaboration, and empowerment (Fallot & Harris, 2009).

Trauma-informed services are particularly important given the extent of historical and contemporary trauma in the lives of Native Americans. A trauma-informed approach is destigmatizing and moves away from a deficit perspective that explores *what's wrong with you* inherent in many examinations of health and social disparities, to an exploration of *what happened to you*, recognizing the impact of trauma on individuals and communities. A trauma-informed approach minimizes the risk of causing additional trauma or exacerbating trauma symptoms (Harris & Fallot, 2001).

### Safety

Lack of safety continues to be a major issue for many Native Americans. This includes high rates of violence, policies that undermine self-determination, and an unfavorable legal climate that fails to recognize inherent rights based on Indigenous status, collective rights, and human rights. Perhaps the greatest ongoing threat to Native Americans is the loss of children. Native children were removed from families and communities in large numbers during the boarding school era. Removals continued as large numbers of Native children were taken into child welfare and juvenile justice systems, typically being placed in non-Native settings (Myhra & Wieling, 2014). Congress passed the Indian Child Welfare Act (ICWA) in 1978 noting that there is no resource more vital to the continued existence and integrity of Indian tribes than their children and that the United States has a direct interest, as trustee, in protecting Indian children who are members of or are eligible for membership in an Indian tribe; that an alarmingly high percentage of Indian families are broken up by removal, often unwarranted, of their children from them by nontribal public and private agencies and that an alarmingly high percentage of such children are placed in non-Indian foster and adoptive homes and institutions; and that the States, exercising their recognized jurisdiction over Indian child custody proceedings through administrative and judicial bodies, have often failed to recognize the essential tribal relations of Indian people and the cultural and social standards prevailing in Indian communities and families. (p. 1901)

ICWA (1978) affirms that tribes have a vested interest in their children, have a right to exercise jurisdiction when Indian children are removed from their families, and stricter levels of scrutiny and placement preferences apply in child welfare proceedings. Unfortunately, ICWA has never been fully funded, service providers have never been adequately trained to implement this federal mandate, and large numbers of Native American children continue to be removed from their families and communities and placed in non-Native care (Weaver & White, 1999).

Practitioners in child welfare settings must recognize that alienation of Native children from their communities is a long-standing and painful issue. Under ICWA (1978), the tribe can take jurisdiction of a case where an *Indian child*, as defined by ICWA, is at risk of placement outside the home. Tribes must be notified if a tribal member (or a child eligible for membership) is at risk of placement. Cases that remain in county jurisdiction must follow a set of placement preferences.

Understanding ICWA (1978) and its provisions is central to an ability to maximize feelings of safety for Native Americans involved in the child welfare system. Clients can be reassured that all opportunities to maximize cultural continuity for Native children taken into foster care will be upheld and the additional scrutiny required by ICWA will be applied before children are removed from their families.

On the societal level, service providers can advocate for more funding and training so ICWA (1978) can be properly implemented to maximize the safety, security, and integrity of Native families and communities. International discourse on human rights typically has an individual bias and fails to acknowledge collective rights articulated in ICWA's provisions about tribes' rights. Strengthening ICWA is an important step to take that would maximize safety for Native American families.

The UNDRIP (UN, 2007) speaks to the issues involved when Native American children are at risk of removal. It emphasizes the importance of "Recognizing in particular the right of indigenous families and communities to retain shared responsibility for the upbringing, training, education and well-being of their children, consistent with the rights of the child" (UN, 2007, p. 3). Like ICWA (1978), UNDRIP affirms Native children have a right to cultural continuity. The UNDRIP goes beyond most international human rights documents to recognize that Native Peoples possess collective rights. In the context of child welfare, this means that tribes can object to placement of Native American children with non-Native families, even when parents do not object.

Both ICWA and UNDRIP recognize the long-standing history of child removal in Indigenous communities. Taking Indigenous children and raising them outside Indigenous cultural contexts threatens the continued existence of Indigenous Peoples and is a form of cultural genocide. Article 7, Section 2, of UNDRIP states Indigenous Peoples "shall not be subjected to any act of genocide or any other act of violence, including forcibly removing children of the group to another group" (UN, 2007, p. 5).

Child removal has been a deliberate tool of forced assimilation. UNDRIP Article 8 continues with the statement that Indigenous Peoples have a "right not to be subjected to forced assimilation or destruction of their culture" (UN, 2007, p. 5). Beyond this right, states must have mechanisms to prevent and redress forced assimilation of Indigenous Peoples. In this instance, ICWA is an important preventive mechanism that needs further strengthening to fulfill its original intent. Native American families and communities are still losing many children to non-Native systems. Service providers can maximize the safety component of trauma-informed services by being sensitive and informed about the meaning and history of losing Native American children, being knowledgeable about ICWA, and advocating for its full implementation.

### *Trustworthiness*

Maximizing trustworthiness is a key element of providing trauma-informed services. This is important, both on individual and systems levels. The extent of violence against Indigenous women provides an example of how this principle can be applied. Stemming the tide of violence against Indigenous women is hampered by many factors, including perpetuation of stereotypes, vulnerabilities linked to lack of resources, and complicated jurisdictional issues that make prosecution of perpetrators difficult. When violence happens in Indigenous communities, victims are often discouraged from reporting by the network of relationships in communities and potential ripple effects if confidentiality is breached.

Service providers need to understand that Indigenous communities are often highly interrelated. A woman disclosing violence may encounter relatives (her own and those of the perpetrator) at her workplace, school, or the agency where she seeks services. Service providers must demonstrate trustworthiness and extra care in how privacy is protected. A provider or agency that does not demonstrate utmost trustworthiness will become known throughout the community. Under these circumstances, women will not access needed services and will continue to be at risk.

It is also important to recognize how internalized oppression can manifest as violence (Kipp, 2004). Imposed gender roles that undermine equality can lead to both self-harming behaviors and oppression of others (Chenault, 2011). Violence may also manifest in culturally specific ways such as one partner denigrating the other for not being knowledgeable of the culture, history, or language.

On a societal level, providers can maximize trustworthiness by being knowledgeable about jurisdictional issues and being able to advise and serve clients in ways that are most helpful. Practitioners should be aware of the Native-specific provisions of the Violence Against Women Act and how this affects tribal communities (United States Department of Justice, 2018). To be trustworthy and address violence against Native people, practitioners must counteract stereotypes and racism that perpetuate dehumanization and allow a culture of violence to flourish.

### Choice

Maximizing choice is another pillar of trauma-informed services. As per UNDRIP Article 23, "indigenous peoples have the right to be actively involved in developing and determining health, housing and other economic and social programs affecting them and, as far as possible, to administer such programmes through their own institutions" (UN, 2007, p. 9). Service providers can ensure Native clients are offered a range of treatment options. They can also cultivate networks that include tribally based services so they can make appropriate referrals.

In addition to mainstream treatment options, many Native Americans benefit from traditional healing methods. Sometimes Indigenous ways of helping are integrated with Western methods. For example, some substance abuse recovery programs integrate sweat lodge ceremonies as part of healing. Sometimes Native Americans prefer traditional services over mainstream services. Trauma-informed care includes facilitating access to traditional healing, if clients prefer. Different forms of help are valid and should be available. Article 24 of UNDRIP (UN, 2007) states Indigenous Peoples should be able to access traditional or mainstream social and health services. In addition to offering treatment choices to individual Native Americans, service providers can play an important role in ensuring such services are available. One mechanism for doing this is to advocate that social and health agencies employ traditional healers and that these providers qualify for reimbursement for services.

## Collaboration

Collaboration is a component of trauma-informed care that is closely aligned with choice. For example, service providers may collaborate with traditional healers to maximize client choice and to offer holistic, synergistic methods to promote wellness. It is also important that service providers are knowledgeable about and collaborate with Indigenous practitioners and researchers who are developing cutting-edge models of practice-based evidence for effective treatments (Lucero & Bussey, 2015).

Most evidence-based practice has not been normed for or tested with Native American clients and is therefore of unknown utility. On the other hand, the development of practice-based evidence is an organic process that grows from this specific population and is known to be effective (Lucero & Bussey, 2015). Collaborating with practitioners who are developing these models will help service providers make thoughtful choices about interventions. On a societal level, service providers have an important role in advocating for funders and policy makers to set standards based on practice-based evidence. Service providers can also partner with tribes and other Indigenous entities to conduct and promote practice-based research.

## Empowerment

Because Indigenous individuals and nations have been systematically disempowered through colonial processes, empowerment is a particularly important component of trauma-informed care. Service providers must foster self-determination and help clients tap into strengths and resilience to make their own choices.

On the macro-level, maximizing self-determination translates as support for sovereignty and Indigenous nationhood. The AIANCEV (2014) report identified a vital connection between tribal sovereignty and protecting Indigenous children. Service providers can challenge federal policies that undermine sovereignty and promote dependency.

Self-determination is a principle that underlies much of UNDRIP (UN, 2007). The preamble reveals the reasoning behind development of this document. Declaration authors were "convinced that control by indigenous peoples over developments affecting them and their lands, territories and resources will enable them to maintain and strengthen their institutions, cultures and traditions, and to promote their development in accordance with their aspirations and needs" (p. 2). Article 3 elaborates on the need for self-determination, and Article 4 describes the importance of Indigenous Peoples maintaining autonomy or self-governance in internal and local affairs. These priorities align with the principles of trauma-informed services and the social work value of self-determination.

## CONCLUSION

While there is still much to be done, there is growing attention to inclusion of Indigenous Peoples within the human rights discourse. Legal scholars such as Echo-Hawk and Tsosie have established significant bodies of scholarship that critique how laws, policies, and human rights documents have failed to adequately incorporate Indigenous understandings. They also point to the promise of the UNDRIP (UN, 2007) and how this can be a guiding document that leads to more inclusive visions of human rights by making national and international law more accountable to Indigenous Peoples.

The 2017 United Nations Permanent Forum on Indigenous Issues was dedicated to examining the state of the world's Indigenous Peoples in the decade since the passage of UNDRIP (UN, 2007). While significant injustices remain, and the tenets of the document have not been legally incorporated in most countries, they are used as guiding principles around the world. In particular, Indigenous People frequently refer to UNDRIP when calling attention to issues such as the reduction of

Bears Ears National Monument and construction of the Dakota Access Pipeline, both done without tribal consent. Indigenous Peoples also can and do call on the Special Rapporteur to investigate and document ongoing injustices (University of Arizona Rogers College of Law, 2018). Historical and contemporary trauma has an ongoing and significant impact on the well-being of Native Americans. Societal change is required to effectively address root causes of trauma. It is important to recognize that the target for change is often unjust colonial societies that perpetuate disparities and injustice. Without societal change, clinical efforts will remain limited in their effectiveness. The IFSW (2017) policy statement on Indigenous Peoples and the UNDRIP (2007), along with the principles of trauma-informed care provide guidance for service providers, policy makers, and change agents to work with Indigenous individuals, communities, and nations to promote wellness, resilience, and human rights.

## References

Amnesty International. (2004). *Canada stolen sisters: A human rights response to discrimination and violence against indigenous women in Canada.* Retrieved from https://www.amnesty.org/en/documents/amr20/003/2004/en/.

Attorney General's Advisory Committee on American Indian/Alaska Native Children Exposed to Violence. (2014). *Ending violence so children can thrive.* US Department of Justice. Retrieved from https://www.justice.gov/sites/default/files/defendingchildhood/pages/attachments/2015/03/23/ending_violence_so_children_can_thrive.pdf.

Beals, J., Manson, S. M., Croy, C., Klein, S. A., Whitesell, N. R., Mitchell, C. M., & the AI-SUPERPTF Team. (2013). Lifetime prevalence of posttraumatic stress disorder in two American Indian reservation populations. *Journal of Traumatic Stress, 26,* 512–520.

Berliner, L., & Kolko, D. J. (2016). Trauma informed care: A commentary and critique. *Child Maltreatment, 21*(2), 168–172.

Braga, L. L., Mello, M. F., & Fiks, J. P. (2012). Transgenerational transmission of trauma and resilience: A qualitative study with Brazilian offspring of Holocaust survivors. *BMC Psychiatry, 12,* 134–144.

Braine, T. (2016, December 15). North Dakota oil spill leaks more than 176,000 gallons of crude. *Indian Country Today.* Retrieved from https://newsmaven.io/indiancountrytoday/archive/north-dakota-oil-spill-leaks-more-than-176-000-gallons-of-crude-VHoMuVw0RESKvzRnFY4qFQ/.

Brave Heart, M. Y. H., Chase, J., Elkins, J., & Altshul, D. B. (2011). Historical trauma among indigenous peoples of the Americas: Concepts, research, and clinical considerations. *Journal of Psychoactive Drugs, 43*(4), 282–290.

Browne, A. J., Varcoe, C., Lavoie, J. Smye, V., Wong, S. T., Krause, M., ... Fridkin, A. (2016). Enhancing health care equity with indigenous populations: Evidence-based strategies from an ethnographic study. *BMC Health Services Research, 16,* 1–17.

Burnette, C. (2015). Historical oppression and intimate partner violence experienced by indigenous women in the United States: Understanding connections. *Social Service Review, 89*(3), 531–563.

Burnette, C. E., & Figley, C. R. (2017). Historical oppression, resilience, and transcendence: Can a holistic framework help explain violence experienced by indigenous people? *Social Work, 62*(1), 37–44.

Carlisle Indian School Digital Resource Center. (2018). *"Kill the Indian, and save the man": Capt. Richard H. Pratt on the education of Native Americans.* Retrieved from http://carlisleindian.dickinson.edu/teach/kill-indian-and-save-man-capt-richard-h-pratt-education-native-americans.

Cavalieri, C. E. (2013). Situating psychotherapy with tribal peoples in a sovereignty paradigm. *Journal of Social Action in Counseling and Psychology, 5*(3), 25–43.

Chenault, V. S. (2011). *Weaving strength, weaving power: Violence and abuse against indigenous women.* Durham, NC: Carolina Academic Press.

Cobb, N., Espey, D., & King, J. (2014). Health behaviors and risk factors among American Indians and Alaska Natives, 2000–2010. *American Journal of Public Health, 104*(Suppl. 3), S481–S489.

Coleman, J. A. (2016). Racial differences in posttraumatic stress disorder in military personnel: Intergenerational transmission of trauma as a theoretical lens. *Journal of Aggression, Maltreatment and Trauma, 25*(6), 561–579.

Dahre, U. J. (2010). There are no such things as universal human rights: On the predicament of indigenous peoples, for example. *The International Journal of Human Rights, 14*(5), 641–657.

Dunbar-Ortiz, R. (2014). *An indigenous peoples' history of the United States.* Boston, MA: Beacon Press.

Durham, M., & Webb, S. S. N. (2014). Historical trauma: A panoramic perspective. *The Brown University Child and Adolescent Behavioral Letter, 30*(10), 4–6.

Echo-Hawk, W. R. (2013). *In the light of justice: The rise of human rights in Native America and the UN Declaration on the Rights of Indigenous Peoples.* Golden, CO: Fulcrum Publishing.

Evans-Campbell, T. (2008). Historical trauma in American Indian/Native Alaska communities: A multilevel framework for exploring impacts on individuals, families, and communities. *Journal of Interpersonal Violence, 23*(3), 316–338.

Evans-Campbell, T., Lindhorst, T., Huang, B., & Walters, K. L. (2006). Interpersonal violence in the lives of urban American Indian and Alaska Native women: Implications for health, mental health, and help-seeking. *American Journal of Public Health, 96*(8), 1416–1422.

Fallot, R. D., & Harris, M. (2009). *Creating cultures of trauma-informed care (CCTIC): A self-assessment and planning protocol.* Community Connections.

Retrieved from https://traumainformedoregon.org/wp-content/uploads/2014/10/CCTIC-A-Self-Assessment-and-Planning-Protocol.pdf.

Federal Register. (2017, January 17). Indian entities recognized and eligible to receive services from the United States Bureau of Indian Affairs (document citation 82 FR 4915), 62(10), 4915–4920. Retrieved from https://www.federalregister.gov/documents/2017/01/17/2017-00912/indian-entities-recognized-and-eligible-to-receive-services-from-the-united-states-bureau-of-indian.

Gone, J. P. (2009). A community-based treatment for Native American historical trauma: Prospects for evidence-based practice. *Journal of Consulting and Clinical Psychology, 77*(4), 751–762.

Harris, M., & Fallot, R. D. (2001). Envisioning a trauma-informed service system: A vital paradigm shift. In M. Harris & R. D. Fallot (Eds.), *Using trauma theory to design service systems* (pp. 3–22). San Francisco, CA: Jossey-Bass.

Hartmann, W. E., & Gone, J. P. (2014). American Indian historical trauma: Community perspectives from two Great Plains medicine men. *American Journal of Community Psychology, 54,* 274–288.

Haupton, L. M. (2015). *The Iroquois struggle for survival: World War II to red power.* Syracuse, NY: Syracuse University Press.

Hedrick, C. (2016). Returning the warrior spirit: Native men's wellness gatherings. *News From Native California, 29*(4), 49–51.

Indian Child Welfare Act. (1978). 25 U.S.C. 1901–63.

International Federation of Social Workers. (2017). *Indigenous peoples.* https://www.ifsw.org/indigenous-peoples/.

Kipp, W. (2004). *Viet Cong at Wounded Knee: The trail of a Blackfeet activist.* Lincoln, NE: University of Nebraska Press.

Klopotek, B., Lintinger, B., & Barbry, J. (2008). Ordinary and extraordinary trauma: Race indigeneity, and Hurricane Katrina in the Tunica-Biloxi history. *American Indian Culture and Research Journal, 32*(2), 55–77.

Lucero, N. M., & Bussey, M. (2015). Practice-informed approaches to addressing substance abuse and trauma exposure in urban Native families involved with child welfare. *Child Welfare, 94*(4), 97–117.

Mann, C. C. (2005). *1491: New revelations of the Americas before Columbus.* New York, NY: Vintage Books.

Mohatt, N. V., Thompson, A. B., Thai, N. D., & Tebes, J. K. (2014). Historical trauma as public narrative: A conceptual review of how history impacts present-day health. *Social Science and Medicine, 106,* 128–136.

Myhra, L. L. (2011). "It runs in the family": Intergenerational transmission of historical trauma among urban American Indians and Alaska Natives in culturally specific sobriety maintenance programs. *American Indian and Alaska Native Mental Health Research, 18*(2), 17–40.

Myhra, L. L., & Wieling, E. (2014). Psychological trauma among American Indian families: A two-generation study. *Journal of Loss and Trauma, 19,* 289–313.

Norris, T., Vines, P. L., & Hoeffel, E. M. (2012). *The American Indian and Alaska Native population: 2010*. United States Census Bureau. Retrieved from https://www.census.gov/history/pdf/c2010br-10.pdf.

Nutton, J., & Fast, E. (2015). Historical trauma, substance use, and indigenous peoples: Seven generations of harm from a "Big Event". *Substance Use and Misuse, 50,* 839–847.

Ostler, J. (2010). *The Lakotas and the Black Hills: The struggle for sacred ground*. New York, NY: Penguin Books.

Pember, M. A. (2016). *Intergenerational trauma: Understanding Natives' inherited pain*. Indian Country Today Media Network.

Perry, B. (2009). "There's just places ya' don't wanna go": The segregating impact of hate crime against Native Americans. *Contemporary Justice Review, 12*(4), 401–418.

Salazar, M. (2016). State recognition of American Indian tribes. *National Conference of State Legislatures, 24*(39). Retrieved from http://www.ncsl.org/research/state-tribal-institute/state-recognition-of-american-indian-tribes.aspx.

Substance Abuse and Mental Health Services Administration. (2014). *Understanding historical trauma when responding to an event in Indian Country*. Retrieved from https://store.samhsa.gov/product/Understanding-Historical-Trauma-When-Responding-to-an-Event-in-Indian-Country/sma14-4866.

Swoyer, A. (2017, June 19). Supreme court ruling against censoring The Slants' name bolsters Washington Redskins trademark case. *Washington Times*. Retrieved from http://www.washingtontimes.com/news/2017/jun/19/washington-redskins-trademark-fight-aided-by-supre/.

Tsosie, R. (2012). Reconceptualizing tribal rights: Can self-determination be actualized within the U.S. constitutional structure? *Lewis and Clark Law Review, 15*(4), 923–950.

Turner, S. L., & Pope, M. (2009). North America's native peoples: A social justice and trauma counseling approach. *Multicultural Counseling and Development, 37,* 194–205.

United Nations. (1948). *Universal declaration of human rights*. Retrieved from http://www.un.org/en/universal-declaration-human-rights/.

United Nations. (2007). *United nations declaration on the rights of indigenous peoples*. Retrieved from https://www.un.org/development/desa/indigenous-peoples/declaration-on-the-rights-of-indigenous-peoples.html.

United Nations. (2018). *State of the world's indigenous peoples (SOWIP)*. Retrieved from https://www.un.org/development/desa/indigenouspeoples/publications/state-of-the-worlds-indigenous-peoples.html.

United States Department of Justice. (2018). *Violence Against Women Act (VAWA) Reauthorization 2013*. Retrieved from https://www.justice.gov/tribal/violence-against-women-act-vawa-reauthorization-2013-0.

University of Arizona Rogers College of Law. (2018). *Indigenous Resistance to the Dakota Access Pipeline: Criminalization of Dissent and Suppression of Protest*. Report to the United Nations Special Rapporteur on the Rights of Indigenous Peoples, Victoria Tauli-Corpuz.

Venables, R. W. (2004). *American Indian history: Five centuries of conflict and coexistence*. Santa Fe, NM: Clear Light Publishing.

Walls, M. L., & Whitbeck, L. B. (2012). The intergenerational effects of relocation policies on indigenous families. *Journal of Family Issues, 33*(9), 1272–1293.

Weaver, H. N., & White, B. J. (1999). Protecting the future of indigenous children and nations: An examination of the Indian Child Welfare Act. *Journal of Health and Social Policy, 10*(4), 35–50.

Whitbeck, L. B., Adams, G. W., Hoyt, D. R., & Chen, X. (2004). Conceptualizing and measuring historical trauma among American Indian people. *American Journal of Community Psychology, 33*(3/4), 119–130.

# CHAPTER 5

# Black Trauma in the US and the Pursuit of Human Rights: A Brief History

*Christopher St. Vil and Noelle M. St. Vil*

Up until 1862 in the US, there was never a question about the place or role of Persons of African Descent (PAD). They were relegated to a menial class with few rights and viewed as beasts in need of control, hence chattel slavery. It never registered in the minds of the colonists that PAD would or could serve any other purpose than to serve as slaves. In 1862, newspaper headlines during the Civil War would often offer a variant of a perplexing question. The question was, "What shall we do with the Negro?" (Escott, 2009). This was the Negro Question that the US needed to answer in much the same way that Europe felt a need to answer the Jewish Question (Dawidowicz, 1975). How could PAD in the US be expected to engage fully in civic matters, equal to Whites? The US answered that question with policies and practices: policies and practices that constituted human right violations as defined in the Universal Declaration of Human Rights (UDHR; United Nations

C. St. Vil · N. M. St. Vil (✉)
School of Social Work,
University at Buffalo, Buffalo, NY, USA
e-mail: noellst@buffalo.edu

C. St. Vil
e-mail: cstvil@buffalo.edu

© The Author(s) 2019
L. D. Butler et al. (eds.), *Trauma and Human Rights*,
https://doi.org/10.1007/978-3-030-16395-2_5

[UN], 1948) and that continue today through structural violence. Many of these state-sanctioned policies and practices, over time, have produced longitudinal economic, educational, and health impacts on the Black community that manifest for some individuals, families, and communities as historical trauma. Some of these policies included the Black Slave Codes and Vagrancy laws, housing segregation laws, and Separate but Equal policies. Some practices included redlining, the prevention of free participation in the progressive phases of capitalist development, voter suppression, unequal protection under the law, lynching, and the omission of historical facts that obscured significant contributions by Blacks thereby reinforcing perceptions of intellectual and moral inferiority and the implied superiority of White individuals.

Domestic efforts to assuage these conditions experienced by PAD in the US abound throughout US history, and the efforts during the 1960s in particular—which often receive disproportionate attention—were couched in a civil rights framework. Less known are the attempts to present the plight of PAD in the US to an international platform, the United Nations, specifically, the Human Rights Council, and to re-frame these issues from a civil rights framework to a human rights framework from both an activist and civil perspective. The former has often been met with rebuff in the US, while the latter is the current dominant approach to human right issues around the world. Those leading the struggle for human rights believed that bringing their case before a world stage—the UN—would draw helpful international attention and pressure on the US to address these issues. This chapter seeks to shed light on some of those efforts.

This chapter begins with an introduction to the concept of the historical trauma framework. It has been employed to explain mental health outcomes among European Jews and Native Americans. We apply this framework to Blacks in the US through a 3-stage framework that nests the Black experience within a historical perspective. That discussion is followed by a description of a framework that seeks to explain the consequences of Black historical trauma. We then describe efforts to bring the Negro Question (Allen, 1936) in the US to the world stage via the UN and their outcome. The relationship between PAD and human rights in the US is a complicated one and one that mental health practitioners should be privy to when working with PAD. We use the term PAD and Black interchangeably to refer to people of African descent in the US. These terms are inclusive of African Americans, Caribbeans and Africans, and those who identify as such and are perceived as being Black in the US. The justification for this all-encompassing definition is couched in the reality that in public discourse, the first thing one sees and uses as a basis of judgment is race not ethnicity, thereby making all Blacks in the diaspora subject to cultural definitions and stereotypes of Blackness in the US.

## Historical Trauma

Whether the plight of PAD has improved or not since slavery is not much of a debate. Remnants of "chattel slavery" remind us of the vast improvement of the social position of PAD in the US. However, the historical remnants of such a history, where the human rights of PAD suffered state-sanctioned physical and psychological assaults that continue through the impacts of structural racism, have led to a legacy of historical trauma that has resulted in maladaptive responses such as vacant esteem and internalized racism (DeGruy, 2005).

*Historical trauma* (HT) is a framework that seeks to explain behaviors as a function of one generation's trauma on subsequent generations (Danieli, 1998). This framework was originally employed to explain how the children of Jewish Holocaust survivors tend to absorb some of the psychological burdens of their parents and the parental transmission of the trauma associated with the atrocities of the Jewish Holocaust (Danieli, 1982; Kellerman, 2001). HT is defined as "the cumulative and collective psychological and emotional injury sustained over a lifetime and across generations resulting from massive group trauma experiences" (Brave Heart, 2003). The main characteristic of the HT framework is that populations historically subjected to long-term, mass trauma exhibit psychological emotional, attitudinal, and behavioral outcomes similar to posttraumatic stress disorder symptoms, and pass those symptoms on to successive generations through social and physiological pathways which can manifest in a variety of ways resulting in an intergenerational cycle of trauma response (Brave Heart & DeBruyn, 1998; Danieli, 1982; DeGruy, 2005; Estrada, 2009).

In the case of the Jewish Holocaust, between 1933 and 1945, state-sponsored legislation, specifically the Nuremberg Laws, led to the segregation, marginalization, detainment, and eventual genocide of 6 million Jews (Benz, 2001). State-sanctioned violence against those who identified as Jewish and those whom the Nazis decided were Jewish (or Gypsies, homosexual, or disabled) could easily be characterized as human right violations. Jews in Germany were stripped of their citizenship and civil rights including the right to work in legal professions and civil service, suggesting a form of state-sanctioned workplace discrimination. Additionally, the state sanctioned the boycott of Jewish businesses (Danieli, 1998). Many Jewish Holocaust survivors had a difficult time adjusting after the trauma of surviving the concentration camps, and many suffered direct effects from the trauma (Kellerman, 2001). That the same trauma symptoms of the actual survivors who experienced such horrible events are exhibited in their children and grandchildren is evidence of the intergenerational transmission of HT.

Brave Heart and DeBruyn (1998) applied the literature on HT to Native Americans in the US and argue that the issues facing Native Americans now are the result of unresolved grief stemming from HT. Since the 1500s, Indigenous peoples of the Americas have experienced massacres, torture, terrorism, sexual abuse, military occupations, forced removal from lands, and a state-sanctioned policy of extermination (Stannard, 1993). Additionally, they endured the seizure and placement of Native American children in boarding schools and federal assimilation policies (Brave Heart & DeBruyn, 1998). From a colonization standpoint, the Native Americans also experienced forced abandonment of religious and cultural practices, the destruction of resources necessary for native survival, disease, addiction, and the disruption of kinship and family relations (Legters, 1988). From these historical atrocities came huge health disparities that render Native Americans the highest among demographic groups in the US in poverty, and the lowest in income and education (Denny, Holtzman, Goins, & Croft, 2005). Most notably, Brave Heart and DeBruyn (1998) cite internalized oppression and identification with the aggressor as a consequence of this trauma, manifested through high rates of alcohol abuse, suicide, and violence and low rates of educational attainment, to name a few.

What is clear from this brief overview of HT among Native Americans and European Jews is that the trauma and terror that both groups experienced are attributable to state policies that were indifferent to both groups' human rights. In the case of the Jews, it was the Nuremberg Laws in Germany; with Native Americans, it was policies that gave way to westward expansion in the US, resulting in cultural suppression, forced assimilation, and extermination. The HT framework suggests that these state-sanctioned atrocities left indelible marks on the historical legacies of these two groups and their overall functioning. In the next section, applying this same framework to PAD, we begin with a description of the experiences of PAD in the US, which can be divided into 3 time periods that were a result of state-sanctioned human right violations that are still having an impact today in the US: the slavery generation, the legalized segregation and discrimination generation, and the race-neutral generation.

## THE AFRICAN AMERICAN HOLOCAUST/BLACK EXPERIENCE IN THE US

Similar to the condition of Native Americans and European Jews, the rights and human dignity of PAD in the US were violated and the conditions in which they were forced to live and endure led to negative effects on their psychological and physical health. Today, in the advent of the twenty-first century, PAD, second only to Native Americans, are the least healthy ethnic group in the US as a result of years of racial and social injustice (Noonan, Velasco-Mondragon, & Wagner, 2016). Consequently, we argue that the social and physical disparities that Black families in the US contend with and the historical trauma that they have experienced are a direct result of human right violations in the form of structural violence, manifested through federal, state, and local policies and laws that have severely constrained their opportunities to improve their health and accumulate financial assets and capital (Gaskin, Headen, & White-Means, 2005). From this perspective, we employ Galtung's (1969) definition of violence which views violence as "the cause of the difference between the potential and the actual" (p. 168). In other words, "the avoidable disparity between the potential ability to fulfill basic needs and their actual fulfillment" expands the definition of violence to include policies (Ho, 2007, p. 1).

The Black experience in the US can be divided into three periods (Gaskin et al., 2005): (1) the slavery generation which lasted 246 years (1619–1865), (2) the legalized segregation and discrimination generation which lasted 100 years (1865–1965), and (3) the race-neutral generation which is what we are presently in which has lasted about 53 years (1965–2018). The sum of these three periods, 399 years, is the length of time that PAD have lived in the US. Thus, 62% of the Black tenure in the US was spent in the institution of chattel slavery and an additional 25% of the time after chattel slavery Blacks were still segregated and experiencing legal discrimination. Thus, for only 13% of the Black tenure in the US has there been a lessening of the severity of legal statutes and policies that severely restricted the movement and freedoms of PAD. PAD endured significant assaults to their human rights throughout these three periods similar to the Jewish and Native American Holocausts.

## *Slavery Generation*

The experience of PAD in the US begins with the slavery generation or "Chattel Slavery," with the first Blacks arriving in Jamestown Virginia in 1619 as indentured servants (Franklin & Moss, 1994). This period lasted until 1865, the year the Emancipation Proclamation was ratified. The treatment of PAD during this period was characterized by extreme brutality and trauma. This trauma has been documented in slave narratives that provide vivid examples of violent encounters perpetuated on PAD by Whites not limited to whippings, lynchings, abuse, and the rape of both enslaved women (Douglass, 1845; Equiano, 1789; Smith, 1798) and boys (Foster, 2011). The cruel and inhumane treatment of PAD was sanctioned by law with the first known statutory recognition of slavery taking place in 1661 defining the Negro's subordinate position in society (Degler, 1959; Franklin & Moss, 1994). These laws, known as slave codes, regulated every aspect of a Black person's life and impressed the conception that slaves are not people but property.

Male slaves were denied the right to perform the role of husband, provider, or protector, and they and their families had to defer to the plantation owner for their needs (Black, 1997). Black families lived consistently under the threat of violence or family breakup through the threat of sale (Dunaway, 2003). Slaves had no standing in court or legal recourse including being party to a lawsuit or providing testimony except against another PAD; they could make no contracts or engage in business without the permission of their master; ownership of property was forbidden; they had no right to strike a White person, even in self-defense; and the death of a PAD was rarely regarded as murder. The rape of a Black female was permitted by slave masters and regarded as a crime if anyone other than the slave master raped her only because it involved trespassing (Franklin & Moss, 1994). PAD could not leave plantations without permission, and if they did any White person regardless of position or status could capture them and turn them into public officials for a reward; PAD could not possess firearms; they could not buy or sell goods, and often times PAD would watch helplessly as family members were flogged and whipped (Dunaway, 2003; Franklin & Moss, 1994).

The most debilitating and lasting impact of this period, beyond the physical and psychological abuse, is the cementing in the minds of most Americans, including PAD, the permanent association of Blackness with inferiority. During this period in the US, Christian theology was used to legitimize the treatment toward Native Americans as well as PAD. Both groups were characterized as soulless heathens or savages: non-humans at best, beasts at worst, deserving of the treatment bestowed upon them by God (Willhelm, 1973). These deep-rooted beliefs that had 246 years to fester led to deep-rooted stereotypes of the inferiority of PAD that have persisted through the seventeenth century to today (Plous & Williams, 1995). It is the end of this period that the Negro Question is posed in the US. Sending them back from where they were stolen/kidnapped from was not an option. The individual slave, 246 years later, was no longer African and knew nothing of Africa. After living under such wretched conditions for close to 250 years, how can these new Americans be assimilated into the fabric of US society?

### *Legalized Segregation and Discrimination Generation*

Slavery did not necessarily end in 1865. The legalized segregation and discrimination generation began the year the Emancipation Proclamation was ratified in 1865. This period lasted until 1965 with the passage of the civil rights movement that outlawed legal segregation. This period is distinguished from the first in that PAD were no longer under a system of chattel slavery. Two practices endured during this period which challenged the gains of the Emancipation Proclamation: (1) convict leasing and (2) peonage. In an effort to replenish the labor that was lost as a result of the prohibition of slavery, many states instituted "Black Codes" or "Vagrancy Laws" which were laws, modeled on the slave codes, intended to restrict Black freedoms and make it easy to secure their arrest and conviction for minor infractions so they could be committed to state-sanctioned involuntary labor (Blackmon, 2008). These Black Codes prohibited Blacks from voting, bearing arms, learning how to read or write, and being out after dark. Any violation of these laws led to unlawful arrest and inhumane detainment (Mancini, 1996). Once detained, the men would be leased to US companies for cheap labor (Blackmon, 2008). This practice became known as *convict leasing* and continued officially in Alabama until 1928 and North Carolina until 1933 (Fierce, 1994). It is during this period that the penal institutions transitioned from being predominately White to predominately Black and also when the association between criminality and Blackness was solidified in the US (Muhammad, 2010). Convict leasing is the official beginning of the prison industrial complex.

*Peonage*, akin to slavery, is a type of involuntary servitude where laborers have little control over their employment conditions (Freeman, 1999). After the Civil War, freedmen who could not afford their own land would farm another person's land in exchange for a portion of the crops (Blackmon, 2008). However, in order to farm that land, the freedmen would need to buy the seeds and tools from the landowner at inflated prices. Unable to pay, freedmen would be relegated to perpetual indebted servitude (Daniel, 1990). The treatment of those trapped in this arrangement mirrored the conditions of slavery. Both convict leasing and peonage were practiced widely to remind PAD of their place in US society even though chattel slavery as an official policy ended.

In addition to convict leasing and peonage, the legal segregation and discrimination period also included the implementation of separate and unequal Jim Crow Laws (Woodward, 1955); the peak of the practice of lynching (of men, women, and children), which was tolerated by state and federal officials between the years 1877 and 1950, and which was more prevalent than previously reported (Equal Justice Initiative, 2017); the formation of the Ku Klux Klan (Goldberg, 1996); and the Brown decision (Weinstein, Gregory, & Strambler, 2004). PAD and Whites were still legally prohibited from marrying in many places throughout the country as evidenced by the Loving's case (Douglas, 2008). That the practices of peonage, convict leasing, lynching, and denying the right to marriage based on race persisted well into the 1960s suggest that in some respects, this period was not much different from the previous one; it just took a different form.

### Race-Neutral Generation

The race-neutral period begins in 1965, a year after the passage of the Civil Rights Act of 1964. We are currently 53 years into this period and are the beneficiaries of said legislation. That we are still discussing issues around the treatment of PAD in the US in 2018 is a testimony to the glacial pace of social and legal change in this country. In spite of rhetoric about a post-racial America, human rights issues of today that continue to impact PAD in the current period are residential segregation and the prison industrial complex, which violate Articles 7, 17, and 9 of the UDHR (UN, 1948), respectively.

The second part of Article 7 of the UDHR (UN, 1948) states "All are entitled to equal protection against any discrimination in violation of this Declaration and against any incitement to such discrimination." Article 17 states, "Everyone has the right to own property alone as well as in association with others and no one shall be arbitrarily deprived of his property." Blacks received no protection against discrimination from the federal government in a number of areas including employment, the use of public spaces, and schools. The inability of PAD to secure housing during the legal segregation period and the outcomes of those practices are being felt now in the race-neutral period. According to Richard Rothstein (2017), the US government engaged in de jure segregation between the 1920s and the 1970s by refusing to insure home loans for PAD, out of a desire to keep the races segregated. The US government coordinated with real estate agents to deny PAD access to better housing stock that they would have been able to afford and that would have improved their social and financial capital. Rothstein makes the argument that PAD were unconstitutionally denied the right to integrate middle-class neighborhoods. This denial led to marginalization, social isolation, and a dearth of financial assets and social and cultural capital that would have accumulated generational wealth for many Black families and may have resulted in lower poverty rates and lower rates of concentrated poverty among Black families (Gaskin et al., 2005). Rothstein (2017) argues that since the denial to middle-class housing was state-sponsored, then the state is obligated to remedy it. This act by the US federal government and its result (concentrated poverty) is a violation of Articles 7 and 17 of the UDHR and a form of structural violence in that it denied the right of Blacks to purchase property when they possessed the financial means to do so.

Now if we conceptualize the impact that incarceration has on social and financial capital, we understand the stigma associated with incarceration and how it leads to unemployment and criminal recidivism. The effects on an individual are devastating and debilitating. However, when a whole community of able-bodied individuals are shut out from opportunities because of stigma, then it becomes systematic. Article 9 of the UDHR (UN, 1948) addresses unlawful arrest and detention. It states, "No one shall be subjected to arbitrary arrest, detention, or exile." The mass incarceration of Black men in the US has reached epic proportions, and the growth of the prison industrial complex has been concentrated among poor Black men with little education (Western, 2006). According to a recent US Department of Justice report, although Black men make up roughly 7% of the US population, they represent about 37% of the state and federal male population in comparison with 32% for White males and 22% for Hispanic males (Carson, 2014). The same report goes on to state that almost 3% of Black male US residents of all ages were imprisoned in December 2013 compared to 1% of Hispanic males and 0.5% of White males. These percentages translate into rates of imprisonment of 2805, 1134, and 466 per 100,000 for Black, Hispanic, and White men, respectively. Among incarcerated males between the ages of 25 and 39, Black males were disproportionately imprisoned at a rate of at least 2.5 times greater than Hispanic males and 6 times greater than White males. When we observe this same trend among males aged 18–19, Blacks were more than 9 times more likely to be imprisoned than Whites (Carson, 2014).

The disproportionate incarceration of Black males without remedy is a violation of Article 9 of the UDHR (UN, 1948). Now we cannot ignore during this current period the justified and unjustified shootings and assaults of Black men and women by law enforcement as well as the employment issues around hiring as a result of one's race and criminal background. From this depiction of the Black experience in the US, it can be summarized that trauma, human right violations, and structural violence characterized PAD's reality for 89% of the time they have been on US soil. This period demonstrates that the US response to the Negro Question is still playing out. The next section highlights the impact of living under such conditions for PAD.

## The Impact of the Black Experience in the US

### Post Traumatic Slave Syndrome/Historical Trauma

Similar to the way the historical trauma framework was applied to survivors of the Jewish and Native American Holocausts, DeGruy (2005) applies it to the Black Holocaust in the US. According to DeGruy, the cumulative result of the treatment of PAD during the chattel slavery and legal segregation generations led to the adoption of attitudes and behaviors that ensured PAD survival. Those same attitudes and behaviors that have served as survival strategies during the slavery and legal segregation periods in the current context prove un-useful today. They are behaviors that exist as a consequence of the multigenerational oppression of PAD and their descendants. These same behaviors are sustained because of the absence of opportunities to heal and continued oppression. This historical trauma results in predictable patterns of behavior called Post Traumatic Slave Syndrome (PTSS) which DeGruy categorizes into three areas: (1) vacant esteem, (2) marked propensity for anger and violence, and (3) internalized racism. Vacant esteem is defined as the state of believing oneself to have little or no worth, exacerbated by the group and societal pronouncement of inferiority (DeGruy, 2005). Esteem is developed through the messages we receive from society, our community, and our families about our capacity to perform or do things. On a societal level in the US, messages abound about the inferiority of Blacks (Burrell, 2010). Beginning with Bible teachings, PAD and Americans alike were socialized into thinking that the subordinate role of Blacks was their rightful place in the social order (Willhelm, 1973). This socialization reinforced an ethos of White supremacy and Black inferiority that we as a nation struggle to reconcile. This socialization continues today through contemporary television and radio advertisements (Burrell, 2010). The consequences of vacant self-esteem include hyper-vulnerability and hyper-vigilance, lack of appreciation for the achievement of peers, and feeling responsible for the entire community when one commits an egregious act (DeGruy, 2005).

A marked propensity for anger and violence is, according to DeGruy (2005), the most pronounced behavior pattern of PTSS. Now Blacks in the US are often accused of being angry and aggressive, especially Black men. DeGruy's argument is in line with Merton's theory of anomie. Merton (1938) argued that society puts pressure on people to achieve socially accepted goals but provides no means for a significant number of people to achieve them, which leads them to experience strain. The argument is similar for DeGruy's (2005) concept of a propensity for anger except that she replaces strain with anger. In relation to PTSS, DeGruy argues that anger and the propensity for violence are natural responses to blocked goals. Often times people respond to the blocked opportunity, if it's perceived to have happened by chance and not by prejudice, with motivation to try again. However, when it appears that goals are blocked over time as a result of social inconsistency (Chestang, 1972), then the slight becomes significant and results in the possibility of failure which produces fear, a fear that can then be released as anger. PAD in the US have often had opportunities closed to them because of nothing else other than their race. What DeGruy (2005) is pointing out is the long-term consequence of these feelings, how these feelings breed cynicism and hopelessness for change, and how this cynicism and hopelessness for societal change is passed down generationally. For over 340 years in the US, Blacks have been told they are equal and that they have the same rights as Whites only to realize that the majority of America did not buy into that part of the constitution, including the government.

The last aspect of PTSS, internalized racism, is related to the first, vacant esteem. As stated earlier, one of the most debilitating impacts of the 399-year tenure of PAD in the US is the cumulative impact of being brought up within a system where you are taught to devalue yourself and to value the lifestyle, perspective, and ethos of another's culture. The foundation of the US value system was the belief that all things associated with Whiteness were superior and that all things associated with Blackness were inferior. As a result, many Blacks in the US have taken on the attitude of the oppressor over time as a normalized perspective and view themselves and their peers through the racialized view of American society. Essentially, PAD were taught to hate themselves, and this internalized racism has become a pillar in the continued subjugation of the Black experience.

It is important to note that PTSS resulting from the three periods that make up the Black experience has been exacerbated through numerous violations of human rights especially during the first two periods such as rape, mass executions, forced labor, and false imprisonment. PTSS cannot be addressed without addressing the human rights atrocities experienced by PAD. Within this 399 year odyssey, there were attempts to present the Black plight in the US to the UN to remedy it, since domestic attempts had fallen short. Through these attempts, Black leaders sought to re-frame the problem of PAD in the US from civil rights to human rights for two reasons. First, they thought that bringing the issue of American segregation and racism to the world stage would draw sympathy from the world and bring international attention to their plight, which would increase pressure on the US to improve conditions for Blacks in spite of their promises. Second, Black leaders felt that the change in terminology from civil rights to human rights would align their cause and efforts with other oppressed groups and colonies around the world who were achieving higher levels of success in their respective countries with international support (Nier, 1997). These efforts are highlighted in the next section.

## BLACKS IN THE US AND THE UNITED NATIONS: ATTEMPTED REMEDIES

The UDHR was proclaimed by the UN General Assembly in Paris on December 10, 1948 (Twiss, 2004), 4 years after Gunnar Myrdal's publication "The American Dilemma" which documented the horrid conditions of PAD in the US. Ralph Bunche, a political scientist from Howard University, along with Eleanor Roosevelt, was instrumental in the creation and adoption of the UDHR (McFadden, 1971). Now, it is important to note that the year in which the UDHR was proclaimed, the Black experience in the US was in the legal discrimination period, the US military was still not yet integrated, and housing discrimination was rampant and gradually reaching its zenith of concentrated poverty and social isolation. This is important to note because it demonstrates the hypocrisy of the US political system in being party to a document that emphasizes the rights of human beings abroad but simultaneously denies those rights based on race to human beings within her domestic borders. The attempts at bringing the Black case before the UN were undergirded by individual efforts as well as bodies representing the UN.

### Individual Efforts: W.E.B. DuBois and Malcolm X

Prior to the passage of the UDHR (1948), W.E.B. Dubois was a staunch advocate of bringing the US before the UN for its treatment of Blacks. In 1945, DuBois attended the establishment of the UN as a member of a special delegation from the National Association for the Advancement of Colored People (NAACP) (Horne, 2009) held at the Dumbarton Oaks estate in Washington, DC. The meeting was formally called the Washington Conversations on International Peace and Security Organization and attendees deliberated over proposals for the establishment of an organization to maintain peace and security around the world.

At this inaugural meeting, the NAACP delegation, headed by DuBois, requested that the Dumbarton Oaks Proposal (named after the location of the historic meeting) endorse racial equality and formally call an end to the colonial era. Although the proposal received support from other countries, the request was ignored and not included in the United Nations Charter. After this perceived slight, DuBois went on to criticize the persistence of colonial rule in the controversial publication, *Color and Democracy: Colonies and Peace* (Lewis, 2009; Mazower, 2004).

Two years later after the first snub, another attempt by DuBois to bring the Black plight to the UN was attempted when he submitted a document titled, "An Appeal to the World: A Statement of Denial of Human Rights to Minorities in the Case of Citizens of Negro Descent in the United States of America and an Appeal to the United Nations for Redress" to the human rights division of the UN in 1947 (NAACP, 2017). Eleanor Roosevelt refused to take part in the presentation of this document for political reasons, specifically that it would put her in a position to defend the racial policies of the US, and this petition, like the first, was thus ignored as well. The next attempt at bringing the Black issue to the UN as an individual effort was committed by Malcolm X.

### Malcolm X

In 1964, Malcolm X along with the Organization of Afro/African American Unity (OAAU) prepared a document for submission to the UN entitled: *Outline for Petition to the United Nations Charging Genocide against 22 million Black Americans* (Nier, 1997). Malcolm X believed in taking advantage of the UDHR and that the plea for civil rights should be replaced by a plea for human rights so that the struggle could be expanded from a domestic jurisdiction to an international one (Handler, 1964). The OAAU was a Pan-Africanist organization founded by Malcolm X in 1964 and modeled after the Organization of African Unity (OAU) (Perry, 1991). The OAU was established in May 1963 and represented a sort of UN of countries from the continent of Africa. At the time of its disbanding, 53 of the 54 African states were members of the OAU. It was disbanded in July 2002 by its last chairperson, South African President Thabo Mbeki, and replaced by the African Union.

Malcolm presented his plan to the second meeting of the OAU to garner their support. Because the US would not allow Malcolm X to address the UN, he sought the assistance of the OAU to assist him with a sponsorship to speak. In order to address the UN, a member state would have to sponsor him and allow him to address the member states.

The OAU responded with a worded declaration of acknowledgment of the 1964 Civil Rights Act along with a tempered statement citing their disturbance with racial bigotry and an urging of the US to deal with discrimination based on race (Nier, 1997). Despite the OAU's reluctance to support Malcolm X, he sought to submit the document to the UN anyway. Prior to submitting the draft to the UN Malcolm X was assassinated in February 1965. Both DuBois and Malcolm X attempted to engage the UN as activists and recruit international allies in the quest for Black equality in the US. DuBois's attempts preceded the establishment of the UDHR, and Malcolm X's were well after it. The next attempts were initiated by the UN "monitoring bodies that work to improve government's practice in the specified areas of human rights" (Hafner-Burton & Tsutsui, 2005, p. 1374).

### Efforts by Official Bodies of the United Nations

The UN consists of two entities to promote and protect human rights: charter bodies and treaty bodies. *Charter bodies* are groups established for the purpose of making decisions and guiding the work of the UN. More specifically, these bodies review the human rights record of every UN member and promote international coordination. The charter bodies include the Human Rights Council and the Office of the UN High Commissioner for Human Rights. *Treaty bodies*, in contrast, are tasked with the responsibility of monitoring and promoting compliance with a particular human rights treaty. Treaty bodies collect, consider, and report on measures member states have adopted to carry out their obligations under the treaty and make recommendations as to how the state can improve their compliance with the treaty. It is important to note that a finding by a treaty body that a member state has violated an individual's human rights is not legally binding, and individuals can only make complaints to treaty bodies if they have exhausted all domestic remedies and if the relevant state has recognized the competence of the treaty body to hear the complaint. There have been a number of treaty-monitoring bodies established to supervise the implementation of treaty obligations such as the Human Rights Committee, the Committee against Torture, the Committee on Migrant Workers, and the Committee on the Elimination of Discrimination (CERD) against Women. Another treaty-monitoring body includes the *International Convention on the Elimination of Racial Discrimination* (ICERD; UN, 1965).

ICERD is a human rights treaty designed to protect individuals and groups from discrimination based on race. The US ratified ICERD in 1994, which bound it to all provisions of the treaty including a periodic compliance review conducted by the UN CERD. The third CERD review of the US took place in August of 2014. The concluding report was submitted by the CERD on August 29, 2014. The report identified areas of improvement such as the implementation of strategies to remove barriers to equal employment, the adoption of the Fair Sentencing Act, and the adoption of the Matthew Shepard and James Byrd Jr. Hate Crimes Prevention Acts passed in 2009. It took the report one single page to list the areas of positive regard for the US review under section "B." Section "C" in contrast begins on page 2 and ends on page 14. Areas of concern for the CERD included, among others, that the definition of racial discrimination used in federal and state legislation should conform more closely with the UN definition, which requires state parties to prohibit and eliminate racial discrimination in all its forms; strengthen and preserve affirmative action to eliminate disparities in employment; intensify efforts to combat racial profiling and illegal surveillance; enforce federal voting rights and reinstate voting rights to persons convicted of a felony; intensify efforts to eliminate housing segregation, and ensure equal access to education and health care. The fourth periodic report demonstrating how the previously identified concerns were addressed by the US was due November 20, 2017.

More recently, a Universal Periodic Review (UPR) took place in the US. A UPR is a process which involves a periodic review of the human rights records of all 193 UN member states. It provides an opportunity for all states to declare what actions they have taken to improve the human rights situations in their countries. The UPR was established when the Human Rights Council was created on March 15, 2006 by the UN General Assembly (UN, 2006). The most recent US government UPR took place on May 11, 2015, and resulted in 348 recommendations to the US which included: 6 recommendations on creating a National Action Plan for racial justice; 47 recommendations on racial and religious discrimination; 44 recommendations on racial profiling and the use of excessive force; 13 recommendations on gender equality and women's rights; 10 recommendations on the rights of Indigenous Peoples; and 29 recommendations on torture, prison conditions, and detention, just to name a few (UN, 2015).

Finally, between the dates of January 19 and 29, 2016, the Working Group of Experts on People of African Descent (WGEPAD) visited the US as a follow-up to a 2010 visit to assess the situation of African Americans and people of African descent. The WGEPAD was established in 2002 by the Commission on Human Rights Resolution 2002/68 (UN, 2002). The WGEPAD was created by the World Conference against Racism, Racial Discrimination, Xenophobia and Related Intolerance held in Durban, South Africa 2001. This conference adopted the Durban Declaration and Program of Action which specifically "requests the Human Rights Council to consider establishing a working group of the UN to study the problems of racial discrimination faced by people of African Descent living in the African Diaspora and make proposals for the elimination of racial discrimination against people of African descent" (UN, 2019, n.p.). The group released a balanced statement to the media applauding improvements in many areas and highlighting concerns (UN, 2016). Among the concerns were: (1) no real commitment to reparations and to truth and reconciliation for people of African descent and the continuous negative impact of white supremacy; (2) contemporary police killings; (3) racial bias and disparities in the criminal justice system, mass incarceration, and tough on crime policies; (4) eroding constitutional rights as a result of the Patriot Act with a disproportionate impact on Blacks; (5) stand your ground laws; and (6) the low number of cases where police officers have been held accountable in the killings of Blacks just to name a few. These efforts at presenting the plight of PAD in the US indicate that the US, as a permanent and influential member of the UN and world community, has a lot of work to do in addressing human right violations among members of her own population.

## IMPLICATIONS FOR BECOMING MORE TRAUMA-INFORMED

One aspect of being trauma informed for mental health workers and social service providers alike is recognizing the impact of violence and victimization on clients' development and coping strategies (Butler, Critelli, & Rinfrette, 2011). One theoretical framework that can be used to explain the impact of 399 years of differential treatment on Blacks in the US is the historical trauma framework (Brave Heart, 2003). In much the same manner, it has been employed to explain the outcomes of the children of the survivors of the Jewish Holocaust and the descendants of the Native American Holocaust, PTSS (DeGruy, 2005) can be used to understand the long-term impact of historical, state-sanctioned, oppressive treatment among PAD. Additionally, knowledge of previous efforts by PAD to address their concerns on the human rights level unsuccessfully also shed light on how some Blacks may continue to feel social injustice, social inconsistency, and impotence now in the present. This knowledge is beneficial to mental health practitioners and social service providers in a number of ways.

First, this knowledge offers mental health practitioners not familiar with the historical treatment of US policies toward Blacks an alternative explanation to draw from in attempting to understand responses to trauma as well as the world view of clients of African descent. This education alone may change the perspective that some practitioners hold of Blacks as a group. It's one thing to argue "get over it" when you think oppression ended with slavery 150 years ago, but it's another when you understand that Blacks have been symbolically free of legal social restraints for only 48 years. Many older Blacks who have experienced negative interactions with the government, agents of the state, and Whites pass those stories and the negative and pessimistic attitudes associated with them onto their children and grandchildren who then inherit this cynical perception of US society.

Second, given the history of the US government's role in advocating and supporting racist and discriminatory practices, practitioners should be receptive to and validate feelings of injustice shared by clients on a micro level, and advocate for greater transparency and adherence to human rights principles by their local and governmental institutions on a macro-level on behalf of those clients. Not all Black clients seeking services will present with the symptoms of historical trauma. Not all Black clients presenting with the symptoms of historical trauma will present with the same symptoms or the same exact antecedents and triggers. The healing process and approach will differ based in part on the background (family and community factors) and the type of trauma or traumas experienced on an individual or group basis. Also, a paradigm shift is underway for demands of accountability from nations who have engaged in or turned a blind eye toward state-sanctioned atrocities against their own citizens (Kritz, 1997). Advocating for federal accountability on the issues of the prison industrial complex as well as justice toward the unconstitutional housing policies, described by Rothstein (2017), on behalf of Black clients are actions that can be taken to heal racial wounds of the past and to chip away at institutions that have implemented racial policies that have inflicted such grave damage on our society. Emphasis should not be placed on the resiliency of individuals within a hostile environment solely. An overemphasis on resiliency has done a disservice to Blacks by diverting the focus to their ability to survive within a racist structure, instead of focusing on the racist structure itself. Emphasis should shed light on why hostile social structures and institutions are able to continue their oppressive practices in a democratic society for so long and why so many individuals freely go along with policies that marginalize and oppress other groups.

Third, the manner in which we portrayed the Black experience in the US is indicative of structural causes responsible for constrained agency. From this view, one can make the leap of characterizing US policies disproportionately impacting Blacks (and Native Americans) as forms of structural violence that can be perceived as the structural violation of human rights (Ho, 2007). This framework is useful to mental health practitioners who appreciate the expansion of the term *violence* to include indirect acts of policy making as forms of violence that impact individual lives and families.

## Conclusion

The purpose of this chapter was to integrate a perspective on trauma with an emphasis on human rights for PAD in the US. We launched from a trauma-informed standpoint, describing the experience of PAD in the US. The forms of terrorism that Germany and the US inflicted on European Jews and Native Americans, respectively, share similarities with the terrorism inflicted on PAD. All of the terrorism among all three groups was state-sponsored and undergirded by currents of racism, prejudice, and bigotry. All three groups experienced unimaginable assaults on their human rights and collective conscious that impact how their group copes with the facts and memories of state-sponsored violence. There are also differences between the European Jewish Holocaust and the US-based holocausts as well, specifically in the response to their suffering (Kirmayer, Gone, & Moses, 2014).

First, because of the vastness of the Jewish diaspora, many survivors of the Jewish Holocaust were able to move away from Germany and start new lives with the help of diasporic communities already thriving, thus leaving behind the source of their trauma. Survivors of the Native American and African American Holocaust in contrast were unable to leave the land that served as the source of their trauma, thereby, experiencing re-traumatization and compounded levels of fear. The Native Americans were unable to leave because they were colonized and had their lands taken from them and the PAD were kidnapped from the continent of Africa. In effect, Native Americans and PAD could not flee to areas they felt were safe unlike the European Jews who survived the Holocaust.

Second, survivors of the Jewish Holocaust had a culture to return to grounded in the Torah and the Talmud and the communal life of Jews in the diaspora. Native Americans and PAD, in contrast, were forced to give up their culture and practices and assimilate US culture through residential boarding schools and cultural suppression. Their ways of life and cultures were frowned upon and viewed as primitive. Consequently, the customs and rituals of many of the PAD and Native American cultures have been lost and discontinued as a result of the long tenure of oppression. There are now Native Americans who never experienced traditional tribal rituals and practices and PAD in the US have shed their African-based rituals, religions, identity, and practices due to their separation from the African continent and becoming African American. Although the Nazi regime sought the destruction of European Jewish culture through the burning of historical artifacts and books, it did not succeed. Given the size of the Jewish Diaspora and the rich history preserved through the diaspora, such a task would have been monumental.

Third, the Jewish Holocaust, although it took place in Germany, has enjoyed widespread recognition in the US and the world through the media, general discourse, and educational materials. The US government and education system go to great lengths to make Americans aware of an atrocity that took place in another country, whereas the stories of the atrocities and holocausts that took place on US soil are just being recognized following centuries of purposeful omission and inaccuracies from educational curricula and texts and challenged in some instances by those who claim that some of the atrocities never happened. These differences are highlighted not to strike comparisons between events of suffering, but rather, to emphasize the point that the experience of Native Americans and PAD in the US reflects a continued oppression through their inability to relocate outside of the US, the deliberate suppression of their cultural practices, and through the deliberate omission and re-framing of their story from US general discourse. The occupation of Native American lands and the disregard for their autonomy continue as evidenced by the recent court ruling of the Dakota Access Pipeline, and the oppression of PAD, largely focused on the poor and marginalized, continue through the prison industrial complex, concentrated poverty, unequal school resources, and police shootings of unarmed PAD.

Lastly, the international response to the three holocausts differed. International human rights law was made necessary in large part because of the atrocities committed by the Nazis against the Jews during World War II. The reference to "barbarous acts" in the preamble of the UDHR (UN, 1948) was motivated by the actions of the Nazis against the Jews (Karpf, Klug, Rose, & Rosenbaum, 2008), and to this day, the Jews continue to receive reparations for the Holocaust. A New York Times article revealed that the Conference on Jewish Material Claims against Germany has collected over $89 billion in compensation to mostly Jewish victims of Nazi crimes over six decades and continue to meet regularly to expand and revise the plan with the support of the international community (Eddy, 2012).

In contrast, the first United Nations Conference on Indians in the Americas wasn't held until 1977. Thirty years later, in 2007, after continuous and relentless advocacy on the part of Native Americans, the UN General Assembly overwhelmingly adopted the *UN Declaration on the Rights of Indigenous Peoples* with tallies of 143 in favor of the Declaration, four opposed, and eleven abstaining. The US was one of the opposed (Gottschalk & Runs Him, n.d.). In 2012, a UN investigator exploring acts of discrimination against Native Americans called on the US government to return some of the land stolen from Indian tribes (McGreal, 2012). As recently as 2016, the UN has moved forward on establishing a body to monitor the implementation of the Declaration. That body is called the Expert Mechanism on the Rights of Indigenous People (EMRIP) (Gottschalk & Runs Him, n.d.). In many respects, the movement for human rights among Indigenous Peoples, including Native Americans from the US, is just beginning.

The first time the phrase "the Negro Question" appeared was in the *New York Times* in 1862 (Escott, 2009). Since then, the question has appeared again as the title of a book by James S. Allen, *The Negro Question in the United States*, in 1936. After the establishment of the UN, Albert Einstein used it for the title of a speech, "The Negro Question," in 1946 (Gillis, 2016). Paul D. Escott most recently used for the title of his book, *What Shall We Do with the Negro* in 2009. That question is still being posed in 2018, and hopefully, the international order can help answer it this time around.

## REFERENCES

Allen, J. S. (1936). *The Negro question in the United States.* New York, NY: International Publishers.

Benz, W. (2001). Death toll. In W. Lacqueur (Ed.), *The holocaust encyclopedia* (pp. 137–145). New Haven, CT: Yale University Press.

Black, D. P. (1997). *Dismantling black manhood: A historical and literary analysis of the legacy of slavery.* New York, NY: Routledge.

Blackmon, D. A. (2008). *Slavery by another name: The re-enslavement of Black Americans from the Civil War to World War II.* New York, NY: Anchor Books.

Brave Heart, M. Y. H. (2003). The historical trauma response among natives and its relationship with substance abuse: A Lakota illustration. *Journal of Psychoactive Drugs, 35*(1), 7–13.

Brave Heart, M. Y. H., & DeBruyn, L. M. (1998). The American Indian Holocaust: Healing historical unresolved grief. *American Indian and Alaska Native Mental Health Research, 8*(2), 60–82.

Burrell, T. (2010). *Brainwashed: Challenging the myth of black male inferiority.* New York, NY: SmileyBooks.

Butler, L. D., Critelli, F. M., & Rinfrette, E. S. (2011). Trauma-informed care and mental health. *Directions in Psychiatry, 31*(3), 197–212.

Carson, E. A. (2014). *Prisoners in 2013: Bureau of Justice Statistics* (NCJ 247282). Washington, DC: US Department of Justice, Office of Justice Programs. Retrieved from http://www.bjs.gov/content/pub/pdf/p13.pdf.

Chestang, L. W. (1972). *Character development in a hostile environment* (Occasional Paper No. 3, Series, pp. 1–12). Chicago, IL: University of Chicago Press.

Daniel, P. (1990). *The shadow of slavery: Peonage in the south, 1901–1969.* Urbana, IL: University of Illinois Press.

Danieli, Y. (1982). Families of survivors and the Nazi holocaust: Some short- and long-term effects. In C. D. Spielberger, G. Sarason, & N. Milgram (Eds.), *Stress and anxiety* (Vol. 8, pp. 405–423). Washington, DC: Hemisphere.

Danieli, Y. (1998). *International handbook of multigenerational legacies of trauma.* New York, NY: Plenum.

Dawidowicz, L. S. (1975). *The war against the Jews: 1933–1945.* New York, NY: CBS Educational & Professional Publishing.

Degler, C. N. (1959). Slavery and the genesis of American race prejudice. *Comparative Studies in Society and History, 2*(1), 49–66.

DeGruy, J. (2005). *Post Traumatic Slave Syndrome: America's legacy of enduring injury and healing.* Portland, OR: Joy DeGruy Publications.

Denny, C. H., Holtzman, D., Goins, T., & Croft, J. B. (2005). Disparities in chronic disease risk factors and health status between American Indian/Alaska Native and White elders: Findings from a telephone survey, 2001 and 2002. *American Journal of Public Health, 95*(5), 825–827. https://doi.org/10.2105/AJPH.2004.043489.

Douglas, M. (2008, May 6). Mildred Loving, who battled ban on mixed-race marriage, dies at 68. *The New York Times*. Retrieved from https://www.nytimes.com/2008/05/06/us/06loving.html?searchResultPosition=1.

Douglass, F. (1845). *Narrative of the life of Frederick Douglass, an American slave*. Boston, MA: Simon & Brown.

Dunaway, W. A. (2003). *The African-American family in slavery and emancipation*. Cambridge, UK: Cambridge University Press.

Eddy, M. (2012, November 17). For 60th year, Germany honors duty to pay holocaust victims. *The New York Times*. Retrieved from https://www.nytimes.com/2012/11/18/world/europe/for-60th-year-germany-honors-duty-to-pay-holocaust-victims.html.

Equal Justice Initiative. (2017). *Lynching in America: Confronting the legacy of racial terror* (3rd ed.). Retrieved from https://lynchinginamerica.eji.org/report/.

Equiano, O. (1789). *The interesting narrative and the life of "Olaudah Equiano" or Gustavus Vassa, the African*. Retrieved from https://www.gutenberg.org/files/15399/15399-h/15399-h.htm.

Escott, P. D. (2009). *"What shall we do with the Negro"? Lincoln, white racism and civil war America*. Charlottesville, VA: University of Virginia Press.

Estrada, A. L. (2009). Mexican Americans and historical trauma theory: A theoretical perspective. *Journal of Ethnicity in Substance Abuse, 8*(3), 330–340.

Fierce, M. (1994). *Slavery revisited: Blacks and the southern convict lease system, 1865–1933*. New York, NY: Africana Studies Research Center, Brooklyn College, City University of New York.

Foster, T. A. (2011). The sexual abuse of black men under American slavery. *Journal of the History of Sexuality, 20*(3), 445–464.

Franklin, J. H., & Moss, A. A. (1994). *From slavery to freedom: A history of African Americans* (7th ed.). New York, NY: McGraw-Hill.

Freeman, G. A. (1999). *Lay this body down: The 1921 murders of eleven plantation slaves*. Chicago, IL: Chicago Review Press.

Galtung, J. (1969). Violence, peace, and peace research. *Journal of Peace Research, 6*(3), 167–191.

Gaskin, D. J., Headen, A. E., & White-Means, S. I. (2005). Racial disparities in health and wealth: The effects of slavery and past discrimination. *Review of Black Political Economy, 32*(3–4), 95–110.

Gillis, T. T. (2016). *Albert Einstein's essay on racial bias in 1946*. Retrieved from https://onbeing.org/blog/albert-einsteins-essay-on-racial-bias-in-1946/.

Goldberg, D. J. (1996). Unmasking the Ku Klux Klan: The northern movement against the KKK, 1920–1925. *Journal of American Ethnic History, 15*(4), 32–48.

Gottschalk, K. J., & Runs Him, H. W. (n.d.). *United Nations and indigenous peoples*. Retrieved from https://www.narf.org/cases/declaration-indigenous-rights-un/.

Hafner-Burton, E. M., & Tsutsui, K. (2005). Human rights in a globalizing world: The paradox of empty promises. *American Journal of Sociology, 110*(5), 1373–1411.

Handler, M. S. (1964, August 13). *Malcolm X seeks U.N. Negro debate; He asks African states to cite US over rights*. NYTimes.com. Retrieved from http://query.nytimes.com/gst/abstract.html?res=9C01E4DC113FEE32A-25750C1A96E9C946591D6CF&src=DigitizedArticle&legacy=true.

Ho, K. (2007). Structural violence as a human rights violation. *Essex Human Rights Review, 4*(2), 1–17.

Horne, G. (2009). *W.E.B. DuBois: A biography*. Denver, CO: Greenwood Press.

Karpf, A., Klug, B., Rose, J., & Rosenbaum, B. (Eds.). (2008). *A time to speak out: Independent Jewish voices on Israel, Zionism, and Jewish identity*. London, UK: Verso.

Kellerman, N. P. F. (2001). Transmission of holocaust trauma—An integrative view. *Psychiatry: Interpersonal and Biological Processes, 64*, 256–267.

Kirmayer, L. J., Gone, J. P., & Moses, J. (2014). Rethinking historical trauma. *Transcultural Psychiatry, 51*(3), 299–319.

Kritz, N. J. (1997). Coming to terms with atrocities: A review of accountability mechanisms for mass violations of human rights. *Law and Contemporary Problems, 59*(4), 127–152.

Legters, L. H. (1988). The American genocide. *Policy Studies Journal, 16*(4), 768–777.

Lewis, D. L. (2009). *W.E.B. DuBois: A biography 1868–1963*. New York, NY: Holt.

Mancini, M. J. (1996). *One dies, get another: Convict leasing in the American South, 1866–1928*. Columbia, SC: University of South Carolina Press.

Mazower, M. (2004). The strange triumph of human rights, 1933–1950. *The Historical Journal, 47*(2), 379–398.

McFadden, R. D. (1971, December 10). Dr. Bunche of U.N., Nobel winner, dies. *The New York Times*. Retrieved from http://www.nytimes.com/learning/general/onthisday/bday/0807.html.

McGreal, C. (2012, May 4). US should return stolen land to Indian tribes, says United Nations: UN correspondent on Indigenous Peoples urges government to act to combat 'racial discrimination' felt by Native Americans. *The Guardian*. Retrieved from https://www.theguardian.com/world/2012/may/04/us-stolen-land-indian-tribes-un.

Merton, R. K. (1938). Social structure and anomie. *American Sociological Review, 3*, 672–682. https://doi.org/10.2307/2084686.

Muhammad, K. G. (2010). *The condemnation of Blackness: Race, crime, and the making of modern urban America*. Cambridge, MA: Harvard University Press.

NAACP. (2017, October 23). *An appeal to the world*. Retrieved from https://www.naacp.org/latest/an-appeal-to-the-world/.

Nier, C. L. (1997). Guilty as charged: Malcolm X and his vision of racial justice for African Americans through utilization of the United Nations international human rights provisions and institutions. *Penn State International Law Review, 16*(1), 149–189.

Noonan, A. S., Velasco-Mondragon, H. E., & Wagner, F. A. (2016). Improving the health of African Americans in the USA: An overdue opportunity for social justice. *Public Health Reviews, 37*(12). Retrieved from https://publichealthreviews.biomedcentral.com/articles/10.1186/s40985-016-0025-4.

Perry, B. (1991). *Malcolm: The life of a man who changed Black America.* Barrytown, NY: Station Hill Press.

Plous, S., & Williams, T. (1995). Racial stereotypes from the days of American slavery: A continuing legacy. *Journal of Applied Social Psychology, 25*(9), 795–817.

Rothstein, R. (2017). *The color of law: A forgotten history of how our government segregated America.* New York, NY: Norton.

Smith, V. (1798). *A narrative of the life and adventures of venture, a native of Africa: But resident above sixty years in the United State of America.* New London, CT: Aeterna.

Stannard, D. E. (1993). *American holocaust: The conquest of the new world.* New York, NY: Oxford University Press.

Twiss, S. B. (2004). History, human rights and globalization. *Journal of Religious Ethics, 32*, 39–70.

United Nations. (1948). Universal declaration of human rights. Retrieved from http://www.un.org/en/universal-declaration-human-rights/.

United Nations. (1965). *International convention on the elimination of all forms of racial discrimination.* Retrieved from http://www.refworld.org/docid/3ae6b3940.html.

United Nations. (2002). *Racism, racial discrimination, xenophobia and related intolerance.* Commission on Human Rights resolution 2002/68. Retrieved from http://ap.ohchr.org/documents/e/CHR/resolutions/E-CN_4-RES-2002-68.doc.

United Nations. (2006). *Resolution adopted by the general assembly* (A/RES/60/251). Retrieved from https://www.ohchr.org/en/hrbodies/hrc/pages/aboutcouncil.aspx.

United Nations. (2015). *Draft report of the working group on the Universal Periodic Review: United States* (A/HRC/WG.6/22/L.10). Retrieved from https://www.upr-info.org/sites/default/files/document/united_states/session_22_-_may_2015/a_hrc_wg.6_22_l.10.pdf.

United Nations. (2016, January 29). *Statement to the media by the United Nations' working group of experts on people of African descent, on the conclusion of its official visit to USA, 19–29 January 2016.* Retrieved from http://www.ohchr.org/EN/NewsEvents/Pages/DisplayNews.aspx?NewsID=17000.

United Nations. (2019). *Working group of experts on people of African descent.* Retrieved from https://www.ohchr.org/en/issues/racism/wgafricandescent/pages/wgepadindex.aspx.

Weinstein, R. S., Gregory, A., & Strambler, M. J. (2004). Intractable self-fulfilling prophecies fifty years after Brown v. Board of Education. *American Psychologist, 59*(6), 511–520.

Western, B. (2006). *Punishment and inequality in America.* New York, NY: Russell Sage.

Willhelm, S. M. (1973). Equality: America's racist ideology. In J. A. Ladner (Ed.), *The death of white sociology* (pp. 136–157). New York, NY: Random House.

Woodward, C. V. (1955). *The strange career of Jim Crow.* New York, NY: Oxford University Press.

# CHAPTER 6

# Children's Experiences of Trauma and Human Rights Violations Around the World

*Molly R. Wolf, Shraddha Prabhu, and Janice Carello*

The Convention on the Rights of the Child (CRC; United Nations [UN], 1989) affirms and comprehensively delineates the fundamental civil, political, economic, social, and cultural human rights of all children below the age of 18. By defining and recognizing every child's right to survival, development, and protection from all forms of violence, the CRC establishes the global standard for child protection and promotion of child well-being. Further, it delineates children's right to participation and representation in all areas of social, political, economic, and cultural life that impacts them. As of November 2017, 196 countries have ratified the CRC; the United States remains the only member of the UN that

M. R. Wolf (✉) · S. Prabhu
Department of Social Work, Edinboro University of Pennsylvania, Edinboro, PA, USA
e-mail: mrwolf@edinboro.edu

S. Prabhu
e-mail: sprabhu@edinboro.edu

J. Carello
Department of Social Work, Edinboro University, Edinboro, PA, USA
e-mail: jcarello@edinboro.edu

© The Author(s) 2019
L. D. Butler et al. (eds.), *Trauma and Human Rights*,
https://doi.org/10.1007/978-3-030-16395-2_6

has signed but not ratified the CRC (Office of the High Commissioner for Human Rights [OHCHR], 2017). Additionally, three optional protocols to the CRC have been approved. The Optional Protocol to the CRC on the sale of children, child prostitution, and child pornography has been ratified by 174 state parties; the Optional Protocol to the CRC on the involvement of children in armed conflict has been ratified by 167 state parties; and the Optional Protocol to the CRC on a communications procedure has been signed by 39 state parties (OHCHR, 2017).

This univocal commitment to the recognition of children as individuals with specific human rights has not translated into expeditious actualization of these rights, particularly as they relate to child protection. There has been considerable progress in some respects to meeting the obligations related to children's rights to survival and development. For example, according to a report from the Bill and Melinda Gates Foundation (2017), targeted efforts for preventing and redressing child malnutrition have resulted in a notable reduction in the prevalence of stunting among children under the age of five globally, from a prevalence rate of 36% in 1990 to 26% in 2016. Similar gains have been noted on child survival and development indicators such as child mortality rates for children under the age of 5 years, neonatal mortality, access to immunizations and vaccines, and access to education (Bill and Melinda Gates Foundation, 2017). However, as discussed in this chapter, child protection remains a formidable challenge around the world.

There is a growing body of interdisciplinary research documenting the profound impact of traumatic exposure on the brains, minds, and bodies of children, youth, and adults (e.g., Brown, Thacker, & Cohen, 2013; Dvir, Ford, Hill, & Frazier, 2014; Espelage, Hong, & Mebane, 2016; Finkelhor, Turner, Hamby, & Ormrod, 2011; Ports, Ford, & Merrick, 2016; Turner, Finkelhor, & Ormrod, 2006; van der Kolk, 2005, 2015). An understanding of the developmental, immediate, and long-term impact of potentially traumatic experiences and incorporation of this understanding at the micro-, mezzo-, and macro-levels of child protection initiatives is integral to meeting our commitments to child protection.

In this chapter, we examine the intersections of class, gender identity, race, caste, disability, sexuality, and sociocultural practices for their impact on the extent and nature of vulnerability experienced by children. Further, we discuss how trauma-informed approaches organically uphold the core principles of children's rights. Central also to integrating a trauma-informed, human rights approach to intervention is the recognition that individuals and communities can be supported to realize and build their resilience.

## TRAUMA EXPOSURE AMONG CHILDREN: PREVALENCE, NATURE, AND CONTEXT

Violence against children is endemic in human societies. Forms of violence faced by children include physical, verbal, and emotional abuse, homicide, sexual abuse, and sexual and economic exploitation. These violations of children's rights continue to occur within homes, at school, at work, in communal spaces, and over the Internet. Societal crises such as armed conflicts or natural disasters and their aftermath can further precipitate direct and vicarious exposure to violence (United Nations Children's Fund [UNICEF], 2017). Intersections of sociocultural identities related to sexual orientation, gender identity, caste, class, race/ethnicity, citizenship status, age, and disability often compound vulnerability and experienced exposure to potentially traumatic experiences.

It is important to note that reported numbers of childhood traumatic experiences outlined below are likely underestimates for several reasons. Interpersonal and betrayal traumas tend to happen in private (in the child's own home, for instance) and are rarely observed by others. Compounding this issue is the fact that when children experience physical violence, it is legal in most countries (i.e., disciplinary violence), and when that type of violence crosses the line into abuse, the child often thinks this is appropriate and normal, particularly in regions where physical punishment is considered customary (Rebellon & Strauss, 2017; Ridgely, 2016). Also, the stigmatizing nature of emotional, physical, or sexual victimization induces shame in children, which greatly inhibits disclosure (Saunders & Adams, 2014). Finally, a subset of traumatized individuals may experience dissociative amnesia from their traumatic experience and may not remember it well into adulthood, if at all (Williams, 1994; Wolf & Nochajski, 2013).

### *Physical, Verbal, and Emotional Abuse*

Corporal punishment within the home, at school, at places of employment, and in long and short-term residential care facilities has been found to be widespread and often accompanied by verbal and emotional abuse (UNICEF, 2014). Violent discipline as a part of child rearing still remains very common across the world, with younger children experiencing the highest risk for exposure (Global Initiative to End All Corporal Punishment of Children [Global Initiative], 2015;

UNICEF, 2017). Between 2005 and 2016, an estimated 300 million children ages 2–4 years experienced violent discipline regularly. Further, data from 30 countries suggest that, during this time period, 250 million children aged 12–23 months were subjected to violent disciplinary methods (such as hitting or slapping child on the face, head, or ears repeatedly), and for half of the children in this age group, physical violence was accompanied by verbal abuse.

In most countries where data were available, children in the poorest and richest households were equally likely to experience violent discipline, which implicates larger cultural and social norms in the prevalence of this form of violence against children. Globally, an estimated 1.1 billion parents/caregivers viewed physical punishment as necessary for raising and educating children (UNICEF, 2017). Only 9% of children globally live in countries that provide full legal protection from corporal punishment within the home (UNICEF, 2017).

Children also continue to experience corporal punishment outside the home. Despite specific mandates in the CRC that require state parties to protect children from physical discipline in schools, children living in 73 countries do not have full legal protection against corporal punishment at school (Global Initiative, 2015; UNICEF, 2017). Data from 63 countries suggest varying rates of prevalence for the use of corporal punishment in school, ranging from 13% of students in Kazakhstan to 97% in Cameroon. In at least 20 of those countries, corporal punishment at school was perpetrated against 70–90% of the students (Gershoff, 2017).

Corporal punishment at school has several tangible impacts, including interference with learning, risk for physical injury, and increased risk for emotional and behavioral problems (Gershoff, 2017). Additionally, preliminary research suggests that gender (Makwanya, Moyo, & Nyenya, 2012; Ogando, Portela, & Pell, 2015), race or ethnicity (Gershoff & Font, 2016), and disability (Alyahri & Goodman, 2008; Covell & Becker, 2011; Dunne, Humphreys, & Leach, 2006; Lee, 2015) increased the vulnerability to violent discipline faced by children in school.

Children and adolescents who report exposure to physical abuse are often also exposed to verbal, emotional, and psychological abuse within and outside the home (UNICEF, 2014). In addition to corporal punishment, other forms of violence experienced by children in schools include bullying, sexual harassment and/or abuse, school shootings, and vulnerability to attack during conflicts, especially in the aftermath of natural and manmade disasters (International Labour Organization [ILO], 2017a; Office of the Special Representative of Secretary General for Child and Armed Conflict, 2013; UNICEF, 2014, 2017). Many children are also exposed to intimate partner violence within their homes. Worldwide, 1 in 4 children under the age of 5 lives with a mother who is experiencing intimate partner violence (UNICEF, 2017). Each of these experiences of violence individually and cumulatively makes schools emotionally and psychologically unsafe for children and increases the risks of truancy and of dropping out (UNICEF, 2017).

Intersections of gender and sexuality can increase vulnerability to violence and its impact. Discrimination and violence against gay, lesbian, bisexual, transgender, and gender-variant children and youth remain understudied and under-documented globally. In countries where the experiences of these children and youth have been documented, the risk factors and resultant outcomes for survival, well-being, and development are alarming. In the United States, rejection by family members and verbal and physical violence within the home, at school, and in the community have found to be widespread and significant risk factors for exponential increase in suicidality and suicide attempts among LGBT youth (Centers for Disease Control and Prevention, 2017; Mustanski, Garofalo, & Emerson, 2010; Ryan, Huebner, Diaz, & Sanchez, 2009). Homophobia, bi-phobia, and transphobia are still a norm in most societies around the world and codified through legislation that severely undermines the human rights of LGBTQ children (Equaldex, 2018).

Systems charged with the care of children can also perpetuate a cycle of victimization. Children and adolescents find themselves interfacing with the justice systems for a variety of reasons, including victimization, perpetration, witnessing violence, asylum seeking, being detained with caregivers, or being targeted due to aspects of identity such as race, gender, sexual orientation, or religion (UNICEF, 2009, 2011). Corporal punishment as a legalized form of punishment, within juvenile penal and out of home placement institutions, is also not uncommon with children being subjected to whipping, flogging, caning, and amputation (Child Rights International Network [CRIN], n.d.). Additionally, while in detention, children and adolescents are often exposed to various forms of violence, including torture, physical, sexual, and emotional abuse, and solitary confinement (Chynoweth, 2017; UNICEF, 2011).

## Homicide

Approximately 90% of all homicides of children and adolescents occur in middle- and low-income countries. Although only 1 in 20 of the world's children and adolescents resides in Latin America and the Caribbean, some countries in these regions account for a quarter of all homicide-related deaths among children and adolescents, outside of regions experiencing collective/mass conflict (UNICEF, 2014). In 2015, in some Latin American and Caribbean countries, adolescents were found to be at equal or higher risk for homicide than adolescents in certain conflict-affected regions in the world (UNICEF, 2017).

Ethnicity has also been found to increase vulnerability to homicide among children and adolescents in non-conflict areas. In the United States, black adolescent boys are 19 times more likely to die from homicide than white adolescent boys. Although African-American boys aged 10–19 years make up 16% of the male adolescent population in the United States, they account for 66% of adolescent homicide victims. Homicide is also the leading cause of death among black adolescent girls in the United States (UNICEF, 2017). Likewise, in Brazil, in 2015, boys of African or multi-racial descent aged 10–19 were at highest risk for homicide, with 3 out of 4 child and adolescent victims of homicide belonging to these ethnicities.

Gender differences have also been noted in the context in which children and adolescents are killed. Globally, while females are more likely to be killed by family members or intimate partners, males are more likely to be killed by strangers or due to their involvement in crime- or gang-related activity or a high prevalence of community violence (UNICEF, 2014). Child marriage, honor killings, and female feticide (sex-selective abortion of female fetus), and infanticide are significant gender-specific risks for homicide experienced by child and adolescent girls in South Asia (UNICEF, 2017).

State-sanctioned violence against children also remains a significant risk to survival for children in some parts of the world. In 15 countries around the world, children can be sentenced to death by lethal injection, hanging, shooting, or stoning (CRIN, 2017). Unfortunately, schools within certain sociopolitical contexts can increase children's vulnerability to homicide. An estimated 158 million school-age children and adolescents live in 24 countries and regions affected by armed conflict. In 2016 alone, there were 400 verified attacks or threat of attacks on schools (UNICEF, 2017). School shootings are another sociocultural phenomenon that creates significant risks for homicide among children and adolescents. The largest number of school shootings, a total of 288 since 2009, have occurred in the United States (Grabow & Rose, 2018, May 21).

### Sexual Abuse and Exploitation

Sexual abuse and exploitation remains one of the most insidious forms of violence against children. In 2014, UNICEF estimated that globally, 120 million girls (i.e., 1 in 10 girls) under the age of 20 were forced to have sexual intercourse or engage in other forced sexual acts at some point during their life (UNICEF, 2014). While children of all ages are vulnerable to various forms of sexual abuse and exploitation, analysis of data collected in 28 countries between 2005 and 2016 indicates that 9 out of 10 adolescent girls who reported forced sex also reported that their first assault occurred between the ages of 10 and 19 years (UNICEF, 2017). In most countries that have studied child sexual abuse and exploitation (including the United States, Tanzania, Zimbabwe, Malawi, Kenya, Cambodia, and Haiti), about one-third to one-fourth of girls reported sexual violence, whereas one-sixth to one-tenth of boys reported it (Chiang et al., 2016; Saunders & Adams, 2014), and the numbers were doubled for physical violence. Additionally, children with disabilities were 75% more likely to experience victimization (Berg, Shiu, Msall, & Acharya, 2015).

The increase in travel, the growth of tourism, and the ubiquity of the Internet have also created new avenues for sexual exploitation of children and adolescents (End Child Prostitution, Child Pornography and Trafficking of Children for Sexual Purposes [ECPAT] International, 2016). Children living in poverty and/or in marginalized communities, such as indigenous, homosexual, and transgender children, have been found to be particularly vulnerable to sex trafficking and sexual exploitation (EPACT International, 2016).

Children and adolescents make up the majority of the victims of sexual violence during conflicts and in the aftermath of conflicts (Save the Children, 2013). During armed conflict, the recruitment and/or displacement of children increases their vulnerability to sexual abuse and exploitation by family members, community members, traffickers, armed forces, peacekeeping troops, and camp/detention personnel (Inspector

General U.S. Department of Defense, 2017; Save the Children, 2013). The prevalence of sexual abuse and exploitation of children below the age of 18 in conflict-affected regions ranges from 50% to over 80% (Chynoweth, 2017; Inspector General U.S. Department of Defense, 2017; Save the Children, 2013). In non-conflict contexts, the prevalence of sexual abuse is reported at lower rates by boys than girls; however, during conflicts, sexual abuse, sexual exploitation, and sexual slavery as tools of control, exploitation, and humiliation are frequently used against boys, as has been documented in Afghanistan and Syria (Chynoweth, 2017; Inspector General U.S. Department of Defense, 2017).

*Child Labor*

According to the ILO, between 2012 and 2016, one-tenth of the world's children, an estimated 152 million children ages 5–17, were engaged in labor. Of these, 73 million children were engaged in hazardous work, including as slaves and/or bonded laborers (ILO, 2017a, b). The highest rate of child labor and the greatest number of working children in absolute numbers live and work in Africa. Together, Africa and Asia-Pacific regions are home to 9 out of 10 children working as laborers (ILO, 2017a). Armed conflicts and humanitarian emergencies such as disasters significantly increase the risk of child labor; the incidences of child labor and children involved in hazardous work in regions affected by conflict were 77% and 50% higher, respectively, than global averages (ILO, 2017a). Working children, particularly children involved in hazardous work, are often denied adequate nutrition, required to work long hours, and denied adequate access to health care and schooling. Further, these children often do not receive fair wages, are not provided adequate space and opportunities for recreation, and are required to perform labor that negatively impacts their physical and emotional health and exposes them to hazardous substances. Further, child laborers also often experience physical, verbal, and sexual abuse (ILO, 2017a).

## IMPACTS OF CHILDHOOD TRAUMA

As the previous section of this chapter attests, human rights violations are often experienced as traumatic events. In this section, we will address some of the most common impacts of childhood trauma events on individuals.

## Posttraumatic Stress Disorder

The rates of *posttraumatic stress disorder* (PTSD) in children vary by type of trauma experienced, as well as geographical region of the world (Feldman, Vengrober, Eidelman-Rothman, & Zagoory-Sharon, 2013; Gabbay, Oatis, Silva, & Hirsch, 2004; Heiervang et al., 2007). However, it is safe to say that a subset of children who experience trauma in every studied geographic region of the world will meet criteria a lifetime diagnosis of PTSD (Breslau, Wilcox, Storr, Lucia, & Anthony, 2004; Giaconia, et al., 1995; Perkonigg, Kessler, Storz, & Wittchen, 2000). In addition to PTSD, some of the more common symptoms of childhood trauma include psychiatric disorders such as anxiety and depression (Copeland et al., 2007), suicidal ideation, (Paolucci, Genuis, & Violato, 2001), comorbidity (Widom, DuMont, & Czaja, 2007), and emotional and behavioral disorders (Heiervang et al., 2007).

## Developmental Trauma

Bessel van der Kolk (2005) advises that the term *PTSD* does not adequately capture the developmental trauma sustained by children who are exposed to chronic trauma. In an attempt to bridge the gap between the term PTSD and the actual experience of developmental trauma, he proposes the use of a different diagnosis: Developmental Trauma Disorder (DTD; see van der Kolk, 2005, for a complete description of this diagnosis). In order to receive a diagnosis of DTD, a child would have to survive chronic exposure to interpersonal trauma, and then have symptoms in three different areas: dysregulation of self (e.g., dissociative amnesia, cutting oneself, etc.), distorted worldview (such as thinking that everyone is a possible assailant), and functional impairment (e.g., an inability to maintain healthy relationships.) Studies suggest that van der Kolk's proposal is both useful and accurate, as cumulative childhood trauma seems to influence the complexity of adult symptomology in a way that traumas survived in adulthood do not (Cloitre et al., 2009). Better diagnosis also means better treatment, which is why it is important for helping professionals to conceptualize children's trauma responses in terms of child development (D'andrea, Ford, Stolbach, Spinazzola, & van der Kolk, 2012).

## *Adverse Childhood Experiences (ACE)*

The Adverse Childhood Experiences (ACE) Study was the first and largest study to date to examine the relationship between traumatic experiences in childhood and negative health effects later in life (Felitti et al., 1998). The ACE Study is also important because it reveals the ripple effect trauma has on the child experiencing it. The original ACE researchers studied ten types of experiences related to household dysfunction: verbal abuse, physical abuse, sexual abuse, emotional abuse, intimate partner violence against mother, substance abuse in household, mental illness in household, separation/divorce of parents, neglect, and incarceration of parents. More recent studies have also included community-level experiences: witnessing violence, feeling discriminated, living in an unsafe neighborhood, experience bullying, and living in foster care (Cronholm et al., 2015). These experiences are highly interrelated; therefore, evidence of one ACE should prompt assessment of the rest (Dong et al., 2004). The original and subsequent ACE studies found that children who experienced four or more ACEs grew up to be adults at exponentially higher risk for engaging in health risk behaviors such as alcoholism/substance abuse (Anda et al., 2002; Dube et al., 2002; Wolf, Nochajski, & Farrell, 2015) and risky sexual behaviors (Hillis, Anda, Felitti, & Marchbanks, 2001) that can lead to disease and early death (Brown et al., 2009; Felitti et al., 1998), as well as major psychological, social, and interpersonal relationship problems (Anda et al., 2007; Chapman et al., 2004).

## *Hidden Wounds*

The effects found in the original ACE study and subsequent studies can also be considered to be 'hidden wounds,' as the effects of childhood trauma are often not realized until later in life. Some of the adolescent and adult physical health effects that can be attributed to child trauma are cardiovascular issues and diabetes (Basu, McLaughlin, Misra, & Koenen, 2017), autoimmune disease (Dube et al., 2009), chronic obstructive pulmonary disease (Anda et al., 2008; Cunningham et al., 2014), headaches (Anda, Tietjen, Schulman, Felitti, & Croft, 2010), inflammation (Danese, Pariante, Caspi, Taylor, & Poulton, 2007), lung cancer (Brown et al., 2010), obesity (Danese & Tan, 2013; Gooding, Milliren, Austin, Sheridan, & McLaughlin, 2015), sexually transmitted diseases (Hillis, Anda, Felitti, Nordenberg, & Marchbanks, 2000), and somatic and neurobiological issues (Anda et al., 2006).

'Hidden wounds' also present as psychological effects, such as PTSD (Kaplow, Saxe, Putnam, Pynoos, & Lieberman, 2006), depression (Anda et al., 2002; Chapman et al., 2004), other mental health issues (such as anxiety and dysthymia) (Greger, Myhre, Lydersen, & Jozefiak, 2015), sleep issues (Chapman et al., 2013), memory disturbance (Brown et al., 2007; Edwards, Fivush, Anda, Felitti, & Nordenberg, 2001; Wolf & Nochasjki, 2013), and suicidal ideation (Hadland et al., 2015). Children who have been traumatized grow up to become adults who are at much higher risk for needing (and being prescribed) psychotropic medication (Anda et al., 2007), which makes sense in terms of needing to ameliorate the posttrauma symptoms that are rampant in this population.

In addition to emotional and physical reactions to trauma, there are often social and interpersonal problems such as homelessness (Bender, Brown, Thompson, Ferguson, Langenderfer, 2015; Herman, Susser, Struening, & Link, 1997), intimate partner violence (Whitfield, Anda, Dube, Felitti, 2003), impaired job performance (Anda et al., 2004), and unintended pregnancies (Dietz et al., 1999). Teenaged boys who experience adverse childhood experiences are more likely to impregnate teenaged girls (Anda et al., 2001). All of these issues are viewed as 'presenting problems' in social service agencies, yet the root cause is child trauma. It is possible (and probable) that if child trauma were treated at the time that it occurred, many of these 'presenting problems' may be prevented altogether (Berkowitz, Stover, & Marans, 2011).

## TRAUMA-INFORMED CHILD WELFARE PRACTICE AND POLICY

Taking all of these physical, emotional, health, and societal consequences into account, it is clear that child trauma is a global public health issue (Magruder, McLaughlin, & Borbon, 2017) as well as a human rights issue. In the past two decades, there have been numerous initiatives in the United States to bring both trauma-specific services and trauma-informed approaches to child welfare systems in order to address child trauma as a public health issue at the micro-, mezzo-, and macro-levels of practice.

*Trauma-specific services* refer to prevention, intervention, and treatment services that are designed to ameliorate traumatic stress symptoms and syndromes (Harris & Fallot, 2001; Substance Abuse and Mental

Health Services Administration [SAMHSA], 2014). By contrast, *trauma-informed approaches* refer to organizational change efforts guided by a set of principles that influence organizational structures, policies, and procedures designed to minimize the risk of retraumatization and promote resilience of both clients and staff (Bowen & Murshid, 2016; Harris & Fallot, 2001; SAMHSA, 2014). The trauma-informed approach adopted by SAMHSA (2014) comprises six key principles: (1) Safety, (2) Trustworthiness and Transparency, (3) Peer Support, (4) Collaboration and Mutuality, (5) Empowerment, Voice, and Choice, and (6) Cultural, Historical, and Gender Issues.

### Trauma-Specific Services for Children

The most commonly used evidence-based treatments recommended for children who have experienced trauma are trauma-focused cognitive behavioral therapy (TF-CBT) (Cohen & Mannarino, 2008; de Arellano et al., 2014), narrative exposure therapy (Robjant & Fazel, 2010), eye-movement desensitization and reprocessing (EMDR) (Rodenburg, Benjamin, de Roos, Meijer, & Stams, 2009), and play therapy (Reyes & Asbrand, 2005). (See also Child Welfare Information Gateway, 2015, and Jennings, 2008, for additional evidence supported treatment models.) It is important to note that in trauma treatment for children, there is no 'one size fits all' approach, because different types of trauma and different types of symptoms necessitate different approaches (Cohen, Berliner, & Mannarino, 2000). For young children, however, the interventions for *complex trauma* (i.e., chronic, repetitive, prolonged trauma) tend to focus heavily on the relationship between the child and the caregiver (Cook et al., 2017).

While these interventions have been shown to be effective with children in middle- and high-income countries, there is also emerging evidence that some of these treatments are also effective in developing countries. For instance, narrative exposure therapy (NET) was originally developed for civilian survivors of war (Neuner, Schauer, Klaschik, Karunakara, & Elbert, 2004; Onyut et al., 2005). However, many regions of the world have successfully used different interventions with traumatized children. For instance, in the Democratic Republic of the Congo, researchers tested trauma-focused and non-trauma-focused interventions with children who were traumatized from war, and both types of interventions were successful at reducing psychological distress (O'Callaghan, McMullen, Shannon, & Rafferty, 2015).

Another example would be the Adaptation and Development After Persecution and Trauma (ADAPT) intervention, which is a community mental health model that explores the trauma experience of refugees (resettled in Australia) in terms of psychosocial adaptive processes (McGregor, Melvin, & Newman, 2016). In fact, whereas in the United States there is a focus on personal or group therapy as a modality for treating trauma, a common modality for treating trauma in other countries is community-based (Jordans, Pigott, & Tol, 2016). In low- and middle-income countries, a school-based or community-based mental health treatment model has also been shown to be beneficial as well as feasible (Fazel, Patel, Thomas, & Tol, 2014), but more research is needed on this approach before considering it to be evidence-based.

### Trauma-Informed Child Welfare Systems

One of the primary ways children and families access support and services is through the child welfare system. As Ko et al. (2008) observe, of all systems that serve children, child welfare systems may encounter the greatest number of children with trauma histories. Not all child welfare agencies provide trauma-specific services; however, there have been numerous initiatives to help agencies in the United States to become trauma-informed. At the federal level, the Children's Health Act of 2000 authorized SAMHSA to develop the National Child Traumatic Stress Initiative (NCTSI) and the National Child Traumatic Stress Network (NCTSN). NCTSI and NCTSN comprise a network of providers, researchers, and family members who collaborate to increase awareness and treatment of child and adolescent trauma. The Every Student Succeeds Act (2015) mandates trauma-informed mental health services and trauma-informed classroom management practices. And, most recently, the Trauma-Informed Care for Children and Families Act (2017) was introduced 'To address the psychological, developmental, social, and emotional needs of children, youth, and families who have experienced trauma' (n.p.).

As a result of increasing awareness of the impact of trauma and available funding for trauma-informed research and training, there are now initiatives to integrate awareness of trauma and/or ACEs in all 50 US states (see Prewitt, 2018). A few of the most notable include the Trauma and Learning Policy Initiative sponsored by Massachusetts Advocates for Children and Harvard Law School (www.traumasensitiveschools. org), Trauma-Informed Oregon (https://traumainformedoregon. org/), and the Sanctuary Model (http://www.sanctuaryweb.com/), all of which provide implementation guidelines as well as a variety of training, assessment, and advocacy tools and policy recommendations to assist individuals, organizations, and community partners in becoming trauma-informed.

## CONCLUSION

Human rights violations against children and youth are grievous, widespread, and reinforced through sociocultural norms and systemic failures to safeguard and enforce children's rights. However, we would be remiss not to note that children, families, and communities with adequate and appropriate support can be resilient. The presence of factors that promote resilience at the individual, community, and societal levels serve to buffer the impact of potentially traumatic experiences. Therefore, many survivors of childhood trauma go on to live happy and fulfilling lives with or without trauma-specific interventions (Willis, DeSanto-Madeya, & Fawcett, 2015). In this regard, the achievements of the global child rights movement are heartening and invigorating. The global child rights movement has been instrumental in: (a) holding governments, non-governmental organizations, and private entities accountable for willful violations, such as sexual abuse and exploitation by peacekeeping forces; (b) informing public policy and reforming of systems of care that implement commitments explicated in the CRC; and (c) providing outreach, public education, and social consensus building regarding the need to protect children's rights and ensure their well-being.

Reading a chapter such as this one can be emotionally draining. Terrible things can and do happen to children, and the types of violations and negative effects we have summarized in this chapter are far from exhaustive. Importantly, the policy and practice interventions we have summarized are also far from exhaustive. Clearly, there are many ways those who love, serve, and protect children can and do help. Numerous individuals, organizations, and government bodies worldwide are collaborating to address children's experiences of trauma and human rights violations. The more we learn as a global society about the prevalence and impact of trauma, and the more we apply a human rights perspective in our work as helping professionals, researchers, educators, child welfare workers, criminal justice professionals, and child's rights advocates, the better positioned we will be to develop and implement effective interventions at the micro-, mezzo-, and macro-levels to prevent and heal childhood trauma and to secure children's rights.

## References

Alyahri, A., & Goodman, R. (2008). Harsh corporal punishment of Yemeni children: Occurrence, type and associations. *Child Abuse & Neglect, 32,* 766–773. https://doi.org/10.1016/j.chiabu.2008.01.001.

Anda, R. F., Brown, D. W., Dube, S. R., Bremner, J. D., Felitti, V. J., & Giles, W. H. (2008). Adverse childhood experiences and chronic obstructive pulmonary disease in adults. *American Journal of Preventive Medicine, 34*(5), 396–403.

Anda, R. F., Brown, D. W., Felitti, V. J., Bremner, J. D., Dube, S. R., & Giles, W. H. (2007). Adverse childhood experiences and prescribed psychotropic medications in adults. *American Journal of Preventive Medicine, 32*(5), 389–394.

Anda, R. F., Felitti, V. J., Bremner, J. D., Walker, J. D., Whitfield, C. L., Perry, B. D., ... Giles, W. H. (2006). The enduring effects of abuse and related adverse experiences in childhood: A convergence of evidence from neurobiology and epidemiology. *European Archives of Psychiatry and Clinical Neuroscience, 56*(3), 174–186.

Anda, R. F., Felitti, V. J., Chapman, D. P., Croft, J. B., Williamson, D. F., Santelli, J., ... Marks, J. S. (2001). Abused boys, battered mothers, and male involvement in teen pregnancy. *Pediatrics, 107*(2), e19.

Anda, R. F., Fleisher, V. I., Felitti, V. J., Edwards, V. J., Whitfield, C. L., Dube, S. R., & Williamson, D. F. (2004). Childhood abuse, household dysfunction and indicators of impaired worker performance in adulthood. *The Permanente Journal, 8(1),* 30–38.

Anda, R., F., Tietjen, G., Schulman, E., Felitti, V., & Croft J. (2010). Adverse childhood experiences and frequent headaches in adults *Headache, 50*(9), 1473–1481.

Anda, R. F., Whitfield, C. L., Felitti, V. J., Chapman, D., Edwards, V. J., Dube, S. R., et al. (2002). Adverse childhood experiences, alcoholic parents, and later risk of alcoholism and depression. *Psychiatric Services, 53*(8), 1001–1009.

Barron, I. G., Abdallah, G., & Smith, P. (2013). Randomized control trial of a CBT trauma recovery program in Palestinian schools. *Journal of Loss and Trauma, 18*(4), 306–321.

Basu, A., McLaughlin, K. A., Misra, S., & Koenen, K. C. (2017). Childhood maltreatment and health impact: The examples of cardiovascular disease and type 2 diabetes mellitus in adults. *Clinical Psychology: Science and Practice, 24*(2), 125–139.

Becker-Blease, K. A. (2017). As the world becomes trauma–informed, work to do. *Journal of Trauma and Dissociation, 18*(2), 131–138.

Bender, K., Brown, S. M., Thompson, S. J., Ferguson, K. M., & Langenderfer. (2015). Multiple victimizations before and after leaving home associated with PTSD, depression, and substance use disorder among homeless youth. *Child Maltreatment, 20*(2), 115–124.

Berg, K. L., Shiu, C. S., Msall, M. E., & Acharya, K. (2015). Victimization and depression among youth with disabilities in the US child welfare system. *Child: Care, Health and Development, 41*(6), 989–999.

Berkowitz, S. J., Stover, C. S., & Marans, S. R. (2011). The child and family traumatic stress intervention: Secondary prevention for youth at risk of developing PTSD. *Journal of Child Psychology and Psychiatry, 52*(6), 676–685.

Bill and Melinda Gates Foundation. (2017). *Goalkeepers: The stories behind the data 2017*. Seattle, Washington: Bill Gates and Melinda Gates. Retrieved from https://datareport.goalkeepers.org/assets/downloads/Stories_behind_the_data_2017.pdf.

Bowen, E. A., & Murshid, N. S. (2016). Trauma-informed social policy: A conceptual framework for policy analysis and advocacy. *American Journal of Public Health, 106*(2), 223–229.

Breslau, N., Wilcox, H. C., Storr, C. L., Lucia, V. C., & Anthony, J. C. (2004). Trauma exposure and posttraumatic stress disorder: A study of youths in urban America. *Journal of Urban Health, 81*, 530–544.

Brown, D. W., Anda, R. F., Edwards, V. J., Felitti, V. J., Dube, S. R., & Giles, W. H. (2007). Adverse childhood experiences and childhood autobiographical memory disturbance. *Child Abuse & Neglect, 31*, 961–969.

Brown, D. W., Anda, R. F., Felitti, V. J., Edwards, J., Malarcher, A. M., Croft, J. B, & Giles, W. H. (2010). Adverse childhood experiences are associated with the risk of lung cancer: A prospective cohort study. *BMC Public Health, 10*(1), 20.

Brown, D. W., Anda, R. F., Tiemeier, H., Felitti, V. J., Edwards, V. J., Croft, J. B., et al. (2009). Adverse childhood experiences and the risk of premature mortality. *American Journal of Preventive Medicine, 37*(5), 389–396.

Brown, M. J., Thacker, L. R., & Cohen, S. A. (2013). Association between adverse childhood experiences and diagnosis of cancer. *PloS One, 8*(6), e65524. https://doi.org/10.1371/journal.pone.0065524.

Burns, B. J., Phillips, S. D., Wagner, H. R., Barth, R. P., Kolko, D. J., Campbell, Y., & Landsverk, J. (2004). Mental health need and access to mental health services by youths involved with child welfare: A national survey. *Journal of the American Academy of Child and Adolescent Psychiatry, 43*, 960–970.

Centers for Disease Control and Prevention. (2017). *LGBT youth*. Retrieved from https://www.cdc.gov/lgbthealth/youth.htm.

Chapman, D. P., Liu, Y., Presley-Cantrell, L. R., Edwards, V. J., Wheaton, A. G., Perry, G. S., & Croft, J. B. (2013). Adverse childhood experiences and frequent insufficient sleep in 5 US States, 2009: A retrospective cohort study. *BMC Public Health, 13*(1). https://doi.org/10.1186/1471-2458-13-3.

Chapman, D. P., Whitfield, C. L., Felitti, V. J., Dube, S. R., Edwards, V. J., & Anda, R. F. (2004). Adverse childhood experiences and the risk of depressive disorders in adulthood. *Journal of Affective Disorders, 82*, 217–225.

Chiang, L. F., Kress, H., Sumner, S. A., Gleckel, J., Kawemama, P., & Gordon, R. N. (2016). Violence Against Children Surveys (VACS): Towards a global surveillance system. *Injury Prevention, 22*(Suppl 1), i17–i22.

Child Rights International Network. (n.d.). *Inhuman sentencing: Campaign reports.* https://archive.crin.org/en/home/campaigns/inhuman-sentencing.html.

Child Rights International Network. (2017, March 20). *Death penalty: Submission for the UN secretary-general's report to the Human Rights Council on the question of the death penalty.* Retrieved from https://archive.crin.org/en/home/campaigns/inhuman-sentencing/problem/death-penalty.html.

Child Welfare Information Gateway. (2015). *Developing a trauma-informed child welfare system.* Washington, DC: U.S. Department of Health and Human Services, Children's Bureau.

Chynoweth, S. (2017). *"We keep it in our heart:" Sexual violence against men and boys in the Syria Crisis.* UN High Comissioner for Refugees (UNCHR). UNCHR: Geneva, Switzerland. Retrieved from http://www.refworld.org/docid/5a128e814.html.

Cloitre, M., Stolbach, B. C., Herman, J. L., Kolk, B. V. D., Pynoos, R., Wang, J., & Petkova, E. (2009). A developmental approach to complex PTSD: Childhood and adult cumulative trauma as predictors of symptom complexity. *Journal of Traumatic Stress, 22*(5), 399–408.

Cohen, J. A., Berliner, L., & Mannarino, A. P. (2000). Treating traumatized children: A research review and synthesis. *Trauma, Violence, & Abuse, 1*(1), 29–46.

Cohen, J. A., & Mannarino, A. P. (2008). Trauma-focused cognitive behavioural therapy for children and parents. *Child and Adolescent Mental Health, 13*(4), 158–162.

Cook, A., Spinazzola, J., Ford, J., Lanktree, C., Blaustein, M., Cloitre, M., ... Mallah, K. (2017). Complex trauma in children and adolescents. *Psychiatric Annals, 35*(5), 390–398.

Copeland, W. E., Keeler, G., Angold, A., & Costello, E. J. (2007). Traumatic events and posttraumatic stress in childhood. *Archives of General Psychiatry, 64*, 577–584.

Covell, K., & Becker, J. (2011). *Five years on: A global update on violence against children, report for the NGO advisory council for follow-up to the UN secretary-general's study on violence against Children.* New York, NY: United Nations.

Cronholm, P. F., Forke, C. M., Wade, R., Bair-Merritt, M. H., Davis, M., Harkins-Schwartz ... & Fein, J. A. (2015). Adverse childhood experiences: Expanding the concept of adversity. *American Journal of Preventative Medicine, 49*(3), 354–361.

Cunningham, T. J., Ford, E. S., Croft, J. B., Merrick, M. T., Rolle, I. V., & Giles, W. H. (2014). Sex-specific relationships between adverse childhood experiences and chronicobstructive pulmonary disease in five states. *International Journal of COPD, 9*, 1033–1042.

D'andrea, W., Ford, J., Stolbach, B., Spinazzola, J., & van der Kolk, B. A. (2012). Understanding interpersonal trauma in children: Why we need a developmentally appropriate trauma diagnosis. *American Journal of Orthopsychiatry, 82*(2), 187–200.

Danese, A., Pariante, C. M., Caspi, A., Taylor, A., & Poulton, R. (2007). Childhood maltreatment predicts adult inflammation in a life-course study. *Proceedings of the National Academy of Sciences, 104*(4), 1319–1324. https://doi.org/10.1073/pnas.0610362104.

Danese, A., & Tan, M. (2013). Childhood maltreatment and obesity: Systematic review and meta-analysis. *Molecular Psychiatry, 19*(5), 544–554. https://doi.org/10.1038/mp.2013.54.

Danese, A., & van Harmelen, A. L. (2017). The hidden wounds of childhood trauma. *European Journal of Psychotraumatology, 8*, 1–3.

de Arellano, M. A. R., Lyman, D. R., Jobe-Shields, L., George, P., Dougherty, R. H., Daniels, A. S., ... Delphin-Rittmon, M. E. (2014). Trauma-focused cognitive-behavioral therapy for children and adolescents: Assessing the evidence. *Psychiatric Services, 65*(5), 591–602.

Derluyn, I., Broekaert, E., Schuyten, G., & De Temmerman, E. (2004). Post-traumatic stress in former Ugandan child soldiers. *The Lancet, 363*(9412), 861–863.

Dietz, P. M., Spitz, A. M., Anda, R. F., Williamson, D. F., McMahon, P. M., Santelli, J. S., ... Kendrick, J. S. (1999). Unintended pregnancy among adult women exposed to abuse or household dysfunction during their childhood. *JAMA, 282*(14), 1359–1364.

Dong, M., Anda, R. F., Felitti, V, J., Dube, S. R., Williamson, D. F., Thompson, R. J., ... Giles, W. H. (2004). The interrelatedness of multiple forms of childhood abuse, neglect, and household dysfunction. *Child Abuse & Neglect, 28*, 771–784. https://doi.org/10.1016/j.chiabu.2004.01.008.

Dube, S. R., Anda, R. F., Felitti, V. J., Edwards, V. J., & Croft, J. B. (2002). Adverse childhood experiences and personal alcohol abuse as an adult. *Addictive Behaviors, 27*(5), 713–725.

Dube, S. R., Fairweather, D., Pearson, W. S., Felitti, V. J., Anda, R. F., & Croft, J. B. (2009). Cumulative childhood stress and autoimmune disease. *Psychom Med., 71*(2), 243–250.

Dunne, M., Humphreys, S., & Leach, F. (2006). Gender violence in schools in the developing world. *Gender and Education, 18,* 75–98. https://doi.org/10.1080/09540250500195143.

Dvir, Y., Ford, J. D., Hill, M., & Frazier, J. A. (2014). Childhood maltreatment, emotional dysregulation, and psychiatric comorbidities. *Harvard Review of Psychiatry, 22*(3), 149–161.

Dyb, G., Jensen, T. K., & Nygaard, E. (2011). Children's and parents' posttraumatic stress reactions after the 2004 tsunami. *Clinical Child Psychology and Psychiatry, 16*(4), 621–634.

Edwards, V. J., Fivush, R., Anda, R. F., Felitti, V. J., & Nordenberg, D. F. (2001). Autobiographical memory disturbances in childhood abuse survivors. *Journal of Aggression, Maltreatment, & Trauma, 4*(2), 247–263.

Eiling, E., Van Diggele-Holtland, M., Van Yperen, T., & Boer, F. (2014). Psychosocial support for children in the Republic of South Sudan: An evaluation outcome. *Intervention, 12*(1), 61–75.

End Child Prostitution, Child Pornography and Trafficking of Children for Sexual Purposes [ECPAT] International. (2016). *Offenders on the move: Global study on sexual exploitation of children in travel and tourism.* Bangkok: ECPAT International. Retrieved from https://www.ecpat.org/wp-content/uploads/2019/06/Offenders-on-the-move-Global-Study-on-the-Sexual-Exploitation-of-Children-in-Travel-and-Tourism.pdf.

Equaldex. (2018). *Status of LGBTQ laws by country.* Retrieved from http://www.equaldex.com/.

Espelage, D. L., Hong, J. S., & Mebane, S. (2016). Recollections of childhood bullying and multiple forms of victimization: Correlates with psychological functioning among college students. *Social Psychology of Education, 19*(4), 715–728.

Every Student Succeeds Act. (2015). S. 1177, 114th Congress, Public Law 95. Retrieved from https://www.congress.gov/bill/114th-congress/senate-bill/1177/text.

Farley, M., Baral, I., Kiremire, M., & Sezgin, U. (1998). Prostitution in five countries: Violence and post-traumatic stress disorder. *Feminism & Psychology, 8*(4), 405–426.

Fazel, M., Patel, V., Thomas, S., & Tol, W. (2014). Mental health interventions in schools in low-income and middle-income countries. *The Lancet Psychiatry, 1*(5), 388–398.

Feldman, R., Vengrober, A., Eidelman-Rothman, M., & Zagoory-Sharon, O. (2013). Stress reactivity in war-exposed young children with and without posttraumatic stress disorder: Relations to maternal stress hormones, parenting, and child emotionality and regulation. *Development and Psychopathology, 25,* 943–955.

Felitti, V. J., Anda, R. F., Nordenberg, D., Williamson, D. F., Spitz, A. M., Edwards, V., ... Marks, J. S. (1998). Relationship of childhood abuse and household dysfunction to many of the leading causes of death in adults: The Adverse Childhood Experiences (ACE) study. *American Journal of Preventive Medicine, 14*(4), 245–258.

Finkelhor, D., Turner, H. A., Hamby, S. L., & Ormrod, R. (2011). *Polyvictimization: Children's exposure to multiple types of violence, crime, and abuse.* Washington, DC: Office of Juvenile Justice and Delinquency Prevention, Office of Justice Programs, U.S. Department of Justice.

Gabbay, V., Oatis, M. D., Silva, R. R., & Hirsch, G. (2004). Epidemiological aspects of PTSD in children and adolescents. In R. R. Silva (Ed.), *Posttraumatic stress disorder in children and adolescents: Handbook* (pp. 1–17). New York: Norton.

Gershoff, E. T., & Font, S. A. (2016). Corporal punishment in U.S. public schools: Prevalence, disparities in use, and status in state and federal policy. *Society for Research in Child Development, 30*(1), 1–25.

Gershoff, E. (2017). School corporal punishment in global perspective: Prevalence, outcomes, and efforts at intervention. *Psychology, Health & Medicine, 22*(sup1), 224–239. https://doi.org/10.1080/13548506.2016.1271955.

Giaconia, R., Reinherz, H., Silverman, A., Bilge, P., Frost, A., & Cohen, E. (1995). Traumas and posttraumatic stress disorder in a community population of older adolescents. *Journal of the American Academy of Child and Adolescent Psychiatry, 34,* 1369–1380.

Global Initiative to End All Corporal Punishment of Children. (2015). *Towards non-violent schools: Prohibiting all corporal punishment.* Global report 2015. Retrieved from http://endcorporalpunishment.org/wp-content/uploads/thematic/Schools-report-2015-EN.pdf.

Gooding, H. C., Milliren, C., Austin, S. B., Sheridan, M. A., & McLaughlin, K. A. (2015). Exposure to violence in childhood is associated with higher body mass index in adolescence. *Child Abuse & Neglect, 50,* 151–158.

Grabow, C., & Rose, L. (2018, May 21). *The US had 57 times as many school shootings as the other major industrialized nations combined.* Cable News Network [CNN]. Retrieved from https://www.cnn.com/2018/05/21/us/school-shooting-us-versus-world-trnd/index.html.

Greger, H. K., Myhre, A. K., Lydersen, S., & Jozefiak, T. (2015). Previous maltreatment and present mental health in a high-risk adolescent population. *Child Abuse & Neglect, 45,* 122–134.

Hadland, S. E., Wood, E., Dong, H., Marshall., B. D. L., Kerr, T., Montaner, J. S., & DeBeck, K. (2015). Suicide attempts and childhood maltreatment among street youth: A prospective cohort study. *Pediatrics, 136*(3), 440–449.

Harris, M., & Fallot, R. D. (Eds.). (2001). *Using trauma theory to design service systems.* San Francisco, CA: Jossey-Bass.

Hasanović, M., Srabović, S., Rašidović, M., Šehović, M., Hasanbašić, E., Husanović, J., et al. (2009). Psychosocial assistance to students with post-traumatic stress disorder in primary and secondary schools in post-war Bosnia Herzegovina. *Psychiatria Danubina, 21*(4), 463–473.

Heiervang, E., Stormarkph, K. M., Lundervold, A. J., Heimann, M., Goodman, R., Posserud, M. B., .... Gillberg, C. (2007). Psychiatric disorders in Norwegian 8- to 10-year-olds: An epidemiological survey of prevalence, risk factors, and service use. *Journal of the American Academy of Child & Adolescent Psychiatry, 46*(4), 438–447.

Herman, D. B., Susser, E. S., Struening, E. L., & Link, B. L. (1997). Adverse childhood experiences: Are they risk factors for adult homelessness? *American Journal of Public Health, 87*(2), 249–255.

Hillis, S. D., Anda, R. F., Felitti, V. J., & Marchbanks, P. A. (2001). Adverse childhood experiences and sexual risk behaviors in women: A retrospective cohort study. *Family Planning Perspective, 33*(5), 206–211.

Hillis, S. D., Anda, R. F., Felitti, V. J., Nordenberg, D., & Marchbanks, P. A. (2000). Adverse childhood experiences and sexually transmitted diseases in men and women: A retrospective study. *Pediatrics, 106*(1), e11.

Hsu, C. C., Chong, M. Y., Yang, P., & Yen, C. F. (2002). Posttraumatic stress disorder among adolescent earthquake victims in Taiwan. *Journal of the American Academy of Child and Adolescent Psychiatry, 41*, 875–881.

Inspector General U.S. Department of Defense. (2017). *Implementation of DoD Leahy Law regarding allegations of child sexual abuse by members of the Afghan National Defense and Security Forces.* Report No. DODIG-2018-018. Retrieved from https://media.defense.gov/2017/Nov/15/2001843802/-1/-1/1/DODIG-2018-018_CHILD_SEXUAL_ABUSE_V2_508_R_REDACTED.PDF.

International Labour Organization. (2017a). *Global estimates of child labor: Results and trends, 2012–2016.* Geneva: International Labour Organization. Retrieved from http://www.ilo.org/wcmsp5/groups/public/@dgreports/@dcomm/documents/publication/wcms_575499.pdf.

International Labour Organization. (2017b). *Global estimates of modern slavery: Forced labor and forced marriage.* Geneva: International Labour Organization. Retrieved from https://www.ilo.org/wcmsp5/groups/public/@dgreports/@dcomm/documents/publication/wcms_575479.pdf.

Jennings, A. (2008). *Models for developing trauma-informed behavioral health systems and trauma-specific services.* National Center for Trauma-Informed Care. Retrieved from http://www.ct.gov/dmhas/lib/dmhas/trauma/TraumaModels.pdf.

Jordans, M. J., Komproe, I. H., Tol, W. A., Kohrt, B. A., Luitel, N. P., Macy, R. D., & De Jong, J. T. (2010). Evaluation of a classroom-based psychosocial intervention in conflict-affected Nepal: A cluster randomized controlled trial. *Journal of Child Psychology and Psychiatry, 51*(7), 818–826.

Jordans, M. J., Pigott, H., & Tol, W. A. (2016). Interventions for children affected by armed conflict: A systematic review of mental health and psychosocial support in low-and middle-income countries. *Current Psychiatry Reports, 18*(1). https://doi.org/10.1007/s11920-015-0648-z.

Kaplow, J. B., Saxe, G. N., Putnam, F. W., Pynoos, R. S., & Lieberman, A. F. (2006). The long-term consequences of early childhood trauma: A case study and discussion. *Psychiatry, 69*(4), 362–375.

Ko, S. J., Ford, J. D., Kassam-Adams, N., Berkowitz, S. J., Wilson, C., Wong, M., … Layne, C. M. (2008). Creating trauma-informed systems: Child welfare, education, first responders, health care, juvenile justice. *Professional Psychology, Research and Practice, 39*(4), 396–404.

Kroll, J. (2003). Posttraumatic symptoms and the complexity of responses to trauma. *JAMA, 290*(5), 667–670.

Lee, J. H. (2015). Prevalence and predictors of self-reported student maltreatment by teachers in South Korea. *Child Abuse and Neglect, 46*, 113–120. https://doi.org/10.1016/j.chiabu.2015.03.009.

Magruder, K. M., McLaughlin, K. A., & Elmore Borbon, D. L. (2017). Trauma is a public health issue. *European Journal of Psychotraumatology, 8*(1), 1–9.

Makwanya, P., Moyo, W., & Nyenya, T. (2012). Perceptions of the stakeholders towards the use of corporal punishment in Zimbabwean schools: A case study of Bulawayo. *International Journal of Asian Social Science, 2*, 1231–1239.

McFarlane, A. C. (1987). Posttraumatic phenomena in a longitudinal study of children following a natural disaster. *Journal of the American Academy of Child and Adolescent Psychiatry, 26*, 764–769.

McGregor, L. S., Melvin, G. A., & Newman, L. K. (2016). An exploration of the adaptation and development after persecution and trauma (adapt) model with resettled refugee adolescents in Australia: A qualitative study. *Transcultural Psychiatry, 53*(3), 347–367.

Mustanski, B. S., Garofalo, R., & Emerson, E. M. (2010). Mental health disorders, psychological distress, and suicidality in a diverse sample of lesbian, gay, bisexual, and transgender youths. *American Journal of Public Health, 100*(12), 2426–2432.

Neuner, F., Schauer, M., Klaschik, C., Karunakara, U., & Elbert, T. (2004). A comparison of narrative exposure therapy, supportive counseling, and psychoeducation for treating posttraumatic stress disorder in an African refugee settlement. *Journal of Consulting and Clinical Psychology, 72*(4), 579–587.

O'Callaghan, P., McMullen, J., Shannon, C., & Rafferty, H. (2015). Comparing a trauma focused and non trauma focused intervention with war affected Congolese youth: A preliminary randomised trial. *Intervention, 13*(1), 28–44.

Office of the High Commissioner for Human Rights. (n.d.) *Committee on the Rights of the Child: Monitoring children's rights.* Retrieved from http://www.ohchr.org/EN/HRBodies/CRC/Pages/CRCIntro.aspx.

Office of the High Commissioner for Human Rights. (2017). [Interactive map of the world identifying status of ratification] Status of Ratification: Convention on the Rights of the Child (CRC) and Optional Protocols to the CRC. Retrieved from: http://indicators.ohchr.org/.

Office of the Special Representative of Secretary General for Child and Armed Conflict. (2013). *The six grave violations against children during armed conflict: A legal foundation.* New York, NY: United Nations. Retrieved from https://childrenandarmedconflict.un.org/publications/WorkingPaper-1_SixGraveViolationsLegalFoundation.pdf.

Ogando Portela, M. J., & Pells, K. (2015). *Corporal punishment in schools: Longitudinal evidence from Ethiopia, India, Peru, and Viet Nam* (Innocenti Discussion Paper No. 2015-02). Florence, Italy: UNICEF Office of Research. Retrieved from https://www.unicef-irc.org/publications/series/22/.

Onyut, L. P., Neuner, F., Schauer, E., Ertl, V., Odenwald, M., Schauer, M., & Elbert, T. (2005). Narrative exposure therapy as a treatment for child war survivors with posttraumatic stress disorder: Two case reports and a pilot study in an African refugee settlement. *BMC Psychiatry, 5*(1). https://doi.org/10.1186/1471-244x-5-7.

Paolucci, E. O., Genuis, M. L., & Violato, C. (2001). A meta-analysis of the published research on the effects of child sexual abuse. *Journal of Psychology, 135,* 17–36.

Perkonigg, A., Kessler, R. C., Storz, S., & Wittchen, H. U. (2000). Traumatic events and post-traumatic stress disorder in the community: Prevalence, risk factors and comorbidity. *Acta Psychiatrica Scandinavica, 101,* 46–59.

Perkonigg, A., Pfister, H., Stein, M.B., Höfler, M., Lieb, R., Maercker, A., & Wittchen, H. U. (2005). Longitudinal course of posttraumatic stress disorder and posttraumatic stress disorder symptoms in a community sample of adolescents and young adults. *American Journal of Psychiatry, 162,* 320–1327.

Ports, K. A., Ford, D. C., & Merrick, M. T. (2016). Adverse childhood experiences and sexual victimization in adulthood. *Child Abuse & Neglect, 51,* 313–322.

Prewitt, E. (2018, February 24). *State profiles for 50 states and district of Columbia.* State ACEs Action. Retrieved from https://www.acesconnection.com/g/state-aces-action-group/blog/state-profiles-list-of-50-states-and-district-of-columbia-with-links-to-individual-profiles.

Rebellon, C. J., & Straus, M. (2017). Corporal punishment and adult antisocial behavior: A comparison of dyadic concordance types and an evaluation of mediating mechanisms in Asia, Europe, and North America. *International Journal of Behavioral Development, 41*(4), 503–513.

Reyes, C. J., & Asbrand, J. P. (2005). A longitudinal study assessing trauma symptoms in sexually abused children engaged in play therapy. *International Journal of Play Therapy, 14*(2), 25–47. https://doi.org/10.1037/h0088901.

Ridgely, S. B. (2016). When pain becomes symbolic of commitment: The practice of spanking among adults and children and "focus on the family" childrearing literature. *Journal of Religion and Violence, 4*(3), 373–386.

Robjant, K., & Fazel, M. (2010). The emerging evidence for narrative exposure therapy: A review. *Clinical Psychology Review, 30*(8), 1030–1039.

Rodenburg, R., Benjamin, A., de Roos, C., Meijer, A. M., & Stams, G. J. (2009). Efficacy of EMDR in children: A meta-analysis. *Clinical Psychology Review, 29*(7), 599–606.

Ryan, C., Huebner, D., Diaz, R. M., & Sanchez, J. (2009). Family rejection as a predictor of negative health outcomes in white and Latino lesbian, gay, and bisexual young adults. *Pediatrics, 123*(1), 346–352.

Substance Abuse and Mental Health Services Administration. (2014). *Trauma-informed approach and trauma specific interventions.* Retrieved from https://www.samhsa.gov/nctic/trauma-interventions.

Saunders, B. E., & Adams, Z. W. (2014). Epidemiology of traumatic experiences in childhood. *Child and Adolescent Psychiatric Clinics of North America, 23*(2), 167–184.

Save the Children. (2013). *Unspeakable crimes against children: Sexual violence in conflict.* Retreived from https://www.savethechildren.es/sites/default/files/imce/docs/unspeakable_crimes_report.pdf.

Trauma-Informed Care for Children and Families Act. (2017). H.R. 1757, 115th Congress. Retrieved from https://www.govtrack.us/congress/bills/115/hr1757.

Turner, H. A., Finkelhor, D., & Ormrod, R. (2006). The effect of lifetime victimization on the mental health of children and adolescents. *Social Science & Medicine, 62*(1), 13–27.

United Nations. (1989). *Convention on the Rights of the Child.* Retrieved from http://www.un.org/documents/ga/res/44/a44r025.htm.

United Nations. (2015). *The millennium development goals report.* Retrieved from http://www.un.org/millenniumgoals/2015_MDG_Report/pdf/MDG%202015%20rev%20(July%201).pdf.

United Nations Children's Fund. (2009). *Progress for children: A report card on child protection.* Retrieved from https://www.unicef.org/protection/files/Progress_for_Children-No.8_EN_081309(1).pdf.

United Nations Children's Fund. (2011). *Justice for children.* Retrieved from https://www.unicef.org/protection/57929_57999.html.

United Nations Children's Fund. (2014). *Hidden in plain sight. A statistical analysis of violence against children.* New York: UNICEF. Retrieved from http://files.unicef.org/publications/files/Hidden_in_plain_sight_statistical_analysis_EN_3_Sept_2014.pdf.

United Nations Children's Fund. (2017). *A familiar face: Violence in the lives of children and adolescents.* New York: UNICEF. Retrieved from https://www.

unicef.org/publications/files/Violence_in_the_lives_of_children_and_adolescents.pdf.

van der Kolk, B. A. (2005). Developmental trauma disorder: Toward a rational diagnosis for children with complex trauma histories. *Psychiatric Annals, 35*(5), 401–408.

van der Kolk, B. A. (2015). *The body keeps the score: Brain, mind, and body in the healing of trauma.* New York, NY: Penguin Books.

Whitfield, C. L., Anda, R. F., Dube, S. R., & Felitti, V. J. (2003). Violent childhood experiences and the risk of intimate partner violence in adults: Assessment in a large health maintenance organization. *Journal of Interpersonal Violence, 18*(2), 166–185.

Widom, C. S., DuMont, K., & Czaja, S. J. (2007). A prospective investigation of major depressive disorder and comorbidity in abused and neglected children grown up. *Archives of General Psychiatry, 64,* 49–56.

Williams, L. M. (1994). Recall of childhood trauma: A prospective study of women's memories of child sexual abuse. *Journal of Consulting and Clinical Psychology, 62*(6), 1167–1176.

Willis, D. G., DeSanto-Madeya, S., & Fawcett, J. (2015). Moving beyond dwelling in suffering: A situation-specific theory of men's healing from childhood maltreatment. *Nursing Science Quarterly, 28*(1), 57–63.

Wolf, M. R., & Nochajski, T. H. (2013). Child sexual abuse survivors with dissociative amnesia: What's the difference? *Journal of Child Sexual Abuse, 22*(4), 462–480.

Wolf, M. R., Nochajski, T. H., & Farrell, M. (2015). The effects of childhood sexual abuse and other trauma on drug court participants. *Journal of Social Work Practice in the Addictions, 15*(1), 44–65. https://doi.org/10.1080/15 33256X.2014.996228.

# CHAPTER 7

# Women, Trauma, and Human Rights

*Filomena M. Critelli and Jane McPherson*

Women have long experienced discrimination, violence, and oppression due to their unequal position in society, but only recently have these assaults to women's dignity and personal safety been recognized and addressed as rights violations within the human rights framework. In 1993, 45 years after the adoption of the *Universal Declaration of Human Rights* (UDHR; United Nations [UN], 1948), the UN World Conference on Human Rights in Vienna confirmed that women's rights were human rights. That same year the UN *Declaration on the Elimination of Violence Against Women* (UN, 1993) was approved to recognize this critical global human rights violation. Women are more likely to experience gender-based violence and unequal treatment than are men. The effects of this violence and inequality go far beyond the immediate physical damage to the victim. Indeed, women's exposure to traumatic events results in significant psychological harms that are linked to a variety of negative health and social consequences; although it is important to note that responses to trauma are highly individual and

F. M. Critelli (✉)
School of Social Work, University at Buffalo, Buffalo, NY, USA
e-mail: fmc8@buffalo.edu

J. McPherson
School of Social Work, University of Georgia, Athens, GA, USA
e-mail: jmcpherson@uga.edu

© The Author(s) 2019
L. D. Butler et al. (eds.), *Trauma and Human Rights*,
https://doi.org/10.1007/978-3-030-16395-2_7

shaped by a range of contextual factors (Kimerling, Weitlauf, Iverson, Karpenko, & Jain, 2013). Still, women experience post-traumatic stress disorder (PTSD) at about twice the rate that men do (Kimerling et al., 2013; Tolin & Foa, 2006). Existing research also suggests that, in part, women are more susceptible to PTSD because they are more likely than men to experience the kinds of traumatic events that are typically associated with higher risk for PTSD, such as sexual assault and child sexual abuse (Tolin & Foa, 2006).

This chapter will discuss some common human rights violations experienced by women, provide an overview of women's protections under current human rights law, and explore the way that evolving trauma theory has shifted our understanding of those violations. Finally, this paper will provide two case studies for how human rights and trauma-informed frameworks are combined to help women successfully assert their right to dignity.

## Prevalent Human Rights Violations in Women's Lives

Despite the progress made globally by women's rights movements and advances in international human rights law, women still experience a multitude of rights violations and potentially traumatizing events. Intersecting forms of discrimination due to age, ethnicity, nationality, religion, health status, marital status, education, disability, sexual orientation, socioeconomic factors, and migration status may exacerbate these violations (Office of the High Commissioner for Human Rights [OHCHR], 2014).

### Gender-Based Violence

Globally, violence against women and girls is one of the most pervasive human rights violations and is a prominent manifestation of gender-based discrimination (Amnesty International, 2004). No country has successfully eliminated it. Violence against women comes in many forms and occurs within various contexts, but the experience or threat of violence inhibits women everywhere from fully exercising and enjoying their human rights.

Domestic violence or intimate partner violence is the most common type of violence against women. It includes murder, rape, and battery by intimate partners. A 2013 World Health Organization (WHO) analysis found that almost one-third (30%) of all women worldwide who have been in a relationship have experienced physical and/or sexual violence by their intimate partners. Furthermore, as many as 38% of all murders of women were committed by intimate partners (WHO, 2013). Intimate partner violence is common, but women experience sexual violence from other men as well: Available data indicates that throughout the world, 7% of women report experiencing a sexual assault by someone other than a partner (WHO, 2013). Girls are especially vulnerable to sexual violence, and 20% of women report having been victims of sexual violence as children (WHO, 2013). Violence results in health and mental health consequences, such as serious injuries, increased likelihood of miscarriage, depression, post-traumatic stress and other anxiety disorders, sleep difficulties, eating disorders, and suicide attempts (WHO, 2013).

Women are also likely to comprise the greatest proportion of adult civilians killed in war and targeted for abuse, as well as the majority of refugees and internally displaced people forced to flee their homes because of armed conflict. Conflict-related sexual violence may include rape, sexual slavery, forced prostitution, forced pregnancy, enforced sterilization, and other forms of sexual violence perpetrated against women or girls connected directly or indirectly to a conflict (UN, 2017). Rape is employed as a weapon of war and is used to terrorize populations, break up families, destroy communities, and as a strategy for ethnic cleansing. Between 100,000 and 250,000, women were raped in Rwanda, during the three months of genocide in 1994. In the former Yugoslavia (1992–1995), as many as 60,000 women were victimized, and at least 200,000 rapes of women took place in the Democratic Republic of the Congo since 1998 (UN, 2014).

At present, the UN documents 19 countries in conflict, post-conflict, or situations of concern where sexual violence is exercised (UN, 2017). In Syria, a nation facing one of the greatest humanitarian crises of our time, sexual violence continues to be employed by various parties within the conflict as a systematic tactic of warfare, terrorism, and torture. Another massive crisis is playing out in Myanmar (Burma) where Burmese security forces have committed widespread rape against women and girls as part of a campaign of ethnic cleansing against Rohingya Muslims in Burma's Rakhine State (Human Rights Watch, 2017a).

Sexual violence perpetrates a "double traumatization" of its victims because of the shame, discrimination, and lack of assistance victims' experience, even beyond the physical and emotional trauma the attacks leave behind (UN, 2017). Post-conflict nations are still coping with the enduring effects of past sexual crimes including socioeconomic marginalization and stigma of survivors.

## Trafficking in Women and Girls

Trafficking in women and girls is another growing problem, in spite of the fact that international law and the laws of 158 countries criminalize trade in human beings. The most common forms of trafficking involve sexual exploitation and forced labor (Deshpande & Nawal, 2013). The vast majority of the 20.9 million persons who are trafficked are women and girls, and they comprise 71% of the victims (United Nations Office on Drugs and Crime [UNODC], 2017). Women and children are disproportionately impacted by some of the root causes of trafficking, including poverty, lack of education, lack of equal employment opportunities, discrimination, violence, and armed conflict, and therefore, they are the most vulnerable. Women become captive in these situations through promises of employment, false marriage, or relationship offers; parents may barter their children for a cash advance and/or promises of future earnings; or victims may be abducted outright. Once brought to their destination, women have no control over the nature or place of work, or the terms or conditions of employment, and find themselves in coerced and abusive situations from which escape is both difficult and dangerous. The victims are often controlled by using their vulnerabilities against them, for example, the need for drugs, if they have become addicted, or the lack of legal papers, if they are illegal migrants. Officials often treat those apprehended as undocumented migrants or prostitutes, rather than acknowledging them as victims (Human Rights Watch, 2000; Wilson, Critelli, & Rittner, 2015). Debt bondage, also known as bonded labor, is another form of contemporary slavery. Women may become bonded laborers when they are coerced into work as a means of repayment for a loan, often for a very small amount. Once in debt, the victim is forced to work long hours for very little or no pay. The original debt is inflated through charges for food, transport, and interest on loans, making it impossible to repay and trapping the worker in a cycle of debt that may never be fully repaid. Bonded laborers are disproportionately members of groups that are discriminated against, including scheduled castes, religious and ethnic minorities, indigenous people, and migrant workers (Global Alliance against Traffic in Women, n.d.).

## Sexual Harassment

Sexual harassment operates as a barrier to the equal rights of women and is a powerful mechanism that maintains women's subordinate social status. It threatens women's freedom of assembly, ability to work, vote, shop, or participate in public spaces. Sexual harassment includes behaviors such as sexual advances or propositions, sexual assault and rape, inappropriate touching, offensive questions or comments about physical appearance or sex life, sexual jokes and insults, leering or the display of pornographic material, and condescending or paternalistic remarks (UN Commission on Human Rights, 2003). It is difficult to quantify the prevalence of sexual harassment due to low reporting rates, yet data gathered by the UN indicate that it is a pervasive human rights violation experienced by women everywhere. For example, between 40 and 50% of women in the European Union report some form of sexual harassment or unwanted sexual behavior in the workplace, while small surveys in Asia-Pacific countries indicate that 30–40% of women workers report some form of harassment either verbal, physical, or sexual (UN, 2006). In the United States, recently there has been heightened awareness of the breadth of this violation following a cascade of sexual harassment allegations that have come forth from women against prominent men in the entertainment and news industries and have stirred a national conversation on this issue using the hashtag, #metoo.

## Gender-Based Traditional Practices

Female genital mutilation (FGM), honor crimes, stoning, child marriage, and dowry-related violence and killings are gender-based traditional practices that seek to control the sexuality and reproductive capacity of women and girls. As they have been practiced over many generations, they are justified by their perpetrators as accepted cultural practices (UN Commission on Human Rights, 1999).

*Female genital mutilation* refers to procedures that involve partial or total removal of the external female genitalia or other injury to the female genital organs for non-medical reasons (WHO, 2017). More than 200 million girls and women today have experienced one of these procedures, which are traditionally practiced in Africa, the Middle East, and Asia (UNICEF, 2016), but have more recently been reported in the EU and United States, as well (Krupa, 2017). FGM is mostly carried out on young girls between infancy and age 15. There are no health benefits to this practice. Rather, it poses health risks to girls and women including direct negative effects on sexuality and sexual health. While far too many cases of FGM persist, attitudes are changing about the acceptability of this practice. Prevalence rates have declined by 41 percentage points in Liberia, 31 in Burkina Faso, 30 in Kenya, and 27 in Egypt over the last 30 years (UNICEF, 2016). Five countries also have passed national legislation criminalizing the practice. However, the overall rate of progress may not keep up with population growth so that if current trends continue the number of girls and women subjected to FGM will increase significantly over the next 15 years.

The practice of child marriage is another manifestation of gender inequality that has long-term adverse consequences on young women's lives and contributes to intergenerational poverty. Globally, more than 700 million women alive today were married before their 18th birthday, and about 250 million were married even younger, before age 15 (UNICEF, 2014). Child marriage among girls is most common in South Asia and sub-Saharan Africa, and the 10 countries with the highest rates are located in these two regions. Child marriage impedes access to basic human rights, such as education and health, including sexual and reproductive health (UNICEF, 2014). The mortality rate of girls aged 15–20 during pregnancy or childbirth is twice that of women who marry in their twenties.

Child brides are often married to considerably older men, leaving them unable to negotiate safer sex, and therefore more vulnerable to sexually transmitted infections, HIV, early pregnancy, sexual assault, and domestic violence than women who marry later (UNFPA and UNICEF, 2011; UNICEF, 2014). This practice is often driven by poverty or the parents' belief that a married girl is "protected" from harm with a regular male guardian. On a positive note, the practice of child marriage is slowly declining, in particular with regard to girls under age 15 (UNICEF, 2014). Concern about the harmful effects of early marriage extends to the Global North as well. In New York State in the years 2001–2010, 3850 children under 18 were married. In 27 other US states, there is no limit to how young a child can marry if a judge authorizes the marriage. Human rights advocates succeeded in getting the Governor of NY state to sign legislation to limit such marriages (Human Rights Watch, 2017b).

Dowry-related violence is continuous harassment and torture by husbands and in-laws in an effort to extort an increased *dowry*, which are the gifts, money, goods, or property given from the bride's family to the groom or in-laws before, during, or after the marriage. These crimes are most prevalent in South Asian nations. The most common forms of dowry-related violence are battering, marital rape, acid attacks, and wife burning. These attacks often involve violence disguised as suicides or accidents, such as stove or kerosene disasters (stove burnings), to maim or kill women for failing to meet dowry demands (Advocates for Human Rights, n.d.). Acid attacks are another form of violence, usually triggered by refusal of sexual advances or marriage proposals, or failure to pay dowry, or by land disputes. The perpetrators are generally people known to the victim. Such attacks are devastating to women, as they can cause disfigurement and damage to the eyes, and also affect the victim's self-esteem and social and economic well-being. These crimes also take place primarily in South Asian nations (Acid Survivors Foundation, 2016).

Honor crimes encompass a variety of manifestations of violence against women including "honor killings," assault, confinement or imprisonment, and interference with choice in marriage (Welchman & Hossain, 2005). At least 5000 women around the world are murdered by family members yearly (WHO, 2012). The motive of these acts is to eliminate a woman for allegedly having brought shame to or dishonor on the family, thereby restoring the family's honor. Suspicion of adultery, premarital sex, an unsanctioned relationship, being a victim of rape or sexual assault, refusing to enter an arranged marriage, seeking divorce, trying to escape marital violence, and falling in love with someone who is unacceptable to the victim's family are common justifications for these acts (Advocates for Human Rights, 2008). Honor crimes often remain unpunished by the law. Women who have fled their country for fear of hate crimes or honor killings may be eligible for asylum in countries that have ratified the 1951 Refugee Convention (Advocates for Human Rights, 2010).

*Stoning* is a method of execution by which an organized group throws stones or rocks at the person they wish to execute. The practice has grown to be associated with Islam and Muslim culture, although there is no mention of stoning in the Qur'an. Stoning to death is largely carried out, whether by law or by custom, for the crime of "adultery of married persons," but may also be used to punish premarital or homosexual acts (Women Living Under Muslim Laws, 2014). Iran and Somalia have actually conducted stoning as a death penalty in recent years, and stoning continues on the law books in several countries, including Brunei, Iran, Mauritania, Nigeria (in one-third of the country's states), Pakistan, Qatar, Saudi Arabia, Somalia, Sudan, the United Arab Emirates, and Yemen. Stoning may also take place extra-judicially and has occurred in Afghanistan, Iraq, Pakistan, and Mali (Women Living Under Muslim Laws, 2014).

### *Violations of Women's Rights to Sexual and Reproductive Health*

Women also suffer from violations of their rights to sexual and reproductive health and the right to safe and healthy pregnancy. These can result in losses that are traumatic to individuals, children, and the family as a whole. Every day, approximately 830 women die from preventable causes related to pregnancy and childbirth, with 99% of these deaths occurring in the Global South (WHO, 2018). Family planning, skilled attendance at birth, and emergency obstetric and newborn care play a fundamental role in reducing maternal mortality (WHO, 2016). The World Health Organization (2016) reports some positive advances in that maternal mortality dropped by about 44% between 1990 and 2015 worldwide, in part due to the goals of reducing maternal mortality as part of the Millennium Development Goals (MDGs). The United States has the worst maternal mortality rate in the developed world, and the US rate is actually rising (Martin & Montagne, 2017). At 26.4 deaths per 100,000 live births, the US rate is nearly three times that of the UK (9.2 per 100,000), and much higher than the Netherlands, Spain, Australia, Ireland, Italy, Denmark, and others, where the maternal death rate is under 7 deaths per 100,000 live births (GBD 2015 Maternal Mortality Collaborators, 2016).

*Virginity testing*—the forcible examination of the genitalia to look for damage to the hymen—is another violation of women's sexual and reproductive rights. Although it is ineffective as a test for virginity or rape, its use continues in countries including Afghanistan, South Africa, and India (Women and Global Human Rights, n.d.). The government of Turkey was forced to rescind a law that allowed schoolgirls suspected of having premarital sex to be given these tests after they were attributed to suicide attempts by girls forced to undergo them (Women Living Under Muslim Laws, 2004).

Other violations of women's sexual and reproductive rights include both forced abortion and sterilization, as well as the lack of access to abortion services. These violations are often state-sanctioned or conducted where there are weak policies to protect patients' rights (Eggers, 2017; Open Society Foundation, 2011). Forced sterilization has occurred among poor women and members of ethnic and racial minorities in the United States, against Roma women in the Czech Republic, Slovakia and Hungary, indigenous women in Latin America, HIV positive women, and among women with disabilities in many parts of the world (Open Society Foundation, 2011). Since 1979, the Chinese government has been involved in regulating population growth through family planning policies that included the one-child policy. The process of phasing it out began in 2015, but according to Amnesty International (2015), Chinese women remain at risk of intrusive forms of contraception and coerced or forced abortions. Conversely, women are also deprived access to abortion services in countries that criminalize the procedure (e.g., Chile, Ireland) or in nations like the United States where abortion providers face increasing restrictions (Eggers, 2017; Jones & Jerman, 2017).

## WOMEN'S RIGHTS ARE HUMAN RIGHTS

Over the past seventy years, since the initial signing of the UN's UDHR in 1948, the understanding of women's specific vulnerability to human rights violations has grown stronger. Within the UN framework, equality of rights for all people was a basic principle articulated in the UDHR, yet many gaps persisted regarding the protection of women's human rights. Even though the UDHR, the *International Covenant on Civil and Political Rights* (ICCPR; UN, 1966a), and the *International Covenant on Economic, Social and Cultural Rights* (ICESCR; UN, 1966b) specifically ban discrimination based on sex, the human rights legal framework conceptualized human rights in a way that did not fully take account of the gendered violations that routinely affect women in both the domestic and cultural spheres.

Still, ICCPR and ICESCR treaties did specifically attempt to protect women. The ICCPR guarantees the right to life, the right to marry with free and full consent, the right to be of marriageable age, and also asserts equality in marriage. The ICESCR preserves women's right to an adequate standard of living, including the equal rights of women to housing, to work, to just conditions of work, to food, to the highest attainable standard of health, to social security, and to education (ICESCR, 1966b). These rights carry particular significance in the lives of women because they are core issues that underlie women's poverty and inequality, and access to these rights is essential for women's day-to-day survival, economic security, and physical safety (International Network for Economic, Social and Cultural Rights, 2013). Article 12 of the ICESCR carries great significance from a women's rights perspective as it protects "the enjoyment of the highest attainable standard of physical and mental health," and specifically highlights sexual and reproductive health. The ICESCR interprets reproductive health as the freedom to decide if and when to reproduce, the right to be informed, and to have access to safe, effective, affordable, and acceptable methods of family planning of their choice. It also guarantees access to appropriate health-care services that will enable women to safe through pregnancy and childbirth, thereby reducing women's health risks, lowering rates of maternal mortality, and protecting women from domestic violence (Global Initiative for Economic, Social and Cultural Rights, 2016).

Beginning in the 1960s, due to greater awareness of gender oppression as a result of the global women's movement, criticisms emerged that the human rights framework reflected a male bias and therefore perpetuated patriarchal violations of women's human rights (Dauer, 2001). At that time, the human rights framework focused on actions directly attributable to State agents such as torture, killings, and arbitrary detention, while violence and repression committed within the private sphere were not considered as human rights violations (OHCHR, 2014). Within the UN system, there were calls for a new conceptualization of human rights that would require States to protect women from violations committed by third parties, including in the private sphere (OHCHR, 2014).

In 1963, the UN Commission on the Status of Women was asked to draft a declaration combining international standards articulating the equal rights of men and women in a single instrument. This culminated in the Declaration on the Elimination of Discrimination against Women, adopted by the General Assembly in 1967. As a Declaration, it lacked the contractual force of a treaty, but within five years, momentum gathered for the creation of a comprehensive and binding international instrument to eliminate discrimination against women. In 1979, the *Convention on the Elimination of All Forms of Discrimination Against Women* (CEDAW) was adopted by the UN General Assembly and it entered into force in September 1981, bringing to fruition the UN efforts to codify international legal standards for women.

CEDAW (UN, 1979) is the most comprehensive treaty on the rights of women. It guarantees equal political, economic, social, cultural, and civil rights to women. It defines what constitutes discrimination against women and sets up an agenda for action to end such discrimination. The Convention also pays specific attention to particular phenomena (such as trafficking), to certain groups of women (for instance, rural women), and to specific matters where there are special risks to women's full enjoyment of their human rights (e.g., marriage and the family).

CEDAW (UN, 1979) states that there should be equal political, economic, social, cultural, and civil rights for women regardless of their marital status and requires States to enact national legislation banning discrimination. States are obligated to address not only discriminatory laws, but also discriminatory traditional practices and customs, and any discrimination against women by private actors. It obliges States to modify any social or cultural patterns based on the supposed inferiority or superiority of either sex. States are also obliged to take all necessary measures, including legislation, to suppress all forms of trafficking and any other sexual exploitation of women. Sexual harassment is prohibited. Rights related to health care include non-discriminatory health services for women, access to family planning, and the right to a safe and healthy pregnancy. To date, one hundred and eighty-seven member states have ratified the Convention, so it has the second highest ratifications of any human rights treaty after the *Convention on the Rights of the Child* (UN, 1989). Yet, challenges persist that have undermined the strength of the Convention and have demanded ongoing attention.

For example, CEDAW (UN, 1979) calls on States to "abolish existing laws, customs, regulations and practices which are discriminatory against women, and to establish adequate legal protection for equal rights of men and women," yet governments have been allowed to defend discriminatory customs as part of their cultural or national identity. Governments may "enter a reservation," and thereby exempt themselves from a particular element of a treaty, provided that the reservations are not incompatible with the purpose of the Convention. CEDAW is the most heavily reserved treaty in the UN human rights system, and Articles 2, 5, and 16, which call for the modification of discriminatory social and cultural practices (including in matters relating to marriage and family) have the greatest number of reservations lodged (Freeman, 2009).

CEDAW (1979) does not explicitly mention violence against women; rather, violence is addressed under the umbrella of discrimination. Over the years since CEDAW's ratification, there have been increased efforts to direct broader attention to the various forms of violence against women and affirm the universality of women's rights. A number of significant actions occurred in the 1990s. The CEDAW committee General Recommendations (OHCHR, n.d.-a) No. 12 (1989) and No. 19 (1992) provided detailed clarification on how the Convention prohibits violence against women, and also requires appropriate services for victims of violence, including legal protection, shelter, counseling, rehabilitation, and support services. Gender-sensitive training of judiciary and law enforcement is also mandated. Bolstering these recommendations, ICCPR General Comment (OHCHR, n.d.-b) No. 20 (1992) elaborated on the prohibition of torture and recognized that private torture, such as extreme forms of domestic violence, are as acute and harmful as official torture.

Finally, in 1993—45 years after the adoption of the UDHR—women's rights were declared as human rights at the UN World Conference on Human Rights in Vienna. The Vienna Declaration and Program of Action adopted at the conference also emphasized the importance of protecting women from violence. That same year, the UN *Declaration on the Elimination of Violence Against Women* (UN, 1993) proclaimed violence as a critical global human rights violation, confirming the duty of States to extend protection of women from violations committed in the private sphere. The Declaration goes on to define "violence against women" as "any act of gender-based violence that results in, or is likely to result in, physical, sexual or psychological harm or suffering to *women*, including threats of such acts, coercion or arbitrary deprivation of liberty, whether occurring in public or in private life."

This definition is noteworthy in that it recognizes that violence causes harm and/or suffering and detrimental effects on women, physically as well as psychologically; in other words, it is traumatizing. The 1995 Beijing Platform for Action advanced this position further as it identified specific actions for governments to take to prevent and respond to violence against women and girls and expanded the definition of violence to include harmful cultural practices and sexual violence during conflict (UN, 1995). Finally, The Optional Protocol to the Convention on the Elimination of All Forms of Discrimination Against Women (OP-CEDAW) was adopted in 1999. It establishes complaint and inquiry mechanisms for CEDAW, which allow individuals to voice complaints or inquire into "grave or systematic violations" of the Convention. The Protocol has led to a number of decisions against member states on issues such as domestic violence, parental leave, and forced sterilization. It also paved the way for a UN investigation into the systematic killing of women in the Mexican city of Ciudad Juárez (OP-CEDAW, 1999).

## TRAUMA, HUMAN RIGHTS, AND THE GENDERED EFFECTS OF VIOLENCE

As the gendered nature of human rights was being understood and codified, there was a parallel advance in the visibility of the gendered dimensions of trauma. Activists, feminists, and mental health advocates brought women-centered discussions of rape, sexual abuse, and domestic violence into the public arena. The feminist slogan "the personal is political" highlighted that women's experiences of violence were not isolated and individual, but connected to larger social and political structures. Beginning in the mid-1970s, a body of research began to emerge on rape and sexual assault and later domestic violence. Women's activists established programs such as rape crisis centers and shelters for victims of domestic violence. In the course of these efforts, they generated the direct knowledge of women's lived experiences that helped to forge broader definitions of what constitutes trauma. This shift was invaluable for those working with women, as most of the early research on trauma and PTSD focused on males, particularly on their combat experience and war-related trauma (Ringel, 2012). Early studies of women's sexual assault experiences found that rape-exposed women's responses were similar to those experienced by combat-exposed men; this research resulted in the identification of a new trauma-related condition, Rape Trauma Syndrome (Burgess & Holmstrom, 1974). Feminist therapists also contested the original criteria for trauma in the Diagnostic and Statistical Manual of Mental Disorders (DSM). They asserted that traumatic experiences in the lives of women were not "outside the range of usual human experience," as indicated in the DSM–III definition of trauma, but were in fact, so common as to be normative (Brown, 2004).

Judith Herman's work, *Trauma and Recovery* (1992), was groundbreaking on several counts. Herman explicitly included interpersonal violence among traumatic stressors, and insisted that the then-current PTSD diagnosis did not fully capture the severe psychological harm that occurs with prolonged, repeated trauma. She posited a spectrum of traumatic disorders ranging from the effects of a single overwhelming event to the more complex effects of prolonged and repeated abuse. Previously, mental health practitioners had often failed to recognize the impact of trauma in the lives of women, especially in women diagnosed with other mental illnesses, including severe personality disorders (Herman, 1992). Herman and other clinicians recommended that a new diagnostic category of Complex PTSD be established (Courtois, 2004; Herman, 1992; van der Kolk, 1996), although it has yet to be included in the DSM. Complex PTSD is caused by long-term trauma or traumas, where victims are brutalized over multiple events, by multiple perpetrators, or are held in a state of captivity, physically or emotionally. It may be the diagnosis of choice for the impact of severe human rights violations, including long-term domestic violence, captivity in a brothel or prison, and other chronic stressors in which a victim is under the control of the perpetrator and unable to get away from the danger (National Center for PTSD, n.d.).

Herman's (1992) work also and paved the way for research on gender and trauma that enabled a more comprehensive understanding of gendered dimensions of PTSD, especially the heightened vulnerability of women to the diagnosis. Research suggests that women may be more susceptible to PTSD because they are more likely to experience chronic exposure to trauma than men, such as within the context of ongoing marital violence (Kimerling et al., 2013). Other researchers theorize that women's gendered social roles—such as wife, mother, or caretaker—may also compound the negative impact of trauma exposure, as women could experience additional role strain when traumatic experiences or stress reactions interfere with their ability to fulfill these roles (Olff, Langeland, Draijer, & Gersons, 2007).

Finally, Herman's work forges a critical link between trauma, human rights, and women. She draws parallels between child abuse, spousal abuse, and incest—forms of domestic abuse—and rape, torture, war, captivity, and other forms of political terror. This shift moved the discourse away from individualistic perspectives that position the "problem" within the person and places trauma within social, political, historical, and economic contexts.

Trauma and human rights violations are viewed as arising from acts of violence and oppression that have a basis in patriarchy and gender inequality. Here, trauma-informed and rights-based paradigms converge: Recovery does not solely lie with the victims, but requires official accountability and larger systemic change. Services are required for the individual, as well as the society. While mental health practitioners are needed for individuals and families, the international human rights legal system provides an important tool for macro-level change. States and authorities can be held accountable and have a duty to act to protect women from human rights violations. Unifying the concepts of trauma and human rights enables mental health practitioners, activists, and human rights defenders to work as allies, using a common language and framework to protect women from human rights violations and facilitate healing.

## Applying a Trauma-Informed and Human Rights Framework with Women

To conclude this chapter, we discuss the elements of a trauma-informed human rights approach. We provide examples of how professionals and activists have collaboratively used this framework to address personal traumas and assert women's right to dignity in the face of domestic violence.

The experience of domestic violence—including physical, psychological, sexual, and economic abuse—is a traumatic experience that threatens its victims' physical and psychological integrity, and even their lives (Herman, 1992). Though women are at greatest risk, children are also at risk of violence and even homicide in the context of domestic violence (Hamilton, Jaffe, & Campbell, 2013). In the United States, trauma-informed principles increasingly underlie the provision of care (Sullivan, Goodman, Virden, Strom, & Ramirez, 2017), and they are endorsed by prominent mental health bodies to improve agency- and systems-level responses to survivors of domestic and sexual violence (National Center on Domestic Violence, Trauma & Mental Health, 2015; Substance Abuse and Mental Health Services Administration [SAMHSA], 2014). Though research is only beginning to emerge on the effectiveness of trauma-informed models, one study of over 50 women in Ohio showed an association between trauma-informed methods and women's increased self-efficacy and safety-related empowerment (Sullivan et al., 2017). It is especially notable that larger doses of trauma-informed intervention were associated with greater gains in both self-efficacy and empowerment (Sullivan et al., 2017).

To be a trauma-informed practitioner, one must develop an ability to listen for and respond to the impact of violence and victimization in the lives of clients and must apply that understanding to all aspects of the service design and implementation (Butler, Critelli, & Rinfrette, 2011). Further, one must employ the principles of trauma-informed care: safety, trustworthiness, choice, collaboration, empowerment, and attention to cultural, historical, and gender issues (Harris & Fallot, 2001; SAMHSA, 2014). These principles stress the importance of the client being safe, well-informed, in control, and enabled to heal.

Rights-based professional bases one's practice in similar principles. Human rights principles of participation, non-discrimination, and accountability also focus on an individual's rights to self-determination, full information, and ethical professional behavior (Androff, 2015; McPherson, 2015a). Rights-based practitioners' methods reinforce the trauma-informed principle of empowerment by emphasizing capacity-building and using strengths-based methods (McPherson & Abell, 2018). The rights-based framework extends the trauma framework through its focus on changing the world beyond the individual and family. Due diligence, which is a foundational human rights principle, requires proactive measures to prevent violence against women and girls and for governments to provide individuals with access to courts and to adequate and effective remedies when their rights are violated (Amnesty International, 2014). Applying the human rights lens, domestic violence is more than a private family matter; it is a form of systematic violence into which the state has an obligation to intervene—and beyond intervention, it has a duty to change social norms and promote social justice (Hidalgo, 2015). A human rights framework calls for a comprehensive plan to end gender-based violence. To achieve these goals, rights-based professionals must employ additional methods, like interdisciplinary collaboration and activism to bring justice. Rights-based practitioners view their clients' lives through a rights-based lens, and therefore define clients' traumas as potential rights violations; also, they work toward rights-based goals (McPherson, Siebert, & Siebert, 2017). With regard to domestic violence, these would be framed as rights to life and freedom from cruel and degrading treatment, the right to basic needs such as safe shelter, adequate housing, and access to health care, as well as appropriate medical, psychological, legal, and support services to redress the harm and consequences of violence (Amnesty International, 2014). In summary, a combined trauma-informed and rights-based approach is deeply compassionate, avoids victim-blaming, engages the victim in all aspects of treatment and strategy planning, and seeks healing on both personal and societal levels.

### Freedom from Domestic Violence Is a Human Right

The human rights framework has been employed to affirm freedom from domestic violence as a basic human right in many parts of the world. Regional human rights treaties have also been developed that focus specifically on women's rights and have resulted in seminal decisions in cases of violence against women. These include the Protocol to the African Charter on the Rights of Women in Africa, known as the "Maputo Protocol," that addresses issues of particular importance in Africa, such as genital mutilation (African Union, 2003); the Inter-American Convention on the Prevention, Punishment and Eradication of Violence Against Women (Organization of American States, 1994), known as the "Convention of Belém do Pará," that recognizes the rights of women to be free from violence in both the public and private spheres, and the Council of Europe Convention on Preventing and Combating Violence against Women and Domestic Violence known as the "Istanbul Convention" (Council of Europe, 2011). Key legal decisions have been made regarding violence against women in countries such as Brazil, Mexico, Turkey, Croatia, and Austria, to name a few (International Justice Resource Center, n.d.).

Human rights principles are also integrated into programs that assist survivors of violence. For example, in Brazil, social workers, psychologists, and lawyers are collaborating to create a rights-based model of care at the Reference Center for Women from Maré in Rio de Janeiro (Martins Costa, Felix, & Vargas Silva, 2011; McPherson, 2015b). As with similar shelters in the United States, the Reference Center provides a variety of services, including shelter for women and children, assistance with accessing state welfare services, legal assistance, and psychological support. Consistent with the human rights framework, they also provide capacity-building classes that promote economic self-sufficiency, and others that focus on building women's gender- and class-related knowledge in order to promote political and cultural change (Reference Center, n.d.). Women are introduced to national and international human rights conventions, like the Inter-American Convention on the Prevention, Punishment and Eradication of Violence against Women (Organization of American States, 1994), which has been ratified by Brazil and 32 other American countries (though not the United States or Canada). It promises every woman the "free and full exercise of her civil, political, economic, social and cultural rights" (Article 5), as well as the right to be free from violence in both public and private spheres (Article 3; Organization of American States, 1994). Beyond education, the Reference Center holds groups, inspired by Freire's (1984) pedagogy, that promote reflection about gender, class, and race in Brazilian society. For example, within the low-income and low-resource neighborhood where the shelter is located, professionals and women discuss together the ways in which poverty, gender, race, and government neglect have made women vulnerable to violence and other human rights violations (McPherson, 2015b). In all their services, violence against women is presented as a violation of human rights, and the goals of intervention are individual, cultural, and political change (Martins Costa et al., 2011).

The United States is one of a handful of nations that has not ratified CEDAW (UN, 1979), but it has witnessed growing momentum for a human rights approach to violence against women nationally and at the grassroots level (Amnesty International, 2014). In 1998, San Francisco became the first city in the world to adopt an ordinance reflecting the principles of CEDAW and has led other cities to follow suit (San Francisco Department on the Status of Women, n.d.). The human rights framework has also been successfully employed as a pathway toward change through the groundbreaking advocacy of Jessica Lenahan and her legal team. This case, which began with a crime in 1999, has led to an international human rights judgment, as well as a domestic campaign to have "freedom from domestic violence" declared a human right for US women.

To understand these developments, it is important to know the basic facts of Jessica's case. In the summer of 1999, Jessica, a domestic violence survivor living in Castle Rock, CO, had filed for divorce from Simon Gonzales and obtained multiple restraining orders against him protecting herself and her three young daughters. Not long after she obtained her orders, Simon abducted the girls. Jessica immediately called the police, and though she called continually over several hours, her calls for help went unheeded. Nearly 10 hours later, Simon arrived at the police station and opened fire from his truck. Simon was killed in the ensuing firefight, and the dead bodies of Jessica's three girls were found in the truck (Bettinger-Lopez, 2013).

Seeking justice, Jessica Lenahan filed a lawsuit claiming that her restraining orders, coupled with Colorado's mandatory arrest law, had entitled her to a response from the police. The case went all the way to the US Supreme Court, but in 2005, the Court ruled that enforcement of her restraining order was not mandatory (Bettinger-Lopez, 2013). In making their decision, the Supreme Court relied on a previous ruling, *DeShaney v. Winnebago County Department of Social Services* (1989), which declared that the government has no duty to protect individuals from private acts of violence. The Supreme Court's denial of Jessica's rights—and by extension the rights of every other survivor of domestic abuse—prompted a "swift, intense, and united reaction" from domestic violence advocates, women's rights activists, and civil rights lawyers (Bettinger-Lopez, 2013, p. 214). Initially, that reaction was outrage, but also, inaction. As Jessica's lawyer, Caroline Bettinger-Lopez, explains it, at the Supreme Court, "we had reached the end of the line, legally speaking" (Bettinger-Lopez, 2013, p. 215).

But there was one more option: An international human rights tribunal. As Leigh Goodmark (2014) writes, "The movement to apply human rights norms in cases of intimate partner abuse in the United States was sparked by the deaths of the three daughters of Jessica Lenahan" (p. 710). Jessica and her family were not willing to give up after the Supreme Court's decision, and with the support of their legal team, they petitioned the Inter-American Commission on Human Rights (IACHR), claiming that the United States government was responsible for human rights violations that Jessica and her daughters had experienced (Bettinger-Lopez, 2013). In August 2011, the IACHR issued a landmark decision finding that the United States had violated Jessica's family's rights to life, non-discrimination, and judicial protection, and that all of this was in violation of the American Declaration on the Rights and Duties of Man (Organization of American States, 1948). Thus, though no US Court has acknowledged wrongdoing, an international court called attention to the systematic discrimination that women experience when seeking redress for private violence, and emphasized the disproportionate impact of this discrimination on low-income and minority women; finally, the IACHR recognized the "governmental duty to protect and prevent private acts of violence" (Bettinger-Lopez, 2013, p. 223). The IACHR further called on the United States to provide retribution to the Lenahan family, and recommended that the United States adopt procedures, training, and legislation to improve the enforcement of domestic violence concerns. Though these recommendations are unenforceable, in the wake of the IACHR decision, the Department of Justice voluntarily began to work toward improved policing (Bettinger-Lopez, 2013).

This case has energized the US movement to legally recast domestic violence as a human rights issue. Between 2011 and May 2017, 31 US counties, towns, and municipal governments—including Miami, Chicago, Seattle, Dallas, and Washington, DC—have passed local resolutions that recognize freedom from domestic violence as a human right (Cornell Law School, 2017a). Though these resolutions differ between localities, Albany, NY, Baltimore, MD, and Chicago, IL all state that government has a responsibility to secure women's right to be free from domestic violence; in Florida, Miami, and Jacksonville specifically note that government has a moral responsibility to do so, and the resolutions commonly declare that state and local governments should secure the right for all (Cornell Law School, 2017b). This movement is ongoing and new ordinances are being written all over the country.

In conclusion, as Bettinger-Lopez (2013) writes, "By framing domestic violence as a human rights violation, the *Lenahan* decision challenges advocates and policymakers to rethink the United States' approach to domestic violence, and to ask whether fundamental rights are being respected, protected, and fulfilled" (p. 228). Indeed, this is the challenge we are all left with: To engage with our own work in ways that focus on women's traumatic experiences as human rights violations, and thereby allow us to respond in ways that enhance the gender equity within our societies, reduce all women's vulnerability to violence, and improve access to human rights for all.

## REFERENCES

Acid Survivors Foundation. (2016). *Acid violence*. Retrieved from http://www.acidsurvivors.org/Acid-Violence.

Advocates for Human Rights. (2008). *Crimes committed in the name of "honor"*. Retrieved from http://www.stopvaw.org/honor_killings.

Advocates for Human Rights. (2010). *Gender-based asylum*. Retrieved from http://www.stopvaw.org/gender-based_asylum.

Advocates for Human Rights. (n.d.). *Dowry-related violence*. Retrieved from http://www.stopvaw.org/dowry-related_violence.

African Union. (2003, July 11). *Protocol to the African charter on human and people's rights on the rights of women in Africa.* Retrieved from http://www. achpr.org/instruments/women-protocol/.

Amnesty International. (2004). *It's in our hands—Stop violence against women.* https://www.amnesty.ie/wp-content/uploads/2016/05/Its-in-our-Hands.pdf.

Amnesty International. (2014). *Domestic violence & sexual assault in the United States: A human rights based approach & practice guide.* Retrieved from http://www.law.columbia.edu/sites/default/files/microsites/human-rights-institute/files/dv_sa_hr_guide_reduce.pdf.

Amnesty International. (2015). *China: Reform of one-child policy not enough.* Retrieved from https://www.amnesty.org/en/latest/news/2015/10/china-one-child-reform/.

Androff, D. K. (2015). *Practicing rights: Human rights-based approaches to social work practice.* New York, NY: Routledge.

Bettinger-Lopez, C. (2013). Introduction: Jessica Lenahan (Gonzales) v. United States of America: Implementation, litigation, and mobilization strategies. *Journal of Gender, Social Policy & the Law, 21,* 207–229.

Brown, L. (2004). Feminist paradigms of trauma treatment. *Psychotherapy Theory Research & Practice, 41*(4), 464–471.

Burgess, A. W., & Holstrom, L. L. (1974). Rape trauma syndrome. *American Journal of Psychiatry, 131*(9), 981–986.

Butler, L. D., Critelli, F. M., & Rinfrette, E. S. (2011). Trauma-informed care and mental health. *Directions in Psychiatry, 31*(3), 197–209.

Cornell Law School. (2017a). *Freedom from domestic violence as a fundamental human right resolutions, presidential proclamations, and other statements of principle.* Retrieved from http://www.lawschool.cornell.edu/womenandjustice/DV-Resolutions.cfm.

Cornell Law School. (2017b). *Discussion of resolutions by county, town, and municipal governments.* Retrieved from http://www.lawschool.cornell.edu/womenandjustice/Resolutions-by-County-Town-and-Municipal-Governments.cfm.

Council of Europe. (2011, May 11). *Council of Europe Convention on preventing and combating violence against women and domestic violence.* Retrieved from https://rm.coe.int/168008482e.

Courtois, C. A. (2004). Complex trauma, complex reactions: Assessment and treatment. *Psychotherapy: Theory, Research, Practice, Training, 41*(4), 412–425.

Dauer, S. (2001). Indivisible or invisible: Women's human rights in the public and private sphere. In M. Agosín (Ed.), *Women, gender, and human rights: A global perspective.* Piscataway, NJ: Rutgers University Press.

Deshpande, N., & Nawal, N. (2013). Sex trafficking of women and girls. *Reviews in Obstetrics and Gynecology, 6*(1), 22–27.

Eggers, M. (2017). The criminalization of women for abortion in Chile. In S. Choudhury, J. Erausquin, & M. Withers (Eds.), *Global perspectives on women's sexual and reproductive health across the lifecourse* (pp. 173–188). New York, NY: Springer.

Freeman, M. (2009). *Reservations to CEDAW: An analysis for UNICEF.* Retrieved from https://www.unicef.org/gender/files/Reservations_to_CEDAW-an_ Analysis_for_UNICEF.pdf.

Freire, P. (1984). *Pedagogy of the oppressed.* New York, NY: Continuum.

GBD 2015 Maternal Mortality Collaborators. (2016). Global, regional, and national levels of maternal mortality, 1990–2015: A systematic analysis for the Global Burden of Disease Study 2015. *Lancet, 388,* 1775–1812. Downloaded from www.thelancet.com/pdfs/journals/lancet/PIIS0140-6736(16)31470-2.pdf.

Global Alliance Against Traffic in Women. (n.d.). *Debt bondage in the world: An underestimated and forgotten scourge.* Retrieved from https://www.gaatw. org/162-materials/advocacy-statements-2009-10/589-debt-bondage-in-the-world-an-underestimated-and-forgotten-scourge.

Global Initiative for Economic, Social and Cultural Rights. (2016). *The International Covenant on Economic, Social and Cultural Rights at 50: The significance from a women's rights perspective.* Retrieved from http://globalini-tiative-escr.org/wp-content/uploads/2016/10/ICESCR-and-Womens-ESC-Rights-FINAL.pdf.

Goodmark, L. (2014). "Law and justice are not always the same": Creating community-based justice forums for people subjected to intimate partner abuse. *Florida State University Law Review, 42,* 707–763.

Hamilton, L. H. A., Jaffe, P. G., & Campbell, M. (2013). Assessing children's risk for homicide in the context of domestic violence. *Journal of Family Violence, 28*(2), 179–189. https://doi.org/10.1007/s10896-012-9473-x.

Harris, M., & Fallot, R. D. (2001). Envisioning a trauma informed service system: A vital paradigm shift. In M. Harris & R. D. Fallot (Eds.), *Using trauma theory to design service systems* (pp. 3–22). San Francisco, CA: Jossey Bass.

Herman, J. L. (1992). *Trauma and recovery: The aftermath of violence—From domestic abuse to political terror.* New York, NY: Basic Books.

Hidalgo, R. (2015). Advancing a human rights framework to reimagine the movement to end gender violence. *University of Miami Race & Social Justice Law Review, 5*(2), 559–578.

Human Rights Watch. (2000). *International trafficking of women and children.* Retrieved from https://www.hrw.org/news/2000/02/21/international-trafficking-women-and-children.

Human Rights Watch. (2017a). *"All of my body was pain": Sexual violence against Rohingya women and girls in Burma.* Retrieved from https://www.hrw.org/report/2017/11/16/all-my-body-was-pain/ sexual-violence-against-rohingya-women-and-girls-burma.

Human Rights Watch. (2017b). *US: New York governor signs anti-child marriage law: One of first states to act; others should follow.* Retrieved from https://www.hrw.org/news/2017/06/20/us-new-york-governor-signs-anti-child-marriage-law.

International Justice Resource Center. (n.d.). *Women's human rights.* Retrieved from http://www.ijrcenter.org/thematic-research-guides/womens-human-rights/.

International Network for Economic, Social and Cultural Rights (ESCR-Net). (2013). *Claiming women's economic, social and cultural rights: A resource guide to advancing women's economic, social and cultural rights.* Retrieved from https://www.escr-net.org/sites/default/files/Guide%20on%20Women%27s%20ESCR%20-%20Final.pdf.

Jones, R. K., & Jerman, J. (2017). Abortion incidence and service availability in the United States, 2014. *Perspectives on Sexual and Reproductive Health, 49,* 17–27. Downloaded from https://www.guttmacher.org/sites/default/files/article_files/abortion-incidence-us.pdf.

Kimerling, R., Weitlauf, J. C., Iverson, K. M., Karpenko, J. A., & Jain, S. (2013). Gender issues in PTSD. In M. J. Friedman, T. M. Keane, & P. A. Resick (Eds.), *Handbook of PTSD: Science and practice* (pp. 313–330). New York, NY: Guilford Press.

Krupa, M. (2017, July 14). The alarming rise of female genital mutilation in America. *CNN.* Retrieved from http://www.cnn.com/2017/05/11/health/female-genital-mutilation-fgm-explainer-trnd/index.html.

Martin, N., & Montagne, R. (2017, May 12). US has the worst rate of maternal deaths in the developed world. *NPR.* Retrieved from https://www.npr.org/2017/05/12/528098789/u-s-has-the-worst-rate-of-maternal-deaths-in-the-developed-world.

Martins Costa, A. L., Felix, A., & Vargas Silva, C. (2011). *O imperativo da interdisciplinaridade na busca da humanização dos direitos* [The importance of an interdisciplinary approach to humanize human rights]. Paper presented at the Second International Colloquium on Human Rights, Faculty of Law, Federal University of Rio de Janeiro, Rio de Janeiro, Brazil.

McPherson, J. (2015a). *Human rights practice in social work: A rights-based framework & two new measures* (Doctoral dissertation). Retrieved from ProQuest Dissertations and Theses (Accession Order No. AAT 3705877).

McPherson, J. (2015b). Human rights practice in social work: A US social worker looks to Brazil for leadership. *European Journal of Social Work, 18,* 599–612. https://doi.org/10.1080/13691457.2014.947245.

McPherson, J., & Abell, N. (2018). *Measuring rights-based practice: Introducing the human rights methods in social work scale.* Manuscript submitted for publication.

McPherson, J., Siebert, C. F., & Siebert, D. C. (2017). Measuring rights-based perspectives: A validation of the human rights lens in social work scale.

*Journal of the Society for Social Work Research, 8*(2), 233–257. https://doi. org/10.1086/692017.

National Center for PTSD. (n.d.). *Complex PTSD.* Retrieved from https://www. ptsd.va.gov/professional/treat/essentials/complex_ptsd.asp.

National Center on Domestic Violence, Trauma & Mental Health. (2015). *Promising practices and model programs: Trauma-informed approaches to working with survivors of domestic and sexual violence and other trauma.* Retrieved from http://www.nationalcenterdvtraumamh.org/publications-products/ promising-practices-and-model-programs/.

Office of the High Commissioner on Human Rights. (2014). *Women's rights are human rights.* Retrieved from http://www.ohchr.org/Documents/Events/ WHRD/WomenRightsAreHR.pdf.

Office of the High Commissioner on Human Rights. (n.d.-a). *Committee on the elimination of discrimination against women: General recommendations.* Retrieved from https://www.ohchr.org/EN/HRBodies/CEDAW/Pages/ Recommendations.aspx.

Office of the High Commissioner on Human Rights. (n.d.-b). *Human rights treaty bodies—General comments: CCPR.* Retrieved from https://www.ohchr. org/EN/HRBodies/Pages/TBGeneralComments.aspx.

Olff, M., Langeland, W., Draijer, N., & Gersons, B. P. R. (2007). Gender differences in posttraumatic stress disorder. *Psychological Bulletin, 133,* 183–204.

Open Society Foundation. (2011). *Against her will: Forced and coerced sterilization of women worldwide.* Retrieved from https://www.opensocietyfounda- tions.org/sites/default/files/against-her-will-20111003.pdf.

Organization of American States. (1948). *American declaration of the rights and duties of man.* Retrieved from https://www.cidh.oas.org/basicos/english/ basic2.american%20declaration.htm.

Organization of American States. (1994). *Inter-American convention on the pre- vention, punishment and eradication of violence against women ('Convention of Belem do Para').* Retrieved from http://www.oas.org/juridico/english/trea- ties/a-61.html.

Reference Center for Women from Maré. (n.d.). Retrieved from http://www. nepp-dh.ufrj.br/crmm/ingles/apresentacao.html.

Ringel, S. (2012). Overview. In S. S. Ringel & J. R. Brandell (Eds.), *Trauma: Contemporary directions in theory, practice, and research* (pp. 1–12). New York, NY: Sage.

San Francisco Department on the Status of Women. (n.d.). *Implementing CEDAW as a local ordinance.* Retrieved from https://sfgov.org/dosw/sites/ default/files/Cities%20for%20CEDAW%20Fact%20Sheet_0.pdf.

Substance Abuse and Mental Health Services Administration. (2014). *Trauma- informed care in behavioral health services: Treatment improvement protocol (TIP) Series 57* (HHS Publication No. [SMA] 13-4801). Rockville, MD:

Substance Abuse and Mental Health Services Administration. Retrieved from https://store.samhsa.gov/product/TIP-57-Trauma-Informed-Care-in-Behavioral-Health-Services/SMA14-4816.

Sullivan, C. M., Goodman, L. A., Virden, T., Strom, J., & Ramirez, R. (2017). Evaluation of the effects of receiving trauma-informed practices on domestic violence shelter residents. *American Journal of Orthopsychiatry, 88*(5), 563. https://doi.org/10.1037/ort0000286.

Tolin, D. F., & Foa, E. B. (2006). Sex differences in trauma and posttraumatic stress disorder: A quantitative review of 25 years of research. *Psychological Bulletin, 132,* 959–992.

UNFPA and UNICEF. (2011). *Women's & children's rights: Making the connection.* Retrieved from https://www.unfpa.org/sites/default/files/pub-pdf/Women-Children_final.pdf.

UNICEF. (2014). *Ending child marriage: Progress and prospects.* Retrieved from https://www.unicef.org/media/files/Child_Marriage_Report_7_17_LR.. pdf.

UNICEF. (2016). *Female genital mutilation/cutting: A global concern.* Retrieved from https://www.unicef.org/media/files/FGMC_2016_brochure_final_UNICEF_SPREAD.pdf.

United Nations. (1948). *Universal Declaration of Human Rights.* Retrieved from http://www.un.org/en/universal-declaration-human-rights/.

United Nations. (1966a). *International Covenant on Civil and Political Rights.* Retrieved from http://www.ohchr.org/EN/ProfessionalInterest/Pages/CCPR.aspx.

United Nations. (1966b). *International Covenant on Economic, Social and Cultural Rights.* Retrieved from http://www.ohchr.org/EN/ProfessionalInterest/Pages/CESCR.aspx.

United Nations. (1979). *Convention on the Elimination of All Forms of Discrimination Against Women.* Retrieved from http://www.un.org/women-watch/daw/cedaw/text/econvention.htm#article6.

United Nations. (1989). *Convention on the Rights of the Child.* Retrieved from https://www.ohchr.org/en/professionalinterest/pages/crc.aspx.

United Nations. (1993). *Declaration on the Elimination of Violence Against Women.* Retrieved from http://www.un.org/documents/ga/res/48/a48r104.htm.

United Nations. (1995, October 27). *Beijing Declaration and Platform of Action, Adopted at the Fourth World Conference on Women.* Retrieved from http://www.un.org/womenwatch/daw/beijing/pdf/BDPfA%20E.pdf.

United Nations. (1999). *Optional Protocol to the Convention on the Elimination of All Forms of Discrimination Against Women.* Retrieved from http://www.un.org/womenwatch/daw/cedaw/protocol/.

United Nations. (2006, July 6). *In-depth study on all forms of violence against women: Report of the Secretary-General, A/61/122/Add.1.* Retrieved from http://www.un.org/womenwatch/daw/vaw/SGstudyvaw.htm#more.

United Nations. (2014). *Background information on sexual violence used as a tool of war.* Retrieved from http://iknowpolitics.org/en/knowledge-library/report-white-paper/background-information-sexual-violence-used-tool-war-r wanda.

United Nations. (2017). *Report of the Secretary-General on conflict-related sexual violence.* Retrieved from http://www.undocs.org/S/2017/249.

United Nations Commission on Human Rights. (1999). *Report of the Special Rapporteur on violence against women, its causes and consequences.* Retrieved from https://documents-dds-ny.un.org/doc/UNDOC/GEN/G99/103/26/PDF/G9910326.pdf?OpenElement.

United Nations Commission on Human Rights. (2003). *Report of the special rapporteur on violence against women, its causes and consequences.* Retrieved from https://digitallibrary.un.org/record/489001.

United Nations Department for Economic and Social Affairs. (2009). *The millennium development goals report 2009.* Retrieved from http://www.un.org/en/development/desa/publications/millennium-development-goals-report-2009.html.

United Nations Office on Drugs and Crime. (2017). *Human trafficking.* Retrieved from https://www.unodc.org/unodc/en/human-trafficking/what-is-human-trafficking.html.

van der Kolk, B. A. (1996). The complexity of adaptation to trauma: Self-regulation, stimulus discrimination, and characterological development. In B. A. van der Kolk, A. McFarlane, & L. Weisaeth (Eds.), *Traumatic stress* (pp. 182–213). New York, NY: Guilford Press.

Welchman, L., & Hossain, S. (2005). *"Honour" crimes, paradigms, and violence against women.* New York, NY: Zed Books.

Wilson, B., Critelli, F. M., & Rittner, B. (2015). Transnational responses to commercial sexual exploitation: A comprehensive review of interventions. *Women's Studies International Forum, 48,* 71–80.

Women and Global Human Rights. (n.d.). *Virginity testing.* Retrieved from http://faculty.webster.edu/woolflm/wandghrwebpage.html.

World Health Organization. (2012). *Understanding and addressing violence against women: Femicide.* Retrieved from https://apps.who.int/iris/bitstream/handle/10665/77421/WHO_RHR_12.38_eng.pdf;jsessionid=2B553EB4BAF740B9EDB256A25154A8FB?sequence=1.

World Health Organization. (2013). *Global and regional estimates of violence against women: Prevalence and health effects of intimate partner violence and nonpartner sexual violence.* Retrieved from https://www.who.int/reproductivehealth/publications/violence/9789241564625/en/.

World Health Organization. (2016). *Maternal mortality.* Retrieved from http://www.who.int/mediacentre/factsheets/fs348/en/.
World Health Organization. (2017). *Female genital mutilation fact sheet.* Retrieved from http://www.who.int/mediacentre/factsheets/fs241/en/.
World Health Organization. (2018). *Maternal mortality.* Retrieved from https://www.who.int/news-room/fact-sheets/detail/maternal-mortality.
Women Living Under Muslim Laws. (2004). *Turkey moves to ban virginity tests.* Retrieved from http://www.wluml.org/node/1556.
Women Living Under Muslim Laws. (2014). *Stoning: Legal or practised in 16 countries and showing no signs of abating: WLUML's submission to the UN Secretary General on the question of the death penalty to the 27th session of the Human Rights Council.* Retrieved from http://www.wluml.org/sites/wluml.org/files/WLUML%20Submission%20on%20the%20Question%20of%20the%20Death%20Penalty%20HRC%2030%2003%2014.pdf.

CHAPTER 8

# The Lives of Lesbian, Gay, Bisexual, and Transgender People: A Trauma-Informed and Human Rights Perspective

*Diane E. Elze*

Since the 1969 Stonewall Rebellion, lesbian, gay, bisexual, transgender, queer/questioning (LGBTQ) Americans have witnessed remarkable gains in social acceptance and legal protections (e.g., same-sex marriage, the decriminalization of same-sex sexual behavior, and state- and local-level LGBT non-discrimination laws). LGBTQ youths, their families, and LGBTQ activists have advanced LGBTQ youths' rights to safety and equitable, appropriate treatment in public service sector systems through litigation, advocacy, and education.

Although the country has advanced well beyond its former practices of routinely imprisoning and/or executing gender-variant and same-sex-loving people, labeling them as mentally ill, and subjecting them to castration, hypothalamotomy, hormone injections, clitoridectomy, hysterectomy, or ovariectomy to change their orientation and behavior (Silverstein, 1991), discrimination, violence, and other human

D. E. Elze (✉)
School of Social Work, University at Buffalo, Buffalo, NY, USA
e-mail: deelze@buffalo.edu

© The Author(s) 2019
L. D. Butler et al. (eds.), *Trauma and Human Rights*,
https://doi.org/10.1007/978-3-030-16395-2_8

rights violations persist. The 45th Administration in Washington and Republican-controlled state legislatures across the country are designing new, emerging attacks on LGBTQ human rights (Movement Advancement Project [MAP], 2017).

During the first five months of 2017, state legislators introduced over 100 anti-LGBT bills in 20 states (Miller, 2017). Within the first month post-inauguration, the 45th Administration rescinded joint guidance from the US Departments of Education and Justice that directed educational institutions to include gender identity within Title IX sex discrimination protections, an action criticized by the Organization of American States' Inter-American Commission on Human Rights (IACHR, 2017). The Administration has tried multiple times to ban transgender people from military service (Bebinger, 2018). Early in 2018, the Administration announced the creation of the Conscience and Religious Freedom Division within the US Department of Health and Human Services to protect health professionals when they refuse to care for patients based on their own religious or moral beliefs (Cha & Eilperin, 2018).

This chapter discusses human rights violations against LGBTQ people in the USA, primarily, and reviews research on adverse childhood experiences and minority stressors (e.g., stigma, discrimination) affecting LGBTQ adults and youth. The chapter highlights advances in LGBTQ inclusion on the United Nations' (UN) human rights agenda and historic achievements of the international LGBTQ movement in securing recognition of LGBTQ rights as human rights. An integration of LGBTQ-affirmative practice with trauma-informed (TI) service delivery principles provides guidance for professional practice with LGBTQ populations.

## LGBTI Human Rights Organizations and Terminology

Although many international, regional, and national organizations advocate globally for lesbian, gay, bisexual, transgender, and intersex (LGBTI) human rights, this chapter frequently refers to the International Lesbian, Gay, Bisexual, Trans, and Intersex Association (ILGA) and ARC International (ARC), as they spearhead much of the international LGBTI advocacy. ILGA, founded in 1978, is a global federation of over 1200 member organizations across Asia, Europe, Latin

America and the Caribbean, North America, Oceania, and Pan Africa (Karsay, Dos Santos, & Mosquera, 2016). ARC International, founded in 2003, and ILGA directly advocate with UN Member States and human rights mechanisms and facilitate Civil Society Organizations' (CSOs) engagement with UN and other international human rights structures (Karsay et al., 2016). ILGA and ARC International utilize definitions of sexual orientation and gender identity found in the Yogyakarta Principles, which specify states' obligations to ensure human rights for people of diverse sexual orientations, gender identities, and sex characteristics (Alston et al., 2017).

*Sexual orientation* refers to an individual's "capacity for profound emotional, affectional and sexual attraction to, and intimate and sexual relations with, individuals of a different gender or the same gender or more than one gender" (Karsay et al., 2016, p. 15). *Gender identity* is a person's "deeply felt internal and individual experience of gender, which may or may not correspond with the sex assigned at birth," and incorporates one's "personal sense of the body" and "other expressions of gender, including dress, speech and mannerisms" (Karsay et al., 2016, p. 14). The definition recognizes that people may or may not choose to modify their body through medical and other procedures.

*Transgender* is "an umbrella term for people whose gender identity and/or gender expression differs from what is typically associated with the sex assigned to them at birth" (Karsay et al., 2016, p. 15). *Intersex* people are "born with physical sex characteristics that do not fit medical norms for female or male bodies" (Karsay et al., 2016, p. 14). *Sex characteristics* refer to "each person's physical features related to sex, including genitalia and other sexual and reproductive anatomy, chromosomes, hormones, and secondary physical features emerging from puberty" (Alston et al., 2017, p. 6). *Gender expression* is newly defined as each individual's presentation of their gender "through physical appearance including dress, hairstyles, accessories, cosmetics—and mannerisms, speech, behavioral patterns, names and personal references" (Alston et al., 2017, p. 6).

The UN and the LGBTI international human rights organizations utilize the phrases and acronyms "sexual orientation, gender identity, gender expression, and sex characteristics" (SOGIESC); "sexual orientation, gender identity, and intersex" (SOGII); and "lesbian, gay, bisexual, transgender, and intersex" (LGBTI). Derivatives of these acronyms are also used (i.e., LGBT, SOGI, and SOGIE) when human rights issues related to intersex and sex characteristics are excluded from consideration (Carroll & Mendos, 2017). In this chapter, "LGBTQI2-S" (i.e., lesbian, gay, bisexual, transgender, queer, intersex, two-spirit), "LGBTQ" (i.e., queer and questioning), "LGB" and "LGBT" are used when research, policies, and practices apply to those populations. *Two-spirit* is a contested term used by some American Indian/Alaska Native people who are "not male and not female" or as an umbrella term for LGBT or "alternatively gendered" and Native (Bearse, 2012, p. 91).

## INTERSECTIONALITY AND LGBTI HUMAN RIGHTS

An intersectional lens is critical to understanding LGBTI people's vulnerability and experiences with traumatic events and state-sponsored/state-sanctioned human rights violations in the USA. An intersectional analysis recognizes that systems of oppression based on race, class, gender, and other social identities intersect to produce different patterns of intragroup oppression, "the complexities of compoundedness" (Crenshaw, 1989, p. 166). The Sexual Rights Initiative (SRI), another international human rights coalition, called for an intersectional analysis in global LGBTI advocacy and policy development. The SRI asserted that SOGIE-based human rights violations do not affect LGBTI people equally, that LGBTI peoples' multiple, intersecting identities uniquely shape their experiences with systems of oppression, violence, and discrimination. LGBTI people's vulnerability to human rights violations and traumatic events varies based on their multiple, intersecting identities, including race, class, gender identity, gender expression, national origin, disability status, age, and geographic location (Carroll & Itaborahy, 2015).

US LGBTQ adults and youth of color, for example, experience disproportionate contact with law enforcement, and abusive, discriminatory treatment by police and within criminal justice systems, and asylum and detention facilities (Center for American Progress [CAP] & MAP, 2016). LGBTQ Americans continue to face discrimination in education, employment, housing, and health care, with LGBTQ people of color at greatest risk (Human Rights Campaign [HRC], 2018; Human Rights Watch, 2016; Palmer, Greytak, & Kosciw, 2016).

## WHAT ARE LGBTI HUMAN RIGHTS?

LGBTI activists, human rights organizations, and CSOs have utilized the UN's major human rights monitoring mechanisms, under the auspices of the Human Rights Council, to advocate for LGBTI inclusion: the Universal Periodic Review (UPR); the Special Procedures; and the Complaint Procedure (ARC International, 2015; Karsay et al., 2016). The Special Procedures include the special rapporteurs, independent experts, special representatives, and working groups charged with human rights investigations and reports (ARC International, 2015).

After decades of activism, LGBTI activists and CSOs dedicated to LGBTI human rights achieved, on June 30, 2016, a historic UN Human Rights Council resolution, which established an Independent Expert on the protection against violence and discrimination based on sexual orientation and gender identity (Karsay et al., 2016). Members of the Group of African States and the Organization of Islamic Cooperation (OIC), which had long-opposed efforts to promote SOGIESC human rights at the UN, organized multiple unsuccessful attempts to block the mandate during General Assembly processes. Sadly, opposing states vocalized their intentions to not cooperate, recognize, nor engage with the Independent Expert (ARC & ILGA, 2016).

Every SOGIESC-related human rights victory with UN bodies has required overcoming the historical inertia of UN entities on SOGIESC human rights issues and strong, hostile opposition from some of its 193 Member States (Karsay et al., 2016). Not until 2011 did the Human Rights Council adopt its first SOGI-specific resolution, which called for the Office of the High Commissioner for Human Rights (OHCHR) to document worldwide SOGI-related discriminatory laws, practices, and violence (Karsay et al., 2016). Several States walked out of a panel discussion on SOGI-related violence and discrimination convened the following year by the Human Rights Council, the first time a UN body formally debated SOGI issues (OHCHR, 2017). Perceiving a slowdown in progress, ILGA delivered a joint civil society statement, signed by over 500 CSOs from over 100 countries, challenging the Council to fulfill its responsibility to address systemic human rights violations against LGBTI people (ILGA et al., 2014). A second Human Rights Council resolution followed which requested an update from the OHCHR on SOGI-related violence and discrimination (Karsay et al., 2016).

The OHCHR (2017) has identified States' core legal obligations to protect the human rights of LGBTI persons: (a) protect them from bias-motivated violence; (b) prevent torture and cruel, inhumane, and degrading treatment; (c) decriminalize homosexuality; (d) prohibit SOGI-related discrimination in employment, health care, and access to services; and (e) respect freedom of association, expression, and peaceful assembly. Twelve UN entities, in 2015, issued a precedent-setting joint statement calling upon Member States to "urgently" end violence and discrimination against LGBTI adults, adolescents, and children, and the OHCHR organized the first UN meeting devoted to intersex human rights (OHCHR, 2017).

## The Yogyakarta Principles

The Yogyakarta Principles, developed in 2006 and expanded in 2017 by international panels of human rights experts, apply the rights embodied in international human rights law to people of diverse sexual orientations, gender identities, gender expressions, and sex characteristics (Alston et al., 2017). An intersectional lens is reflected in the Yogyakarta Principles' recognition that SOGIESC-related discrimination may be compounded by discrimination and persecution based on many other social categories (e.g., race, ethnicity, disability, marital or family status, class, HIV status, language, religion, political orientation, migration status, national origin) (Alston et al., 2017).

The Yogyakarta Principles specifically assert LGBTI individuals' rights to equality and non-discrimination in public and private spheres; freedom of opinion and expression, including gender expression through dress, speech, and other means; and privacy, which necessitates that states end the criminalization of same-sex sexual activities between persons over the age of consent. Freedom of opinion and expression includes freedom of peaceful assembly and association and guaranteed access to SOGIE-related information and ideas, including relevant safer sex information, and the dissemination of affirmative and accurate SOGIESC-related information in educational programs.

The principles affirm rights to an adequate standard of living (e.g., food, clothing, shelter, housing, social security, and social insurance) without SOGI-related discrimination; safe and healthy work conditions;

equal access to employment and unemployment benefits, health insurance, parental leave, and other family benefits. LGBTI people have rights to education, including higher education that is equally accessible, and to the enjoyment of the highest attainable standard of physical and mental health. States are obligated to protect families, recognize the diversity of family structures without subjecting them to SOGI-based discrimination, ensure non-discrimination toward all children for reasons related to their parentage, and safeguard access to adoption and assisted procreation, including alternative insemination.

The principles assert LGBTI individuals' rights to change state-issued gendered identity documents. The principles call for simple, accessible mechanisms to change names, and an end to sex/gender markers on identity documents (e.g., birth certificates, passports, driver licenses). Whenever sex/gender markers are used, states must not require surgical and other medical procedures, or psychological and diagnostic conditions to change sex/gender markers, as such conditions violate the human rights to self-determination, and bodily and mental integrity (Alston et al., 2017).

The principles affirm LGBTI individuals' rights to life, liberty, and security of person, free from violence, harassment, and degrading treatment or punishment. States must take measures to prevent hate violence, vigorously investigate incidents, prosecute the perpetrators, and conduct public awareness campaigns aimed at eliminating SOGIE-related prejudice that underlies hate violence. The principles call for the repeal of laws criminalizing sex work, abortion, and unintentional HIV transmission, and the enactment of measures to hold police accountable for violence, abuse, and intimidation based on people's SOGIESC. The right to humane treatment while incarcerated obligates states to provide adequate physical and mental health care, including gender-affirming interventions; protect LGBT people from rape and sexual assault; and avoid subjecting LGBT people to solitary confinement.

To safeguard children's self-determination and bodily and mental integrity, states must protect them from coercive, involuntary, and irreversible modification of their sex characteristics, such as with disorders of sexual development, without children's full, free, and informed consent. States must also prohibit medical and psychological interventions that pathologize and claim to change SOGI diversity (Alston et al., 2017).

## GLOBAL TRENDS IN HUMAN RIGHTS AND VIOLATIONS

Since 2006, ILGA has annually summarized Member States' laws that promote or violate SO-related human rights (Carroll & Mendos, 2017) and recently began mapping laws and administrative procedures governing transgender people (Chiam, Duffy, & Gil, 2016). Global trends are toward decriminalization of same-sex sexual activities, protection from discrimination and hate crimes, and recognition of LGB relationships and families (Carroll & Mendos, 2017).

However, state-sponsored and state-sanctioned human rights violations toward LGBTI people persist, including the criminalization of same-sex sexual acts between consenting adults, with eight nations allowing the death penalty; prohibitions on public promotion or expression of SOGIE issues; and barriers to the founding and/or recognition of SOGIE-related CSOs. Nearly, all nations allow conversion therapies, employment discrimination, and prohibit same-sex marriage. Hate-motivated violence against LGBTI people by police officers, other State officials, extremist organizations, and other non-State actors is pervasive globally, with many States failing to investigate and prosecute these crimes (Carroll & Mendos, 2017).

## LGBTI HUMAN RIGHTS VIOLATIONS IN THE USA

Neither the US government nor public discourse typically view the persecution of LGBTI people as human rights issues. Historically hostile toward the idea that economic and social policies and practices are human rights issues (Reichert, 2007), the USA never ratified the International Covenant on Economic, Social and Cultural Rights (ICESCR) (UN, 1966). However, the rights embodied in the ICESCR, essential to the well-being of all residents of the USA, are found in the Universal Declaration of Human Rights (UN, 1948), which the USA did ratify. Little chance exists for human rights advances at the federal level given the 45th Administration's contempt for the UN (Landler, 2017) and its determination to diminish human rights for the American people (Alston, 2017), particularly for LGBT people (Caspani, 2018; MAP, 2017).

### Poverty

The UN Special Rapporteur on extreme poverty and human rights toured areas in the USA in 2017, as part of the UN Human Rights

Council's accountability mechanisms that apply to all Member States. In his final report, Dr. Philip Alston remarked that the USA is "alone among developed countries in insisting that while human rights are of fundamental importance, they do not include rights that guard against dying of hunger, dying from a lack of access to affordable healthcare, or growing up in a context of total deprivation" (Alston, 2017, para. 8). Alston projected that the Republicans' tax reform package and promised cuts to welfare programs will further exacerbate the country's inequality levels that already dwarf those of other countries, as the US endeavors "to become the most unequal society in the world" (para. 2).

Research with US LGBT populations points to their heightened vulnerability to poverty, particularly for LGBT people of color, although poverty rates have increased for many US residents. LGBT Americans are more likely to live in poverty than are heterosexual/cisgender Americans, particularly LGBT females and people of color (CAP & MAP, 2014). Of the 27,715 participants in a national transgender survey, 29% reported living in poverty, 15% lacked employment, and 30% experienced homelessness in the previous year. Transgender people of color reported higher poverty and unemployment rates compared to white transgender people. Over one-third (38%) of African-Americans lived in poverty; 41% of American Indians; 40% of multiracial persons, and 43% of Latinos/Latinas. Nearly 25% of transgender people of color lacked employment, compared to 12% of whites (James et al., 2016).

### Health Care Access

The Affordable Care Act (ACA) prohibited LGBT- and HIV-related discrimination in the health insurance marketplaces, health plans offering essential benefits, and health programs and providers receiving federal funds (Kates, Ranji, Beamesderfer, Salganicoff, & Dawson, 2017). However, only 13 states and the District of Columbia ban insurance exclusions for transgender health care (HRC, 2018). Although the ACA and the legalization of same-sex marriage helped many LGBT people acquire health insurance (Kates et al., 2017), 15% of LGBT Americans still lacked insurance in 2017, compared to 7% of their heterosexual/cisgender counterparts; 25% of transgender people were uninsured, compared to 8% of cisgender people (Baker & Durso, 2017). LGBT people, especially transgender people of color, continue to report disturbing incidents of mistreatment, humiliation, and discrimination from health care providers, which dissuade them from seeking needed care (Mirza &

Rooney, 2018). Republican attacks on the ACA, Medicaid, and Planned Parenthood disproportionately threaten health care access for women, particularly low-income women, women of color, and LGBT individuals (MAP, 2017).

### State-Sanctioned/State-Sponsored Discrimination

Basic civil rights protections for US LGBT people and their families vary widely among and within the states. Of the estimated 9.5 million LGBT adults residing in the USA, approximately 52% live in states that permit SOGI-based discrimination, which are states in which African-American LGBT individuals more highly concentrated (Hasenbush, Flores, Kastanis, Sears, & Gates, 2014). Although same-sex couples can now marry across the USA, they risk losing their jobs if they do. No federal laws ban SOGI-based discrimination in employment, housing, and public accommodations (Carroll & Mendos, 2017).

Only 21 states and the District of Columbia prohibit SOGI-based employment and housing discrimination (HRC, 2018), and only 19 states and the District of Columbia prohibit SOGI-based discrimination in public accommodations (HRC, 2018). In 2016, state legislatures considered over 30 bills attacking transgender access to public accommodations (Singh & Durso, 2017). Research with a national representative sample of LGBT people found that, during 2016, up to 28% of LGB workers and 27% of transgender workers reported some form of employment discrimination. A quarter of transgender respondents reported avoiding stores and restaurants, 11% avoided public transportation, 12% avoided getting needed services, and 27% deliberated carefully on where to shop (Singh & Durso, 2017). Nearly one-third (30%) of the participants in the national transgender survey reported experiences with GI/GE-based employment discrimination, promotion denials, firings, workplace verbal harassment and physical assault, and interference with their use of sanitation facilities (James et al., 2016).

During the US's Second Universal Periodic Review, the UN Working Group urged the USA to strengthen its efforts to eradicate SOGII-related discrimination and to prohibit SOGI-related discrimination based on religious beliefs (UN, 2015). Unfortunately, the 45th Administration is seeking to legalize SOGI-related discrimination through the US Supreme Court, executive orders, federal guidance and regulations, and religious exemption laws. Religious exemptions laws permit private businesses, social service agencies, federal contractors, and/or government agencies to deny services to LGBT people for religious reasons. Such laws exist in Kansas, Mississippi, South Dakota, and Texas (MAP, 2017). Illinois, Tennessee, Mississippi, and Alabama allow health professionals to deny medical treatment to LGBT people (MAP, Public Rights/Private Conscience Project, & SAGE, 2017).

### School-Based Discrimination

Alabama, Arizona, Louisiana, Mississippi, Oklahoma, South Carolina, and Texas restrict school-based discussions of LGBT issues via laws that malign SOGI-diverse people (i.e., "No Promo Homo" laws). Alabama and Texas' laws, for example, declare that "homosexual conduct is a criminal offense" under state law (despite the Supreme Court decision overturning sodomy laws) and that homosexuality is not "a lifestyle acceptable to the general public" (Human Rights Watch, 2016, p. 12). Such laws create hostile environments for LGBT youth and prevent them from accessing accurate HIV- and sexuality-related information. During 2016, legislators in nearly 20 states introduced bills to limit transgender students' access to school bathrooms congruent with their gender identity (Human Rights Watch, 2016). LGB youth, particularly girls, disproportionately endure police stops, school expulsions, juvenile arrests and convictions, and adult convictions, despite no higher rates of misbehavior compared to their heterosexual peers (Himmelstein & Bruckner, 2011). With school-based zero-tolerance policies, school officials disproportionately levy punitive sanctions against LGBT youth, particularly youth of color, for minor infractions (Palmer et al., 2016).

### Sexual Orientation Change Efforts

Sexual orientation change efforts (SOCE) refer to discredited methods (e.g., behavioral and psychoanalytic therapies; medical, religious, and spiritual approaches) used by mental health professionals, self-help groups, religious ministries, and other non-professionals aimed at changing a person's sexual orientation. These practices, sometimes called "conversion" or "reparative" therapy, are grounded in the assumption that homosexuality is a mental illness, maladaptive, or a developmental or spiritual failing. No research demonstrates the efficacy or effectiveness of using SOCE to alter sexual orientation (Drescher et al., 2016). The Pan American Health Organization (PAHO) denounced SOCE, deeming them unethical and unjustifiable for causing harm, lacking in scientific evidence and medical justification, and violating human rights (PAHO/WHO, 2012). All major health and mental health professional associations have issued position statements against these practices (Drescher et al., 2016).

Young people subjected to SOGE have reported their experiences on social media (Shear, 2015), before policy makers (Margolin, 2014), and in lawsuits (Stern, 2015). LGBTI youth advocates have challenged, locally to globally, SOCE that target LGBTI adolescents, developing and lobbying for state and federal legislation banning these practices. Only 10 states and the District of Columbia ban mental health professionals from using conversion therapy with minors (HRC, 2018). The UN Committee against Torture (CAT) raised serious concerns with the US State Department about the use of conversion therapy with LGBT youth, upon hearing testimonies from LGBTI activists and survivors of conversion therapy at its meeting in Geneva (Margolin, 2014). This marked the first time in history that the Committee against Torture, a UN Treaty Body, addressed conversion therapy as a global human rights issue under the Convention against Torture and other Cruel, Inhuman or Degrading Treatment or Punishment, although other Treaty Bodies had previously addressed the issue (Kirichenko, 2017).

### Surgical Procedures on Intersex Children

Surgical interventions to alter genitalia are still performed on US children with atypical sex characteristics, despite recommendations to delay such procedures until children can actively participate in the decision-making process (Human Rights Watch & InterACT-Advocates for Intersex Youth, 2017). Massachusetts-based interACT (Advocates for Intersex Youth), which promotes intersex human rights internationally, submitted a report to CAT documenting the use of premature surgery and other medical treatments on US intersex children; CAT requested a response from the US government, asking for the number of children subjected to such surgeries (UN CAT, 2017).

### Hate Violence

To fulfill their obligations to protect LGBTI people from violence, States should specify SOGI as protected characteristics in hate crime laws

(OHCHR, 2017). However, only 30 states and the District of Columbia include sexual orientation in hate crime laws, of which 18 also include gender identity (HRC, 2018). Hate violence against LGBTQ and HIV-affected people in the USA appears to be increasing, with people of color, transgender and gender non-conforming (TGNC) people at greatest risk (National Coalition of Anti-violence Programs [NCAVP], 2017). NCAVP, which annually publishes hate violence incidents reported to its member programs, recorded 36 hate-motivated homicides of LGBTQ and HIV-affected people by August 23, 2017, a 29% increase from 2016; 75% of the victims were people of color (NCAVP, 2017). The national transgender survey found that sexual and physical violence and verbal abuse against TGNC people are pervasive, with violence beginning early in life, occurring in multiple settings and across a lifetime, with revictimization common (James et al., 2016). Undocumented TGNC people are at high risk for violence; 24% of undocumented respondents in the national survey reported physical assaults (James et al., 2016).

### Persecution Within Criminal Justice, Asylum, and Immigration Systems

Discrimination, harassment, and abuse of LGBT and HIV-affected people by US law enforcement officials are widespread, particularly against LGBT people of color (James et al., 2016; Lambda Legal, 2015). Mistreatment takes the form of profiling LGBT youth and adults as criminals; physical and sexual assaults; verbal harassment and abuse; arbitrary searches; entrapment; criminalizing people living with HIV; and unjustified arrests (Lambda Legal, 2015). Over 30 states have laws that target consensual sex, impose harsher penalties on persons living with HIV, and reflect ignorance about HIV transmission (Lambda Legal, 2015). Findings from the national transgender survey revealed that more than half (58%) of the respondents that had interacted with police reported mistreatment (e.g., physical or sexual assault, verbal harassment) (James et al., 2016). NCAVP (2017) found that 41% of the 1036 LGBT hate crime survivors interacted with law enforcement, of which approximately one-third found police indifferent or hostile. Black survivors were nearly three times more likely to experience excessive force than were other survivors (NCAVP, 2017).

Within prisons and immigration detention facilities, LGBT people are disproportionately subjected to rape, sexual harassment, other assaults by staff and inmates, and solitary confinement and, if transgender, denied medically necessary health care and housed, dangerously, according to their sex assigned at birth (Lambda Legal, 2015). Prior to the US's sixth periodic review before CAT, the Treaty Body asked the USA for clarification on the care of transgender detainees, including use of solitary confinement and sexual assaults within detention facilites (UN CAT, 2017). Serious deficiencies exist with the Prison Rape Elimination Act's implementation, including lack of full state compliance, corrections industry resistance, lack of vigorous promotion by the USDOJ and inconsequential penalties for noncompliance (Sontag, 2015). Recently, the US Bureau of Prisons rescinded prior protections for transgender inmates and declared its intent to house transgender inmates according to their sex assigned at birth, elevating their risk for rape and other assaults (Caspani, 2018).

### Barriers to Changing Sex/Gender Markers

US states vary widely on criteria for changing sex/gender markers on birth certificates, driver licenses, and other documents. Approximately 22 states in the USA require proof of sex reassignment surgery (SRS) to change birth certificates, and 13 states require such proof to modify driver licenses. Tennessee (legally) and Idaho (procedurally) forbid correction of a birth certificate for transgender people and require SRS to change a driver license, while California, in contrast, requires a licensed physician's statement attesting that the individual has undergone clinically appropriate treatment for gender transitioning. Most states allow modifications of driver licenses without SRS, but with Social Security Administration-approved name changes, documents from medical professionals, and court orders (Chiam et al., 2016). However, under the Yogyakarta Principles, these barriers constitute human rights violations (Alston et al., 2017).

## ADVERSE CHILDHOOD EXPERIENCES, STRUCTURAL STIGMA, MINORITY STRESS, AND ASSOCIATED HEALTH OUTCOMES

LGBT populations experience adverse childhood experiences (ACEs) at rates that exceed those of their heterosexual/cisgender counterparts (Andersen & Blosnich, 2013; Hughto, Reisner, & Pachankis, 2015). Multiple studies with LGB populations reveal higher rates of childhood sexual abuse, parental physical and emotional abuse, and peer victimization, compared to heterosexuals (Friedman et al., 2011), with childhood abuse and other forms of interpersonal trauma accounting for disparities in PTSD (Roberts, Austin, Corliss, Vandermorris, & Koenen, 2010; Roberts, Rosario, Corliss, Koenen, & Austin, 2012). Among veterans, LB women report higher rates of trauma across the life span than do their heterosexual peers (Lehavot & Simpson, 2014). Higher ACE scores among LGB people have been associated with adverse health outcomes and health disparities (Austin, Herrick, & Proescholdbell, 2016; McLaughlin, Hatzenbuehler, Xuan, & Conron, 2012).

LGBT youth consistently report greater exposure to family, school, and community violence, compared to their heterosexual/cisgender peers (Eisenberg et al., 2017; Mitchell, Ybarra, & Korchmaros, 2014). LGBTQ adolescents have reported high rates of diverse forms of victimization, with 41% reporting polyvictimization (Sterzing et al., 2017). Although evidence exists that victimization decreases for many LGBT youths as they enter early adulthood, the cumulative victimization experienced by some youths has deleterious effects on their mental health (Mustanski, Andrews, & Puckett, 2016).

Structural stigma (Hatzenbuehler et al., 2014) and the minority stress model (Brooks, 1981; Meyer, 2003, 2016) provide two frameworks for conceptualizing the associations between structural inequalities, minority stressors, and adverse health outcomes among LGBT people. Research with LGBT adults and youth points to the role of *structural stigma* (i.e., anti-LGBT laws, policies, and cultural norms) in explaining adverse health outcomes and health disparities (Hughto et al., 2015). For example, LGB adults living in highly prejudicial communities suffer from elevated suicide, homicide, and cardiovascular death rates (Hatzenbuehler et al., 2014). Transgender veterans living in states without SOGI-inclusive employment non-discrimination laws are at higher risk for mood disorders (Blosnich et al., 2016). LGB youths' risk for adverse health outcomes increases when they reside in neighborhoods with higher rates of anti-LGBT hate crimes, and in counties with fewer school districts with SOGI-inclusive anti-bullying policies (Hatzenbuehler & Pachankis, 2016).

The *minority stress model* (MSM) has informed nearly four decades of research on LGB health and health disparities (Brooks, 1981; Meyer, 2016), and, more recently, emerging research on the well-being of TGNC populations (Testa et al., 2017). The MSM and the *Gender Minority*

*Stress and Resilience* (GMSR) *model* posit that the chronic psychosocial stress related to anti-LGBT prejudice, discrimination, and stigmatization could explain the higher prevalence of physical and mental health problems among LGBT populations. The models distinguish between distal or external stressors (i.e., actual experiences of discrimination, violence, rejection, and identity non-affirmation by individuals, institutions, and communities), and internal or proximal stressors (i.e., expectations of rejection and discrimination, identity concealment or non-disclosure, chronic vigilance, and internalized homophobia/transphobia) (Meyer, 2003; Testa, Harbarth, Peta, Balsam, & Bockting, 2015).

Extant research has shown relationships between minority stressors and a diverse array of adverse physical and mental health outcomes in LGB (Baams, Grossman, & Russell, 2015; Goldbach, Tanner-Smith, Bagwell, & Dunlap, 2014; Lick, Durso, & Johnson, 2013), and TGNC people (Bariola et al., 2015; Bockting, Miner, Romine, Hamilton, & Coleman, 2013; Gonzalez, Gallego, & Bockting, 2017; Testa et al., 2017). Researchers have investigated the role of protective factors in mitigating poor health outcomes associated with minority stressors (Goldbach & Gibbs, 2017; Hoy-Ellis et al., 2017) and the role of psychological processes (Hatzenbuehler, 2009) and other risk factors in mediating relationships between stressors and outcomes (Mereish, Goldbach, Burgess, & DiBello, 2017). The GMSR model explicitly incorporates resilience factors (i.e., community connectedness and pride) that may attenuate the impact of stressors on TGNC individuals' well-being (Testa et al., 2015).

## THE RESILIENCE OF LGBTQ POPULATIONS

LGBTQ people exhibit tremendous *resilience* in the face of oppression, if resilience means successful, adaptive functioning when confronted with adversity (Meyer, 2015). LGBTQ people have faced decades of oppression with increased visibility and political activism; the creation of diverse family constellations and affirming community organizations; the proliferation of local to global advocacy organizations; and public/private celebratory events. Researchers have noted the importance of individual- and community-based resilience factors in mitigating minority stressors among LGBT populations (Breslow et al., 2015; Meyer, 2015).

## LGBTQ-AFFIRMATIVE PRACTICE AND TRAUMA-INFORMED SERVICE DELIVERY

The Substance Abuse and Mental Health Services Administration (SAMHSA) has long recognized the trauma and health disparities affecting LGBT populations and has engaged with LGBT communities to addresses their behavioral health care needs since the early 1990s (Craft & Mulvey, 2001; SAMHSA, 2014a). SAMHSA has collaborated with other entities to enhance policy and service delivery to LGBTQI2-S youth and their families in systems of care and to disseminate LGBTQI2-S-affirmative practice guidelines (Fisher, Poirier, & Blau, 2012). Best practice guidelines, training curricula, standards for care, and model policies exist to guide delivery of culturally sensitive services to LGBTQI2-S youth in diverse service settings and systems (Fisher et al., 2012; Hadland, Yehia, & Makadon, 2016; Poirier, 2015).

LGBTQ-affirmative practice and TI service delivery share some underlying principles that inform both the delivery of care and organizational transformation (Mallon, 2009; SAMHSA, 2014b). However, TI service delivery requires LGBTQ-affirmative practice. Services that are not LGBTQ-affirmative are inherently not trauma-informed. Just as TI services recognize the potential for any client to possess a trauma history, LGBTQ-affirmative services understand that any client could identify as LGBTQ. Whenever individual providers and service delivery systems assume that clients are heterosexual and/or cisgender, the principles of TI service delivery are immediately lacking for LGBTQ clients. Both TI- and LGBTQ-affirmative practices demand that providers take a stance of curiosity, asking, "What happened to this person?," rather than "What is wrong with this person?" (American Psychological Association [APA], 2012, 2015; SAMHSA, 2014b).

Guidelines for LGBTQ-affirmative service delivery have evolved over decades of scholarship and practice by researchers and clinicians in the health and mental health professions (APA, 2012, 2015; Chang & Singh, 2016). LGBTQ-affirmative guidelines essentially provide a map for executing TI principles with LGBTQ people. LGBTQ-affirmative services recognize that LGBTQ clients may possess trauma histories similar to those of heterosexual/cisgender people. They also recognize that LGBTQ clients may come with histories of bias-motivated traumatic experiences, which have far-reaching impact on LGBTQ individuals, their families, and their communities (APA, 2012, 2015; SAMHSA, 2014b). LGBT-affirmative providers, however, understand that LGBT clients may seek services for problems unrelated to their sexual orientation and/or gender identity (APA, 2012, 2015).

LGBTQ-affirmative practitioners understand the distinctions between gender identity, gender expression, and sexual orientation and interrogate their own biases, beliefs, values, and attitudes about SOGIE diversity. They affirm and value clients' diverse sexual orientations, gender identities, and preferred pronouns; recognize that same-gender desire, romantic and sexual attractions, and behaviors are normal, positive variations of human sexuality; and understand that heterosexist oppression is the problem, not sexual orientation or gender identity per se. They possess accurate knowledge about the diversity of LGBTQ people and their life experiences, including identity development trajectories; relationships with friends, families of origin and families of choice; romantic and/or sexual partners; and unique challenges and risks they face over the life span (APA, 2012, 2015).

LGBTQ-affirmative practitioners are knowledgeable about the societal manifestations of heterosexism and intersecting systems of oppressions, and their potential impact on LGBTQ people's development, life options, access to resources, and physical, emotional, social, and spiritual well-being. They possess knowledge about the pervasiveness of violence, harassment, discriminatory laws and policies, and other traumas and human rights violations affecting LGBTQ people (e.g., APA, 2012, 2015; Chang & Singh, 2016; Singh & dickey, 2016), and they advocate on behalf of clients (APA, 2012; Singh & dickey, 2016). As they practice, they obtain LGBTQ-knowledgeable supervision and consultation and address insensitive organizational climates and discriminatory policies, procedures, and practices (APA, 2012, 2015).

Organizational transformation toward becoming LGBTQ-affirmative and TI requires administrative support and investment; policies and procedures that reflect LGBTQ-affirmative and TI principles; changes in the physical environment to promote safety and inclusion; engagement with LGBTQ service recipients, trauma survivors, and family members in implementing the principles; and asserting LGBTQ-affirmative and TI principles in cross-sector collaborations (Mallon, 2009; SAMHSA, 2014b). LGBTQ-TI affirmative services screen, assess, and treat clients utilizing culturally appropriate, evidence-based, or evidence-informed instruments and interventions, particularly those that have shown efficacy or effectiveness with LGBTQ populations (APA, 2012, 2015).

SAMHSA and its collaborators developed ten standards of care, congruent with principles underlying TI-organizational transformation, to guide agencies and systems in evaluating policies and procedures for LGBTQI2-S cultural and linguistic sensitivity across youth-serving systems (Fisher et al., 2012).

## CONCLUSION

When this chapter was readied to go to press, the USA was in the throes of a partial government shutdown that was imposed by the 45th Administration in late December, demanding billions of dollars from Congress for a border wall. Following its first submission date, the US Senate confirmed an anti-reproductive freedom, anti-regulatory, pro-corporate, anti-worker individual to the US Supreme Court, amid sexual assault allegations, with a documented "stunningly expansive view of presidential power and impunity" (The Editorial Board, 2018), as an unindicted co-conspirator sits in the White House. Additionally, November midterm elections returned control of the House of Representatives to the Democrats, sending an unprecedented number of women, African-American, and Latino/a citizens to Congress, among them the first two Muslim women (i.e., a Somali-American and a Palestinian-American) and the first two Native American women, one of whom is a lesbian (Newberger, 2019). Within the first week of the new year, the US House of Representatives adopted a rules package protecting LGBTQ congressional employees from discrimination (Clymer, 2019), and the newly-elected governors of Wisconsin (Metzger, 2019a) and Michigan (Metzger, 2019b) signed executive orders protecting LGBTQ state employees from discrimination. However, state policies profoundly impact people's daily lives, and Republicans still hold the majority of governorships. Just before the new year, Governor Kasich (R-Ohio) signed legislation banning the most common method of abortion used in the second trimester of pregnancy (i.e., dilation and evacuation), with no exceptions for pregnancies resulting from rape or incest (Rosenberg, 2018). We can expect the 45th Administration and some of the states to continue their wars on people of color, women, LGBTQ communities, immigrants and refugees, and people who are poor. LGBTQ people, our families, our advocacy organizations are resilient. LGBTQ people will continue to fight for LGBTQ human rights and populate the ranks of the resistance across all social justice issues. There is no conclusion.

## REFERENCES

Alston, P. A. (2017, December 15). *Statement on visit to the USA, by Professor Philip Alston, United Nations Special Rapporteur on extreme poverty and human rights*. Retrieved from http://www.ohchr.org/EN/NewsEvents/Pages/DisplayNews.aspx?NewsID=22533.

Alston, P., Brands, I. K., Brown, D., Grinspan, M. C., Cameron, E., Carpenter, M., ... Zieselman, K. (2017). *The Yogyakarta Principles plus 10: Additional principles and state obligations on the application of international human rights law in relation to sexual orientation, gender identity, gender expression and sex characteristics to complement the Yogyakarta Principles*. Retrieved from http://yogyakartaprinciples.org/wp-content/uploads/2017/11/A5_yogy-akartaWEB-2.pdf.

American Psychological Association. (2012). Guidelines for psychological practice with lesbian, gay, and bisexual clients. *American Psychologist, 67*(1), 10–42. https://doi.org/10.1037/a0024659.

American Psychological Association. (2015). Guidelines for psychological practice with transgender and gender nonconforming people. *American Psychologist, 70*(9), 832–864. http://dx.doi.org/10.1037/a0039906.

Andersen, J. P., & Blosnich, J. (2013). Disparities in adverse childhood experiences among sexual minority and heterosexual adults: Results from a multi-state probability-based sample. *PLoS One, 8*(1), e54691. https://doi.org/10.1371/journal.pone.0054691.

ARC International. (2015). *The U.N. Special Procedures: A guide for advocates working on human rights relating to sexual orientation and gender identity*. Retrieved from http://arc-international.net/wp-content/uploads/2011/08/ARC-Special-Procedures-Guide-2015.pdf.

ARC International & International Lesbian, Gay, Bisexual, Trans and Intersex Association. (2016). *Compilation of the adoption of the 2016 SLGI resolution*. Retrieved from https://ilga.org/compilation-adoption-2016-sogi-resolution.

Austin, A., Herrick, H., & Proescholdbell, S. (2016). Adverse childhood experiences related to poor adult health among lesbian, gay, and bisexual individuals. *American Journal of Public Health, 106*, 314–320. https://doi.org/10.2105/AJPH.2015.302904.

Baams, L., Grossman, A. H., & Russell, S. T. (2015). Minority stress and mechanisms of risk for depression and suicidal ideation among lesbian, gay, and bisexual youth. *Developmental Psychology, 51*(5), 688–696. https://doi.org/10.1037/a0038994.

Baker, K., & Durso, L. E. (2017, March 22). *Why repealing the Affordable Care Act is bad medicine for LGBT communities*. Center for American Progress. Retrieved from https://www.americanprogress.org/issues/lgbt/news/2017/03/22/428970/repealing-affordable-care-act-bad-medicine-lgbt-communities/.

Bariola, E., Lyons, A., Leonard, W., Pitts, M., Badcock, P., & Couch, M. (2015). Demographic and psychosocial factors associated with psychological distress and resilience among transgender individuals. *American Journal of Public Health, 105,* 2108–2116. https://doi.org/10.2105/AJPH.2015.302763.

Bearse, M. L. (2012). Becoming who we are meant to be: Native Americans with two-spirit LGBT, and/or related tribal identities. In S. K. Fisher, J. M. Poirier, & G. M. Blau (Eds.), *Improving emotional and behavioral outcomes for LGBT youth: A guide for professionals* (pp. 87–109). Baltimore, MD: Paul H. Brooks Publishing.

Bebinger, M. (2018, March 24). *Trump swaps complete ban for 'qualified ban' on transgender military service.* National Public Radio. Retrieved from https://www.npr.org/2018/03/24/596656712/trump-swaps-complete-ban-for-qualified-ban-on-transgender-military-service.

Blosnich, J. R., Marsiglio, M. C., Gao, S., Gordon, A. J., Shipherd, J. C., Kauth, M., ... Fine, M. J. (2016). Mental health of transgender veterans in US States with and without discrimination and hate crime legal protection. *American Journal of Public Health, 106,* 534–540. https://doi.org/10.2105/ajph.2015.302981.

Bockting, W. O., Miner, M. H., Romine, R. E. S., Hamilton, A., & Coleman, E. (2013). Stigma, mental health, and resilience in an online sample of the US transgender population. *American Journal of Public Health, 103*(5), 943–951. https://doi.org/10.2105/AJPH.2013.301241.

Breslow, A. S., Brewster, M. E., Velez, B. L., Wong, S., Geiger, E., & Soderstrom, B. (2015). Resilience and collective action: Exploring buffers against minority stress for transgender individuals. *Psychology of Sexual Orientation and Gender Diversity, 2*(3), 253–265. https://doi.org/10.1037/sgd0000117.

Brooks, V. R. (1981). *Minority stress and lesbian women.* Lexington, MA: Lexington Books.

Carroll, A., & Itaborahy, L. P. (2015). *State-sponsored homophobia: A world survey of laws—Criminalization, protection and recognition of same-sex love* (10th ed.). Retrieved from http://ilga.org/downloads/ILGA_State_Sponsored_Homophobia_2015.pdf.

Carroll, A., & Mendos, L. R. (2017). *State-sponsored homophobia: A world survey of sexual orientation laws—Criminalization, protection and recognition* (12th ed.). Retrieved from http://ilga.org/downloads/2017/ILGA_State_Sponsored_Homophobia_2017_WEB.pdf.

Caspani, M. (2018, May 12). U.S. rolls back protections for transgender prison inmates. *U.S. News & World Report.* Retrieved from https://www.usnews.com/news/top-news/articles/2018-05-12/us-rolls-back-protections-for-transgender-prison-inmates.

Center for American Progress & Movement Advancement Project. (2014). *Paying an unfair price: The financial penalty for being LGBT in America.* Retrieved from http://www.lgbtmap.org/file/paying-an-unfair-price-full-report.pdf.

Center for American Progress & Movement Advancement Project. (2016). *Unjust: How the broken criminal justice system fails LGBT people of color.* Retrieved from http://www.lgbtmap.org/criminal-justice-poc.

Cha, A. E., & Eilperin, J. (2018, January 18). New HHS civil rights division charged with protecting health care workers with moral objections. *The Washington Post.* Retrieved from https://www.washingtonpost.com/news/to-your-health/wp/2018/01/18/new-hhs-civil-rights-division-charged-with-protecting-health-workers-with-moral-objections/?utm_term=.05e9da15172a.

Chang, S. C., & Singh, A. A. (2016). Affirming psychological practice with transgender and gender nonconforming people of color. *Psychology of Sexual Orientation and Gender Diversity, 3*(2), 140–147. https://doi.org/10.1037/sgd0000153.

Chiam, Z., Duffy, S., & Gil, M. G. (2016, November). *Trans legal mapping report: Recognition before the law* (1st ed.). Retrieved from http://ilga.org/downloads/TLMR_ENG.pdf.

Clymer, C. (2019, January 4). *Historic: House rules package includes gender identity & sexual orientation protections.* Human Rights Campaign. Retrieved from https://www.hrc.org/blog/house-rules-package-includes-SOGI-protections.

Craft, E. M., & Mulvey, K. P. (2001). Addressing lesbian, gay, bisexual, and transgender issues from the inside: One federal agency's approach. *American Journal of Public Health, 91*(6), 889–891.

Crenshaw, K. (1989). De-marginalizing the intersection of race and sex: A black feminist critique of antidiscrimination doctrine, feminist theory and antiracist politics. *University of Chicago Legal Forum, 1*(8), 139–167.

Drescher, J., Schwartz, A., Casoy, F., McIntosh, C. A., Hurley, B., Ashley, K., … Tompkins, D. A. (2016). The growing regulation of conversion therapy. *Journal of Medical Regulation, 102*(2), 7–12.

Eisenberg, M. E., Gower, M. L., McMorris, B. J., Rider, G. N., Shea, G., & Coleman, E. (2017). Risk and protective factors in the lives of transgender/gender nonconforming adolescents. *Journal of Adolescent Health, 61*(4), 521–526. https://doi.org/10.1016/j.jadohealth.2017.04.014.

Fisher, S. K., Poirier, J. M., & Blau, G. M. (Eds.). (2012). *Improving emotional & behavioral outcomes for LGBT youth: A guide for professionals.* Baltimore, MD: Paul H. Brookes Publishing.

Friedman, M. S., Marshal, M. P., Guadamuz, T. E., Wei, C., Wong, C. F., Saewyc, E. M., & Stall, R. (2011). A meta-analysis of disparities in childhood sexual abuse, parental physical abuse, and peer victimization among sexual minority and sexual nonminority individuals. *American Journal of Public Health, 101*, 1481–1494. https://doi.org/10.2105/AJPH.2009.190009.

Goldbach, J. T., & Gibbs, J. J. (2017). A developmentally informed adaptation of minority stress for sexual minority adolescents. *Journal of Adolescence, 55*, 36–50. https://doi.org/10.1016/j.adolescence.2016.12.007.

Goldbach, J. T., Tanner-Smith, E. E., Bagwell, M., & Dunlap, S. (2014). Minority stress and substance use in sexual minority adolescents: A meta-analysis. *Prevention Science, 15*, 350–363. https://doi.org/10.1007/s11121-013-0393-7.

Gonzalez, C. A., Gallego, J. D., & Bockting, W. O. (2017). Demographic characteristics, components of sexuality and gender, and minority stress and their associations to excessive alcohol, cannabis, and illicit (non-cannabis) drug use among a large sample of transgender people in the United States. *Journal of Primary Prevention, 38*(4), 419–445. https://doi.org/10.1007/s10935-017-0469-4.

Hadland, S. E., Yehia, B. R., & Makadon, H. J. (2016). Caring for lesbian, gay, bisexual, transgender, and questioning youth in inclusive and affirmative environments. *Pediatric Clinics of North America, 63*, 955–969. https://doi.org/10.1016/j.pcl.2016.07.001.

Hasenbush, A., Flores, A. R., Kastanis, A., Sears, B., & Gates, G. J. (2014). *The LGBT divide: A data portrait of LGBT people in the Midwestern, Mountain, & Southern states.* Los Angeles, CA: The Williams Institute, UCLA School of Law. Retrieved from https://williamsinstitute.law.ucla.edu/wp-content/uploads/LGBT-divide-Dec-2014.pdf.

Hatzenbuehler, M. L. (2009). How does sexual minority stigma "get under the skin"? A psychological mediation framework. *Psychological Bulletin, 135*(5), 707–730. https://doi.org/10.1037/a0016441.

Hatzenbuehler, M. L., Bellatorre, A., Lee, Y., Finch, B. K., Muennig, P., & Fiscella, K. (2014). Structural stigma and all-cause mortality in sexual minority populations. *Social Science and Medicine, 103*, 33–41. https://doi.org/10.1016/j.socscimed.2013.06.005.

Hatzenbuehler, M. L., & Pachankis, J. E. (2016). Stigma and minority stress as social determinants of health among lesbian, gay, bisexual, and transgender youth: Research evidence and clinical implications. *Pediatric Clinics of North America, 63*, 985–997. https://doi.org/10.1016/j.pcl.2016.07.003.

Himmelstein, K. E. W., & Brückner, H. (2011). Criminal justice and school sanctions against nonheterosexual youth: A national longitudinal study. *Pediatrics, 127*(1), 49–57. https://doi.org/10.1542/peds.2009-2306.

Hoy-Ellis, C. P., Shiu, C., Sullivan, K. M., Kim, H. J., Sturges, A. M., & Fredriksen-Goldsen, K. I. (2017). Prior military service, identity stigma, and mental health among transgender older adults. *Gerontologist, 57*(S1), S63–S71. https://doi.org/10.1093/geront/gnw173.

Hughto, J. M. W., Reisner, S. L., & Pachankis, J. E. (2015). Transgender stigma and health: A critical review of stigma determinants, mechanisms, and interventions. *Social Science and Medicine, 147,* 222–231. https://doi. org/10.1016/j.socscimed.2015.11.010.

Human Rights Campaign. (2018). *State Maps of Laws & Policies.* Retrieved from https://www.hrc.org/state-maps.

Human Rights Watch. (2016). *"Like walking through a hailstorm": Discrimination against LGBT youth in US schools.* Retrieved from https:// www.hrw.org/sites/default/files/report_pdf/uslgbt1216web_2.pdf.

Human Rights Watch, & InterACT-Advocates for Intersex Youth. (2017). *I want to be the way nature made me: Unnecessary surgeries on intersex children in the US.* Retrieved from https://www.hrw.org/sites/default/files/report_ pdf/lgbtintersex0717_web_0.pdf.

Inter-American Commission on Human Rights. (2017, March 15). *IACHR expresses concern over setbacks in federal protections for trans and gender non-conforming students in the United States.* Organization of American States. Retrieved from http://www.oas.org/en/iachr/media_center/pre-leases/2017/033.asp.

International Lesbian, Gay, Bisexual, Trans and Intersex Association, et al. (2014, June 24). *NGO joint statement—Item 8 general debate, 26th session of the Human Rights Council.* ARC International. Retrieved from http://arc-international.net/wp-content/uploads/2014/06/NGO-Joint-statement-Eng-Final1.pdf.

James, S. E., Herman, J. L., Rankin, S., Keisling, M., Mottet, L., & Anafi, M. (2016). *The report of the 2015 U.S. transgender survey.* Washington, DC: National Center for Transgender Equality. Retrieved from https://www. transequality.org/sites/default/files/docs/USTS-Full-Report-FINAL.PDF.

Karsay, D., Dos Santos, H. R., & Mosquera, D. C. P. (2016). *Sexual orientation, gender identity and expression, and sex characteristics at the Universal Periodic Review.* Geneva, Switzerland: ARC International, International Bar Association, & ILGA. Retrieved from http://ilga.org/downloads/ SOGIESC_at_UPR_report.pdf.

Kates, J., Ranji, U., Beamesderfer, A., Salganicoff, A., & Dawson, L. (2017, August). *Health and access to care and coverage for lesbian, gay, bisexual, and transgender individuals in the U.S. (Issue Brief).* The Henry J. Kaiser Family Foundation. Retrieved from http://files.kff.org/attachment/Issue-Brief-Health-and-Access-to-Care-and-Coverage-for-LGBT-Individuals-in-the-US.

Kirichenko, K. (2017). *United Nations Treaty Bodies: References to sexual orientation, gender identity, gender expression, and sex characteristics 2016.* Geneva, Switzerland: International Lesbian, Gay, Bisexual, Trans and Intersex Association. Retrieved from http://ilga.org/downloads/Treaty_Bodies_ SOGIESC_references_2016_ILGA.pdf.

Lambda Legal. (2015). *Human rights abuses related to the criminalization and incarceration of LGBT people and people living with HIV in the United States*. New York, NY: Lambda Legal. Retrieved from http://www.lambdalegal.org/sites/default/files/us_20150915_upr-contribution.pdf.

Landler, M. (2017, December 21). "We'll save a lot": Trump warns he'll cut aid if crossed at U.N. *The New York Times*, pp. A1, A12.

Lehavot, K., & Simpson, T. L. (2014). Trauma, posttraumatic stress disorder, and depression among sexual minority and heterosexual women veterans. *Journal of Counseling Psychology, 61*(3), 392–403. https://doi.org/10.1037/cou0000019.

Lick, D. J., Durso, L. E., & Johnson, K. L. (2013). Minority stress and physical health among sexual minorities. *Perspectives on Psychological Science, 8*(5), 521–548. https://doi.org/10.1177/1745691613497965.

Mallon, G. P. (2009). A call for organizational trans-formation. In G. P. Mallon (Ed.), *Social work practice with transgender and gender variant youth* (2nd ed., pp. 163–174). New York, NY: Routledge.

Margolin, E. (2014, November 13). *UN panel questions gay conversion therapy in US*. MSNBC. Retrieved from http://www.msnbc.com/msnbc/gay-conversion-therapy-un-committee.

McLaughlin, K. A., Hatzenbuehler, M. L., Xuan, Z., & Conron, K. J. (2012). Disproportionate exposure to early-life adversity and sexual orientation disparities in psychiatric morbidity. *Child Abuse and Neglect, 36*, 645–655. https://doi.org/10.1016/j.chiabu.2012.07.004.

Mereish, E. H., Goldbach, J. T., Burgess, C., & DiBello, A. M. (2017). Sexual orientation, minority stress, social norms, and substance use among racially diverse adolescents. *Drug and Alcohol Dependence, 178*, 49–56. https://doi.org/10.1016/j.drugalcdep.2017.04.013.

Metzger, I. (2019a, January 7). Wisconsin governor Tony Evers signs executive order protecting LGBTQ state employees. *Human Rights Campaign*. Retrieved from https://www.hrc.org/blog/wisconsin-governor-tony-evers-signs-order-protecting-lgbtq-employees.

Metzger, I. (2019b, January 8). Michigan governor Gretchen Whitmer signs executive directive protecting LGBTQ state employees. *Human Rights Campaign*. Retrieved from https://www.hrc.org/blog/michigan-governor-gretchen-whitmer-signs-directive-protecting-lgbtq.

Meyer, I. H. (2003). Prejudice, social stress, and mental health in lesbian, gay, and bisexual populations: Conceptual issues and research evidence. *Psychological Bulletin, 129*(5), 674–697. https://doi.org/10.1037/0033-2909.129.5.674.

Meyer, I. H. (2015). Resilience in the study of minority stress and health of sexual and gender minorities. *Psychology of Sexual Orientation and Gender Diversity, 2*(3), 209–213. https://doi.org/10.1037/sgd0000132.

Meyer, I. H. (2016). The elusive promise of LGBT equality. *American Journal of Public Health, 106*(8), 1356–1358. https://doi.org/10.2105/AJPH.2016.303221.

Miller, S. (2017, June 1). Onslaught of anti-LGBT bills in 2017 has activists 'playing defense.' *USA Today*. Retrieved from https://www.usatoday.com/story/news/nation/2017/06/01/onslaught-anti-lgbt-bills-2017/102110520/.

Mirza, S. A., & Rooney, C. (2018, January 18). *Discrimination prevents LGBTQ people from accessing health care*. Center for American Progress. Retrieved from https://www.americanprogress.org/issues/lgbt/news/2018/01/18/445130/discrimination-prevents-lgbtq-people-accessing-health-care/.

Mitchell, K. J., Ybarra, M. L., & Korchmaros, J. D. (2014). Sexual harassment among adolescents of different sexual orientations and gender identities. *Child Abuse and Neglect, 38*(2), 280–295. https://doi.org/10.1016/j.chiabu.2013.09.008.

Movement Advancement Project. (2017, October). *Tipping the scales: The coordinated attack on LGBT people, women, parents, children, and health care*. Retrieved from https://www.lgbtmap.org/file/tipping-the-scales.pdf.

Movement Advancement Project, Public Rights/Private Conscience Project, & SAGE. (2017, December). *Dignity denied: Religious exemptions and LGBT elder services*. Movement Advancement Project. Retrieved from http://www.lgbtmap.org/file/Older-Adults-Religious-Exemptions.pdf.

Mustanski, B., Andrews, R., & Puckett, J. A. (2016). The effects of cumulative victimization on mental health among lesbian, gay, bisexual, and transgender adolescents and young adults. *American Journal of Public Health, 106*, 527–533. https://doi.org/10.2105/AJPH.2015.302976.

National Coalition of Anti-Violence Programs. (2017). *Lesbian, gay, bisexual, transgender, queer, and HIV-affected hate violence in 2016*. New York, NY. Retrieved from http://avp.org/wp-content/uploads/2017/06/NCAVP_2016HateViolence_REPORT.pdf.

Newberger, E. (2019, January 3). *These are the women making history as the 116th Congress is sworn in*. CNBC. Retrieved from https://www.cnbc.com/2019/01/03/these-are-the-women-making-history-as-the-116th-congress-is-sworn-in.html.

Office of the High Commissioner for Human Rights. (2017). *The role of the United Nations in combatting discrimination and violence against individuals based on sexual orientation and gender identity: A programmatic overview*. Retrieved from https://www.ohchr.org/Documents/Issues/Discrimination/LGBT/UN_LGBTI_Summary.pdf.

Palmer, N. A., Greytak, E. A., & Kosciw, J. G. (2016). *Educational exclusion: Drop out, push out, and the school-to-prison pipeline among LGBTQ youth*. New York, NY: Gay, Lesbian, Straight Education Network. Retrieved from https://www.glsen.org/sites/default/files/Educational%20Exclusion_Report_6-28-16_v4_WEB_READY_PDF.pdf.

Pan American Health Organization & World Health Organization. (2012, May 17). *"Therapies" to change sexual orientation lack medical justification and threaten health.* Retrieved from http://new.paho.org/hq/index. php?option=com_content&view=article&id=6803&Itemid=1926.

Poirier, J. M. (2015). *Recommended LGBTQ children, youth and families cultural competence tools, curricula, and resources.* Washington, DC: American Institutes for Research. Retrieved from https://healthysafechildren.org// sites/default/files/LGBTQ%20Tools%20Curricula%20and%20Resources.pdf.

Reichert, E. (2007). *Challenges in human rights: A social work perspective.* New York, NY: Columbia University Press.

Roberts, A. L., Austin, B., Corliss, H. L., Vandermorris, A. K., & Koenen, K. C. (2010). Pervasive trauma exposure among US sexual orientation minority adults and risk of posttraumatic stress disorder. *American Journal of Public Health, 100*(12), 2433–2441. https://doi.org/10.2105/ AJPH.2009.168971.

Roberts, A. L., Rosario, M., Corliss, H. L., Koenen, K. C., & Austin, B. (2012). Elevated risk of posttraumatic stress in sexual minority youths: Mediation by childhood abuse and gender nonconformity. *American Journal of Public Health, 102*, 1587–1593. https://doi.org/10.2105/AJPH.2011.300530.

Rosenberg, G. (2018, December 21). *Kasich signs law banning common abortion method, vetoes 'heartbeat bill.'* Cincinnati Public Radio News. Retrieved from http://www.wvxu.org/post/kasich-signs-law-banning-common-abortion-method-vetoes-heartbeat-bill#stream/0.

Shear, M. D. (2015, April 9). Obama to ask for 'repairing' of gays to end. *The New York Times*, pp. A1, A18.

Silverstein, C. (1991). Psychological and medical treatments of homosexuality. In J. C. Gonsiorek & J. D. Weinrich (Eds.), *Homosexuality: Research implications for public policy* (pp. 101–114). Newbury Park, CA: Sage.

Singh, A. A., & dickey, l. m. (2016). Implementing the APA guidelines on psychological practice with transgender and gender nonconforming people: A call to action to the field of psychology. *Psychology of Sexual Orientation and Gender Diversity, 3*(2), 195–200. https://doi.org/10.1037/sgd0000179.

Singh, S., & Durso, L. E. (2017, May 2). *Widespread discrimination continues to shape LGBT people's lives in both subtle and significant ways.* Center for American Progress. Retrieved from https://www.americanprogress.org/ issues/lgbt/news/2017/05/02/429529/widespread-discrimination-continues-shape-lgbt-peoples-lives-subtle-significant-ways/.

Sontag, D. (2015, May 13). Push to end prison rape loses momentum. *The New York Times*, pp. A1, A14–A15.

Stern, M. J. (2015, February 10). Unconscionable practice: This court ruling could mean the end of gay conversion therapy. *Slate.* Retrieved from http:// www.slate.com/articles/news_and_politics/jurisprudence/2015/02/new_jersey_gay_conversion_therapy_case_blocked_expert_testimony_could_be.html.

Sterzing, P. R., Gartner, R. E., Goldbach, J. T., McGeough, B. L., Ratliff, G. A., & Johnson, K. C. (2017). Polyvictimization prevalence rates for sexual and gender minority adolescents: Breaking down the silos of victimization research. *Psychology of Violence*. Advance online publication. https://doi.org/10.1037/vio0000123.

Substance Abuse and Mental Health Services Administration. (2014a). *A practitioner's resource guide: Helping families to support their LGBT children*. HHS Publication No. PEP14-LGBTKIDS. Rockville, MD: Substance Abuse and Mental Health Services Administration. Retrieved from https://store.samhsa.gov/product/A-Practitioner-s-Resource-Guide-Helping-Families-to-Support-Their-LGBT-Children/PEP14-LGBTKIDS.

Substance Abuse and Mental Health Services Administration. (2014b). *TIP57: Trauma-informed care in behavioral health services*. HHS Publication No. (SMA) 14-4816. Rockville, MD: Substance Abuse and Mental Health Services Administration. Retrieved from https://store.samhsa.gov/product/TIP-57-Trauma-Informed-Care-in-Behavioral-Health-Services/SMA14-4816.

Testa, R. J., Bliss, W., Balsam, K. F., Michaels, M. S., Rogers, M. L., & Joiner, T. (2017). Suicidal ideation in transgender people: Gender minority stress and interpersonal theory factors. *Journal of Abnormal Psychology, 126*(1), 125–136. https://doi.org/10.1037/abn0000234.

Testa, R. J., Harbarth, J., Peta, J., Balsam, K., & Bockting, W. (2015). Development of the gender minority stress and resilience measure. *Psychology of Sexual Orientation and Gender Diversity, 2*(1), 65–77. https://doi.org/10.1037/sgd0000081.

The Editorial Board. (2018. September 7). Confirmed: Brett Kavanaugh can't be trusted. *The New York Times*. Retrieved from https://www.nytimes.com/2018/09/07/opinion/editorials/brett-kavanaugh-confirmation-hearings.html.

United Nations. (1948). *Universal Declaration of Human Rights*. Retrieved from http://www.ohchr.org/EN/UDHR/Documents/UDHR_Translations/eng.pdf.

United Nations. (1966). *International Covenant on Economic, Social and Cultural Rights*. Adopted December 16, 1966. GA Res. 2200A (XXI). Retrieved from http://www.ohchr.org/Documents/ProfessionalInterest/cescr.pdf.

United Nations. (2015). *Report of the Working Group on the Universal Periodic Review: United States of America* (A/HRC/30/12). Retrieved from https://documents-dds-ny.un.org/doc/UNDOC/GEN/G15/159/71/PDF/G1515971.pdf?OpenElement.

United Nations Committee Against Torture (UN CAT). (2017). *List of issues prior to submission of the sixth periodic report of the United States of America* (CAT/C/USA/QPR/6). Retrieved from https://documents-dds-ny.un.org/doc/UNDOC/GEN/G17/019/66/PDF/G1701966.pdf?OpenElement.

CHAPTER 9

# Mental Disability, Trauma, and Human Rights

## *Éva Szeli*

Mental disability rights are human rights. Persons labeled with psychiatric, psychosocial, intellectual, or developmental disabilities—hereinafter collectively referred to as *mental disabilities*—are entitled to the same human rights protections as all other persons, yet the particular ways in which their human rights are restricted and violated are often truly horrifying. Many of these abuses occur in institutional settings around the world. Rights infringed upon—or lost altogether—may include the right to life, the right to liberty, and the right to be free from torture and inhuman or degrading treatment or punishment. These rights and others are protected by numerous international and regional human rights documents.

A history of trauma is often a significant factor in the emergence of the psychiatric or psychosocial problems that may lead to institutionalization. This may include trauma at the societal level, such as war, or at the personal level, such as domestic abuse or other violent crimes. The trauma may be physical, sexual, or emotional and, without proper support or

É. Szeli (✉)
Department of Psychology,
Arizona State University, Tempe, AZ, USA
e-mail: eszeli@asu.edu

© The Author(s) 2019
L. D. Butler et al. (eds.), *Trauma and Human Rights*,
https://doi.org/10.1007/978-3-030-16395-2_9

treatment, may lead to lifelong mental health problems. Furthermore, labeling someone with a psychiatric or psychosocial disability may result in added trauma, particularly if it results in institutionalization. The marginalization and isolation of persons living in psychiatric institutions and other residential facilities make them especially vulnerable to neglect and abuse. Human rights investigations into such facilities have revealed violations of basic human rights, ranging from the institutional detention itself to torturous "treatments" to systematic violence. Such further traumatization is often overlooked, denied, or actively concealed, and natural human responses to the traumatic events are ascribed to mental illness rather than identified as the sequelae of human rights abuses.

The focus of this chapter will be the most egregious systemic abuses against persons with mental disabilities worldwide: their segregation, isolation, and detention in large residential institutions. Disability Rights International (DRI, www.driadvocacy.org; formerly Mental Disability Rights International, or MDRI) is a non-governmental organization that investigates and documents human rights abuses in institutional settings where persons with disabilities—particularly those labeled with mental disabilities—reside, often for life. Much of this chapter is based on the author's own human rights work with MDRI in Hungary (MDRI, 1997), Russia (MDRI, 1999), Kosovo (MDRI, 2002), Bulgaria (Amnesty International, 2002), Serbia (MDRI, 2007), and Ukraine (DRI, 2015b), as well as DRI's continued investigations around the globe, including the USA (MDRI, 2010), Mexico (DRI, 2010, 2015a), Georgia (DRI, 2013), and Guatemala (DRI, 2017, 2018). The abuses and human rights violations discussed in this chapter have been observed by the author and widely documented by MDRI/DRI in the referenced reports, which serve as tools for advocacy and reform.

## TRAUMA AND MENTAL DISABILITIES

The relationship between trauma and mental disabilities is complex and likely reciprocal. Trauma may result in mental health difficulties and clinical diagnoses (Sadock & Sadock, 2011), but the act of labeling people with mental disabilities can also have traumatic consequences, particularly in institutional facilities with inadequate resources, an absence of trauma-informed systems and services, and increased vulnerability to further traumatization. Even formal diagnostic systems have struggled to define the role of trauma within the taxonomy of mental disorders (see Butler & Critelli, this volume).

In the fifth edition of psychiatry's *Diagnostic and Statistical Manual of Mental Disorders* (DSM-5; APA, 2013), "Trauma and Stressor-Related Disorders" (previously subsumed under "Anxiety Disorders") were reorganized into their own separate category. The best-known and most widely applied diagnostic labels in this category—that require exposure to trauma as a key criterion—are *posttraumatic stress disorder* and *adjustment disorders*. However, many other mental disorders may be caused, evoked, or exacerbated by trauma or other stressors. These include depressive disorders (Kendler, Karkowski, & Prescott, 1999), anxiety disorders (Fernandes & Osorio, 2015), dissociative disorders (Waites, 1993), psychotic disorders (including schizophrenia; Read, van Os, Morrison, & Ross, 2005), and even personality disorders (especially borderline personality disorder; Herman, Perry, & van der Kolk, 1989). Diathesis-stress models acknowledge that even when there is a biological predisposition to mental disorders, an interaction with an environmental stressor is often necessary (Ingram & Luxton, 2005). The formulation of *mental illness* is therefore problematic, as a medical model is insufficient or inappropriate to characterize psychosocial problems that are trauma-related and reactive, rather than endogenous. What may be labeled as symptoms may instead be sequelae of trauma, or attempts to cope with acute or chronic trauma; a label of mental disability may obscure such trauma and lead to a misattribution of the source of distress or disorder.

Furthermore, as noted above, the term *mental disabilities* in this chapter includes not only psychiatric and psychosocial problems and their labels, but also developmental and intellectual disabilities, which can predispose children and adults to abuse, neglect, and other traumatic experiences (Govindshenoy & Spencer, 2006; Horner-Johnson & Drum, 2006; Sullivan, 2009; Sullivan & Knutson, 2000). Many residential facilities around the world make little practical distinction in the institutionalization of persons labeled with various mental disabilities, as these populations are often housed in the same places. Consequently, their institutional experiences—and the abuses and human rights violations to which they are subject—are disturbingly similar across the globe, as documented by organizations like MDRI/DRI.

## TRAUMA AND HUMAN RIGHTS MONITORING

Human rights monitoring involves investigation and observation that seek to determine whether human rights standards are being met, especially in institutional settings. It includes the type of investigations conducted by MDRI/DRI to identify and report the human rights violations, described above, as an approach to advocate for systemic change, as well as ongoing efforts to ensure that human rights embodied in international documents are recognized and enforced. Manuals published by the United Nation's (UN) Office of the High Commissioner for Human Rights (OHCHR) provide guidelines on human rights monitoring for its UN human rights officers and other human rights monitors in the field. The recognition of trauma has evolved gradually, through various editions of these documents, but remains inadequately developed. In its updated chapter on interviewing, the OHCHR *Manual on Human Rights Monitoring* (2011) has specifically identified survivors of trauma in its section on "Interviewing specific groups or individuals with particular characteristics." Much of this content was included in the original OHCHR *Training Manual on Human Rights Monitoring* (2001) as guidance for interviewing victims of torture. While persons with disabilities were not discussed in the original manual, they are now specifically identified as one of these "specific groups or individuals with particular characteristics" (p. 25) in the updated chapter on interviewing. However, mental disabilities are largely ignored in this section, with the focus on physical and sensory disabilities.

With the entry into force of the *Convention on the Rights of Persons with Disabilities* (CRPD; UN, 2006) in 2008—and the explicit focus on the human rights of persons with disabilities in an international treaty—the OHCHR published additional guidelines for human rights monitors specifically investigating compliance with the new disability rights treaty. In the introduction to its CRPD *Guidance for human rights monitors*, the OHCHR (2010) acknowledged that:

> [T]he great majority [of 650 million people with disabilities worldwide] face discrimination, exclusion, isolation and even abuse. Many persons with disabilities live in extreme poverty, in institutions, without education or employment opportunities and face a range of other marginalizing factors. In some countries they are denied the right to own property and it is common for persons with disabilities to be denied the right to make decisions for themselves. (p. 7)

However, the CRPD *Guidance* fails to mention trauma specifically, mentioning violence and abuse only obliquely, while recognizing that under CRPD, Article 16(3): "In order to prevent the occurrence of all forms of exploitation, violence and abuse, States Parties shall ensure that *all facilities and programmes designed to serve persons with disabilities are effectively monitored by independent authorities*" (emphasis added).

The mental-disability-rights-specific *ITHACA Toolkit for Monitoring Human Rights and General Health Care in Mental Health and Social Care Institutions* (The ITHACA Project Group, 2010) also fails to mention trauma explicitly in its publication, but recognizes that: "People with disabilities removed from society as the result of placement in mental health institutions (such as psychiatric hospitals) and in social care institutions (such as residential care homes) are particularly vulnerable to neglect and abuse" (p. 4).

As such, the current best practice may be a combination of sources, with the updated OHCHR (2011) manual providing guidance for trauma-sensitive human rights monitoring, and the more content-specific CRPD *Guidance* (OHCHR, 2010) and the ITHACA *Toolkit* (The ITHACA Project Group, 2010) as lenses for mental disability rights issues. However, an explicitly trauma-informed model is clearly needed.

## HUMAN RIGHTS AND MENTAL DISABILITIES

The human rights violations most commonly documented against people labeled with mental disabilities are prohibited by all mainstream international human rights documents. These include both aspirational ("soft law") documents such as the *Universal Declaration of Human Rights* (UDHR; UN, 1948)—which has evolved into customary international law—and binding ("hard law") treaties such as the *International Covenant on Civil and Political Rights* (ICCPR; UN, 1966a) and the *International Covenant on Economic, Social, and Cultural Rights* (ICESCR; UN, 1966b). By far the most significant development in the recognition of the human rights of persons with mental disabilities has been the addition of the *Convention on the Rights of Persons with Disabilities* (CRPD; UN, 2006), adopted on December 13, 2006, and entered into force on May 3, 2008.

Prior to the existence of the CRPD (UN, 2006), advocates and reformers relied on content-specific soft-law documents, such as the *Declaration on the Rights of Mentally Retarded Persons* (the "MR

Declaration"; UN, 1971), the *Protection of Persons with Mental Illness and for the Improvement of Mental Health Care* (the "MI Principles"; UN, 1991), and the *Standard Rules on the Equalization of Opportunities for Persons with Disabilities* (the "Standard Rules"; UN, 1993) to interpret and apply the general human rights treaties to persons with mental disabilities (Rosenthal & Rubenstein, 1993; Rosenthal & Sundram, 2003). The CRPD (UN, 2006) became the first legally binding human rights instrument with comprehensive protection of the rights of persons with disabilities facilitating the identification and documentation of human rights violations—and providing more powerful leverage for mental disability rights advocates. The CRPD did not establish new rights; rather, it reinforced human rights already embodied in existing international documents with a focus on the challenges and abuses faced by persons with disabilities. For persons labeled with mental disabilities— especially those who find themselves institutionalized—this may be especially important in light of the potential rights violations they may face due to the stereotypes and stigma associated with the nature of their disabilities (Corrigan, Markowitz, & Watson, 2004; Drew et al., 2011).

Institutionalization unnecessarily denies persons labeled with mental disabilities the opportunity to live, work, and receive any necessary support or treatment in their communities. On a fundamental level, such detention—with the absence of opportunities for habilitation and rehabilitation, and a loss of social functioning—precludes any meaningful participation in a normal life, in violation of ICCPR (UN, 1966a) Article 10: "All persons deprived of their liberty shall be treated with humanity and with respect for the inherent dignity of the human person." Furthermore, as asserted throughout the MDRI and DRI reports referenced earlier, the conditions in most institutional facilities constitute inhuman and degrading treatment, explicitly prohibited by ICCPR Article 7 and CRPD (UN, 2006) Article 15. When unnecessary institutional placement results in further mental deterioration and loss of function, the human right to the highest attainable standard of mental health (under ICESCR [UN, 1966b] Article 12 and CRPD Article 25) has not been met. Not only is institutionalization a form of arbitrary detention, violating the right to liberty and security of person under ICCPR Article 9 and CRPD Article 14, but the failure to provide appropriate habilitation and rehabilitation undermines any opportunities for community reintegration of persons labeled with a disability, violating the right to live independently and be included in the community under Article

19b of the CRPD: "Persons with disabilities have access to a range of in-home, residential and other community support services, including personal assistance necessary to support living and inclusion in the community, and to prevent isolation or segregation from the community."

The UN *Convention on the Rights of the Child* (CRC; UN, 1989) also embodies these rights, recognizing that "a mentally or physically disabled child should enjoy a full and decent life, in conditions that ensure dignity, promote self-reliance and facilitate the child's active participation in the community" (Article 23.1).

Most broadly, all of the applicable human rights documents—ICCPR (UN, 1966a) Article 26, ICESCR (UN, 1966b) Article 2, CRPD (UN, 2006) Article 5, and CRC (UN, 1989) Article 2—prohibit discrimination, although only the CPRD and the CRC do so explicitly on the basis of disability, while the Covenants impliedly relegate disability non-discrimination guarantees to "other status." Discrimination is the behavioral manifestation of prejudice, and the foundation of all human rights abuses to which persons with mental disabilities are subjected; it forms the basis for systemic inequality. Institutions are the structural manifestations of this discrimination, established to segregate unwanted adults and children—particularly those labeled with a mental disability—from the rest of society.

## INSTITUTIONALIZATION AND MENTAL DISABILITIES

Large, residential facilities for persons with disabilities, abandoned and orphaned children, and other disenfranchised vulnerable populations around the world may be branded as hospitals, schools, care homes, or asylums, but they function as "total institutions." Sociologist Erving Goffman (1968) described a *total institution* as a place "where a large number of like-situated individuals, cut off from the wider society for an appreciable period of time together, lead an enclosed, formally administered round of life" (p. 11). Such institutions tend to be hierarchically organized and highly structured. Staff exert almost complete control over the lives of the residents, allowing for almost no freedom of movement or behavioral choice.

First, all aspects of life are conducted in the same place and under the same single authority. Second, each phase of the member's daily activity is carried out in the immediate company of a large batch of others, all of whom are treated alike and required to do the same things together. Third, all phases of the day's activities are tightly scheduled with one activity leading at a pre-arranged time into the next, the whole sequence of events being imposed from above by a system of explicit, formal rulings and a body of officials. Finally the various enforced activities are brought together into a single rational plan purportedly designed to fulfill the official aims of the institution. (Goffman, 1968, p. 17)

Many of the institutions investigated by the author and MDRI/DRI are in isolated locations, far from municipal infrastructure and family supports. Mortality rates are often high—particularly in the winter months—due to the isolation and lack of access to emergency care. Structural and environmental conditions are often appalling. Buildings are in disrepair and decay—and often dangerous. Electricity, heating, and air conditioning may be limited or non-existent, creating life-threatening conditions during bitter winters and sweltering summers. Inactivity, boredom, and repetition are pervasive and never-ending. Institutionalization in such facilities amounts to warehousing human beings.

Residents are typically depersonalized and dehumanized, stripped of agency, autonomy, and identity. Clothing is often communal; hygiene, restricted; privacy, non-existent. Personal belongings are rare. Staff often have little, if any, training; appropriate medical and dental care are dangerously lacking. Physical and sexual abuse are rampant, and residents may be prostituted or trafficked for sex. Young girls and women with intellectual disabilities are particularly vulnerable (Szeli & Pallaska, 2004).

In facilities with children, overcrowding, understaffing, and underfunding may leave young institutional residents with inadequate age-appropriate, developmentally-necessary sensory and motor stimulation. As a result, some children engage in head-banging, self-scratching, and other self-abusive behaviors. Without the training to understand, prevent, or treat this behavior, these children are often restrained in ways that further limit their sensory experiences and movement, thereby exacerbating the problem. Some children are kept in confined spaces—such as cribs—for so long that they experience muscle atrophy (or "wasting") and severely stunted growth. With prolonged neglect, these children may become uncommunicative and unresponsive to stimuli, creating or reinforcing further disabilities.

Such conditions are abusive and traumatizing. The profound irony is that the purported reason for the institutionalization of persons labeled with mental disabilities is often the need for residential treatment or care. Institutionalization may also be the end of the road for adults and children who have suffered through war, community or domestic violence, or familial neglect, abuse, and abandonment. Prior to institutionalization, many have experienced physical, sexual, or emotional trauma and—without proper support or treatment—may be facing mental health problems. Institutionalization not only fails to prevent mental health problems and treat, or provide support for, existing mental disabilities or past trauma, but it becomes its own form of traumatization.

Particularly in long-term residential institutions and other settings in which trauma has been documented as common, severe, and prolonged, it is important to recognize the difference between mental disabilities and the iatrogenic effects of institutional "care." Stigmatization of mental disabilities leads to stereotyped perceptions of so-labeled persons as the "other" (Gilman, 1985, p. xiii), including presumptions about dangerousness and lack of competency (Corrigan & Watson, 2002). Without a broader perspective, paternalistic systems may attempt to justify institutional isolation and segregation—and even abuse—when the label is one of mental disability. In this author's opinion, institutionalization is almost always unnecessary. Not only do institutions fail to provide adequate treatment and support—especially for those with trauma histories—but they create a fertile environment for a broad range of potential human rights abuses and further traumatization.

## CONCLUSION

MDRI/DRI's reports draw attention to violations of applicable human rights standards and serve as advocacy tools for systemwide reform in mental disability rights. The issue of trauma is deeply embedded in the documentation of institutionalized abuse, which, arguably, rises to the level of torture (MDRI, 2010; DRI, 2015a). MDRI/DRI's recommendations focus on preventing new admissions to institutions, encouraging deinstitutionalization efforts, emphasizing family- and community-based care, and supporting stakeholder initiatives in advocacy, reform, and service-delivery (DRI, 2018).

First and foremost, the institutionalization of children should be prevented at all costs (Rosenthal, 2017; UN Human Rights Council, 2015). While children may be particularly vulnerable to the effects of traumatic experiences, childhood is also a time of resilience. Early intervention is critical in minimizing potential long-term effects of trauma, including mental health problems. Institutionalization not only fails to provide needed support, but it further compounds the trauma and potentially condemns a child to a life of institutional segregation and isolation. Quoted in DRI's (2017) report on Guatemala, Dr. Matt Mason of Georgetown University's Trauma Informed Care Project summed it up: "These institutions are the last place you would want to put a child who survived trauma. These chaotic and unsafe environments only contribute to children's suffering and long-term mental health problems" (p. 2). In contrast, removing children from even the worst institutions taps into their natural resilience and provides them with the opportunity to become successfully integrated into their communities (Hillman, 2005).

More broadly, an explicitly trauma-informed approach to monitoring institutions, advocating for systemic reform, and providing support and services is in order. Guidelines for human rights monitors need to be updated to recognize trauma sequelae in institutionalized populations, to look for signs of ongoing abuse and retraumatization in institutional settings, and to resist questioning the credibility of persons labeled with mental disabilities who make allegations of abuse. Any mental health services provided—whether institutional or community-based—must include critical elements of trauma-informed care (Butler, Critelli, & Rinfrette, 2011), with a particular focus on trauma recovery. Article 16(4) of the CRPD (UN, 2006) demands that:

> States Parties shall take all appropriate measures to promote the physical, cognitive and psychological *recovery, rehabilitation and social reintegration of persons with disabilities who become victims of any form of exploitation, violence or abuse*, including through the provision of protection services. (emphasis added)

The setting must be safe; helpers must be trustworthy; choice and consent must be respected; power must be shared in a collaborative—rather than hierarchical—organizational structure; and trauma survivors must be empowered through an emphasis on their resilience (Butler et al., 2011). This is the antithesis of what exists in the large institutional facilities to which persons with mental disabilities may be banished, often for a lifetime.

In seeking to reconcile a human rights approach with the trauma model, Steel, Bateman Steel, and Silove (2009) stated that "[t]he imperative to recognize and respect *human rights* remains a critical focus for mental health professionals working in the *trauma* field" (p. 363, emphasis added). Likewise, the imperative to recognize *trauma* must be a critical focus for mental disability advocates working in the *human rights* field, particularly when investigating institutional settings where abuse is commonplace. A label of a "mental disability" should not obscure "what happened to the person" (trauma) in presumptive judgments about "what is wrong with the person" (Butler et al., 2011, p. 178).

## REFERENCES

Amnesty International. (2002). *Bulgaria: Far from the eyes of society: Systematic discrimination against people with mental disabilities.* AI Index: EUR 15/005/2002. Retrieved from https://www.amnesty.org/download/Documents/116000/eur150052002en.pdf.

Butler, L. D., Critelli, F. M., & Rinfrette, E. S. (2011). Trauma-informed care and mental health. *Directions in Psychiatry, 31,* 197–210.

Corrigan, P. W., Markowitz, F. E., & Watson, A. C. (2004). Structural levels of mental illness stigma and discrimination. *Schizophrenia Bulletin, 30,* 481–491.

Corrigan, P. W., & Watson, A. C. (2002). Understanding the impact of stigma on people with mental illness. *World Psychiatry, 1,* 16–20.

Disability Rights International. (2010). *Abandoned & disappeared: Mexico's segregation and abuse of children and adults with disabilities.* Retrieved from https://www.driadvocacy.org/wp-content/uploads/Abandoned-Disappeared-web.pdf.

Disability Rights International. (2013). *Left behind: The exclusion of children and adults with disabilities from reform and rights protection in the Republic of Georgia.* Retrieved from https://www.driadvocacy.org/wp-content/uploads/Left-Behind-final-report1.pdf.

Disability Rights International. (2015a). *No justice: Torture, trafficking and segregation in Mexico.* Retrieved from https://www.driadvocacy.org/wp-content/uploads/Sin-Justicia-MexRep_21_Abr_english-1.pdf.

Disability Rights International. (2015b). *No way home: The exploitation and abuse of children in Ukraine's orphanages.* Retrieved from https://www.driadvocacy.org/wp-content/uploads/No-Way-Home-final.pdf.

Disability Rights International. (2017). *After the fire: Survivors of Hogar Seguro Virgen de la Asunción at risk.* Retrieved from https://www.driadvocacy.org/wp-content/uploads/After-the-Fire-March-15.pdf.

Disability Rights International. (2018). *Still in harm's way: International voluntourism, segregation and abuse of children in Guatemala.* Retrieved from https://www.driadvocacy.org/wp-content/uploads/Still-in-Harms-Way-2018.pdf.

Drew, N., Funk, M., Tang, S., Lamichhane, J., Chavez, E., Katontoka, S., ... Saraceno, B. (2011). Human rights violations of people with mental and psychosocial disabilities: An unresolved global crisis. *The Lancet, 378,* 1664–1675.

Fernandes, V., & Osorio, F. L. (2015). Are there associations between early emotional trauma and anxiety disorders? Evidence from a systematic literature review and meta-analysis. *European Psychiatry, 30,* 756–764.

Gilman, S. (1985). *Seeing the insane.* New York, NY: Wiley.

Goffman, E. (1968). *Asylums: Essays on the social situation of mental patients and other inmates.* Harmondsworth, UK: Penguin.

Govindshenoy, M., & Spencer, N. (2006). Abuse of the disabled child: A systematic review of population-based studies. *Child: Care, Health and Development, 33,* 252–258.

Griffin, G., Mcclelland, G., Holzberg, M., Stolbach, B., Maj, N., & Kisiel, C. (2011). Addressing the impact of trauma before diagnosing mental illness in child welfare. *Child Welfare, 90*(6), 69.

Herman, J. L., Perry, J. C., & van der Kolk, B. A. (1989). Childhood trauma in borderline personality disorder. *American Journal of Psychiatry, 146,* 490–495.

Hillman, A. A. (2005). Protecting mental disability rights: A success story in the Inter-American Human Rights system. *Human Rights Brief, 12,* 25–28.

Horner-Johnson, W., & Drum, C. E. (2006). Prevalence of maltreatment of people with intellectual disabilities: A review of recently published research. *Mental Retardation and Developmental Disabilities Research Reviews, 12,* 57–69.

Ingram, R. E., & Luxton, D. D. (2005). Vulnerability-stress models. In B. L. Hankin & J. R. Z. Abela (Eds.), *Development of psychopathology: A vulnerability stress perspective* (pp. 32–46). Thousand Oaks, CA: Sage.

The ITHACA Project Group. (2010). *ITHACA toolkit for monitoring human rights and general health care in mental health and social care institutions.* London, UK: Health Service and Population Research Department, Institute of Psychiatry, King's College London.

Kendler, K. S., Karkowski, K. M., & Prescott, C. J. (1999). Causal relationship between stressful life events and the onset of major depression. *American Journal of Psychiatry, 156,* 837–841.

Mental Disability Rights International. (1997). *Human rights & mental health: Hungary.* Retrieved from https://www.driadvocacy.org/wp-content/uploads/Hungary.pdf.

Mental Disability Rights International. (1999). *Children in Russia's institutions: Human rights and opportunities for reform.* Retrieved from https://www.driadvocacy.org/wp-content/uploads/MDRI-Children-in-Russias-Institutions-1999.pdf.

Mental Disability Rights International. (2002). *Not on the agenda: Human rights of people with mental disabilities in Kosovo.* Retrieved from https://www.driadvocacy.org/wp-content/uploads/KosovoReport.pdf.

Mental Disability Rights International. (2007). *Torment not treatment: Serbia's segregation and abuse of children and adults with disabilities.* Retrieved from https://www.driadvocacy.org/wp-content/uploads/Serbia-rep-english.pdf.

Mental Disability Rights International. (2010). *Torture not treatment: Electric shock and long-term restraint in the United States on children and adults with disabilities at the Judge Rotenberg Center.* Retrieved from https://www.driadvocacy.org/wp-content/uploads/USReportandUrgentAppeal.pdf.

Office of the High Commissioner for Human Rights. (2001). *Training manual on human rights monitoring* (Professional Training Series No. 7). Retrieved from http://www.ohchr.org/EN/PublicationsResources/Pages/MethodologicalMaterials.aspx.

Office of the High Commissioner for Human Rights. (2010). *Monitoring the Convention on the Rights of Persons with Disabilities: Guidance for human rights monitors* (HR/P/PT/17, Professional Training Series No. 17). Retrieved from https://www.ohchr.org/Documents/Publications/Disabilities_training_17EN.pdf.

Office of the High Commissioner for Human Rights. (2011). *Manual on human rights monitoring* (Professional training series No. 7, Rev. 1). Retrieved from https://www.ohchr.org/_layouts/15/WopiFrame.aspx?sourcedoc=/Documents/Publications/OHCHRIntro-12pp.pdf&action=default&DefaultItemOpen=1.

Read, J., van Os, J., Morrison, A. P., & Ross, C. A. (2005). Childhood trauma, psychosis and schizophrenia: A literature review with theoretical and clinical implications. *Acta Psychiatrica Scandinavica, 112,* 330–350.

Rosenthal, E. (2017). A mandate to end placement of children in institutions and orphanages: The duty of governments and donors to prevent segregation and torture. In Center for Human Rights & Humanitarian Law's Anti-Torture Initiative (Ed.), *Protecting children against torture in detention: Global solutions for a global problem* (pp. 303–352). Washington, DC: American University, Washington College of Law. Retrieved from https://www.driadvocacy.org/wp-content/uploads/Rosenthal-Torture-seg-Feb-16.pdf.

Rosenthal, E., & Rubenstein, L. S. (1993). International human rights advocacy under the "Principles for the Protection of Persons with Mental Illness". *International Journal of Law and Psychiatry, 16,* 257–300.

Rosenthal, E., & Sundram, C. J. (2003). Recognizing existing rights and crafting new ones: Tools for drafting human rights instruments for people with mental disabilities. In S. S. Herr, L. O. Gostin, & H. H. Koh (Eds.), *The human rights of persons with intellectual disabilities: Different but equal* (pp. 467–502). New York: Oxford University Press.

Sadock, B. J., & Sadock, V. A. (2011). *Kaplan and Sadock's synopsis of psychiatry*. Philadelphia, PA: Lippincott Williams & Wilkins.

Steel, Z., Bateman Steel, C. R., & Silove, D. (2009). Human rights and the trauma model: Genuine partners or uneasy allies? *Journal of Traumatic Stress, 22*, 358–365.

Sullivan, P. M. (2009). Violence exposure among children with disabilities. *Clinical Child and Family Psychology Review, 12*, 196–216.

Sullivan, P. M., & Knutson, J. F. (2000). Maltreatment and disabilities: A population-based epidemiological study. *Child Abuse and Neglect, 24*, 1257–1273.

Szeli, E., & Pallaska, D. (2004). Violence against women with mental disabilities: The invisible victims in CEE/NIS countries. *Feminist Review, 76*, 117–119.

UN Human Rights Council. (2015). *Report of the Special Rapporteur on torture and other cruel, inhuman or degrading treatment or punishment* (A/HRC/28/68). Retrieved from https://documents-dds-ny.un.org/doc/UNDOC/GEN/G15/043/37/PDF/G1504337.pdf.

United Nations. (1948). *Universal Declaration of Human Rights*. Retrieved from https://www.ohchr.org/EN/UDHR/Documents/UDHR_Translations/eng.pdf.

United Nations. (1966a). *International Covenant on Civil and Political Rights*. Retrieved from http://www.ohchr.org/EN/ProfessionalInterest/Pages/CCPR.aspx.

United Nations. (1966b). *International Covenant on Economic, Social and Cultural Rights*. Retrieved from http://www.ohchr.org/EN/ProfessionalInterest/Pages/CESCR.aspx.

United Nations. (1971). *Declaration on the rights of mentally retarded persons* (A/RES/2856[XXVI]). Retrieved from https://www.ohchr.org/Documents/ProfessionalInterest/res2856.pdf.

United Nations. (1989). *Convention on the Rights of the Child*. Retrieved from https://www.ohchr.org/Documents/ProfessionalInterest/crc.pdf.

United Nations. (1991). *The protection of persons with mental illness and the improvement of mental health care* (A/RES/46/119). Retrieved from http://www.un.org/documents/ga/res/46/a46r119.htm.

United Nations. (1993). *Standard rules on the equalization of opportunities for persons with disabilities* (A/RES/48/96). Retrieved from http://www.un.org/disabilities/documents/gadocs/standardrules.pdf.

United Nations. (2006). *Convention on the Rights of Persons with Disabilities*. Retrieved from http://www.un.org/disabilities/documents/convention/convoptprot-e.pdf.

Waites, E. A. (1993). *Trauma and survival: Post-traumatic and dissociative disorders in women*. New York, NY: W. W. Norton.

# CHAPTER 10

# Refugees and Asylum Seekers

*Isok Kim, S. Megan Berthold, and Filomena M. Critelli*

*Ahmed\* and his wife Fatima have been referred to a refugee health clinic by their immigration lawyer. Ahmed has been experiencing insomnia and has lost a lot of weight in the last 3 months. Fatima has had several recent episodes of severe panic with hyperventilation and heart palpitations that resulted in visits to the emergency department of the local hospital. Ahmed and Fatima, originally from Syria, arrived in the United States in 2015 and applied for asylum. Fatima gave birth last month to a baby girl, named Zada. Zada is a US citizen, and Ahmed and Fatima are facing the threat of possible deportation back to Syria, where Ahmed (an anti-government journalist) had been detained and tortured by government forces. After the government barrel bombed Aleppo, Ahmed and Fatima fled Syria. During their escape, Fatima was raped by a group of armed men while Ahmed was*

I. Kim (✉)
School of Social Work, University at Buffalo, The State University of New York, Buffalo, NY, USA
e-mail: isokkim@buffalo.edu

S. M. Berthold
School of Social Work, University of Connecticut, Hartford, CT, USA
e-mail: megan.berthold@uconn.edu

F. M. Critelli
School of Social Work, University at Buffalo, Buffalo, NY, USA
e-mail: fmc8@buffalo.edu

© The Author(s) 2019
L. D. Butler et al. (eds.), *Trauma and Human Rights*,
https://doi.org/10.1007/978-3-030-16395-2_10

*forced to watch. Not only do they fear for their safety if they are deported, but they are terrified that they will either have to leave Zada behind in the United States or bring her with them where her life may be endangered. There have been multiple hate crimes in recent months targeting Muslims in the city in the United States where they live. Ahmed and Fatima are Muslim. Fatima has been harassed for wearing a hijab several times when she has taken the bus to go grocery shopping, and she no longer feels safe going out without her husband. Ahmed was assaulted as he left work last week by two of his coworkers who threatened that he should go back to Syria. Ahmed was too afraid to report the incident. He tells the social worker at the clinic, "I thought we would be safe in America – but now I no longer feel safe here."*

*\*This is a composite case, and all names and other identifying information have been changed.*

People like Ahmed and his family have been migrating across the world for centuries in order to find safe and secure living situations. However, we are presently witnessing a migration surge that is historically unprecedented. Although the proportion of international migrants has stayed fairly constant in the past few decades, the total number of global migrants surpassed the 244 million mark in 2015, making the current number of global migrants greater than ever before (United Nations [UN], 2016). Half of the global migrants can be found in ten developed countries, including Australia, Canada, and the United States, and most of them end up in urban cities (International Organization for Migration, 2015).

Migration is inextricably linked with issues of human rights and trauma, frequently occurring in such contexts as war, ethnic conflicts, state-sponsored persecution, and/or situations that deprive people of their economic, civil, or political rights. Of the 244 million global migrants, 65.3 million individuals have been forcibly displaced due to war-related violence or sociopolitical conflict. The UN High Commissioner for Refugees (UNHCR, 2016) indicated that about one-third, or 22.5 million, of the forcibly displaced people are refugees, desperately needing immediate response to their unpredictable plight. Over half of these refugees are under the age of 18, highlighting the fact that the majority of displaced people are at risk for living in psychosocially unstable and educationally unpredictable circumstances. Another 2.8 million people were seeking asylum in 2016, looking for international protection, but their refugee status was yet to be determined (UNHCR, 2016). People like Ahmed and Fatima normally find themselves in this kind of limbo for years.

## DISTINCTIONS BETWEEN VARIOUS MIGRANT GROUPS

Each of these 244 million individuals has their own reasons for leaving or attempting to leave their country of birth. Their decisions could be borne out of various needs, such as economic, educational, religious, or political needs. Many of the global migrants migrate *proactively* in order to seek better jobs or educational opportunities. These migrants are often referred to as "economic migrants" or "immigrants," and their migration path is legally approved in advance by the receiving country and the travel plan is carried out in an orderly fashion.

However, a decision to leave one's country may not always be pre-planned. These migrants have no other viable choices than to leave *in reaction to* systematic political, social, or religious persecution and may be classified into two categories: refugees and asylum seekers. According to the UNHCR (2011), *refugees* are people who have been forced to flee their country because of persecution, war, or violence. Once someone is identified as a refugee by the international community, he or she is deemed to have "a well-founded fear of being persecuted because of his or her race, religion, nationality, membership of a particular social group or political opinion; and is unable or unwilling to avail him or herself of the protection of that country, or to return there, for fear of persecution" (UNHCR, 2016, p. 3). For these reasons, refugees cannot go back home or are afraid to return for fear of persecution or even death. Being identified as a refugee affords individuals a certain level of legal protection, such as the right to petition for third country resettlement and material resources.

*Asylum seekers* have similar reasons for fleeing their home country as refugees do. However, an asylum seeker must apply and go through the legal process to become an *asylee* in the country where he or she wants to live—this means that anyone who seeks asylum must find a way to arrive at a third country (usually Western European countries, such as Australia, Canada, Germany, and the United States) to petition in person. An asylee has the right to be recognized and receive the same legal protection and material assistance that are afforded to someone with refugee status. Even though asylum seekers may have experienced exactly the same type of persecution as refugees have, they must petition their case through the legal options available in the country where they are physically present, not through the UNHCR.

In 2016, Germany received the largest number of new asylum applications with 722,400 cases, followed by the United States (UNHCR, 2016). Asylum seekers have the burden of proving, with or without the help of legal counsel, that they meet the definition of refugee. This legal process often takes several years or more in the United States because of severe backlogs; more than 690,000 cases were pending as of 2018 (American Immigration Council, 2018). Aside from the severe backlogs, an important caveat in fighting asylum cases in the US immigration court system is the variable success rates of each case depending on who and where the case is being heard. A recent Reuters' report (Rosenberg, Levinson, & McNeill, 2017) revealed that an asylum seeker's chance of winning his or her case is as much as four times better in San Francisco, California than in Charlotte, North Carolina. So, Ahmed and Fatima's fate can look very much different depending on where their case is filed and which immigration judge hears the case.

Lastly, there is another type of international migrant, namely an *"undocumented"* or *"unauthorized" immigrant*, whose legal status cannot be neatly folded into any other category. According to the Pew Research Center (Krogstad, Passel, & Cohn, 2017), there are approximately 11 million undocumented immigrants in the United States. Contrary to popular belief, their population has been decreasing slowly since 2007, when the estimate reached its all-time high at 12.2 million. Eight million of these migrants are part of the US workforce, meaning they are either currently working or are unemployed and looking for work, accounting for about five percent of the entire workforce in the United States (Krogstad et al., 2017). However, they are overrepresented in farming (26%) and construction (15%), where there is perennial shortage of workers. Undocumented migrants are unable to receive benefits or have access to legal protection, which makes them especially vulnerable to low wages as well as exploitation.

## DIFFERENT STAGES OF THE MIGRATION PROCESS

Any international migration involves three broad stages: pre-migration and departure, transit, and resettlement and post-migration adjustment (Bhugra & Becker, 2005; Drachman, 1992). The pre-migration and departure stage may involve different decisions and preparations depending on whether a migration was proactively planned—for immigrants— or reactively happened—for refugees and asylum seekers. Due to physically and psychologically threatening circumstances, or even the death of significant others, experiencing separation from family and clan members may be a common occurrence for refugees and asylum seekers during this stage (Drachman, 1992). Because of the urgency and lack of time to prepare for departure, the transit stage can often include an unpredictable and dangerous journey to safety. Many arrive at temporary, makeshift camps made for refugees in nearby host countries, where many languish for years. The UNHCR refers to this type of circumstances as a "protracted refugee situation," where a group of refugees have been in exile for more than five years since their initial displacement (UNHCR, 2004). As of 2010, two-thirds of refugees worldwide were thought to be in this protracted situation (Milner & Loescher, 2011). Lastly, third country resettlement is the last hurdle for refugees to overcome. There are three durable solutions available for forcibly displaced people. First, voluntary repatriation is to return back to the country of origin on your own; second is local integration, which is to be absorbed into the host country; and lastly, third country resettlement, which is to permanently relocate to another country, such as the United States. Third country resettlement is afforded to only about one percent of all refugees worldwide in any given year (UNHCR, n.d.), further exacerbating the protracted situation around the world. Once the refugee is resettled, cultural and linguistic adjustment processes take center stage during the post-migration stage. Some emerging adjustment issues may include learning different views on health, education, and employment (Drachman, 1992). Sociocultural norms, such as how to communicate interpersonally or seek help, may prove to be the most challenging issues as the refugees resettle in a culturally foreign society.

## RELEVANT INTERNATIONAL HUMAN RIGHTS LAWS AND TREATIES

The human rights of migrants transcend national and regional borders, so a body of international instruments, conventions, and treaties have evolved to provide a framework for humane conditions for international migration. Applying a trauma-informed human rights (TI-HR) framework with migrants requires familiarity with human rights treaties and laws affecting international migrants. The following is a summary of key human rights treaties, highlighting the most relevant provisions.

The *Universal Declaration of Human Rights* (UDHR) of 1948 contains articles that are essential to the rights of migrants. The key principles that underlie the UDHR and all subsequent human rights documents are the universality of human rights as inherent to the dignity of every person and nondiscrimination (UN, 1948, Articles 1 & 7). The fundamental rights belong to all people irrespective of nationality or citizenship. The human rights prohibition on discrimination provides equal protection to citizens and migrants. Fundamental rights protections formulated in the UDHR are integrated into the subsequent core international human rights instruments.

The refugee crisis that ensued in the aftermath of the Second World War led to recognition of the need for greater protection of refugees. The *Convention Relating to the Status of Refugees* was adopted in 1951 (UNHCR, 2011). It established the right of persons to seek asylum from persecution. The Convention defines a *refugee* as any person who is outside their country of origin and who has a "well-founded fear of being persecuted for reasons of race, religion, nationality, membership of a particular social group or political opinion" and is therefore unable or unwilling to return to that country (UNHCR, 2011). The Convention also lays down minimum standards for the treatment of refugees and establishes the legal obligation of States to protect them. One fundamental principle is that of *non-refoulement*, which prohibits the expulsion or forcible return of persons with refugee status. A refugee is not to be returned to a country or territory where she or he is at risk of serious human rights violations. Later, The *Convention Against Torture and Other Cruel, Inhuman or Degrading Treatment or Punishment* (CAT) specified a definition of torture and expanded the principle of non-refoulement by prohibiting the return of a person to a country where he or she may be tortured (UN, 1984).

The *International Covenant on Civil and Political Rights* (ICCPR) recognizes civil and political rights of all individuals in each State Party to the Covenant "within its territory and subject to its jurisdiction," including "illegal aliens" (UN, 1966a). It absolutely prohibits all forms of slavery and slave-trade, servitude, and forced or compulsory labor. It also protects the right to liberty and to freedom from arbitrary detention. The ICCPR also entitles those who are arrested or held in detention to due process, which includes the right to be informed of the reasons for detention, to prompt judicial review, to legal counsel, and to consular assistance (UN, 1966a). Humane treatment in detention is also established as a right. Protection against arbitrary or collective expulsion is codified in Article 13, which states that an alien lawfully in the territory of a State Party ... may be expelled ... only ...in accordance with law including fair procedures, except where national security is an issue (UN, 1966a).

Other rights set out in the ICCPR (UN, 1966a) include equality before the courts, the right of peaceful assembly, and the right to freedom of association. The right to family life or unity is protected by Articles 23 and 17(1), whereby the State must take into account a family's interest in remaining intact in any action to expel or deport a person from its territory or family reunification in situations where a family has been separated. Finally, equality before the law and the prohibition of discrimination and protections for members of ethnic, religious, or linguistic minorities are outlined in Articles 26 and 27, respectively (UN, 1966a).

*The International Covenant on Economic, Social and Cultural Rights* (ICESCR) obliges States to respect the economic, social, and cultural rights of all individuals, including all migrant workers and their families. These include the right to health, to education, to an adequate standard of living, to social security, and to just and favorable conditions of work (UN, 1966b). Article 12(1) of the ICESCR specifically recognizes "the right of everyone to the enjoyment of the highest attainable standard of physical and mental health." At a minimum, all migrants, including irregular migrants, should have the same access to emergency medical care as nationals and to essential drugs and medicines (UN, 1966b).

Migrants' rights are frequently compromised by racism, racial discrimination, and xenophobia in their host states (Amnesty International, 2006; Critelli, 2008). These issues fall within the scope of *The International Convention on the Elimination of All Forms of Racial Discrimination* (ICERD) that requires states to undertake "to prohibit and to eliminate racial discrimination ... and to guarantee the right of everyone, without distinction as to race, color, or national or ethnic origin, to equality before the law ... the enjoyment of ... the rights to work, to free choice of employment, to just and favorable conditions of work. ..." (UN, 1965).

Decades of rising concern among international bodies regarding illegal transportation of labor, the exploitation of workers, and discriminatory treatment of foreign workers stimulated a movement advocating for a treaty focused specifically on migrant workers. It culminated in the creation of the *International Convention on the Protection of the Rights of All Migrant Workers and Their Families* (ICMW) that was adopted by the UN in 1990 but did not enter into force until 13 years later, in 2003. The ICMW stipulates a comprehensive set of rights for migrants, including those living and/or working abroad irregularly (i.e., undocumented). Although the ICMW recognizes that legal migrants have the legitimacy to claim more rights than undocumented migrants do, it emphasizes that undocumented migrants must also see their fundamental human rights respected (UN, 1990).

All migrants, including both regular and irregular migrants (documented or undocumented), are guaranteed general human rights that include the right to life (UN, 1990, Article 9), prohibition of torture or cruel, inhuman and degrading treatment (Article 10), humane living and working conditions (Articles 11, 25), the right to liberty and security of their person and humane conditions of detention (Article 16), the right to legal equality and freedom from disproportionate penalties such as expulsion (Articles 17–20, 22), the right to participate in trade unions (Article 26), freedom of thought, expression and religion (Articles 12 and 13). Access to education, urgent health care, and social services are guaranteed in Articles 27–28 and 30 (UNESCO, 2005). The ICMW's impact has been constrained because of the low rates of ratification compared with other core treaties. All of the states that have ratified the ICMW to date are sending rather than receiving countries. This is mainly due to concerns among receiving countries of the potential costs of rights provisions to migrant workers (Ruhs, 2012).

Children are affected by migration in various ways that may threaten their well-being. They may be left behind by their migrating parents, they may migrate along with their parents, or increasingly they migrate alone. The rights of all children, regardless of nationality or immigration status, are protected by the *Convention on the Rights of the Child* (CRC). Its provisions include the right to citizenship, physical integrity, health, and education as well as the right to be free from discrimination, exploitation, and abuse. Importantly, Article 9 requires that "States Parties shall ensure that a child shall not be separated from his or her parents against their will, except when … such separation is necessary for the best interests of the child" (UN, 1989).

Human trafficking and migrant smuggling are migration-related issues that are transnational in nature and therefore require international cooperation. The *Protocol to Prevent, Suppress and Punish Trafficking in Persons, Especially Women and Children* (UN, 2000b) and the *Protocol Against* the *Smuggling of Migrants by Land, Air and Sea* (UN, 2000a) were each adopted in 2000 to supplement the *United Nations Convention Against Transnational Organized Crime* (UN, 2001). These laws represent a milestone in global efforts to address human trafficking, a modern form of slavery. In them, clear distinctions are made between trafficking and smuggling of humans, and different state responsibilities are established toward people who have been trafficked and those who have resorted to hiring smugglers to help them migrate. *Smuggling* is defined as procuring "the illegal entry of a person" into a country "in order to obtain, directly or indirectly, a financial or other material benefit" (UN, 2000a). This instrument condemns the practice of smuggling of migrants and makes clear that migrants involved are to be immune from criminal charges and to be swiftly and humanely returned to their country of origin (UN, 2000a).

The *Protocol to Prevent, Suppress and Punish Trafficking in Persons, Especially Women and Children* (UN, 2000b) governs human trafficking and defines trafficking of persons as "the recruitment, transportation, transfer, harboring or receipt of persons," by means of the threat or use of force or other forms of coercion, abduction, fraud, deception, or abuse of power "for the purpose of exploitation." *Exploitation* refers to, "at a minimum, the exploitation of the prostitution of others or other forms of sexual exploitation, forced labor or services, slavery or practices similar to slavery, servitude or the removal of organs" (UN, 2000b, Article 3a). The law requires criminalization of trafficking and, importantly, encourages countries to assist and protect trafficking victims.

## AN INTEGRATED TI-HR APPROACH IN WORKING WITH REFUGEES AND ASYLUM SEEKERS

Understanding the experiences of vulnerable migrants through the integrated lens of TI-HR perspectives allows helping professionals the unique opportunity to combine human rights violations that intentionally target collective groups of people (i.e., macro level) with trauma experienced individually (i.e., micro level). Trauma and human rights are closely linked to one another when it comes to the experiences of refugees and asylum seekers—both are highly sensitive and politicized topics. The study of trauma has been primarily influenced by the addition of the diagnosis of posttraumatic stress disorder (PTSD) in 1980 in the *3rd edition of the Diagnostic and Statistical Manual of Mental Disorders* (DSM-III) (American Psychiatric Association, 1980) and strongly reflects the Western view on trauma's impact on individual persons. Goodman (2015) highlights the fact that the latest definition of traumatic events in the DSM-5 continues to focus on individual, not collective, experiences. The PTSD diagnosis, in turn, implicitly labels the person diagnosed with a deficit and dysfunction. Recovery from traumatic experiences, however, ought to involve both social and cultural processes that help the sufferer regain a sense of control, meaning, purpose, dignity, and values (Herman, 1992, 2015; see also Butler & Critelli, this volume).

The traumatic experiences of refugees and asylum seekers are shared experiences, and, by their nature, these experiences cannot be assessed through merely relying on symptoms expressed by an individual nor using purely individual clinical interventions. When traumatic events are experienced collectively by a group of individuals, their collective stories should inform helping professionals as they listen to the story of each person without judgment and without jumping to clinical and diagnostic conclusions. In another words, building on what Herman (1992, 2015) highlighted, recovery from shared traumatic experiences should additionally include helping professionals learning about and understanding the sociopolitical processes that culminated in collective traumas shared by refugees and asylum seekers.

In this regard, a trauma-informed perspective alone cannot fully describe or explain what some immigrants and refugees have experienced before, during, and after their migration. Combining a trauma-informed perspective with a human rights approach is particularly appropriate for understanding shared experiences of refugees and asylum seekers. The human rights approach can complement the trauma-informed perspective and *vice versa*. By definition, refugees and asylum seekers have been persecuted systematically based on their collective identity, whether it is based on race/ethnicity, political opinion, gender, sexual orientation, nationality, or religious affiliation. It is important to consider the civil, legal, and political rights of the first generation of human rights, the very rights that refugees and asylum seekers were systematically deprived of. To chalk up their trauma experiences to individually targeted phenomena would clearly be a misinterpretation.

Rather than listing components of trauma-informed care and human rights-based approaches sequentially and separately, it is best to have an *integrated* vision of a TI-HR approach by combining both approaches (see Table 10.1). As one way of envisioning this integrated approach, this chapter proposes a synthesis of Androff's (2016) five principles of rights-based social work practice—human dignity, nondiscrimination, participation,

**Table 10.1**  Integrating principles of trauma-informed care and rights-based approaches to social work practice: Identification of integrated TI-HR practice principles for refugees and asylum seekers and human services professionals

| Original principles | | Integrated TI-HR practice principles | |
|---|---|---|---|
| Trauma-informed care (TIC) | Human rights-based (HR) | Refugee/asylum seeker | Human services professional |
| Safety | Nondiscrimination | Rights | Cultural Humility |
| Trustworthiness | Transparency | Protection | Honesty |
| Choice & control | Human dignity | Agency/Self-determination | Opportunity |
| Collaboration | Participation | Strength | Capacity-building |
| Empowerment | Accountability | Recovery | Advocacy |

transparency, and accountability—with the five core values of *trauma-informed care* (TIC)—safety, trustworthiness, choice, collaboration, and empowerment (Fallot & Harris, 2009; Harris & Fallot, 2001).

First, concepts of safety (from TIC) and nondiscrimination (from HR) indicate the need and right to feel safe for a refugee or asylum seeker when seeking services, while human services professionals need to maintain cultural humility when working with this group of clients. Ensuring physical and psychological safety for clients in professional settings may reduce the likelihood that they will feel disregarded and discriminated against due to their sense of vulnerability related to legal status and cultural identity. In order to ensure a sense of safety for clients, it is necessary for human services professionals to learn and practice cultural humility, where they can appropriately address and remedy feelings of apprehension and the perpetual sense of instability. For example, human services providers must carefully apply cultural humility to consider where and when services are offered, the security of the location, and how the location is decorated in order to maximize the sense of safety for the refugees and asylum seekers (Butler, Critelli, & Rinfrette, 2011).

Second, concepts of trustworthiness and transparency address the issues of protection and honesty. In order to open up, refugee/asylum seekers need to be able to trust the human services professionals and realize that they are to provide protection from barriers and challenges. Providing protection also means that the human services professionals need to be honest and transparent about the information and the contexts that affect them. For example, clearly describing the scope of practice and consistent practice of receiving informed consent further creates a sense of trust and transparency (Butler et al., 2011).

Third, concepts of choice/control and human dignity aim to raise the awareness that refugees and asylum seekers should have freedom to decide their own fates. The ability to choose and have control over one's own decisions is inextricably related to the right to dignity for simply being a human. This awareness should be fully supported by the human services professionals through presenting and expanding opportunities for clients (Androff, 2016).

Fourth, concepts of collaboration and participation reinforce the importance of building strengths and capacity among refugees and asylum seekers. Through working together as equal partners, participation in accessing or securing rights can ensure further meaningful collaboration with human services professionals, which can promote capacity-building as well as secure strengths at the individual and community levels. For example, by truly expecting and applying participatory collaboration between refugee and asylum seekers and human services professionals, it is possible to explore non-traditional options that incorporate culturally relevant approaches to resolving various challenges to providing effective services (Androff, 2016; Butler et al., 2011). As popularized by disability rights activism that led to passing of the *Americans with Disabilities Act* in 1990, the slogan "nothing about us, without us" (Scotch, 2009) best exemplifies the importance of participation and collaboration among disenfranchised individuals and communities.

Lastly, concepts of empowerment and accountability highlight the inherent resilience and strengths of refugees and asylum seekers. While helping professionals must ensure protection of refugees and asylum seekers from furthering their physical and psychological traumas, we also must recognize that they are resilient and resourceful in surviving their traumatic experiences and can thrive in challenging situations, including their resettlement processes, with the right types of encouragement and advocacy. This means that human services professionals should allow ample time for refugees and asylum seekers to recover from years of trauma and human rights violations. At the same time, they must be responsible, in their capacities as professionals and citizens, to hold people and systems accountable for real and potential human rights violations that may further retraumatize people. This advocacy effort must involve active participation from refugees and asylum seekers, and creating a structure that promotes empowerment and advocacy will serve human services professionals as well as refugees and asylum seekers.

## APPLYING TI-HR INTERVENTION
## WITH REFUGEES AND ASYLUM SEEKERS: AN EXAMPLE

International and national US standards hold social workers and other helping professionals responsible for advancing human rights as a core professional competency (American Psychiatric Association, 2010; American Psychological Association, 2017; Council on Social Work Education, 2015; IFSW/IASSW, 2004; Marks, 2012). Androff's (2016) five core principles of a rights-based practice are applicable for practitioners working at micro, mezzo, and macro levels. Fundamental to a TI-HR approach to working with refugees and asylum seekers is promoting and safeguarding safety and a respect for the dignity and worth of the migrants. Without these foundations in place, it is unlikely that the helping professional will be able to establish a therapeutic relationship with their refugee or asylum-seeking client which would compromise any intervention efforts.

Additional considerations are recommended to achieve effective human rights-based practice. These include: (1) reframing needs as entitlements or rights; (2) operating from a stance of cultural humility and intersectionality; (3) fostering a therapeutic relationship and reconstructing safety; (4) providing trauma-informed care; (5) drawing from the recovery model; and (6) a strengths and resilience orientation (Berthold, 2015, p. 2).

TI-HR based practitioners should be well versed and up to date on the literature on best practices as well as trained to employ therapies and interventions matched to the given refugee or immigrant (Kronick, 2018; Murray, Davidson, & Schweitzer, 2010; National Partnership for Community Training, 2011; Patel, Kellezi, & Williams, 2014; Rousseau, 2018; Slobodin & de Jong, 2015). Refugees typically present with multiple and complex conditions and needs requiring complex models of care that are interdisciplinary in nature (Rezzoug, Baubet, Broder, Taïeb, & Moro, 2008).

Beyond specific therapeutic approaches such as narrative exposure therapy (Robjant & Fazel, 2010; Schauer, Neuner, & Elbert, 2005), the self-trauma model (Briere, 2002), and TF-CBT (Cohen, Mannarino, & Deblinger, 2006), best practices include supporting the advocacy efforts of migrants to promote and protect the realization of their rights (Berthold, 2015). Maintaining a connection with one's political beliefs or activism has been found to be a protective factor (Başoğlu et al.,

1997). Care must be taken, however, to not expose migrants to safety risks in the process (e.g., speaking publically regarding their own torture when loved ones back home may be targeted as a result). The Torture Abolition and Survivors Support Coalition (TASSC), a non-profit based in Washington DC, utilizes a trauma-informed approach to empowering torture survivors to advocate on Capitol Hill for the prevention of torture (TASSC International, n.d.). Complaint mechanisms of the UN Treaty Bodies can be used by individual survivors to hold states accountable for perpetrating human rights violations (Prasad, 2014).

Civil society groups (including those directly affected by human rights violations such as refugees, as well as practitioners and other stakeholders) are encouraged to participate in the Universal Periodic Review (UPR) of member states of the United Nations through the UN Human Rights Council (UN OHCHR, 2018). Stakeholders can submit a Shadow Report and, in some cases, provide a brief oral statement as part of the UPR process. Such written and oral reports may also be provided to the UN treaty body monitoring committee that is reviewing a given state (e.g., the Committee Against Torture in the case of state parties to the Convention against Torture). These mechanisms can be important pathways for refugees and their providers to provide evidence of rights violations by their home state or in their country of exile.

Legal proceedings are also potential avenues for seeking restorative justice, combating impunity, obtaining redress or reparations, and/or obtaining legal status in a country of exile, although the impact of these proceedings is mixed (Allan & Allan, 2000; Bockers, Stammel & Knaevelsrud, 2011; Henry, 2010; Reicherter & Gray, 2011; Skjelsbæk, Sveaass, & Kvaale, 2015). The Center for Justice and Accountability (CJA; www.cja.org), a US-based legal non-profit, works with survivors to identify and prosecute human rights perpetrators. International human rights tribunals (such as the International Criminal Court, the Inter-American Court of Human Rights, the Extraordinary Chambers in the Courts of Cambodia, the European Human Rights Court) typically put high level perpetrators and/or states on trial on human rights charges such as war crimes, crimes against humanity, and/or genocide. Not all refugee or asylum-seeking survivors of human rights violations have the opportunity to sue or testify against their perpetrators, and court judgments may not meet the expectations of victims/survivors. Further, the legal system often fails to fully accommodate the traumatic experiences of witnesses (Henry, 2010).

Trauma-informed clinicians may be engaged to do forensic assessments of survivors in asylum or other court proceedings, prepare them psychologically for their testimony, and/or provide treatment or accompaniment during and after proceedings. These services can contribute to the therapeutic process for survivors in what otherwise may be an extremely retraumatizing experience (Berthold, 2015; Gangsei & Deutsch, 2007). Clinicians may provide invaluable clinical support to survivors as they prepare and deliver their testimony or other evidence, experiences that often trigger reminders of the original trauma and can be distressing or destabilizing. For those involved in court hearings, particularly those where they must face their abuser in court (such as in the case of prosecution of human traffickers in the US) or where they may be at risk of deportation to their homeland (where their life is in danger), clinicians should monitor the survivor's mental status and ensure that safety and other supports are in place.

## CONCLUSION AND FUTURE DIRECTIONS

This chapter has delineated arguments for integrating trauma-informed care with human rights-based principles when human service practitioners work with refugees and asylum seekers. Using the case scenario of an asylum seeker, Ahmed, and his family, this chapter began by describing diverse types of international migrants, the international conventions and covenants related to refugees and asylum seekers in particular, and applied the integrated TI-HR principles to basic clinical interventions that human service practitioners must consider when working with refugees and asylum seekers. The integrated TI-HR perspective provides potential advantages over applying principles of trauma-informed care or human rights-based approaches separately, because the integrated perspective naturally allows simultaneous considerations of traumatic experiences that are often associated with human rights violations during pre-migration and transit phases experienced by refugees and asylum seekers. The TI-HR perspective also has the potential to bridge between individual-level (micro) practice and community-/policy-level (macro) practice.

However, we also must consider pitfalls of applying the TI-HR perspective, as neither TIC nor HR principles are immune from unexamined assumptions that may create unintended consequences for refugees and asylum seekers. The TI-HR perspective and its principles must be understood and examined through critical lenses that reflect social, political, cultural, historical, and economic realities that define societal norms. Consequently, human service practitioners must hold themselves accountable to make sure that the cultural relativism that may undermine the TI-HR principles be thoroughly examined to see whether it is uncritically applied as a device to bypass societal responsibility and accountability in order to limit an individual's right to have equal treatment and access.

Working with refugees and asylum seekers challenges helping professionals to stay informed of current affairs at all levels of society, and integrate current information in providing and promoting services that these vulnerable individuals naturally deserve because they are human. Applying an integrated TI-HR approach and principles will help to ensure that the sufferings of refugees and asylum seekers are rightfully addressed individually while their rights are advocated for collectively.

## REFERENCES

Allan, A., & Allan, M. M. (2000). The South African truth and reconciliation commission as a therapeutic tool. *Behavioral Sciences & the Law, 18*(4), 459–477.

American Immigration Council. (2018, May). *Asylum in the United States.* Retrieved from https://www.americanimmigrationcouncil.org/research/asylum-united-states.

American Psychiatric Association. (1980). *Diagnostic and statistical manual of mental disorders* (3rd ed.). Washington, DC: Author.

American Psychiatric Association. (2010). *The principles of medical ethics.* Arlington, VA: Author.

American Psychological Association. (2017). *Ethical principles of psychologists and code of conduct.* Washington, DC: Author.

Amnesty International. (2006). *Living in the shadows: A primer on the human rights of migrants.* https://www.amnesty.org/download/Documents/80000/pol330062006en.pdf.

Androff, D. K. (2016). *Practicing rights: Human rights-based approaches to social work practice.* New York, NY: Routledge.

Başoğlu, M., Mineka, S., Paker, M., Aker, T., Livanou, M., & Gök, Ş. (1997). Psychological preparedness for trauma as a protective factor in survivors of torture. *Psychological Medicine, 27*(6), 1421–1433.

Berthold, S. M. (2015). *Human rights-based approaches to clinical social work.* New York, NY: Springer.

Bhugra, D., & Becker, M. A. (2005). Migration, cultural bereavement and cultural identity. *World Psychiatry, 4*(1), 18–240.

Blackwell, D. (2007). Oppression and freedom in therapeutic space. *European Journal of Psychotherapy & Counselling, 9*(3), 255–265. https://doi.org/10.1080/13642530701496856.

Bockers, E., Stammel, N., & Knaevelsrud, C. (2011). Reconciliation in Cambodia: Thirty years after the terror of the Khmer Rouge regime. *Torture, 21*(2), 71–83.

Briere, J. (2002). Treating adult survivors of severe childhood abuse and neglect: Further development of an integrative model. In J. E. B. Myers, L. Berliner, J. Briere, C. T. Hendrix, T. Reid, & C. Jenny (Eds.), *The APSAC handbook on child maltreatment* (2nd ed., pp. 175–202). Newbury Park, CA: Sage.

Butler, L. D., Critelli, F. M., & Rinfrette, E. S. (2011). Trauma-informed care and mental health. *Directions in Psychiatry, 31*(3), 197–212.

Cohen, J. A., Mannarino, A. P., & Deblinger, E. (2006). *Treating trauma and traumatic grief in children and adolescents.* New York, NY: Guilford Press.

Council on Social Work Education. (2015). *Educational policy and accreditation standards for baccalaureate and master's social work programs.* Alexandria, VA: Author.

Critelli, F. M. (2008). The impact of September 11th on immigrants in the United States. *Journal of Immigrant and Refugee Studies., 6*(2), 141–167.

Drachman, D. (1992). A stage-of-migration framework for service to immigrant populations. *Social Work, 37*(1), 68–72.

Fallot, R. D., & Harris, M. (2009). *Creating Cultures of Trauma-Informed Care (CCTIC): A self-assessment and planning protocol.* Community Connection. Retrieved from https://traumainformedoregon.org/wp-content/uploads/2014/10/CCTIC-A-Self-Assessment-and-Planning-Protocol.pdf.

Gangsei, D., & Deutsch, A. C. (2007). Psychological evaluation of asylum seekers as a therapeutic process. *Torture, 17*(2), 79–87.

Goodman, R. D. (2015). A liberatory approach to trauma counseling: Decolonizing our trauma-informed practices. In R. D. Goodman & P. C. Gorski (Eds.), *Decolonizing "multicultural" counseling through social justice* (pp. 55–72). New York, NY: Springer.

Harris, M., & Fallot, R. D. (Eds.). (2001). *Using trauma theory to design service systems.* San Francisco, CA: Jossey-Bass.

Henry, N. (2010). The impossibility of bearing witness: Wartime rape and the promise of justice. *Violence Against Women, 16*(10), 1098–1119.

Herman, J. L. (1992). *Trauma and recovery.* New York, NY: BasicBooks.

Herman, J. L. (2015). *Trauma and recovery: The aftermath of violence— From domestic abuse to political terror* (2015th ed.). New York, NY: Basic Books.

International Federation of Social Workers and International Association of Schools of Social Work [IFSW/IASSW]. (2004). *Ethics in social work, statement of principles.* Retrieved from https://www.ifsw.org/global-social-work-statement-of-ethical-principles/.

238 I. KIM ET AL.

International Organization for Migration. (2015). *World migration report 2015: Migrants and cities: New partnerships to manage mobility*. Geneva, Switzerland: Author. Retrieved from http://publications.iom.int/system/files/wmr2015_en.pdf.

Krogstad, J. M., Passel, J. S., & Cohn, D. V. (2017, April 27). 5 facts about illegal immigration in the U.S. *Pew Research Center*. Retrieved from http://www.pewresearch.org/fact-tank/2017/04/27/5-facts-about-illegal-immigration-in-the-u-s/#.

Kronick, R. (2018). Mental health of refugees and asylum seekers: Assessment and intervention. *The Canadian Journal of Psychiatry, 63*(5), 290–296. https://doi.org/10.1177/0706743717746665.

Marks, J. H. (2012). Toward a unified theory of professional ethics and human rights. *Michigan Journal of International Law, 33*(2), 215–263.

Milner, J., & Loescher, G. (2011). *Responding to protracted refugee situations: Lessons from a decade of discussion*. Refugee Studies Centre. Retrieved from https://www.rsc.ox.ac.uk/files/files-1/pb6-responding-protracted-refugee-situations-2011.pdf.

Murray, K. E., Davidson, G. R., & Schweitzer, R. D. (2010). Review of refugee mental health interventions following resettlement: Best practices and recommendations. *American Journal of Orthopsychiatry, 80*(4), 576–585. https://doi.org/10.1111/j.1939-0025.2010.01062.x.

National Partnership for Community Training. (2011). Best, promising, and emerging practices: A compendium for providers working with survivors of torture. *A Thematic Issue of Torture Journal, 21*(1), 1–66. Retrieved from https://irct.org/publications/torture-journal/115/past-reports/2.

Patel, N., Kellezi, B., & Williams, A. C. (2014). Psychological, social and welfare interventions for psychological health and well-being of torture survivors. *Cochrane Database of Systematic Reviews* (11). https://doi.org/10.1002/14651858.cd009317.pub2.

Prasad, N. (2014). Teaching the use of complaint mechanisms of UN treaty bodies as a tool international social work practice. In K. R. Libal, S. M. Berthold, R. L. Thomas, & L. M. Healy (Eds.), *Advancing human rights in social work education*. Council on Social Work Education: Alexandria, VA.

Reicherter, D., & Gray, G. (2011). Reconciliation in Cambodia. *A letter to the editor. Torture, 22*(1), 58–59.

Rezzoug, D., Baubet, T., Broder, G., Taïeb, O., & Moro, M. R. (2008). Addressing the mother-infant relationship in displaced communities. *Child and Adolescent Psychiatric Clinics of North America, 17*(3), 551–568. https://doi.org/10.1016/j.chc.2008.02.008.

Robjant, K., & Fazel, M. (2010). The emerging evidence for narrative exposure therapy: A review. *Clinical Psychology Review, 30*, 1030–1039.

Rosenberg, M., Levinson, R., & McNeill, R. (2017, October 17). They fled danger at home to make a high-stakes bet on U.S. immigration courts. *Reuters*. Retrieved from http://www.reuters.com/investigates/special-report/usa-immigration-asylum/.

Rousseau, C. (2018). Addressing mental health needs of refugees. *Canadian Journal of Psychiatry, 63*(5), 287–289. Article first published online: December 4, 2017. https://doi.org/10.1177/0706743717746664.

Ruhs, M. (2012). The rights of migrant workers: Why do so few countries care? *American Behavioral Scientist, 56*(9), 1277–1293.

Schauer, M., Neuner, F., & Elbert, T. (2005). *Narrative exposure therapy: A short-term intervention for traumatic stress disorders after war, terror and torture*. Gottingen, Germany: Hogrefe & Huber.

Scotch, R. K. (2009). "Nothing about us without us": Disability rights in America. *OAH Magazine of History, 23*(3), 17–22.

Skjelsbæk, I., Sveaass, N., & Kvaale, R. M. G. (2015). Therapeutic prosecutions? (PRIO Policy Brief, 4). Oslo, Norway: PRIO.

Slobodin, O., & de Jong, J. T. (2015). Mental health interventions for traumatized asylum seekers and refugees: What do we know about their efficacy? *International Journal of Social Psychiatry, 61*(1), 17–26. https://doi.org/10.1177/0020764014535752.

TASSC International. (n.d.). *Advocacy and Outreach: Bringing the Survivor Voice to the Foreward*. Retrieved from https://www.tassc.org/advocacy-and-outreach.

United Nations. (1948). *Universal Declaration of Human Rights*. Retrieved from http://www.un.org/en/universal-declaration-human-rights/.

United Nations. (1965). *International convention on the elimination of all forms of racial discrimination*. Retrieved from https://www.ohchr.org/en/professionalinterest/pages/cerd.aspx.

United Nations. (1966a). *International Covenant on Civil and Political Rights*. Retrieved from https://www.ohchr.org/EN/ProfessionalInterest/Pages/CCPR.aspx.

United Nations. (1966b). *International Covenant on Economic, Social and Cultural Rights*. Retrieved from https://www.ohchr.org/EN/ProfessionalInterest/Pages/CESCR.aspx.

United Nations. (1984). *Convention against torture and other cruel, inhuman or degrading treatment or punishment*. Retrieved from https://www.ohchr.org/en/professionalinterest/pages/cat.aspx.

United Nations. (1989). *Convention on the Rights of the Child*. Retrieved from https://www.ohchr.org/en/professionalinterest/pages/crc.aspx.

United Nations. (1990). *International convention on the protection of the rights of all migrant workers and their families*. Retrieved from https://www.ohchr.org/en/professionalinterest/pages/cmw.aspx.

United Nations. (2000a). *Protocol against the smuggling of migrants by land, sea and air, supplementing the United Nations convention against transnational organized crime.* Retrieved from https://www.unhcr.org/en-us/protection/migration/496323791b/protocol-against-smuggling-migrants-land-sea-air-supplementing-united-nations.html.

United Nations. (2000b). *Protocol to prevent, suppress and punish trafficking in persons, especially women and children, supplementing the United Nations Convention against transnational organized crime.* Retrieved from https://www.ohchr.org/EN/ProfessionalInterest/Pages/ProtocolTraffickingInPersons.aspx.

United Nations. (2001). *United Nations convention against transnational organized crime: Resolution/adopted by the general assembly,* A/RES/55/25. Retrieved from https://www.un.org/en/development/desa/population/migration/generalassembly/docs/globalcompact/A_RES_55_25.pdf.

United Nations. (2016). *International migration report 2015: Highlights* (ST/ESA/SER.A/375). Department of Economic and Social Affairs, Population Division. Retrieved from http://www.un.org/en/development/desa/population/migration/publications/migrationreport/docs/MigrationReport2015_Highlights.pdf.

United Nations Educational, Scientific and Cultural Organization. (2005). *United Nations Convention on Migrants' Rights, Information Kit.* Retrieved from http://unesdoc.unesco.org/images/0014/001435/143557e.pdf.

United Nations High Commissioner for Refugees. (2004). *Protracted refugee situations.* Retrieved from http://www.unhcr.org/en-us/excom/standcom/40c982172/protracted-refugee-situations.html.

United Nations High Commissioner for Refugees. (2011). *The 1951 convention relating to the status of refugees and its 1967 protocol.* Geneva, Switzerland: Author. Retrieved from http://www.unhcr.org/en-us/about-us/background/4ec262df9/1951-convention-relating-status-refugees-its-1967-protocol.html.

United Nations High Commissioner for Refugees. (2016). *Global report 2016.* Geneva, Switzerland: Author. Retrieved from http://reporting.unhcr.org/node/18722.

United Nations High Commissioner for Refugees. (n.d.). *U.S. Resettlement Facts.* Retrieved from http://www.unhcr.org/en-us/us-refugee-resettlement-facts.html.

United Nations Office of the High Commissioner for Human Rights. (2018). *Universal Periodic Review.* Retrieved from http://www.ohchr.org/EN/HRBodies/UPR/Pages/UPRMain.aspx.

# CHAPTER 11

# The Interrelationship Between Aging, Trauma, and the End of Life

*Jacqueline McGinley and Deborah Waldrop*

*Stepping into the Future: Tapping the Talents, Contributions and Participation of Older Persons in Society* was the theme of the United Nations' 2017 International Day of Older Persons. This theme underscores growing recognition that the challenges of the future require the development of pathways that support full and effective participation in later life in accordance with older adults' basic rights, needs, and preferences (United Nations, 2017a). The interrelationship between population aging and the lengthening human life span have been changing both how we live and how we die. Growing recognition of how trauma is experienced and processed across the life span illuminates myriad ways that the coexistence of both existing memories and subsequent traumatic events influence both the quality of life and the dying process. This chapter explores how adverse life events inform the experiences of individuals and their caregivers as they reach older ages and as they die within the context of human rights. The experiences of veterans, prisoners, survivors,

J. McGinley (✉) · D. Waldrop
School of Social Work, University at Buffalo, Buffalo, NY, USA
e-mail: jmmcginl@buffalo.edu

D. Waldrop
e-mail: dwaldrop@buffalo.edu

© The Author(s) 2019                     241
L. D. Butler et al. (eds.), *Trauma and Human Rights*,
https://doi.org/10.1007/978-3-030-16395-2_11

and people who have relocated to long-term care facilities illuminate the intersection of trauma, aging, and dying. Trauma-informed approaches to working with this population are presented. The fundamental role of resilience in empowering people to cope with the changes that accompany the aging process and ultimately to die well is demonstrated.

## POPULATION AGING

The number of older adults in developing and developed countries has been steadily rising due to declining fertility, increased longevity, and international migration (United Nations, 2017b). Population studies now predict that there will be over 1 billion older adults (>60) worldwide by 2025 (Barry, McGwire, & Porter, 2015) and over 2.1 billion by 2050 (United Nations, 2017b). The number of adults over the age of 80 is similarly growing; the oldest-old will triple rapidly in the coming years and account for almost one-third of the 3.2 billion older adults expected globally by 2100 (United Nations, 2017b).

As of 2015, 30% of Japan's population was 65 or older thus earning it the designation as the world's "oldest" country, followed by Germany and Italy, which are expected to be replaced by South Korea and Hong Kong by 2050. The United States is not listed among the top 25 oldest countries; however, the country is also experiencing unprecedented growth in the older adult population. Longer life spans and aging "baby boomers" (a cohort born between the early-to-mid-1940s through the early-to-mid-1960s with distinctly high birthrates) have contributed to significant demographic changes. It is now anticipated that older adults will account for 20% of the country's population by 2030 (US Census Bureau, 2016).

Many recognize the contributions of older adults to the development and betterment of their families, communities, and society; these values are represented in policies and programs that work to enhance the aging population's health and well-being in later life. However, the significant financial and political pressures that will accompany the rapidly growing population of older adults cannot be overstated; systems of healthcare, pensions and retirement, and social protections will continue to be scrutinized and tested in the coming decades (United Nations, 2017b). Innumerable human rights issues can and already are emerging within this environment of increasing demand and limited resources.

## END OF LIFE

Death is inevitable for all; however, the nature of death can vary significantly. Some deaths can be traumatic for those who are dying or those who are bearing witness. *Palliative care*, which is a holistic approach to supporting people with life-limiting illnesses and their families across a variety of settings and often alongside curative treatment, is recognized as an intervention that can be particularly helpful in mitigating the risk for traumatic end-of-life experiences (Ganzel, 2016). The principles of palliative care include: patient-centered, family focused care; attention to and honoring of diverse patient/family preferences; and establishing goals of care, including supporting understanding of diagnoses, clarifying prognoses, promoting informed choice, and facilitating opportunities to negotiate care plans (World Health Organization, 2017).

It is estimated that approximately 40 million people globally need palliative care each year, with approximately 80% of these individuals residing in low- to middle-income countries. In spite of the growing prevalence of non-communicable chronic diseases, less than 14% of those who need or want palliative care receive it. Further, 80% of the world's population do not have access to pain relief medication, such as morphine (Lohman, Schleifer, & Amon, 2010). Currently, 17% of the world's population consumes 92% of the world's morphine with the majority of this consumption occurring in developed nations of Oceania, Western Europe, and North America (Open Society Foundation, 2016).

In the United States, approximately 117 million adults are living with chronic illness and 7 out of 10 will ultimately die from it. The most common chronic conditions include: congestive heart failure, chronic lung disease, cancer, coronary artery disease, renal failure, peripheral vascular disease, diabetes, chronic liver disease, and dementia (Centers for Disease Control & Prevention, 2017). The amount of care delivered and the cost of this care tends to increase with the illnesses' progression; accordingly, 25% of Medicare spending for people over the age of 65 occurs in the last year of life (Cubanski, Neuman, Griffin, & Damico, 2016). Living with and ultimately dying—over time—from multiple chronic comorbid conditions is vastly different than the ways people died a century ago. These changes create challenges for maintaining dignity and upholding human rights as death approaches.

## HUMAN RIGHTS ISSUES IN THE CONTEXT
## OF AGING AND END OF LIFE

As people age and near life's end, numerous human rights issues give rise to and warrant both attention and response (Steel, Bateman Steel, & Silove, 2009). While the rights of older and seriously ill adults are implicit within most core treaties, the following sections identify the specific human rights conventions and declarations that have emerged in response to the unique issues of aging and end of life. The historical context of these conventions is described along with the challenges and opportunities they articulate for practitioners and advocates.

### *Fundamental Human Rights for Older Adults*

*Historical Context*
The United Nations has long acknowledged population aging and the implications of the unprecedented growth of older adults worldwide. Guided by a commitment "to add life to the years that have been added to life" (United Nations, 1999a, para. 1), the United Nations has acted to draw both attention to and encourage adoption of principles that implore nations to safeguard opportunities for all people to age well.

Following the First World Assembly on Aging in Vienna, the United Nations General Assembly endorsed the International Plan of Action on Aging in 1982 (Resolution 37/51). In 1992, the United Nations adopted principles for older persons, which included the following issues: independence, participation, care, self-fulfillment, and dignity (Resolution 47/5). The United Nations General Assembly later declared 1999 the International Year of Older Persons as guided by a conceptual framework consisting of four dimensions: the situation of older persons, individual lifelong development, multi-generational relationships, and development and aging of populations (United Nations, 1999b). For approximately 20 years, the work of the First World Assembly on Aging informed how the international community thought about and responded to the issues brought forth by population aging (United Nations, 2002).

In 2002, there was a turning point in the United Nation's efforts to address the key challenges of population aging with the Madrid International Plan of Action on Ageing and the Political Declaration adopted at the Second World Assembly on Aging. The Political

Declaration included 19 Articles that recognized and committed action across three priority directions: development, health and well-being, and supportive environments (United Nations, 2002). Although these directions were attentive to the human rights of older populations, it was not until 2011 that a Report of the Secretary-General to the United Nations General Assembly focused exclusively on the major challenges older persons faced in terms of human rights (United Nations, 2011). The Report acknowledged that an international human rights prism was essential for understanding and addressing the dire circumstances of many older adults in developing and developed countries throughout the world.

## Challenges

In its Report, *The Human Rights of Older Persons*, the secretary-general acknowledged the heterogeneity of the aging population while also identifying four central challenges that require an international approach to eradication. *Discrimination* based on age, and the intersection of age-based discrimination with other forms, can significantly impact the ability of older adults to enjoy a full range of basic human rights; and yet, the Report acknowledges that ageism is frequently tolerated in societies throughout the world. *Poverty* is recognized in the Report as the most significant and imminent challenge to the welfare of older populations, who often serve as providers to grandchildren and other family members within their households. Poverty is expansive and used to describe homelessness, malnutrition, untreated chronic disease and serious illness, poor access to safe drinking water and sanitation, unaffordable medical care and medications, and income insecurity. *Violence, abuse, and exploitation* of older adults occur worldwide; however, there remain ongoing challenges of under-reported and under-documented physical, emotional, or sexual abuse often when perpetrated by someone in a position of trust. Finally, the Report acknowledges a *lack of specific measures and services* necessary to guarantee the human rights of older adults; specifically, there exist too few specialized residential centers, long-term programs, and home-based services for the rapidly aging population (United Nations, 2011).

## Opportunities

The Report affirms the global recognition of the unique human rights issues older adults face, and it documents the diverse efforts by nations to address these challenges (United Nations, 2011). However, it acquiesces that these efforts have often been inconsistent and insufficient; thus, it cites the remaining calls to action:

- International efforts are needed to develop and carry out a protection regime for older populations.
- Violence against older adults and women in particular must be addressed at all levels, including responding to root causes of disempowerment and implementing strategies to address underreporting particularly among those who are reluctant or unable to seek assistance.
- Comprehensive efforts to eradicate financial exploitation must be pursued, particularly those targeted at new and emergent forms of fraud, theft, deprivation, and expropriation.
- Healthcare policies should include preventative and rehabilitative care, while healthcare services should develop policies, implement programs, and allocate resources toward older adults with recognition that this is an often-underserved population.
- Long-term care services must be made more adequate through high-quality labor and services. Efforts should be made toward developing a legal framework for monitoring and responding to human rights violations in these environments of care.
- Policymakers and politicians must be made accountable to older adults, which can be achieved—at least in part—through their direct and informed participation in policymaking and political life.
- Nations should enact non-discrimination legislation in employment based on age, and the enforcement of these efforts should be closely monitored (United Nations, 2011).

While the report stresses the role of nations in responding to the challenges of population aging, the opportunities for individual actors—including practitioners and advocates—to protect and promote the human rights of older adults are significant and many.

### Fundamental Human Rights for Seriously Ill Adults

#### Historical Context
Similar to those efforts undertaken by the United Nations to use the prism of human rights to describe and address the experiences of aging populations, organizations committed to end-of-life care for people

with serious, life-limiting illnesses have articulated palliative care and pain treatment as a basic human right. This right is regarded as first evident in the Universal Declaration of Human Rights (United Nations, 1948). The Declaration includes 30 Articles, largely informed by and in response to the atrocities observed during World War II, with two regarded as most salient to the human rights of seriously ill adults. Articles 5 posits that "no one shall be subjected to torture or to cruel, inhuman, or degrading treatment or punishment" and is often cited by human rights advocates within end-of-life care; and, Article 25 affirms the right of all people to adequate medical care and the social services necessary to maintain health and well-being across all circumstances, including those beyond their control (United Nations, 1948).

In 1966, the United Nations General Assembly ratified the International Covenant on Economic, Social, and Cultural Rights to further affirm and articulate essential human rights. Several of the Covenant's 31 Articles have applicability to those near life's end, including the affirmation of self-determination (Art. 1) and the assurance of medical services and attention to all who are sick (Art. 12). Within the General Comments of this multilateral treaty, signatories are obligated to assure access to essential medicines irrespective of a person's resources; refrain from denying or limiting access to preventative, curative or palliative health services; and attend to and care for chronically and terminally ill people in a manner that minimizes avoidable pain and enables dignified deaths (United Nations, 2017c).

The Joint Declaration and Statement of Commitment on Palliative Care and Pain Treatment as a Human Right were drafted, published, and made available for signature in 2008 by two palliative care organizations (International Association for Hospice & Palliative Care [IAHPC] and The Worldwide Hospice Palliative Care Alliance [WHPCA]). The Declaration cited the United Nations' Universal Declaration of Human Rights; International Covenant on Economic, Social, and Cultural Rights; Committee on Economic, Social, and Cultural Rights; Declaration on the Promotion of Patients' Rights in Europe; and the International Guidelines on HIV/AIDS and Human Rights as establishing the grounds for palliative care and pain treatment as human rights. The Declaration has been signed by individuals, organizations, and nations worldwide in recognition that access to appropriate care and essential medicines is necessary to relieve suffering; education of healthcare professionals is critical for effective care; and governmental public health strategies are essential for achieving full access to the right to health through serious illness and life's end (IAHPC & WHPCA, 2008).

*Challenges*
IAHPC and WHPCA identified two significant challenges that informed the need to recognize palliative care and pain treatment as a basic human right. At the time of publication, they observed that more than 1 million people worldwide died each week with only a small percentage of these individuals receiving palliative care thus "resulting in widespread unnecessary suffering" (IAHPC & WHPCA, 2008, p. 301). The authors further postulate that pain treatments are significantly underutilized or unavailable in developing nations, noting that these countries represent 80% of the world's population but account for only 6% of global morphine consumption (IAHPC & WHPCA, 2008).

*Opportunities*
The Joint Declaration and Statement of Commitment on Palliative Care and Pain Treatment as a Human Right closes with the identification of opportunities for nations, organizations, and individuals to work collaboratively to assure access to palliative care and pain treatment for those who are seriously ill and near life's end by issuing the following calls to action:

- Governments and policymakers must adopt or change legislation to assure seriously ill patients have access to appropriate care.
- Regulators and policymakers should identify and eliminate barriers to the rational use of controlled medications.
- Manufacturers and regulators of medications required for effective pain treatment must work to improve access and availability, including special formations and guidelines for use with children.
- Governments and policymakers must assure the availability of adequate resources to support and sustain the implementation of palliative care and pain treatment where needed.
- Academic institutions, teaching hospitals, and universities should adopt or change practices to ensure the necessary support to sustain palliative care services.
- International and national organizations dedicated to palliative care and pain treatment should engage in united, global campaigns to recognize these services as human rights (IAHPC & WHPCA, 2008).

The Declaration asserts that organizations and members who regard palliative care and pain treatment as a fundamental human right can advocate for the identification, development, and implementation of the aforementioned strategies.

## TRAUMA-INFORMED ISSUES AND APPROACHES FOR OLDER ADULTS

### Cross-Cutting Issues in Later Life

Increasing attention on pervasive ageism and the myriad ways that older adults are marginalized has contributed to new awareness of the inherent vulnerability of advanced age and how an accumulation of stressors can influence the lived experiences of late life. Gerontological scholars have posited the theory of cumulative advantage and disadvantage, which describes processes by which earlier life opportunities or struggles (e.g., economic, health, security) accumulate over the life course leading to differential late-life trajectories. The cumulative (dis)advantage model illuminates the iterative interaction of (dis)advantages, societal context, racial inequalities, and aging (Crystal & Shea, 1990; Crystal, Shea & Reyes, 2017). The model explicates how early-life advantages and disadvantages persist into late life and demonstrates how intervening contingencies (e.g., loss, trauma) as well as random life events can contribute. Issues associated with diversity and inequality in later life can arise through the effects of cumulative advantage and disadvantage over the life course (Baars, Dannefer, Phillipson, & Walker, 2006).

### Vulnerability in Later Life

There are distinct, yet not inherent, features of the aging process that may make older adults uniquely vulnerable in later life (Graziano, 2004). It is useful to recall that trauma is not an event but the person's experience of that event; it is thus essential that vulnerability be defined as experienced by the older adult and not by those who provide care for or support them. In the following paragraphs, sources of vulnerability in later life are defined and their potential consequences described.

Loss is a common feature of later life; it can include but is not limited to the loss of loved ones, place, vocation, cognitive and physical abilities, and personhood (Grant, 2014). Older adults who experience loss, particularly the compounding of multiple losses, may have fewer resources for self-care and an increased likelihood of mental and physical health issues (Grant, 2014). People may also become increasingly *frail* as they age, experience comorbid chronic conditions and serious illness, and approach the end of life. Frailty may increase an older adult's fear of illness, injury, loss, and short- and/or long-term relocation; reliance on informal and formal caregivers; and sense that their personal agency has been diminished (Fried, Ferrucci, Darer, Williamson, & Anderson, 2004). Older adults may also be susceptible to *abuse, neglect, and bullying* across diverse settings by those known and unknown to them (Graziano, 2004); a national study by Acierno and colleagues (2010) found that more than 1 in 10 older Americans have experienced some type of abuse or neglect in the previous year. These forms of mistreatment may foster fear for future well-being; increase the likelihood of physical and mental health issues; and result in diminished resources in later life (Gagnon, DePrince, Srinivas, & Hasche, 2015).

Dr. Robert Butler (1975) defined *ageism* as:

A process of systematic stereotyping and discrimination against people because they are old, just as racism and sexism accomplish this with skin color and gender. Old people are categorized as senile, rigid in thought and manner, old fashioned in morality and skills ... Ageism allows the younger generations to see older people as different from themselves; thus they subtly cease to identify with their elders as human beings. (p. 71)

Ageism has been associated with diminished mental and physical well-being; decreased opportunities for and efforts to seek out meaningful participation in communities and society; and a changed sense of self in older adults (Butler, 1975).

*Gerodiversity*
The older adult population is expected to become increasingly diverse in the coming decades (Population Reference Bureau, 2016). As of 2010, 1 in 8 (12%) of all people in the United States 65 years and older were foreign born. The majority of these older adults were long-term residents; however, this also includes a smaller population of recent late-life migrants from family reunification and refugee programs (US Census Bureau, 2014b).

Individuals often internalize the values of their culture throughout their lives. Culture can influence how older adults think about and make meaning of the aging process. However, cultures differ in how they conceptualize aging, which in turn influences how people age, where they age, and how they perceive their own aging process. Culture also influences the decisions people make as they near life's end, including preferences regarding goals for care—including curative and palliative care, life-sustaining treatment and pain management, the ideal location at death, and funeral rituals (Kwong, Du, & Xu, 2015). Culture can also offer protective factors. Research suggests that immigrants and refugees have increased longevity and better health on average; further, intergenerational housing contributes to a decreased reliance on long-term care (Population Reference Bureau, 2016).

*Retraumatization of Older Adults*
Early adverse life experiences and cumulative trauma over the life course can shape the late-life experiences of older adults and those connected to them, just as new sources of trauma can arise as people age and reach life's end. Many older adults enter later life having experienced trauma, including the witnessing or experiencing of abuse, neglect, natural disasters, and acts of violence. Felitti and colleagues (1998) found that approximately two-thirds (67%) of those surveyed reported at least one adverse childhood experience. They also found a correlation between adverse childhood experiences and health problems in later life, including higher incidences of disease, disability, obesity, substance use, and mental health issues. These factors contributed to the need for higher levels of care, social and relational challenges, and risk for premature death among the older adults studied.

Further, cumulative disadvantage and stress over the life course, or *cumulative trauma* as it is sometimes referred to within the available literature, can impact older adults' experiences of aging (Davis, 2015). Older adults often experience social isolation, limited choice and empowerment, financial strain, and decrements in their overall functioning. As a result, their abilities to manage past or current trauma might be compromised, new trauma or stress might be experienced, and environments and situations may result in retraumatization (Mallers, Claver, & Lares, 2013). At the end of life, older adults with posttraumatic stress disorder have been observed to experience more emotional distress, poorer quality of life, and a less optimistic medical prognosis (Feldman, 2011). As noted by Davis (2015), "The concept of cumulative trauma represents a lifetime of repetitive exposure to adversity that is linked to anxiety, depression, and physical illnesses in old age" (p. 116).

It is, however, important to consider the specific ways in which perspectives may differ in other countries and contexts. Those who may be at increased likelihood for retraumatization in later life can range from an Israeli Holocaust survivor (King, Cappeliez, Carmel, Bachner, & O'rourke, 2015) to Korean survivors of childhood sexual abuse in Japan's "Comfort Women" system (Park, Lee, Hand, Anderson, & Schleitwiler, 2016) to African-American women who survived interpersonal violence (Bowland, 2015). Other older adults who resided in countries where war, ethnic cleansing, torture, and violence resulted in social disruption and migration may also be more likely to experience the reemergence of symptoms in later life (Graziano, 2004). Other studies have noted that older adults who experienced adverse childhood experiences, such as abuse or neglect, might be more likely to tolerate poorer care in later life and were at increased risk for elder mistreatment (Acierno et al., 2010; Fulmer et al., 2005). It is the obligation of practitioners and advocates to situate an older adult in the context of their unique lived experiences, community, and society to assure culturally competent practices (Rikard, Hall, & Bullock, 2015).

*Trauma-Informed Approaches with Older Populations*
Trauma-informed services require looking at the person, not the symptoms, in a manner that is respectful, client-centered, and strengths-based (Lopez, 2017). For older adults, this includes considering who the person was, who they currently are, and who they can become. Ideally, trauma-informed practices (Fallot & Harris, 2009) for supporting older adults will attend to the following principles:

- *Safety*, e.g., safeguarding older adults against abuse, neglect, and bullying;
- *Choice*, e.g., supporting meaningful opportunities for decision-making across all life domains;
- *Empowerment*, e.g., offering opportunities for older adults to exercise their capacity;
- *Collaboration*, e.g., engaging older adults in the process of advocacy, service development, and policymaking; and
- *Trustworthiness*, e.g., creating an environment where caregivers and agencies are working in the best interest of older adults.

The failure to acknowledge trauma histories can lead to an incomplete understanding of the presenting issues and their context; inappropriate or ineffective treatment and referrals; and increased risk for retraumatization during standard practices that can elicit triggering events (Butler, Critelli, & Rinfrette, 2011). The Post Traumatic Disorder Checklist (Hudson, Beckford, Jackson, & Philpot, 2008), Traumatic Grief Inventory (Jacobs, Mazure, & Prigerson, 2000), the Life Events Checklist (Weathers et al., 2013), and the Adverse Childhood Experiences questionnaire (Ege, Messias, Thapa, & Krain, 2015) have all been utilized to screen and assess trauma histories in older adult populations. Best practices suggest that organizations and practitioners supporting aging and seriously ill adults should have regular assessments protocols that seek to sensitively identify past trauma to limit the risk for inadvertent retraumatization and assure comprehensive service planning. In addition, assessments that identify resilience, such as the Connor–Davidson Resilience Scale (CD-RISC), are also essential for identifying those factors that can be harnessed and strengthened through trauma-informed interventions (Lamond et al., 2008).

Broadly, trauma-informed approaches that seek to ease stress and reduce the risk for retraumatization can facilitate improved outcomes for older adults and those near life's end. This process includes educating practitioners, developing trauma-informed services, implementing trauma-informed policies and practices within organizations, engaging communities through both awareness campaigns and development initiatives, and seeking research partnerships to test these efforts (Grant, 2014). More specifically, aging services must consider the impact of past trauma, including planning for and support of those who have had adverse life experiences. They can also prevent stress and trauma by educating and training staff on trauma-informed approaches, developing services that attend to individual safety, implementing trauma-informed policies that respect individuality and autonomy, and engaging in staffing practices that are attentive to the potential for trauma issues (Graziano, 2004).

*Resilience in Older Adults*
An emphasis on resilience underlies many of the principles of trauma-informed services. It is particularly interesting then that older adults often have higher resiliency when compared to younger cohorts (Gooding, Hurst, Johnson, & Tarrier, 2012). Resilience in older adults is multifaceted and often includes psychological, social, and biological dimensions (MacLeod, Musich, Hawkins, Alsgaard, & Wicker, 2016). Researchers have identified high resilience in older adults as contributing to positive

late-life outcomes. For example, resilience has been associated with improved overall mental and physical health, increased longevity, and highly rated quality of life (Luthar & Cicchetti, 2000).

With recognition that resilience is both high among older adults and has a positive impact on later life, it is important for practitioners and organizations to build and strengthen resilience in this population. Although there have been no studies to date testing a resilience intervention in a heterogeneous group of older adults, there have been numerous efforts undertaken with subpopulations of older adults, some of which are described in the following sections, that may be extrapolated and tested with broader populations of aging and seriously ill adults. Broadly, MacLeod and colleagues (2016) identified strengths-based interventions that emphasize optimism, facilitate positive experiences, support relationships, and integrate physical activity as likely effective in fostering resilience. They also acknowledge that interventions should be person-centered in a manner than it is attentive to individual diversity.

### Subpopulations of Older Adults in Later Life

Trauma is a pervasive human experience but it occurs in differential ways; some groups of older adults have had more frequent and long-lasting exposure to trauma. The impact of trauma can be profoundly life-changing and have significant impact on both adult development and the quality of late life. Deconstructing the types of trauma experienced by subpopulations of older adults affirms dignity and respect, upholding basic human rights. Veterans (who may have experienced trauma in earlier adulthood) in contrast to older prisoners (who may have experienced early-life trauma and live with the potential for daily exposure to additional trauma) suggest the importance of understanding the cognitive processing of early, later, and sustained traumatic experiences. Considering relocation stress as likely to be traumatic for older adults who have been relocated and who also may be experiencing the resurgence of earlier life trauma while adapting to life with decreasing control and decisional-capacity provides a platform for exploring the intersection between trauma, aging, and organizational protocols.

### Veterans

As of 2010, 51.3% of men over the age of 65 and 68.3% of men over the age of 85 were veterans (US Census Bureau, 2014a). Approximately, one-half (49.6%, 11 million) of the veterans who are served by the Veterans Administration are 65 years or older; and, veterans over the age of 80 are among the fastest growing cohort of those served by the Veterans Administration (Taylor, Ureña, & Kail, 2015). These numbers are projected to decrease in the coming years in response to differential war experiences and service expectations. Specifically, the era in which an aging veteran served is often associated with their status (e.g., combat vs. noncombat; drafted vs. enlisted), social and cultural perceptions of the war, and experiences of segregation based on race, gender, and sexual orientation (Spiro, Settersten, & Aldwin, 2015).

Understanding of differential combat stress reactions has evolved overtime. During the Civil War, it was referred to as "soldier's heart," while it was called "shell shock" during World War I and "battle fatigue" during World War II. It was not until the Vietnam War era that posttraumatic stress disorder became formally recognized. Today, all branches of the armed forces recognize the importance of mental health, suicide prevention, issues of housing, and substance abuse risk factors that can follow from traumatic combat and noncombat experiences. Additionally, late-onset stress symptomology (LOSS) is increasingly being observed and acknowledged in aging veterans, including those who had previously been functioning effectively across all life domains. LOSS refers to increased thoughts and responses to earlier combat experiences; it often occurs in the context of aging and significant life events that can accompany older age, such as loss of a loved one, changes in health and functional status, and retirement (Davison et al., 2015).

Increased awareness of the implication of these experiences in the lives of aging veterans has resulted in the identification and utilization of best practices. Central to these approaches is the recognition of and response to the impact of prior military service across multiple domains, including health, psychological well-being, housing, substance use, and social networks. Practitioners are encouraged to facilitate aging veterans' positive recall and reflection of their service, including empowering them to self-define their service and identify associated positive emotions. Chatterjee, Avron, King, King, and Davison (2009) found that 90% of veterans endorsed positive perceptions of their military experiences. Davison and colleagues (2015) moved toward a later-adulthood trauma reengagement (LATR) model that acknowledges veterans' intentional efforts to reengage wartime memories with the hopes of finding meaning and building coherence through reminiscence, although they also acknowledge that this can lead some to experience increased stress symptoms. Finally, it has become a best practice to support interconnectedness by facilitating opportunities for relationships to develop between veterans and others who have benefited from their service (Chatterjee et al., 2009).

An innovative trauma-informed intervention for aging Vietnam War veterans was tested by Daniels, Boehnlein, and McCallion (2015). Based on Erik Erikson's theory of human development, small groups of community-based older veterans convened weekly for approximately two hours. Some of the participant groups received the intervention, a life-review autobiography using the life-review and experiencing form. These participants completed their life-reviews in three parts (pre-military, military/war-zone, and post-military) and progressively shared each part with their group. When compared with similar older veterans who did not receive the intervention but instead participated in standard client-centered, emotion-focused discussions of the impact of PTSD, the older veterans who participated in the life-review had a significant reduction in PTSD and LOSS symptoms and improved rating of overall life-satisfaction. Reminiscence through life-reviews may support older veterans to integrate past trauma within a broader life span perspective.

*Prisoners*

The number of prisoners 55 years and older has increased by 400% since 1993. Older prisoners now represent approximately 10% of the total US prison population, and it is expected that they will account for more than 33% by 2030. The cost to incarcerate older adults is approximately three times higher ($70,000 annually) than it is for a younger prisoner (Bureau of Justice Statistics, 2016). This is due in part to healthcare costs, which are significantly higher for this subset of the incarcerated population because of existing conditions and/or symptom exacerbation while in prison. As of the writing of this chapter, more than 75 prisons in the United States offered hospice services; however, the majority of these programs rely heavily on volunteers for essential functions (Maschi, Viola, & Koskinen, 2015).

There is significant research to suggest that trauma and stress are common among older prisoners. Ninety-three percent (93%) of all prisoners report prior exposure to trauma and stressful life events, and 65% report posttraumatic stress symptoms (Maschi et al., 2015). There is also trauma and stress that have been found to be associated with incarceration broadly, including isolation, boredom, bullying, and assault. There are also sources of additional stress that are common to incarcerated older adults, including shame, poor quality of health and variability in healthcare deliver, concerns for reentry, loneliness, and lack of choices (Maschi & Koskinen, 2015).

When working with aging prisoners, several best practices have been identified. Practitioners are encouraged to support adaptive responses and resilience across physical, cognitive, emotional, social, and spiritual domains. Advocates should assure that adequate and reliable health, psychosocial, and end-of-life care are available during incarceration, while acknowledging the impact of trauma and chronic conditions on late-life outcomes. Increasingly, there have been calls for empathic approaches that seek release and family reunification that also mitigate risks to public safety. These approaches are built upon existing data that suggest recidivism appears to decrease with age. Finally, "Communities that Care & Do" are emerging as models for effective release; these reentry programs assure adequate access to the necessary services, including housing, health, social, and end-of-life care regardless of criminal conviction (Maschi et al., 2015; Maschi & Koskinen, 2015).

At the Northern Nevada Correctional Center, the "True Grit Program" was created by psychologist, Mary Harrison, in partnership with the Nevada Division of Aging Services, to support over 300 incarcerated adults who were over 55 years old. The program integrated physical activity including work-related activities and crafts, therapy, and spirituality into participants' daily routine; the program was intentionally designed in consultation with incarcerated older adults to attend to their unique and often underrepresented needs within the larger prison population. The program, which has been highlighted in the press and publications, has resulted in participants experiencing improved overall health as indicated by decreased number of doctor visits and prescribed medications. The program, as of 2014, also had a recidivism rate of zero among released participants (Nevada Department of Corrections, 2013).

*Institutional Residents*
The majority of people 45 and older state that they want to stay in their current residence for the duration of their lives; however, 70% of people who reach the age of 65 will need long-term care (Joint Center for Housing Studies, 2014). When these needs require relocation, Perry and colleagues (2015) found that 71% of older adults surveyed in Detroit

wanted to return to their home and neighborhood. A study by Laughlin and Parsons (2007) found that late-life transitions, particularly when the move is involuntary, reduce both the quality and quantity of life for older adults.

Relocation in later life may be planned or unplanned, wanted or unwanted, and desired or mandated (Perry et al., 2015). It is the circumstances of the relocation or transition that can inform individual responses. Relocation may also lead to a resurgence of prior trauma symptoms and/or introduce new sources of stress and trauma, including bullying, abuse, and neglect (Jackson, 2015). For some older adults, transitioning to an institutional residence may trigger symptoms of relocation stress syndrome (RSS; Manion & Rantz, 1995). Major symptoms of RSS include anxiety, apprehension, increased confusion, depression, and loneliness. Minor symptoms of RSS include verbalization of unwillingness or needs, sleep disturbances, change in eating habits, increased dependency, gastrointestinal problems, insecurity, lack of trust, restlessness, sad affect, expressions of concern, and withdrawal.

Researchers, practitioners, and advocates have identified strategies for reducing RSS and supporting positive late-life transitions. Older adults should be promptly informed of the need to be moved and thoroughly assessed for their individual needs, preferences, and prior trauma and stressors. Practitioners who are facilitating the transition should provide opportunities for questions to be asked and concerns to be stated; they should listen intently and respond honestly about the ways in which the long-term care setting can honor preferences and be flexible during the transition period. Older adults and their family members should be kept informed, both in writing and in-person during site visits. Family and friends should be encouraged to participate in the transition process but without guilt about the necessity of institutional care. As the transition gets underway, personal possessions should be safeguarded, "place making" should be supported (i.e., decorate a new bedroom), opportunities for control and choice-making should be facilitated, adequate staff—who are educated in the signs and symptoms of RSS—should be on-shift, and the older adult should be helped to become acclimated and monitored for signs of RSS (Wisconsin Board of Aging and Long-Term Care, 2011). More broadly, advocates and policymakers should consider how best to minimize the need for relocation in later life by supporting older adults' ability to age in place (Perry et al., 2015).

Institutional residents often experience transfers during the last months, weeks, and days of life; the impact of these transfers are significant in many ways, including causing new stress for older adults and their caregivers while also potentially triggering past trauma (Phend, 2011). In response to this and the prevalence of traumatic experiences in the lives of most older adults, Feldman (2011) proposed an intervention to integrate trauma-informed services with a palliative approach to support older adults with PTSD at the end of life. This therapeutic intervention includes three progressive stages that a clinician guides a seriously ill client through, including (1) palliating to remediate discomfort and provide social support; (2) providing psychoeducation to enhance coping skills; and (3) treating specific trauma issues, which can include a variety of different approaches as determined clinically appropriate given the older adult's prognosis and willingness. Based on theoretical frameworks and existing literature on PTSD at the end of life, this short-term intervention may maximize the quality of life of seriously ill older adults who previously had been unable or unwilling to engage in long-term interventions to address past trauma and stress.

## CONCLUSION

A trauma-informed, human rights approach can have important implications for the quality of life as people age and reach the end of life. The resurgence of traumatic experiences and memories in later life is fraught with complexity, especially as cognitive and physical decline becomes central. Understanding an aging person's wishes and goals of care while upholding their fundamental human rights to adequate medical care and the social services necessary to maintain health and well-being is essential across all circumstances, including those beyond their control (United Nations, 1948). Suffering often accompanies the dying process but emerging models for trauma-informed care and symptom management have been found to mitigate distress. Special attention to this intense life intersection seems essential to keep people from aging poorly and dying badly. Dr. Ira Byock, one of the foremost leaders in palliative medicine, provides an important frame of reference: "Despite the arduous nature of [dying] when people are relatively comfortable and know that they are not going to be abandoned, they frequently find ways to strengthen bonds with people they love and to create moments of profound meaning in their final passage" (Byock, 1997, p. 10).

# References

Acierno, R., Hernandez, M. A., Amstadter, A. B., Resnick, H. S., Steve, K., Muzzy, W., & Kilpatrick, D. G. (2010). Prevalence and correlates of emotional, physical, sexual, and financial abuse and potential neglect in the United States: The national elder mistreatment study. *American Journal of Public Health, 100*(2), 292–297.

Baars, J., Dannefer, D., Phillipson, C., & Walker, A. (Eds.). (2006). *Aging, globalisation and inequality: The new critical gerontology.* London, UK: Routledge.

Barry, A., McGwire, S., & Porter, K. (Eds.). (2015). *Global agewatch index 2015: Insight report.* London, UK: HelpAge International.

Bowland, S. (2015). Aging in place or being warehoused? African American trauma survivors in mixed-age housing. *Traumatology, 21*(3), 172–180.

Bureau of Justice Statistics. (2016). *Aging of state prison population, 1993–2013.* Retrieved from https://www.bjs.gov/index.cfm?ty=pbdetail&iid=5602.

Butler, L. D., Critelli, F. M., & Rinfrette, E. S. (2011). Trauma-informed care and mental health. *Directions in Psychiatry, 31*(3), 197–212.

Butler, R. N. (1975). *Why survive? Being old in America.* New York, NY: Harper Torchbooks.

Byock, I. (1997). *Dying well: The prospect for growth at the end of life.* Thorndike, ME: Thorndike Press.

Centers for Disease Control and Prevention. (2017). *Chronic disease prevention and health promotion.* Retrieved from https://www.cdc.gov/chronicdisease/index.htm.

Chatterjee, S., Avron, S., King, L., King, D., & Davison, E. (2009). Research on aging military veterans: Lifespan implications of military service. *PTSD Research Quarterly, 20*(3), 1–7.

Crystal, S., & Shea, D. (1990). Cumulative advantage, cumulative disadvantage, and inequality among elderly people. *The Gerontologist, 30*(4), 437–443.

Crystal, S., Shea, D., & Reyes, A. M. (2017). Cumulative advantage, cumulative disadvantage, and evolving patterns of late-life inequality. *The Gerontologist, 57*(5), 910–920.

Cubanski, J., Neuman, T., Griffin, S., & Damico, A. (2016). *Medicare spending at the end of life: A snapshot of beneficiaries who died in 2014 and the cost of their care.* Retrieved from https://www.kff.org/medicare/issue-brief/medicare-spending-at-the-end-of-life/.

Daniels, L. R., Boehnlein, J. K., & McCallion, P. (2015). Life-review and PTSD community counseling with two groups of Vietnam War veterans. *Traumatology, 21*(3), 161–171.

Davis, M. (2015). Dealing with cumulative trauma: A model for transforming trauma across the life course. *The Gerontologist, 55,* 116–117.

Davison, E. H., Kaiser, A. P., Spiro, A., III, Moye, J., King, L. A., & King, D. W. (2015). From late-onset stress symptomatology to later-adulthood trauma reengagement in aging combat veterans: Taking a broader view. *The Gerontologist, 56*(1), 14–21.

Ege, M. A., Messias, E., Thapa, P. B., & Krain, L. P. (2015). Adverse childhood experiences and geriatric depression: Results from the 2010 BRFSS. *The American Journal of Geriatric Psychiatry, 23*(1), 110–114.

Fallot, R. D. & Harris, M. (2009). *Creating cultures of trauma-informed care (CCTIC): A self-assessment and planning protocol.* Retrieved from https://traumainformedoregon.org/wp-content/uploads/2014/10/CCTIC-A-Self-Assessment-and-Planning-Protocol.pdf.

Feldman, D. B. (2011). Posttraumatic stress disorder at the end of life: Extant research and proposed psychosocial treatment approach. *Palliative & Supportive Care, 9*(4), 407–418.

Felitti, V. J., Anda, R. F., Nordenberg, D., Williamson, D. F., Spitz, A. M., Edwards, V., ... Marks, J. S. (1998). Relationship of childhood abuse and household dysfunction to many of the leading causes of death in adults: The Adverse Childhood Experiences (ACE) Study. *American Journal of Preventive Medicine, 14*(4), 245–258.

Fried, L. P., Ferrucci, L., Darer, J., Williamson, J. D., & Anderson, G. (2004). Untangling the concepts of disability, frailty, and comorbidity: Implications for improved targeting and care. *The Journals of Gerontology Series A: Biological Sciences and Medical Sciences, 59*(3), M255–M263.

Fulmer, T., Paveza, G., VandeWeerd, C., Fairchild, S., Guadagno, L., Bolton-Blatt, M., & Norman, R. (2005). Dyadic vulnerability and risk profiling for elder neglect. *The Gerontologist, 45*(4), 525–534.

Gagnon, K. L., DePrince, A. P., Srinivas, T., & Hasche, L. K. (2015). Perceptions of participation in trauma research among older adults. *Traumatology, 21*(3), 237–243.

Ganzel, B. L. (2016). Trauma-informed hospice and palliative care. *The Gerontologist, 58*(3), 409–419. https://doi.org/10.1093/geront/gnw146.

Gooding, P. A., Hurst, A., Johnson, J., & Tarrier, N. (2012). Psychological resilience in young and older adults. *International Journal of Geriatric Psychiatry, 27*(3), 262–270.

Grant, G. (2014). *Working with elders who have trauma histories.* Retrieved from http://ufsac.org/wp-content/uploads/2014/09/Ut-ah-Elders-trauma-2014.pdf.

Graziano, R. (2004). Trauma and aging. *Journal of Gerontological Social Work, 40*(4), 3–21.

Hudson, S. A., Beckford, L. A., Jackson, S. D., & Philpot, M. P. (2008). Validation of a screening instrument for post-traumatic stress disorder in a clinical sample of older adults. *Aging and Mental Health, 12*(5), 670–673.

International Association for Hospice and Palliative Care & Worldwide Palliative Care Alliance. (2008). Joint declaration and statement of commitment on Palliative Care and Pain Treatment as Human Rights. *Journal of Pain & Palliative Care Pharmacotherapy, 22*(4), 300–302.

Jackson, K. (2015). Prevent elder transfer trauma: Tips to ease relocation stress. *Social Work Today, 15*(1), 10. Retrieved from http://www.socialworktoday. com/archive/011915p10.shtml.

Jacobs, S., Mazure, C., & Prigerson, H. (2000). Diagnostic criteria for traumatic grief. *Death Studies, 24*(3), 185–199.

Joint Center for Housing Studies at Harvard University. (2014). *Housing America's older adults*. Retrieved from http://www.jchs.harvard.edu/ research/housing_americas_older_adults.

King, D. B., Cappeliez, P., Carmel, S., Bachner, Y. G., & O'rourke, N. (2015). Remembering genocide: The effects of early life trauma on reminiscence functions among Israeli Holocaust survivors. *Traumatology, 21*(3), 145.

Kwong, K., Du, Y., & Xu, Q. (2015). Healthy aging of minority and immigrant populations: Resilience in late life. *Traumatology, 21*(3), 136–144.

Lamond, A. J., Depp, C. A., Allison, M., Langer, R., Reichstadt, J., Moore, D. J., … Jeste, D. V. (2008). Measurement and predictors of resilience among community-dwelling older women. *Journal of Psychiatric Research, 43*(2), 148–154.

Laughlin, A., & Parsons, M. (2007). Predictors of mortality: Following involuntary interinstitutional relocation. *Journal of Gerontological Nursing, 33*(9), 20.

Lohman, D., Schleifer, R., & Amon, J. J. (2010). Access to pain treatment as a human right. *BMC Medicine, 8*(1), 8. https://doi.org/10.1186/1741-7015-8-8.

Lopez, S.A. (2017). *Trauma-informed practices with older adults [powerpoint slides]*. Retrieved from https://virtualconference.socialworkers.org/.

Luthar, S. S., & Cicchetti, D. (2000). The construct of resilience: Implications for interventions and social policies. *Development and Psychopathology, 12*(4), 857–885.

MacLeod, S., Musich, S., Hawkins, K., Alsgaard, K., & Wicker, E. R. (2016). The impact of resilience among older adults. *Geriatric Nursing, 37*(4), 266–272.

Mallers, M. H., Claver, M., & Lares, L. A. (2013). Perceived control in the lives of older adults: The influence of Langer and Rodin's work on gerontological theory, policy, and practice. *The Gerontologist, 54*(1), 67–74.

Manion, P. S., & Rantz, M. J. (1995). Relocation stress syndrome: a comprehensive plan for long-term care admissions: The relocation stress syndrome diagnosis helps nurses identify patients at risk. *Geriatric Nursing, 16*(3), 108–112.

Maschi, T., & Koskinen, L. (2015). Co-constructing community: A conceptual map for reuniting aging people in prison with their families and communities. *Traumatology, 21*(3), 208–218.

Maschi, T., Viola, D., & Koskinen, L. (2015). Trauma, stress, and coping among older adults in prison: Towards a human rights and intergenerational family justice action agenda. *Traumatology, 21*(3), 188–200.

Nevada Department of Corrections. (2013). *Fiscal year 2013 annual statistical report.* Retrieved from http://doc.nv.gov/uploadedFiles/docnvgov/content/About/Statistics/Annual_Abstracts_by_Fiscal_Year/fy2013.pdf.

Open Society Foundation. (2016). *The link between drug policy and access to medicine.* Retrieved from https://www.opensocietyfoundations.org/explainers/link-between-drug-policy-and-access-medicines.

Park, J. H., Lee, K., Hand, M. D., Anderson, K. A., & Schleitwiler, T. E. (2016). Korean survivors of the Japanese "comfort women" system: Understanding the lifelong consequences of early life trauma. *Journal of Gerontological Social Work, 59*(4), 332–348.

Perry, T. E., Wintermute, T., Carney, B. C., Leach, D. E., Sanford, C., & Quist, L. (2015). Senior housing at a crossroads: A case study of a university/community partnership in Detroit, Michigan. *Traumatology, 21*(3), 244–250.

Phend, C. (2011). Transfers not good for nursing home dementia patients. *MedPage Today.* Retrieved from https://www.medpagetoday.com/geriatrics/dementia/28787.

Population Reference Bureau. (2016). *Fact sheet: Aging in the United States.* Retrieved from http://www.prb.org/Publications/Media-Guides/2016/aging-unitedstates-fact-sheet.aspx.

Rikard, R. V., Hall, J. K., & Bullock, K. (2015). Health literacy and cultural competence: A model for addressing diversity and unequal access to trauma-related health care. *Traumatology, 21*(3), 227–236.

Spiro, A., III, Settersten, R. A., & Aldwin, C. M. (2015). Long-term outcomes of military service in aging and the life course: A positive re-envisioning. *The Gerontologist, 56*(1), 5–13.

Steel, Z., Bateman Steel, C. R., & Silove, D. (2009). Human rights and the trauma model: Genuine partners or uneasy allies? *Journal of Traumatic Stress, 22*(5), 358–365.

Taylor, M. G., Ureña, S., & Kail, B. L. (2015). Service-related exposures and physical health trajectories among aging veteran men. *The Gerontologist, 56*(1), 92–103.

United Nations. (1948). *The Universal Declaration of Human Rights.* Retrieved from http://www.ohchr.org/EN/UDHR/Documents/UDHR_Translations/eng.pdf.

United Nations. (1982). *Resolution 37/51: Question of aging.* Retrieved from http://www.un.org/documents/ga/res/37/a37r051.htm.

United Nations. (1992). *Resolution 47/5: Proclamation on ageing.* Retrieved from https://www.un.org/documents/ga/res/47/a47r005.htm.

United Nations. (1999a). *Principles for older persons.* Retrieved from https://www.un.org/development/desa/ageing/resources/international-year-of-older-persons-1999/principles.html.

United Nations. (1999b). *Conceptual framework.* Retrieved from https://www.un.org/development/desa/ageing/resources/international-year-of-older-persons-1999/conceptual-framework.html.

United Nations. (2002). *Political declaration and Madrid international plan of action on aging.* Retrieved from http://www.un.org/en/events/pastevents/pdfs/Madrid_plan.pdf.

United Nations. (2011). *Report A/66/173: Follow-up to the Second World Assembly on ageing.* Retrieved from https://documents-dds-ny.un.org/doc/UNDOC/GEN/N11/428/83/PDF/N1142883.pdf?OpenElement.

United Nations. (2017a). *International day of older persons—Homepage.* Retrieved from https://www.un.org/development/desa/ageing/international-day-of-older-persons-homepage.html.

United Nations. (2017b). *Ageing.* Retrieved from http://www.un.org/en/sections/issues-depth/ageing/index.html.

United Nations. (2017c). *CESCR general comments.* Retrieved from https://tbinternet.ohchr.org/_layouts/15/treatybodyexternal/TBSearch.aspx?TreatyID=9&DocTypeID=11.

United States Census Bureau. (2014a). *65+ in the United States: 2010.* Retrieved from https://www.census.gov/content/dam/Census/library/publications/2014/demo/p23-212.pdf.

United States Census Bureau. (2014b). *An aging nation: The older population in the United States.* Retrieved from https://www.census.gov/prod/2014pubs/p25-1140.pdf.

United States Census Bureau. (2016). *An aging world: 2015.* Retrieved from https://www.census.gov/content/dam/Census/library/publications/2016/demo/p95-16-1.pdf.

Weathers, F. W., Blake, D. D., Schnurr, P. P., Kaloupek, D. G., Marx, B. P., & Keane, T. M. (2013). *The life events checklist for DSM-5* (LEC-5). Retrieved from www.ptsd.va.gov.

Wisconsin Board of Aging and Long-Term Care. (2011). *Awareness: Relocation stress syndrome.* Retrieved from http://longtermcare.wi.gov/docview.asp?docid=21549.

World Health Organization. (2017). *Palliative care fact sheet.* Retrieved from http://www.who.int/mediacentre/factsheets/fs402/en/.

# CHAPTER 12

# Truth and Reconciliation Commissions, Human Rights, and Trauma

## *David K. Androff*

In August of 2017, white supremacists marched on the grounds of the University of Virginia and in downtown Charlottesville (Stolberg & Rosenthal, 2017). They were protesting the planned removal of a statue of the Confederate General Robert E. Lee, and the renaming of two city parks which had previously been named for Confederate generals, complaining that such changes imperil their historical identity. This action by so-called white nationalist and "alt-right" groups, in open collaboration with white supremacist and racist organizations such as the Ku Klux Klan and neo-Nazis, drew many counter-protesters. Heated confrontations occurred, resulting in several violent clashes injuring people on both sides. The worst violence occurred when one of the white supremacists drove his car into a crowd of dispersing counter-protesters and killed one Charlottesville woman, Heather Heyer.

The Charlottesville City Council had voted to remove the statue earlier in the year as similar Confederate statues were being removed around the country. This trend was part of a growing recognition that such symbols celebrated America's racist past and represented explicit condoning

D. K. Androff (✉)
School of Social Work,
Arizona State University, Phoenix, AZ, USA
e-mail: David.Androff@asu.edu

© The Author(s) 2019
L. D. Butler et al. (eds.), *Trauma and Human Rights*,
https://doi.org/10.1007/978-3-030-16395-2_12

of racist behavior and attitudes in contemporary society. Indeed, the traumatic legacy of America's colonial and racist history has left deep wounds in Native American and African American communities, among others, communities who continue to suffer significant health disparities, civil and political disenfranchisement, great inequality and poverty, and stigmatization and discrimination. Despite progressive social movements such as the Civil Rights Movements, the United States still has not reckoned with its past—a past whose echoes can be heard today.

How should societies address such painful and traumatic histories? Such traumas damage not only individual victims, but also their neighborhoods, communities, and nations. How can a society recover once it has experienced a trauma? Societies around the globe are experiencing disruptions and dislocations that fray the social fabric. Mounting of pressures of overpopulation, climate change, inequality, extremism, and despotism are driving violent conflicts around the world. Can the social bonds of community be repaired after they have been ruptured? Can divided societies be healed?

Truth and Reconciliation Commissions (TRCs) offer one possible solution. TRCs have been employed around the world to help societies recover from the traumas of genocide, civil war, and oppression. TRCs pay particular attention to victims in an effort to heal the trauma suffered by individuals, groups, and communities during the course of human rights violations. TRCs are typically convened by governments to investigate prior human rights abuses. To seek the truth, TRCs bring together victims and perpetrators to testify in public forums about the nature and extent of the human rights violations. In some cases, this information is used for prosecutions; in others, amnesty is offered to incentivize perpetrator participation; still others avoid focus on the perpetrators. The conclusions of the investigation are publicly reported and meant to influence the historical narrative. Discovering and disclosing the truth, as well as bringing victims and perpetrators together, can begin a process of social recovery and healing from trauma. This chapter traces the development of TRCs and describes their connection to human rights and trauma.

## HISTORY OF TRUTH AND RECONCILIATION COMMISSIONS

Truth and Reconciliation Commissions were first developed in Africa and Latin American in the 1970s and 1980s and were used by countries in transition from dictatorships to democracies (Hayner, 2011). TRCs were viewed as one component of democratic reforms. At first TRCs were called simply Truth Commissions. Newly democratic governments used them as legal commissions to investigate large-scale human rights violations such as arrests, detentions, torture, and disappearances often conducted by repressive military regimes.

These early Truth Commissions were frequently criticized by the international human rights community (Teitel, 2014). They were seen as weak alternatives to prosecutions. Following World War II, when the modern human rights architecture was created in response to the Holocaust, the Nuremberg War Crimes Trials were regarded as the aspirational standard for accountability. Anything short of criminal prosecutions and punishment was regarded as a failure of justice. The Allied Powers' decisive victory over the Nazis may have set unrealistic expectations for accountability; the ensuing decades revealed much more nuanced political realities that are often complicated with ongoing conflicts, where victims often have to coexist with perpetrators. Early Truth Commissions were also criticized for offering reparations to the victims as "buying off" the victims. For these reasons, early Truth Commissions were not viewed as successful, despite the successful democratization of Argentina in 1983 and Chile in 1990.

## THE SOUTH AFRICAN INNOVATION

The perception of TRCs changed in the 1990s when the most famous TRC was launched in South Africa after the end of apartheid. The South African TRC was the largest and most ambitious TRC to have been undertaken. The world watched in awe at the peaceful transition of power after centuries of colonialism and decades of apartheid. Coupled with the transformative leadership of Nelson Mandela, the South African TRC represented a cultural moment at the end of the Cold War and before the new millennium: A symbol of what may be possible. The TRC was credited for supporting the new South African constitution and preventing the racial violence that many observers feared (Boraine, 2000; Gibson, 2004; Tutu, 1999).

The South African TRC was organized into three committees. The Human Rights Violations Committee collected over 21,000 survivor statements, the Amnesty Committee granted legal amnesty to over 1167 perpetrators who confessed their politically motivated crimes, and the Reparations and Rehabilitation committee provided payments along with therapeutic and social services to qualified victims (Hayner, 2011). That perpetrators applied for amnesty in return for their testimony was widely criticized as the TRC trading justice for truth. Many survivors and families of victims feared that perpetrators would escape justice, including the family of the murdered activist Steve Biko (Daley, 1999). The police who killed Biko applied for amnesty and testified that his death was accidental. For failing to admit guilt, the TRC denied them amnesty; they were not subsequently prosecuted due to insufficient evidence. However, the TRC did grant amnesty to the murderers of American student Amy Biehl who was killed while she was visiting friends in a black township.

The Amnesty Committee held almost 2000 hearings; not all perpetrators received amnesty for their testimony. In one high profile example, an apartheid death squad commander Eugene de Kock, nicknamed Prime Evil, made comprehensive confessions about his extrajudicial killings, disclosed the locations of weapons caches, and named names of superiors who gave the orders. Despite these confessions, he was not granted amnesty; his case was referred to the courts where he was convicted of crimes against humanity and sentenced to multiple life sentences. During his testimony and afterward in private meetings with the families of his victims, de Kock apologized and asked for forgiveness. He remains highly controversial in South Africa; some survivors have accepted his apologies in good faith, many have refused on the basis that he was among the worst of apartheid's killers.

Gibson (2004) found that the TRC was a successful component in the political transition from apartheid to democracy, and Stein et al. (2008) found the TRC to have met the expectations of the public. Several studies suggest that the TRC benefitted victims psychologically, legitimatized of their suffering, permitted their emotional expression in a safe space, and facilitated cathartic releases (Allan & Allan, 2000; Hamber, 2009). One survivor testified about being shot in the face by police, resulting in the loss of his sight; afterward he described his experience with the TRC as regaining his sight (Hamber, Nageng, & O'Malley, 2000). However, others reported retraumatization and distress following their testimony (de Ridder, 1997).

In addition, the TRC was criticized for failing to adequately meet the needs of victims (Chapman & van der Merwe, 2008). Victims saw the majority of perpetrators go unpunished. While some perpetrators were prosecuted, political elites at the highest levels of the apartheid regime faced no consequences. Furthermore, only some of the victims received small amounts of reparations for their harms suffered during apartheid. The larger structural economic inequalities, which were a core aspect of the apartheid regime, were not addressed or reformed. One TRC Commissioner complained that publicizing human rights violations without rectifying them was like receiving an apology for having your bicycle stolen: You can accept the apology, but you still need your bicycle back (Krog, 1999). This reflects the view that economic reforms and reparations are necessary to recover from traumatic legacies (Hayner, 2011).

The South African TRC is also notable for adding reconciliation to the truth commission formula. The original assumption was that truth-seeking would lead to the discovery of information that could be used in prosecutions of perpetrators that would deliver justice. However, several factors tend to inhibit such prosecutions, such as lack of jurisdiction, weak rule of law, and corruption in the judiciary (Hayner, 2011; Schabas & Darcy, 2004).

Where previous Truth Commissions operated from the traditional assumptions of a retributive justice system, with straightforward goals to investigate evidence, prosecute perpetrators, and punish the guilty, the South African TRC was based on a restorative justice paradigm (Androff, 2013). *Restorative justice* is a different theory of justice which contends that crime ruptures social relationships. Therefore, instead of primarily focusing on punishing the offender, restorative justice approaches focus on repairing the community. Because restorative justice acknowledges that crime injures not just the victim but also the community, these approaches involve all three parties—offenders, victims, and communities—in responding to crime and violence.

South Africa did not have the luxury of a decisive victory that afforded the Allied Powers the opportunity to prosecute war criminals. Rather, the TRC was part of a complex negotiation for a peaceful transition of power from apartheid to democracy. Therefore, a goal of the South African TRC was to promote reconciliation between the white Afrikaners population and the black African population. To accomplish this, the wounds from apartheid era had to be addressed, and if possible, remedied and healed. The black population had suffered significantly during apartheid, first due to policies of discrimination, deprivation, and exclusion and then due to increasingly violent reprisals against protest and resistance. To a much smaller extent, white South Africans had suffered violence on the part of the black liberation movement. The two populations had to coexist in mutual acceptance of each other for the new democratic transition to result in a functioning government that was accepted as legitimate by everyone. This new focus on healing in the South African TRC was represented in slogans such as "revealing is healing." The TRC also promoted the concept of Ubuntu. Ubuntu is a Zulu word and concept that is said to mean "I am me through you," a phrase which underscores how community and a sense of common humanity are at the center of the TRC.

## TRUTH AND RECONCILIATION COMMISSIONS ADAPTATIONS

International attention was captured by the South African TRC. Since then TRCs have become widespread in Africa, Asia, and Latin America as communities struggle to find measures to promote healing rebuilding in post-conflict settings. Since South Africa, all TRCs have focused on both truth-seeking and reconciliation. Liberia, Peru, Sierra Leone, and Timor-Leste are where TRCs proliferated after the popularization of the South African TRC (Hayner, 2011).

More recently, TRCs have been implemented in North America to address historical and contemporary racial discrimination and abuse (Androff, 2012a). The first TRC to be applied in the North American context was in Greensboro, North Carolina (Magarrell & Wesley, 2008). This was a grassroots, community-based effort that operated without official government sanction or mandate, unusual for TRCs. The focus was a 1979 KKK shooting that left five labor union activists dead. However, the TRC used the Greensboro Massacre to examine issues of racism, labor exploitation, and violence in the community.

Tribal groups have pioneered the use of TRCs to examine issues related to the forced schooling of indigenous children (Androff, 2012a). This included a national TRC in Canada and the Maine Wabanaki-State Child Welfare partnership between the US state of Maine and tribal nations. A human rights group started a TRC process in Detroit, Michigan to address federal discrimination in housing policy (known as *redlining*) that contributed to the ghettoization and impoverishment of African-American communities. There have been calls for TRCs to address major US issues such as the War on Terror (Rucker, 2009), Hurricane Katrina (Payton, 2006), police brutality (Davis, 2016), the legacy of slavery (Giridharadas, 2016), and the Trump administration (Baker, 2018).

## MECHANICS OF TRUTH
## AND RECONCILIATION COMMISSIONS

TRCs can be customized to fit local history, politics, culture, religion, and other dynamics (Androff, 2010b). However, there are some common features: They focus on the past; they investigate violations of human rights; they are temporary bodies that conclude with specific recommendations; and they have some form of mandate or sanction (Hayner, 2011). Every TRC is different in its specifics. Some are enacted through legislation, others through judicial decree, and still others as a result of community mobilization. The actors involved vary from politicians to religious leaders, victims' rights groups, and community organizers. Based on the composition of its members, each TRC has a different relationship to the courts. Some have subpoena power and others have differing mandates such as legal, political, or social/community. TRCs vary in the type of violations they investigate and the time frame to which the investigation is limited. TRCs typically incorporate local culture; the Timor-Leste commission incorporated animist shamans in village-level ceremonies (Androff, 2008). The Greensboro TRC relied heavily on volunteers from local faith-based communities and congregations (Androff, 2018).

*Truth-seeking* refers to investigations into the extent and nature of human rights violations. The focus is on discovering who did what to whom, learning what happened, and exposing crimes and abuses. When TRCs have subpoena power, they use it to obtain records and compel testimony. Often TRCs engage in data collection and research projects to analyze violations, such as surveys, censuses, and most commonly, interviews with victims and key informants. TRCs also hold public hearings and forums where victims and perpetrators testify about the human rights violations.

Truth-seeking serves several goals. Through interviewing victims, human rights violations are documented (Androff, 2012b). This is for potential prosecutions, as was the case in Argentina, Chad, and Peru (Hayner, 2011), and so that victims and the public, who are often ignorant about the specific nature of violations, can learn what happened. Often this ignorance is the deliberate result of misinformation on the part of perpetrators to obscure and obfuscate their actions. Frequently to mask their violence, perpetrators deceptively claim justification for military or armed intervention due to chaos or "violence on both sides."

Rigorous and sustained investigation can reveal who was in fact targeting whom. Other times the public is unaware of the specific nature of
violations due to discrimination and stigmatization. When people hold
dehumanizing and stereotypical views of minority groups, they can be
complicit in human rights violations. Therefore, truth-seeking is essential so that everyone can be made aware of what happened to the victims. During times of human rights violations, victims are often silenced.
Victims describe being traumatized twice, first by the act and second by
the silencing when their stories are unheard or discounted.

The truth-seeking of TRCs culminates with the release of a Final
Report when the TRC concludes and is disbanded. Final Reports detail
the findings of the investigation and present recommendations for the
future. The Final Report, as well as publicizing victims' and perpetrators'
public testimony before public hearings and open forums, serves the purpose of countering myths, lies, and stigmatization that persists and perhaps predates the violation. This work can correct the historical record so
that victims' perspectives become part of the larger narrative, education
curriculum, and memorialized in monuments and museums.

Each TRC has approached and delimited truth-seeking differently.
The TRC in Timor-Leste conducted several studies to establish a baseline mortality rate of the population that could be used to prove that
the mortality rate during the Indonesian occupation exceeded that of
the natural rate (Hayner, 2011). The data also exposed the large number
of deaths due to famine in the 1980s. Largely unknown to the outside
world, the Indonesian military destroyed local food supplies and displaced most of the population from their subsistence farming and fish-
ing residences into camps; many fled to the mountains. The Timorese
TRC was able to document and publicize data such as these to coun-
ter the Indonesian military's claim that it was protecting the population
from domestic terrorists and internal militias. Governments often justify
their political violence by claiming to protect the population from danger
(Stanley, 1996). However, the Timorese TRC Report was delayed due
to fear of reprisals from naming Indonesian perpetrators, many of whom
had become high-ranking officials (Hayner, 2011).

The Canadian, Guatemalan, and Moroccan TRCs were mandated
against publicizing the names of individual perpetrators in an effort to
prevent revenge attacks; this was criticized as a failure to hold individuals accountable (Hayner, 2011). The Canadian TRC's truth-seeking
publicized crimes committed in the Indian Residential Schools.

Although generations of victims had already passed away, documenting these abuses facilitated the establishment of museums, monuments, and other memorials. This was important due to the ongoing stigmatization against First Nations, Metis, and Inuit people, who are frequently blamed by the public for their high rates of poverty and substance abuse; their social problems are misunderstood as unrelated to their historical trauma. To address prejudice and ignorance about such legacies of human rights violations several TRC Final Reports, including those of the Canadian and Greensboro TRCs, have been incorporated into local educational curricula.

Reconciliation is the other main objective of TRCs. This part of a TRC's work is more ambiguous, due to varying and sometimes conflicting conceptualizations of reconciliation, and how it is achieved. Reconciliation can occur on the micro-, or interpersonal, level (Androff, 2010a) and also at the macro-, or community, level (Androff, 2012d). Reconciliation has theological connotations which can be reinforced in TRCs and have been popularized by religious leaders such as the Anglican Archbishop Desmond Tutu who chaired the South African TRC (Tutu, 1999). However, reconciliation may be better thought of as something necessary to prevent a return to violence. Reconciliation in this sense can be more minimalistic, having a lower baseline. The most basic expectation of reconciliation should be that perpetrators and victims can coexist peacefully. This type of mutual coexistence or reconciliation can have negative connotations for victims and advocates who regard any accommodation of perpetrators to be a corruption of justice. The main idea is that through the promotion of dialogue between victims and offenders, such as through their public testimony, a peaceful mutual coexistence can be created and sustained (Gibson, 2004).

## THE HUMAN RIGHTS CONTEXT FOR TRUTH AND RECONCILIATION COMMISSIONS

The modern international human rights foundation, beginning with the *Universal Declaration of Human Rights* (United Nations, 1948b), was created in response to the genocide of the Jewish people during the Holocaust of World War II. Over time, the type of human rights violations that TRCs have addressed has evolved as the intervention itself has grown and adapted. Early TRCs focused more on the so-called first-generation rights that are primarily civil and political rights.

For example, early TRCs in Argentina and Chile investigated the crimes of military dictatorships with mandates covering disappearances, imprisonment, torture, and extrajudicial killings. These rights are enumerated in the *International Covenant on Civil and Political Rights* (United Nations, 1966a) which has been ratified by 167 nations, including the United States. Especially, relevant is the *Convention against Torture and Other Cruel, Inhuman or Degrading Treatment or Punishment* (United Nations, 1984), which has been ratified by 153 nations, including the United States.

The South African TRC's mandate focused on all apartheid-era violence, which included both the civil and political rights identified above. However, apartheid was more than just a repressive regime that ultimately relied upon violence to maintain power; it was also a system of economic exploitation and social exclusion. Apartheid violations of human rights extend to the second generation of human rights to include exploitation, denial of education, denial of health care, and refusal to invest in social services for the Black South African population. Although the primary focus of the South African TRC was on politically motivated violence, these types of violations of second-generation rights also came into the picture. This trend continued with the Timor-Leste which extended the scope of truth-seeking to economic and social rights violations such as disruption of the populations' food source, exploitation of natural resources, including coffee and sandalwood, and destruction of physical infrastructure. These rights are laid out in the *International Covenant on Economic, Social, and Cultural Rights* (United Nations, 1966b), which has been ratified by 160 nations, not including the United States. Racial violence, discrimination, and exclusion are also covered under the *International Convention on the Elimination of All Forms of Racial Discrimination* (United Nations, 1965), which has been ratified by 175 nations, including the United States. Many of the TRCs after South Africa, including Timor-Leste, began to focus on how women's rights are especially violated during times of violence. This relates to the *Convention on the Elimination of All Forms of Discrimination against Women* (United Nations, 1979), which has been ratified by 187 nations, not including the United States.

The Canadian TRC and the Maine Wabanaki-State Child Welfare TRC also expanded the scope of which violations TRCs examined with an unprecedented focus on indigenous issues. They both address the genocide of indigenous populations. The removal of children of an ethnic or racial group is the fifth category of genocide as outlined in the *Convention on the Prevention and Punishment of the Crime of Genocide* (United Nations, 1948a), ratified by 147 countries including the United States. Previously it was the primarily the Guatemalan TRC which had focused on human rights violations against indigenous people, mainly of their civil and political rights. The Canadian and Maine TRCs focused on a range of first- and second-generation human rights violations that occurred through policies of forced schooling. This coercive colonial practice involved the forced removal of indigenous children from their homes and their placement into residential schools. Known as *Indian Schools*, these institutions were sites of physical and sexual abuse. Neglect and malnourishment were common; many children, ostensibly in the care of the state via child welfare and education systems, perished. In addition, children were prohibited from speaking their native language and practicing their native religion; the stated policy at the time was to "kill the Indian in the child." Beyond the violations of civil, political, economic, and social rights, this represents violations of cultural rights. The human rights of indigenous people are set forth in the *Indigenous and Tribal Peoples Convention* (International Labour Organization, 1989), which has been ratified by 22 countries, not including the United States. In 2007, the United Nations General Assembly passed the *Declaration on the Rights of Indigenous Peoples* (United Nations, 2007); the United States was one of four member states who voted against the Declaration, with Australia, Canada, and New Zealand; however, the United States endorsed the Declaration in 2010. Although not legally binding, it is a first step toward a stronger international protection for the rights of indigenous peoples.

In the future, it is likely that TRCs will be adapted to an increasingly expanded set of human rights violations. Others are beginning to apply a TRC model to climate justice (Klinsky & Brankovic, 2018). Given the importance of climate to the Sustainable Development Goals (United Nations, 2015b) and the Paris Climate Agreement (United Nations, 2015a), climate issues will become increasingly integrated into existing human rights frameworks. For example, the model of addressing historical harm and trauma could be applied to the environmental damage that industrialized economies have done in the past that disproportionately affect nations in the Global South.

## Trauma, Resiliency, and Truth
## and Reconciliation Commissions

TRCs operate in the aftermath of widespread human rights violations, yet in settings where there is little or no accountability for perpetrators. Victims, their families, and communities are frequently traumatized by violations of civil, political, health, and related human rights. TRCs are trauma-informed because their function is to acknowledge the trauma that occurred, and its products and outcomes are based on the understanding of that trauma (Butler, Critelli, & Rinfrette, 2011).

A core element of addressing human rights violations is addressing trauma in the hope that reconciliation is possible. TRCs understand victims have suffered trauma from having their rights violated. All the rights identified in the previous section, when violated, can cause traumatic reactions. As such TRCs respond to all manner of trauma, including but not limited to torture and injury, having family killed or disappeared, sexual assault and rape, destruction of property, discrimination, denial of care and services, and cultural destruction. However, victims are not engaged on the basis of their trauma; rather, it is on the basis of the violation of their human rights.

TRCs promote recovery, resiliency, and healing from trauma in several ways. These include promoting justice, truth-seeking, and reconciliation. As noted above, TRCs are more closely related to restorative justice than to retributive justice. However, when they do support prosecutions, this can be healing as achieving justice can give victims a sense of safety and closure. Punishing the perpetrators of human rights violations can restore moral boundaries that are often obliterated during times of mass human rights violations. It can help victims see that how they have been wronged has been made right. Restoring a moral foundation and common sense of wrong and right within a society can yield a community-based or social resiliency.

Despite the potential for TRCs to contribute to justice in these ways, TRCs are not, by design, primarily focused on retributive justice. Truth-seeking also contributes to healing from trauma. The process of victims telling their story of having their rights violated can be healing (Androff, 2012c). The main assumption is that victims will experience a cathartic relief that will relieve their traumatic stress and diminish their symptoms. By speaking publicly, the will gain control or even "re-order" their biography and repair their self-identity. Furthermore, testifying before a supportive and receptive audience such as a public commission can give victims acknowledgment and validation. Many victims report that the silencing and denial of their stories can be just as traumatizing. The truth-seeking function of TRCs can help to heal or at least provide opportunity to engage in a recovery from trauma. However, there are risks and limitations as well. TRCs may be supportive, but they are not therapeutic. There is a risk for victims that disclosing personal stories and talking about their traumas can be retraumatizing. Additionally, engaging with a TRC requires a certain level of functioning; severely traumatized victims may be unable to participate. Regardless, all victims should be offered supportive and therapeutic services to assist in their recovery. For example, the South African TRC was one of the few TRCs to have institutional supports for victims. However, these were acknowledged to be understaffed and insufficient to the need (Hamber, 2009). Chile and Timor-Leste made counselors and social workers available to victims during their testimonies at public hearings (Rushton, 2006). The Timorese TRC also incorporated indigenous community-based forms of healing that included local religious and spiritual traditions (Androff, 2008). The Canadian TRC did not include services to victims. Rather, the 2005 Indian Residential Schools Settlement Agreement, the historic Supreme Court decision that created the TRC included $125 million to the Aboriginal Healing Foundation for healing services (Castellano & Archibald, 2007).

If truth-seeking can enable recovery from trauma on an individual level, reconciliation can enable recovery from trauma on a macro-level. While less studied and therefore less conceptually clear than psychological trauma, community, social, and cultural trauma. By bringing perpetrators and victims together, TRCs can promote mutual tolerance among formerly antagonistic groups. This kind of social repair is vital to preventing future violence. TRCs also contribute to recovery from trauma through the education about human rights violations and re-humanization of victims and even perpetrators.

Androff (2010a) developed a typology of interpersonal reconciliation from Greensboro TRC participant experiences. The first stage is cognitive-affective reconciliation. *Cognitive-affective reconciliation* refers to a person's internal changes in attitudes, beliefs, and emotions, including examples such as decreased stigmatization or increased empathy. *Behavioral reconciliation* refers to a change in a person's behavior.

Examples include apologies, gestures, signs of respect, or some outward signal of good faith. It can include also the act of telling one's story. It may be the product of cognitive-affective reconciliation, or it may be otherwise motivated. *Social reconciliation* refers to a change in a relationship or social dynamic between two or more parties. This could be when one person acknowledges or accepts another person's behavioral reconciliation. This typology is interrelated but nonlinear.

## TRUTH AND RECONCILIATION COMMISSIONS AS TRAUMA-INFORMED, RIGHTS-BASED APPROACHES

Truth and Reconciliation Commissions are both trauma-informed and rights-based interventions. TRCs are trauma-informed in that they are created after a community or national trauma or series of traumas. They specifically address the trauma of those who have experienced human rights violations. Rights-based approaches apply human rights into practice and have been used across fields such as public health, international development, and United Nations programs. Androff (2016) has identified five principles of rights-based approaches for helping professionals. These include human dignity, nondiscrimination, participation, transparency, and accountability.

### *Human Dignity and (Re)humanization*

Human dignity underscores other aspects of rights-based approaches. The first and fundamental question of any rights-based approach is to ask: Does it respect people's human dignity? There have been many policies and programs designed to help others that do not. Too often human services and social policies treat people as some combination of needy, inadequate, and objects. This formulation diminishes their agency and denies their strengths, potential, and capabilities, and it can be retraumatizing. People must be seen as having human rights, not necessarily needs; human rights become the basis upon which people deserve safety, health care, social security, an adequate standard of living, and not on the basis of a deficiency. Respecting the dignity of victims of human rights violations also means respecting victims' need for safety (Butler et al., 2011). TRCs respect the human dignity through seeking the truth about human rights violations, acknowledging the harm caused to victims, and bringing perpetrators and victims together to rebuild relationships.

Respecting people's human dignity also means ensuring their self-determination. Self-determination relates to the trauma-informed principles of choice and control (Butler et al., 2011).

A second and related component of human dignity is that rights-based approaches should combat dehumanization and promote (re) humanization. The perpetration of most human rights violations is preceded by the dehumanization of the victim by the offender, typically through stigmatization, discrimination, and scapegoating. History suggests that the act of violating another's rights requires the violator to view the victims as subhuman. At the same time, victims are often dehumanized by the violation of their rights. This relates to the trauma that they have suffered. TRCs promote re-humanization by allowing the victims of human rights violations to tell their stories. TRCs rehumanize victims by giving victims a voice, through the documentation of their violated human rights, their public testimony in forums, and in the Final Report which may influence education and memorials. In sharing their stories, victims can become fully human again.

### Nondiscrimination and the Historically and Socially Excluded

Nondiscrimination means preventing discrimination on any basis, especially based on gender, age, ability, race, ethnicity, immigration status, religion, language, sexual orientation, or sexual identity. In addition to promoting inclusivity, the principle of nondiscrimination also requires attending to those who have been excluded from society. Human rights-based approaches must ask "who has been left out and left behind?" This is the express purpose of TRCs, which are designed to attend to those whose rights have been violated. TRCs inherently address historically marginalized or harmed groups that have suffered trauma.

Nondiscrimination includes promoting nonhierarchical relationships. Human services are often characterized by hierarchical relationships based on a power differential between professionals and the people that they would seek to help. Such inequalities in power between practitioners and clients can reinforce stigmatizations, disempower clients, and inadvertently retraumatize victims (Butler et al., 2011). Nonhierarchical relationships between professional and victims of trauma embody the trauma-informed care principle of collaboration (Butler et al., 2011). TRCs transforming relationships and promote nonhierarchical power dynamics by raising the voices of victims.

## Participation and Engagement

Participation is simultaneously a goal for human rights to achieve and a process for how human rights are to be achieved. People's participation is considered a human right, and enabling and empowering participation is an important avenue for achieving and realizing their human rights. The rights-based principle of participation means ensuring people a voice to influence the decisions that affect their quality of life, as with the trauma-informed care principle of choice (Butler et al., 2011). However, this often requires community development and capacity—building initiatives. When realized, the human right of participation can transform relationships of power and achieve the trauma-informed care principle of collaboration (Butler et al., 2011).

TRCs promote participation by getting people involved in the TRC process. The main ways that people participate are through testimony. This is important and relevant for both the individuals, who can gain validation and healing from telling their story, and also for the TRC, which gains valuable data and informs their findings in the Final Report. TRCs may collect testimony from thousands or tens of thousands of victims.

Overall TRCs are mixed in how much they incorporate participation. Many TRCs have been primarily top down but still create avenues for victim participation and engagement, as with the Timor-Leste TRC (Rothschild, 2017). The worst case for participation is when TRCs have been created by political elites for reconciliation at the top levels, such as the Brazilian TRC, which is regarded as a disappointment to victims (Torelly, 2018), or when the TRC is designed to whitewash painful histories, a criticism of the Burundi TRC (Vandeginste, 2012). Others are created by victims but strive for independence, such as the Greensboro TRC (Magarrell & Wesley, 2008). Ultimately, a TRC's success is largely determined by its public credibility. If people trust the process, such as with the South African, Guatemalan, and Peruvian TRC, then they will engage and support it.

## Transparency and Truth-Seeking

Transparency encompasses anti-corruption, assessment, monitoring, and evaluation. Transparency about human rights violations is critical and the purpose of TRCs' truth-seeking. In the process of discovering who did what to whom, TRCs' truth-seeking acts as a "needs assessment" by publicizing data on where rights have been violated and therefore where rights need to be protected and promoted, ensuring victims' safety. TRCs can expose, document, and even contribute to the prosecution of corruption. The truth-seeking process of TRCs coupled with the production of a Final Report can yield institutional reforms that reform corrupt organizations, agencies, policies, and institutions toward more open, transparent, and democratic norms. In this way, transparency is essential to promoting trustworthiness, a trauma-informed care principle, among victims of human rights violations (Butler et al., 2011). TRCs can promote a rebuilding of trust between victims and political institutions. The South African TRC has been found to have effectively built trust between the new democratic national government and the public (Gibson, 2004).

### Accountability and a Human Rights Culture

Accountability refers to advocacy, lobbying, and community education. It can also mean holding those responsible for human rights violations accountable for their actions. Accountability, more broadly than prosecuting perpetrators, refers to ensuring access to justice for victims as well as promoting democratic traditions and institutions. In a few cases prosecutions have resulted from TRCs; in others, reparations have been paid to victims. This is another form of accountability to repair past wrongs. Engaging survivors of trauma in lobbying and advocacy efforts, particularly in the pursuit of their human rights, can build their confidence and lead to empowerment, another trauma-informed care principle (Butler et al., 2011).

However, in most post-conflict settings, due to myriad limitations on the judiciary, accountability is not achieved through prosecution and punishment. Rather, it occurs through public education, the public's raised awareness about the violations and their consequences. The whole society becomes aware of the actions of the perpetrators and reflects upon how everyone, perpetrators as well as bystanders, facilitated the abuses. Through raising awareness, TRCs promote a human rights culture.

### CONCLUSION

TRCs constitute an important human rights intervention for nations, communities, and individuals recovering from trauma. TRCs have played valuable roles in creating spaces for victims to raise their voices and to seek justice. Despite this, TRCs can do more to increase their potential to contribute to the healing of victims of human rights violations. While victim statements are a core aspect of a TRCs work, TRCs can be made more responsive to the needs of trauma survivors. For example, all TRCs should have dedicated victim support teams available. Victims' testimony should be facilitated by trained clinical interviewers and supported with culturally appropriate counseling. TRCs staff in turn should be given adequate training and support to mitigate the risk of secondary traumatization. Long-term follow-up with victims should extend beyond the temporary term of the TRC. A TRC's success on any level depends on political will; victims are best served where there is the political will to confront the crimes of the past, to hold the perpetrators accountable, to break the silence about what happened to them. Victim healing from trauma should be accompanied by a strong emphasis upon reparations. Victims must be allowed and supported in the exercise of their human rights, especially their political and civil rights, such as advocating for supportive policies and institutional reforms.

Trauma, as a stress reaction, is uniquely tied to the past. Therefore, interventions related to confronting and overcoming the past, dealing with painful memories, and correcting legacies to reflect victims' truths are essential in responding to trauma. Shakespeare wrote, "What's past is prologue" ( *The Tempest*: 2.1.221). The past informs who people are, but it need not define them. Everyone is capable of change. Social change to prevent future human rights violations is an arduous undertaking; TRCs are one piece of the puzzle. Failure to address the echoes of the past can infect the present and indeed the future.

## REFERENCES

Allan, A., & Allan, M. (2000). The South African Truth and Reconciliation Commission as a therapeutic tool. *Behavioral Sciences & the Law, 18,* 459–477.

Androff, D. K. (2008). Working in the mud: Community reconciliation and restorative justice in Timor-Leste. In K. van Wormer (Ed.), *Restorative justice across the East and West* (pp. 123–144). Hong Kong: Casa Verde Publishing.

Androff, D. K. (2010a). 'To not hate': Reconciliation among victims of violence and participants of the Greensboro Truth and Reconciliation Commission. *Contemporary Justice Review, 13*(3), 269–285.

Androff, D. K. (2010b). Truth and Reconciliation Commissions (TRCs): An international human rights intervention and its connection to social work. *British Journal of Social Work, 40*(6), 1960–1977.

Androff, D. K. (2012a). Adaptations of Truth and Reconciliation Commissions in the North American context: Local examples of a global restorative justice intervention. *Advances in Social Work: Special Issue on Global Problems and Local Solutions, 13*(2), 408–419.

Androff, D. K. (2012b). Can civil society reclaim the truth? Results from a community-based Truth and Reconciliation Commission. *International Journal of Transitional Justice, 6*(2), 296–317.

Androff, D. K. (2012c). Narrative healing among victims of violence: The impact of the Greensboro Truth and Reconciliation Commission. *Families in Society, 93*(1), 10–16.

Androff, D. K. (2012d). Reconciliation in a community based restorative justice intervention: Victim assessments of the Greensboro Truth and Reconciliation Commission. *Journal of Sociology and Social Welfare, 39*(4), 73–96.

Androff, D. K. (2013). Truth and Reconciliation Commissions and transitional justice in a restorative justice context. In K. van Wormer & L. Walker (Eds.), *Restorative justice today: Practical applications* (pp. 205–213). Thousand Oaks, CA: Sage.

Androff, D. K. (2016). *Practicing rights: Human rights-based approaches to social work practice.* London, UK: Routledge.

Androff, D. K. (2018). A case study of a grassroots Truth and Reconciliation Commission from a community practice perspective. *Journal of Social Work, 18*(3), 273–287.

Baker, K. (2018, May 17). Nothing in all creation is hidden: Why American needs truth and reconciliation after Trump. *The New Republic.* Retrieved from https://newrepublic.com/article/148270/nothing-creation-hidden.

Boraine, A. (2000). *A country unmasked: Inside South Africa's Truth and Reconciliation Commission.* Oxford, UK: Oxford University Press.

Butler, L. D., Critelli, F. M., & Rinfrette, E. S. (2011). Trauma-informed care and mental health. *Directions in Psychiatry, 31*(13), 197–201.

Castellano, M. & Archibald, L. (2007). Healing historic trauma: A report from the Aboriginal Healing Foundation. *Aboriginal Policy Research Consortium International.* Paper 11. Retrieved from https://ir.lib.uwo.ca/cgi/viewcontent.cgi?article=1333&context=aprci.

Chapman, A. & van der Merwe, H. (Eds.). (2008). *Truth and Reconciliation in South Africa: Did the TRC deliver?* Philadelphia: University of Pennsylvania Press.

Daley, S. (1999, January 11). Officer denied amnesty in the killing of Steve Biko. *New York Times.* Retrieved from https://www.nytimes.com/1999/01/11/world/officer-is-denied-amnesty-in-the-killing-of-steve-biko.html.

Davis, F. (2016). This country needs a Truth and Reconciliation Process on violence against African Americans—Right now. *Yes!* Retrieved from http://www.yesmagazine.org/peace-justice/this-country-needs-a-truth-and-reconciliation-process-on-violence-against-african-americans.

de Ridder, T. (1997). The trauma of testifying: Deponents' difficult healing process. *Track Two: Constructive Approaches to Community and Political Conflict, 6*(3/4). Centre for Conflict Resolution. Retrieved from http://journals.co.za/docserver/fulltext/track2/6/3-4/track2_v6_n3_a14.pdf?-expires=1532637206&id=id&accname=guest&checksum=4FF87F65E-2C28A4BA342722C7E58A593.

Gibson, J. (2004). *Overcoming Apartheid: Can truth reconcile a divided nation?* New York, NY: Russell Sage.

Giridharadas, A. (2016). Turning the call for racial reckonings back on the U.S. *New York Times.* Retrieved from https://www.nytimes.com/2016/07/19/us/truth-reconciliation-commission-slavery.html.

Hamber, B. (2009). *Transforming societies after political violence: Truth, reconciliation, and mental health.* New York, NY: Springer.

Hamber, B., Nageng, D., & O'Malley, G. (2000). "Telling it like it is…" understanding the Truth and Reconciliation Commission from the perspective of survivors. *Psychology in Society, 26,* 18–42.

Hayner, P. (2011). *Unspeakable truths: Transitional justice and the challenge of Truth Commissions* (2nd ed.). New York, NY: Routledge.

International Labour Organization. (1989, June 27). *Indigenous and Tribal Peoples Convention,* C169. Retrieved from https://www.refworld.org/docid/3ddb6d514.html.

Klinsky, S., & Brankovic, J. (2018). *The global climate regime and transitional justice.* New York, NY: Routledge.

Krog, A. (1999). *Country of my skull: Guilt, sorrow, and the limits of forgiveness in the new South Africa.* New York, NY: Three Rivers Press.

Magarrell, L., & Wesley, J. (2008). *Learning from Greensboro: Truth and reconciliation in the United States.* Philadelphia: University of Pennsylvania Press.

Payton, J. (2006). Truth, accountability, and Hurricane Katrina. *Human Rights, 33*(4), 7.

Rothschild, A. (2017). Victims versus veterans: Agency, resistance, and legacies of Timor-Leste's Truth Commission. *International Journal of Transitional Justice, 11*(3), 443–462.

Rucker, P. (2009). Leahy proposes panel to investigate Bush era. *Washington Post.* Retrieved from http://www.washingtonpost.com/wp-dyn/content/article/2009/02/09/AR2009020903221.html.

Rushton, B. (2006). Truth and reconciliation? The experience of Truth Commissions. *Australian Journal of International Affairs, 60*(1), 125–141.

Schabas, W., & Darcy, S. (2004). *Truth commissions and courts: The tension between criminal justice and the search for truth.* Dordrecht, The Netherlands: Kluwer Academic Publishers.

Stanley, W. (1996). *The protection racket state: Elite politics, military extortion, and civil war in El Salvador.* Philadelphia, PA: Temple University Press.

Stein, D., Seedat, S., Kaminer, D., Moomal, H., Herman, A., Sonnega, J., et al. (2008). The impact of the Truth and Reconciliation Commission on psychological distress and forgiveness in South Africa. *Social Psychiatry and Psychiatric Epidemiology, 43*(6), 462–468.

Stolberg, S., & Rosenthal, B. (2017, August 12). Man charged after white nationalist rally in Charlottesville ends in deadly violence. *New York Times.* Retrieved from https://www.nytimes.com/2017/08/12/us/charlottesville-protest-white-nationalist.html.

Teitel, R. (2014). *Globalizing transitional justice: Contemporary essays.* New York, NY: Oxford University Press.

Torelly, M. (2018). Assessing a late Truth Commission: Challenges and achievements of the Brazilian National Truth Commission. *International Journal of Transitional Justice, 12*(1), 194–215.

Tutu, D. (1999). *No future without forgiveness.* New York, NY: Doubleday.

United Nations. (1948a). *Convention on the Prevention and Punishment of the Crime of Genocide.* Retrieved from https://www.ohchr.org/en/professionalinterest/pages/crimeofgenocide.aspx.

United Nations. (1948b). *Universal Declaration of Human Rights.* Retrieved from http://www.un.org/en/universal-declaration-human-rights/.

United Nations. (1965). *International Convention on the Elimination of All Forms of Racial Discrimination.* Retrieved from https://www.ohchr.org/en/professionalinterest/pages/cerd.aspx.

United Nations. (1966a). *International Covenant on Civil and Political Rights.* Retrieved from http://www.ohchr.org/EN/ProfessionalInterest/Pages/CCPR.aspx.

United Nations. (1966b). *International Covenant on Economic, Social and Cultural Rights.* Retrieved from http://www.ohchr.org/EN/ProfessionalInterest/Pages/CESCR.aspx.

United Nations. (1979). *Convention on the Elimination of All Forms of Discrimination Against Women.* Retrieved from http://www.un.org/womenwatch/daw/cedaw/text/econvention.htm#article6.

United Nations. (1984). *Convention Against Torture and Other Cruel, Inhuman or Degrading Treatment or Punishment.* Retrieved from https://www.ohchr.org/en/professionalinterest/pages/cat.aspx.

United Nations. (2007). *United Nations Declaration on the Rights of Indigenous Peoples*. Retrieved from https://www.un.org/development/desa/indigenous-peoples/declaration-on-the-rights-of-indigenous-peoples.html.

United Nations. (2015a, December 12). *Paris Agreement*. Retrieved from https://unfccc.int/process-and-meetings/the-paris-agreement/the-paris-agreement.

United Nations. (2015b). *Transforming our world: The 2030 agenda for sustainable development*. Retrieved from https://sustainabledevelopment.un.org/post2015/transformingourworld.

Vandeginste, S. (2012). Burundi's Truth and Reconciliation Commission: How to shed light on the past while standing in the dark shadow of politics? *International Journal of Transitional Justice, 6*(2), 355–365.

# CHAPTER 13

# Afterword: Human Rights and the Science of Suffering

## Sandra L. Bloom

The twentieth century has become known as the Century of Megadeath. Human beings destroyed other human beings in numbers too astonishing to absorb in the name of many different ideas and ideals and in defiance of the multitude of injunctions from many different wisdom traditions of "Thou Shalt Not Kill." But the last century was not just about the wanton destructiveness pushing humankind to the brink of annihilation.

The human rights movement emerged out of the profound suffering of that century, although as several creative interpreters have pointed out, the discourse about human rights is deeply rooted in earlier conversations in many cultures (Donnelly, 2013; Hunt, 2007; Ishay, 2008; Van Cleef, 2008). The opening words of the *Universal Declaration of Human Rights* ring out today as a clarion call for forever preventing another man-made global catastrophe through the clear assertion that "recognition of the inherent dignity and of the equal and inalienable

S. L. Bloom (✉)
Health Management and Policy, Dornsife School of Public Health,
Drexel University, Philadelphia, PA, USA

© The Author(s) 2019
L. D. Butler et al. (eds.), *Trauma and Human Rights*,
https://doi.org/10.1007/978-3-030-16395-2_13

rights of all members of the human family is the foundation of freedom, justice and peace in the world" (United Nations, 1948).

Trauma theory and all the researches associated with it about the effects of stress, toxic stress, and traumatic stress on body, mind, and soul across the life span also emerged as a product of war, the Holocaust, and other disasters, and it has become what I think of as the science of suffering. This science is accompanied by an anthropology, a sociology, a history, an economics, a religion, and an art of suffering. Trauma is and has been a central organizing principle of all human experience and behavior that has been largely ignored in the full understanding of what it means to be human in part because all of these aspects of suffering are not yet fully integrated as components of an overall paradigm shift in our understanding of human nature. The Declaration of Human Rights and the Convention on the Rights of the Child have encoded this recognition in a set of universal values and principles, making the willful infliction or tolerance of suffering the only true universal—although frequently ignored—taboo.

Something else emerged out of the twentieth century—a new paradigm beginning in quantum physics about the nature of reality, the world, and us. It seems we are all interconnected in a vast networked fabric of existence (Capra, 2002; Laszlo, 2008). The version of this new paradigm in psychiatry was social psychiatry, and it too arose out of the tumult of the twentieth century. As in quantum theory and the emergent field of systems theory, the focus of social psychiatry was a deliberate attempt to move away from ideas about the individual isolated from others and move toward an understanding and practice that connects the individual to others and all people to large-scale events. The emphasis in social psychiatry was not just on treatment but also on *prevention*. It represented the emergence of interdisciplinary studies in which all of the humanities had a voice in informing our understanding of how to prevent the destruction of the century from happening again.

The scientific study of the effects of stress, adversity, and violence on human development similarly emerged in that same era. Beginning with the research of John Bowlby and others after World War II, we began evolving a new perspective on the importance of early childhood relationships. By the end of the century, the Adverse Childhood Experiences Study and all the science about the continuous unfolding aspects of child development had revealed the delicate, complex, and interactional nature of the child and the adult that child becomes. The genome project then revealed to us that all human beings are members of the same family, regardless of the color of our skin, and that the racial divides that have served to justify eons of misery constitute mythological beliefs (Sussman, 2014).

Taken together, these shifts in the scientific paradigm that underlies all that we think, feel, and do have the possibility of rapidly changing our worldview. Changing our worldview is vital if we are to save ourselves and the planet. We have an array of tools for self-destruction surrounding us, drivers of extinction that most of us would rather deny as we deal with our own harried lives. Certainly, civilizations have collapsed before, but life has continued. Never before has our sentient species been confronted with the possibility—and with every passing second, the probability—of extinguishing all life on earth. When we focus on human rights, we are being too restrictive. What we can see now is that the human rights movement is directly connected to the right of life to exist at all. Humanity has become the steward of these rights, a truly terrifying responsibility for which we are largely unprepared.

The authors in this book have taken on the challenge of uncovering ways to integrate two powerful late twentieth-century discourses: human rights and trauma theory, and I feel honored to be asked to write the Afterword for their prodigious work. That these two discourses have even been running down separate tracks is an example of a well-known problem that has emerged in the last several centuries: We have accumulated an enormous amount of data about just about everything but there has been little attempt to *integrate* all of it into a manageable and meaningful whole. This book makes a step forward in that direction. The editors set out the context of the book by making it clear that in the human rights discourse, humanity is being set a moral standard that explains and explores the paradigm shift that we are immersed within. As we learn about the evolution of human rights standards we can begin to see the still vague outline of what health in human cultures could actually look like.

The other authors variously point us toward other key concepts: that women's rights and children's rights are human rights; that monitoring human rights violations at every level of our service delivery system is vital; that many populations have experienced—and continue to experience—multiple, multigenerational trauma that does not just disappear and therefore an overemphasis on resiliency may be doing a disservice to many; that moving from identification and treatment to policy and advocacy is vitally important but also requires different skills and therefore expanded collaborative efforts; that incorporating activism as an important component of trauma treatment and transformation may be a vital component of restoring hope, meaning, and purpose to people's lives.

Without stating it, the editors and all of the authors are setting out frameworks that will be the only form of social immunity available to us as humanity goes through the overwhelming trauma that is coming as a result of climate change. My contribution to this rich collection of powerful and passionate discourses is a historical and philosophical musing triggered by absorbing the wisdom of the chapters of this book and being myself a sentient being traversing through the tumult of this century. The chapter begins with a brief explanation of my own journey of awakening and explores some of my efforts to make sense of what I have learned. Through a brief review of some of the roots of social psychiatric thought that were dominant in the first six decades of the twentieth century, I hope to show the interconnected nature of prior psychiatric thought and the overlap with human rights, explain something about how this knowledge was lost, and then explore how those intertwined discourses have arisen again as a result of traumatic stress studies.

## Reminiscences

I am a child of the 1960s, a postwar baby boomer, growing up in a lower middle-class, safe suburban family of working parents. From adolescence on I was immersed in the feminist slogan that the "personal is political," that all oppression begins within a social context, and that there is therefore no way to avoid the economic and political origins of adversity. I attended college during an era when it was usual to participate in student protest against the conflict in Vietnam, American apartheid, and discrimination against women. Before college, during college, and upon entering medical school I worked summers and holidays at an urban hospital where the results of poverty, community violence, sexism, and racism were abundantly obvious and fundamental components of our approach to medical and psychiatric care.

Once I decided to embark on a career in psychiatry, my mentors were themselves political activists who did not hesitate to connect American politics and economics to the mental health problems we encountered daily. I began my psychiatric studies during an era of community mental health, democratic therapeutic communities, and social psychiatry when it looked like the humanities as disciplines were beginning to converge. Studying sociology, anthropology, history, and philosophy was simply a part of what we did as students to try to grapple with the complexity of human suffering. We were well aware that we existed within an only partially conscious world, that most of what happened within and between people was unconscious and influenced by a multiplicity of factors. As physicians we worked collaboratively with social workers, psychologists, and creative therapists. Each specialty had a different lens for viewing each patient, and being able to view the complexity of a person through multiple lenses lent strength to our shared ability to promote healing and recovery. I learned the value of true collaborative teamwork and of a leveled hierarchy based on mutual respect.

Social psychiatry was embedded in the post-World War II human rights framework that was eagerly extended to those suffering from emotional disorders of all kinds, and before that in the cataclysm of World War I. One prominent spokesperson of the day wrote, "the mentally ill person is seen as a member of an oppressed group, a group deprived of adequate social solutions to the problem of individual growth and development" (Ullman, 1969, p. 263). The goals of social psychiatry—the mainstream and dominant discourse at the time—were extensive and unequivocally political: "To include all social, biological, educational, and philosophical considerations which may come to empower psychiatry in its striving towards a society which functions with greater equilibrium and with fewer psychological casualties" (Jones, 1968b, p. 30).

As a result of this experience, the human rights framework seemed both obvious and necessary. I saw no contradictions between social psychiatry and human rights—they were different levels of analysis and action but dealt with similar issues—what it means to be a suffering human and what it takes to minimize or eliminate human suffering. Human rights workers were acting to change the political contexts within which trauma occurred, while mental health workers including psychiatrists were acting on the results of human rights violations within individuals and families, and sometimes communities.

## THE DEEPER ROOTS OF SOCIAL PSYCHIATRY, EMPOWERMENT, AND HUMAN RIGHTS

These ideas of the mid-twentieth century were the natural evolution of earlier connections made between mental disorder and the social context extending back to the moral treatment movement in the eighteenth century and to social philosophers like Emil Durkheim, George Mead,

Charles Cooley, William McDougall, and John Dewey in the nineteenth and early twentieth centuries (Bloom, 2013). During that period discoveries in physics were beginning to explore the relational nature of the universe. Similarly, psychiatry in America began to shift to a deepening understanding of reciprocal processes and extend the previous work of the social philosophers (Witenberg, 1974).

According to a number of authorities, the origins of the first usage of the words "social psychiatry" are to be found in the work of E. E. Southard, the Director of the Boston Psychopathic Hospital from 1912 to 1920, and in his usage became the practice of applied sociology, an interdisciplinary body of knowledge and practice (Bell & Spiegel, 1969). In an early textbook, he described social psychiatry as a new and promising specialty, "an art now in the course of development by which the psychiatrist deals with social problems" (Southard & Jarrett, 1922, p. 523).

In what was then the new field of psychiatry, Adolf Meyer is considered by many to have been the most influential psychiatrist of the early twentieth century, and his ideas of "psychobiology" and "common sense psychiatry" were still profoundly important during the period of my early training and experience. Interestingly, he had grown up in Switzerland, a democratic republic since the 1200s, and Swiss values of democracy, broadmindedness, practicality, and respect for both individual and collective judgment were said to have a continuous and powerful influence on his understanding of human nature (Lamb, 2014).

Meyer's ideas were supported by progressive reform movements in the United States at the end of the nineteenth century and the start of the twentieth century that expressed an abiding confidence in the interconnectedness and malleability of the individual and society, and, importantly, a belief that deliberate action guided by qualified experts would lead to progress. Along with many peers, he had faith in the ability of humans to ameliorate social problems by means of collective action, economic and political efficiency, and science (Lamb, 2014). For Meyer, mind and body were united and influenced by biology and by culture. Emotional disorders were largely problems of failed adaptation. In 1925, he wrote that "This gives us a science which would mean the acceptance of man as the product of physicochemical, biological, and finally psychobiological interpretation, an intrinsically social type of individual, the heir, structurally and culturally, of a succession of civilizations" (p. 538). The practical application of psychobiology was a systematized study of the working of the various determining factors in mental illness, resulting from disharmony with environment, and a search for factors of adaptation (Lief & Meyer, 1948).

Trigant Burrow, with an MD and a PhD in psychology, and a student of Meyer's, was one of the founders of the American Psychoanalytic Association in 1911 and its president in 1926. After being analyzed by Carl Jung and practicing psychoanalysis for years in Baltimore, he became disillusioned with psychoanalysis as a useful approach to psychopathology that he was conceptualizing in an entirely different way, and in doing so took a radical diversion from his psychoanalytic colleagues. This disillusionment with individual approaches led him to create an alternative community where he and his colleagues practiced what would become group therapy but which they termed *phyloanalysis* because they believed that they were uncovering the deep, inherited, and destructive flaws of the species. In 1927, he wrote,

> the question is often asked whether insanity will ever become curable. The answer can only be that the insanity of the individual cannot be curable as long as there exists the insanity of the social mind about him. It is not humanly possible for the psychiatrist to remedy conditions of mental disorganization as long as he himself is part of the disorganized social mind. (p. 24)

Dr. Burrow spent his long life, from 1875 to 1950, wrestling with the reality he saw that "Individual discord is but the symptom of a social discord" (Burrow, 1926, p. 87). From his studies of individuals and groups, he believed that social insanity was, like smallpox and measles, a communicable process, "We do not recognize that of all communicable diseases the most communicable are mental diseases, that in the sphere of mental disharmonies communicableness is itself the essential disease" (Burrow, 1926, p. 87).

Another giant of American psychiatry characterized as "America's most original modern psychiatrist" (Witenberg, 1974, p. 844), Harry Stack Sullivan sounded a similar theme, articulating a split that continues to haunt American mental health services of all kinds,

> Either you believe that mental disorders are acts of God, predestined, inexorably fixed, arising from a constitutional or some other irremediable substratum, the victims of which are to be helped through an innocuous life to a more or less euthanistic exit.... Or you believe that mental disorder is

largely preventable and somewhat remediable by control of psychosocio-
logical factors. (Albee, 1981; Witenberg, 1974, p. 9)

For Sullivan, a person was constituted by a complex interplay of physiological, psychobiological, and situational factors. These included all the
conditions that inhibit or facilitate the development of the person. As
one of his biographers explained, "From the first mysterious contagion
between child and mother to the last personal interchange of the old
man at the•moment of death, the human person is a being in process—
not a fact but an act" (Witenberg, 1974, p. 844).

Yet another important voice came from Karen Horney, lending a powerful female voice to the evolution of social psychiatric thought in the
twentieth century. Horney, trained in Freudian psychoanalysis as well,
viewed man as a social being who could only become fully human in a
cultural milieu. She felt that the development of psychopathology was significantly determined by the cultural conditions of development and she
focused on three fundamental conditions that foster feelings of helpless-
ness, insecurity, hostile tension, and emotional isolation as well as com-
petitiveness that brings "the germs of destructive rivalry, disparagement,
suspicion, and begrudging envy into every human relationship" (Horney,
1966, p. 173). She believed that economic exploitation, inequality of
rights and opportunities, and an overemphasis on success bred destructive
feelings in those affected. She saw a second set of factors related to cultural contradictions, such as the emphasis on winning and competition, in
conflict with the equal emphasis on love and humility, as well as the cultural emphasis on freedom combined with ever-increasing restrictions and
constraints. A third set of factors related to conflicts in the individual over
what the culture rewards or punishes. She understood the neurotic individual as someone who had experienced injurious influences in childhood
and who had essentially become "a stepchild of our culture" (p. 863).

## PREVENTING ANOTHER WORLD DEVASTATION

After World War II, it became universally obvious that what psychiatrists
of an earlier era had been pointing out was true. Ideas connecting social
stress, the social determinants of psychopathology, and the influence of
society permeated psychiatric knowledge and research (Albee, Joffe, &
Dusenbury, 1988; Caplan, 1961, 1964; Joffe & Albee, 1981b). As one
analyst wrote in 1949,

Our jails and prisons are filled with criminals. Our institutions are filled with insane. Our hospitals are filled with cripples—cripples mangled by war. Wars are made by bullies. Bullies are made by fear. And this kind of fear is made by injury to the child, physical or emotional injury when the child is too young, too helpless, to be able to protect himself. This culture criminally ignores the fact that the question of peace or war tomorrow is in the wombs of the mothers of today. (Moloney, 1949, p. 337)

In the first two and a half decades after World War II, spurred on and made obvious by the devastation of two global wars, the Holocaust, the dropping of the nuclear bombs, and the constant threat of nuclear warfare as well as the growing problems related to totalitarianism and the Cold War efforts to articulate prevention moved to center stage. The Korean conflict, as well as the repeated assassinations of key leaders, accentuated political and philosophical divisions that remain with us today.

By mid-century, George Albee, one of the founders of community psychology, was stating that "the principal noxious agent for emotional disorders is stress. The principle source of stress worldwide is poverty. Poverty is at the root of many of the stresses that have been identified as causing emotional distress" (Albee, 2006, p. 451). The problems that emerged out of the devastating events of the twentieth century made it quite clear that if psychiatry was to find a way not just to treat, but also to prevent mental health problems, we could not ignore the multiple social problems that give rise to war, poverty, discrimination, and inequality. One of the seminal thought leaders of mid-century psychiatry, William Menninger, made the cover of *Time* magazine and wrote that "Every institution in American society has to evaluate its program "in terms of the contribution to individual and group mental health" and that it was vital to determine "the more serious community-caused sources of emotional stress" (Grob, 1991, p. 20).

The movement toward community-based inpatient treatment was aligned with a growing push for deinstitutionalization of the enormous state hospitals that, due to their size alone, were hugely expensive and depersonalized and sometimes abusive. In 1945, the average daily resident population of mental institutions was about 430,000; approximately 85,000 were first-time admissions. Nearly 88% of all patient care episodes occurred in mental hospitals; the remainder were located in general hospital psychiatric units. In 1951, total state expenditures for all current operations were $5 billion. Of this sum, 8% was for mental hospitals (Grob, 2005).

Part of the discourse for closing state hospitals derived from Erving Goffman's (1961) analysis of the impact of "total institutions" like asylums on mentally ill patients in the United States. Beginning in the 1960s and gathering momentum throughout the 1970s, clearing patients out of state hospitals and back into the community was frequently articulated as a human rights issue, and various movements to protect the rights of the mentally ill began to grow in the United States and in Europe (Sheth, 2009). At the same time, others focused on human rights abuses of those termed mentally ill in the Soviet Union and in China and in other countries using torture as a political tool ("Abuse of Psychiatry in the Soviet Union," 1983; American Psychiatric Association, 1985; Nightingale & Stover, 1985). The first committee to oppose political abuse of psychiatry was founded in 1974 and eventually became the Netherlands-based Geneva Initiative on Psychiatry. From then on, pressure on the Soviets and bloc countries mounted with condemnations by the British Royal College of Psychiatrists (BRCP), the American Psychiatric Association, and the World Psychiatric Association (WPA), among others ("Psychiatry and Human Rights Abuses," 2004).

In an important book published in 1955, noted psychologist Erich Fromm echoed earlier social critics when he wrote:

> many psychiatrists and psychologists refuse to entertain the idea that society as a whole may be lacking in sanity. They hold that the problem of mental health in a society is only that of the number of 'unadjusted' individuals, and not of a possible unadjustment of the culture itself. (p. 15)

He then went on to define what he meant:

> An unhealthy society is one which creates mutual hostility [and] distrust, which transforms man into an instrument of use and exploitation for others, which deprives him of a sense of self, except inasmuch as he submits to others or becomes an automaton. (pp. 71–72)

Fromm recognized that disconnecting the utilization of scientific concepts from ethical principles could have devastating results. It meant that a man could kill a hundred or a thousand people by pushing a button and not react emotionally to his act, though that same man might experience overwhelming feelings of guilt and shame were he to injure one helpless person (Witenberg, 1974).

As the connections between social conditions and the development of emotional problems were becoming abundantly more obvious, many other psychiatric workers began to address prevention, particularly those at the "coalface" of community mental health. Like Albee and associates, they sought to define and discuss *preventative psychiatry* (Albee et al., 1988; Caplan, 1961, 1964; Joffe & Albee, 1981b). The purpose of this expansion of knowledge was to (1) find ways to reduce the incidence of mental disorder of all types in a community (primary prevention); (2) reduce the duration of a significant number of those disorders which do occur (secondary prevention); and (3) reduce the impairment which may result from those disorders (tertiary prevention) (Caplan, 1964). The role of psychiatrists was to expand because they needed to acquire knowledge of a much wider range of issues—social, economic, political, administrative, and so forth—anything that would enable them to plan and implement programs that focused not only on individual patients but beyond them on the community problems of which they were a part.

## CREATING DEMOCRATIC THERAPEUTIC ENVIRONMENTS

As the influence of deinstitutionalization was growing and was perceived as not just a medical issue, but also a human rights issue, many people still needed extensive services which then had to be delivered within the community. One of the key sites for secondary as well as tertiary prevention was the acute care inpatient psychiatric setting usually called *therapeutic milieu settings*. The 1960s saw the rise of both democratic therapeutic communities and therapeutic milieus across the United States.

These programs, often in community hospitals, were based on principles that grounded an understanding of psychopathology of all kinds in terms of power dynamics and rights: "The fundamental premise of any therapeutic milieu is the sharing of power between all members of the community" (Kennard, 1998, p. 60). A primary assumption was that people had become mentally ill within the context of a social environment and that a psychiatric inpatient program was a microcosm of society which could be seen as a kind of laboratory for social change (Tucker & Maxmen, 1973). As was pointed out at the time, "In the United States, in the United Kingdom, and in other parts of the world, the therapeutic community impulse furthered the idea that a community created in the 'reverse image' of a society at large can be therapeutic for the casualties of that society" (Kennard, 1983, p. 34). By this time, there was a widespread understanding about the dangers of authoritarianism and the totalitarianism that follows in its wake that had been so evident in the events of the previous decades. At the same time, social movements including the feminist movement, the anti-war movement, and the civil rights movement were demonstrating clearly that "the personal is political" and the growing discourse around human rights served the purpose of bringing a value-based philosophical conversation into all of these activist movements.

From the beginning of its development, therapeutic milieu ideas were meant to be applied to a wide variety of settings and populations including schools and prisons (Bloom, Bennington-Davis, Farragher, McCorkle, Nice-Martini, & Wellbank, 2003; Jones, 1962; Kennard, 2004). One of the key founders of the therapeutic community, Maxwell Jones (1968a; see also 1968b), wrote:

> What distinguishes a therapeutic community from other comparable treatment centers is the way in which the institution's total resources, staff, patients, and their relatives, are self-consciously pooled in furthering treatment. That implies, above all, a change in the usual status of patients. (pp. 85–86)

The therapeutic community was designed to be a living-learning situation where everyone had the opportunity to learn from everyone else. To make that possible, power had to be distributed in a very different way, a way that was defined as both permissive, tolerant, respectful, and democratic. In such an environment there needed to be an emphasis on creating a culture of inquiry where basic assumptions about oneself and the other could be re-examined and potentially changed within the context of real life experiences within the therapeutic community. Although largely unshared beyond the world of mental health treatment, therapeutic communities were actually uncovering the necessary substructure of participatory, democratic processes.

The therapeutic community (TC) approach was found to be particularly essential for the post-World War II treatment of returning and troubled veterans and former prisoners of war, and then for the chronically unemployed who had serious personality problems (Jones, 1953; Wilmer, 1958). These were all people—initially men—who had been exposed to traumatic and often very abusive childhood, adolescent, and/or adult experiences with the abusive use of power and the violation of human rights, so the ways in which the issue of power was addressed in any therapeutic milieu became an essential focus.

The TC model represents an attempt to erode the traditional hierarchy existing between clients and staff, replacing this with a more collaborative and power-sharing relationship. When successful, the effect is to produce a more "equal" and symmetrical state of affairs. Each of the parties knows where it stands in relation to the other, in terms of role expectations and, importantly, also the limits of these. Achieving this reciprocity comes via the delegation to the clients of much of the authority conventionally invested in the professional role. (Norton & Bloom, 2004, p. 251)

The foundational ideas around therapeutic environments, patient empowerment, democratic processes, and social responsibility were derived from the experiences of war and survival on the psychiatric community in Europe and in the United States. There was little question in minds of these innovators by the end of World War II that

It seems eminently reasonable to view the concept of the trauma itself as a potential opportunity for growth; we must seek to determine appropriate procedures as a function of the interaction between the subject, significant others in his social world, and socially skilled professional workers during the period of stress,

wrote Maxwell Jones (1968a, p. 86).

The 1960s also saw the rise of "anti-psychiatry" largely coming from clinicians who were mobilizing powerful critiques to psychoanalysis, Kraepelinian diagnostic ideology, coercive forms of treatment, racial and social injustice, and social stigma. In some ways, they picked up the baton of Trigant Burrow and carried it forward but with even more strident critiques. There were many voices of radical psychiatry, representing different ideas including David Cooper, Thomas Szasz, R. D. Laing, and Claude Steiner. Consistent with the questioning and challenging environment of young people in this era, young psychiatrists were also asking some fundamental questions through this discourse:

In this field most particularly, in the midst of people in extreme situations, one experiences the Zen 'doubt sensation' - why am I here, who put me here, or why have I put myself here (and what is the difference between these questions), who is paying me for what, what shall I do, why do anything, why do nothing, what is anything and what is nothing, what is life and death, sanity and madness? (Cooper, 2007, Preface)

For R. D. Laing and David Cooper, both practicing psychiatrists in the UK, the hallmark characteristic of psychiatry was a misunderstanding of "madness," a decontextualization from the social and political context of psychosis and its relationship to disordered family functioning. Laing described the diagnosis of schizophrenia as a theory, not a fact, and Cooper (2007) noted that "Over the last century psychiatry, in the view of an increasing number of present-day psychiatrists, has aligned itself far too closely with the alienated needs of the society within which it functions" (Preface). Thomas Szasz (1974), on the other hand, declared that the very idea of mental illness was a myth, that problems in living were an entirely different category than illnesses of the body, and that he particularly opposed coercive measures used in psychiatry. He perceived much of the problem with psychiatry as centering on the abuse of individual rights.

## THE PERSONAL IS POLITICAL, RIGHTS AND SCIENCE

By the 1970s, it was clear to those of us who were young practitioners that we were engaged not only in medical treatment but also in working to further human rights. The second wave feminist slogan asserting the close connection between our personal lives and the social and political context was evident in the work we were engaged in. Each of us had to figure out how to balance respect for fundamental rights of our patients with protection of ourselves and others in the environment when violence was threatened, but at a deeper philosophical level, there was no contradiction in the discourses. The postwar therapeutic community experiences had shown that paying attention to the social norms of the environment, practicing democratic values, and becoming constantly aware of the interplay of power dynamics within and among every member of a community were all vital if we were to create nonviolent environments (Wilmer, 1958, 1964). We could see in our own lives at home and at work that the personal was indeed political.

For those workers involved in community mental health and preventive psychiatry, it was impossible to ignore the deep and clear connections between emotional disturbance, power inequities, and income inequality. As the political context for psychiatry became increasingly obvious, workers in mental health were increasingly vocal about the undermining of equality that was damaging individuals and our society as a whole. Albee and colleague (Joffe & Albee, 1981a), ever vigilant, summarized their findings pointing out the political, economic, and social conditions promoting mental health problems:

There is a strong tendency in our society to separate and isolate social problems. We have a social problem labeled violence against children in the family, and others labeled battered wives, sexism, racism, abuse of elderly persons, family disruption, poverty and unemployment, the incarceration and decarceration of persons we call mentally ill, the neglect of the mentally retarded, and the isolation of the physically handicapped, to name just a few. What do all these problems involving different groups have in common? We have suggested, for your consideration, the best answer we can come up with. It is their powerlessness. People without power are commonly exploited by powerful economic groups who explain the resulting psychopathology by pointing to the defectiveness of the victims. The rest of us do not rush to the defense of the victims because we are caught up in the ideology that puts 'justice' in the hands of those with power. We join the groups "blaming the victims.".... If we see all these groups as powerless because of socioeconomic conditions, then a logical approach is to determine whether there might be an equitable redistribution of power.... Without meaning to be simplistic, we would like to suggest that we examine the arguments in the papers for a redistribution of power through a redistribution of wealth in our society. (p. 322)

This blatant criticism of the existing social structure came at a time when typical American values were being challenged on every front—in the family, the workplace, communities, schools, and in society as a whole. Could materialistic values give way to increasing concerns about the results of economic inequity and ecological destruction? Could women and African-Americans be given equal protection and equal rights? Could warfare finally be prevented through increasing democratization at home and around the globe? Could technology be the key to creating a global civilization, and in doing all this, could human rights finally come onto center stage as humanity's fundamental priority? General systems theory of the late 1960s and early 1970s began to provide a way of thinking about complex adaptive systems consistent with these emerging values but further research on complex systems was going to have to wait for the development of computer technology that could meet the needs of complexity (Marmor, 1983; Von Bertalanffy, 1974).

At this point most of us were unaware of Thomas Kuhn's seminal work, *The Structure of Scientific Revolutions*, that was originally published in 1962 (Kuhn, 1970). In it, Kuhn had recognized the role of values in science, that there is no such thing as a values-free application of theory. Scientists have often pretended that values can be completely independent from the human beings performing the science and endorsed a concept that without the burden of moral decision-making, progress in science occurs smoothly, while theories and models are continually being refined and replaced by newer and more accurate versions (Capra & Luisi, 2014). Kuhn exposed this notion as invalid, recognizing that underlying all theory choices are deeper assumptions of belief and of value.

Developing these ideas further, Capra and Luisi (2014) asserted that there is a recurrent historical tension in science: "the basic tension is one between the parts and the whole. The emphasis on the parts has been called mechanistic, reductionist, or atomistic; the emphasis on the whole, holistic, organismic, or ecological" (p. 4). They pointed out that these are two very different lines of inquiry that have been in competition with one another throughout our scientific and philosophical tradition. For most of the time, the study of matter—of quantities and constituents—has dominated. But every now and then the study of form—of patterns and relationships—came to the fore (Capra & Luisi, 2014). During the Scientific Revolution of the seventeenth century, values had been separated from fact and here, values were being drawn back into the discussion about the etiology of mental disorders. It was being asserted that if we changed our values to those being described by feminists, civil rights workers, ecologists, and human rights workers, then we could prevent most of the problems plaguing humanity.

But mainstream psychiatry was uncomfortable and largely unprepared to address these enormous political, economic, and social dilemmas, and the need for revolutionary change if mental illness, as being articulated, was to be prevented. The wheel was turning. As causal explanations were becoming ever more complex by the mid-1970s, psychiatry was turning away from a systemic way of viewing fundamental problems as patterns and back toward the ages-old focus on mechanism and number via a biological explanation for mental illness and in doing so, taking up the cudgel of diagnosis.

## The Wheel Turns

Beginning in the 1970s, psychiatry began to radically change with mounting opposition to preventive psychiatry, the community mental health movement, and all aspects of social psychiatry. Vehement criticism arose in the pages of influential journals. In 1979 came one attack on efforts at primary prevention with a criticism of the "fuzziness of the concepts" and the "assumption – which is yet unproved – that difficult life circumstances lead to mental illness"....while going on to state that the "cause and effect relationship between social conditions and mental illness is extremely questionable" (Lamb & Zusman, 1979, p. 13). In another article, the same authors state that

> recent research....in particular, the adoption studies of Kety and others (1976)....indicates that major mental illness is in large part genetically determined; therefore, it is probably not preventable and at best only modifiable. Even that it can be modified is questioned by many, and there is little hard evidence one way or the other. (Lamb & Zusman, 1982, p. 22)

By the end of the 1980s, biological psychiatry had achieved dominance and had successfully displaced psychoanalysis, psychodynamic, and systems theory as the driving forces within the discipline, completely overshadowing the biopsychosocial model derived from Meyerian psychiatry of the earlier decades. This abrupt turning away from previous experience and the failure to integrate the knowledge gained over the prior century was influenced by many factors. The development of psychiatric drugs, the economic power of the psychopharmaceutical industry, the urgent pressure for rapid deinstitutionalization, frustration with psychoanalytic and psychodynamic approaches, and a repressive reaction to widespread social unrest led to a dramatic upswing in the medicalization of what had been previously understood as complex and interactive individual and social problems (Hari, 2018).

A new generation of psychiatrists were being selected and trained, often by psychiatric residency directors who were eager to bring about change as well as garner economic support for their programs from research grants coming from pharmaceutical companies. As an anthropologist who studied these changes wrote,

> These psychiatrists saw themselves as scientists, and to them that word set them apart from psychoanalysis, to which many of them were openly hostile and which few of them regarded as scientific. ... The psychiatric scientists were committed to what they called strict standards of evidence, and they tended to view psychoanalytic theories of causation as neither provable nor disprovable by those standards. They were determined to create a psychiatry that looked more like the rest of medicine, in which patients were understood to have diseases and in which doctors identified the diseases and then targeted them by treating the body, just as medicine identified and treated cardiac illness, thyroiditis, and diabetes. (Luhrmann, 2000, p. 225)

With increasing fervor and the power of advertising, the public began being given repeated messages. One was that psychiatric diagnosis was as firm and definitive as medical diagnoses. The subsequent diagnostic categorization schemes of the DSM-III, III-R, IV, IV-R, and 5[1] each introduced ever-widening definitions of mental illness (Frances, 2014; Greenberg, 2013). This diagnostic fervor was said to be so important because discoveries had been made showing clearly that mental illnesses are biochemically induced and often genetically determined and although not preventable by known means, could be treated effectively with pharmaceutical preparations (Whitaker & Cosgrove, 2015).

By the 1980s, George Albee, along with Justin Joffee, edited a seminal text about preventing psychopathology titled *Prevention Through Political Action and Social Change* (Joffe & Albee, 1981b), a book that can almost be viewed as a "cri de coeur" for what was by then the disappearing idea of prevention in mental health discourse. In the opening chapter, Albee (1981) wrote:

> Back in the days when the world was a much simpler place, a great many of us held firmly to the belief that scientific judgments were based on facts and that social policy changed with accumulating scientific findings, and that theories were held only so long as they were supported by objective evidence. Those who thought of themselves as politically liberal held to the conviction that the world was slowly and steadily changing for the better, and that with improved education, more scientific research, new evidence, and practice society would eventually reach a condition of universal justice and fairness. I am a slow learner. I no longer believe these things to be true. I now believe that the thirst for power is an addiction, far more dangerous than any other addiction... Power needs override the tempering consequences of human empathy and blind the addict to considerations of justice and fairness. (p. 5)

Since that time, psychiatry has consistently been powerfully influenced by a restrictive and reductionist medical model. Although there is an abundance of sound data showing that psychotherapy plus medication gives a significant benefit over either approach alone, many insurance plans refuse to cover psychotherapy or cover only a minimum of sessions. And new psychiatric residents do not receive the intensive psychotherapy training that was characteristic of earlier training experiences (Luhrmann, 2000). The concerns of human rights activists pointed out in this book, that political, social, and economic injustice and oppression is in danger of being medicalized and individualized, should not be overlooked, since that is exactly what has occurred in psychiatry during the last few decades. Psychiatric thought leaders became those who were focused on the molecular level of brain disorders and largely away from the social situations that may have been creating those molecular-level problems.

More disturbing yet are the multiple critiques that expose the enormity of corrupt influence that raise consistent questions about whether or not the medications now prescribed in epic quantity are actually effective, confirming Albee's prescient comments about the addictive nature of power—and the money that trails along with it (Barber, 2008; Bentall, 2009; Hari, 2018; Healy, 2012; Whitaker, 2010; Whitaker & Cosgrove, 2015).

## TRAUMATIC STRESS AND ADVERSITY: RETURN OF THE REPRESSED

The war in Vietnam stretched from 1955 to 1975. It was a devastating time in American culture as the older generation and the younger generation polarized not unlike the polarization we see today between liberal and conservative, except then the dividing line was age and experience. But it was also in the 1970s that the human rights movement, as it is currently understood, gained credibility around the globe after the failure of the multiple totalitarian utopias of the twentieth century became apparent (Moyn, 2012). Veterans from the Vietnam war, their families, psychiatrists, and other activists campaigned to get a diagnosis of post-traumatic stress disorder because the previous diagnostic category that had been applied to sufferers of combat-related psychiatric disorders had been removed from the diagnostic manual in 1968, and as a consequence these men and some women could not get treatment or benefits from the VA. The diagnosis of PTSD arrived in 1980, and that can be seen as a marker for the beginning of the traumatic stress field. The International Society for Traumatic Stress Studies (ISTSS) had its first formative meeting in 1985, while what is now the International Society for the Study of Trauma and Dissociation (ISSTD) formed around the same time. From the beginning of trauma studies, it was clear that values could not be omitted from traumatic stress science when it was perfectly obvious that most trauma occurred in the context of the abusive use of power and that exposure to adversity was largely determined by the political, social, and economic context of individuals' life experience.

The original stated purpose of the ISTSS was "to advance knowledge about the immediate and long-term human consequences of extraordinarily stressful events and to promote effective methods of preventing or ameliorating the unwanted consequences" (Figley, 1986, p. xxvi). In 1998, I served a term as the President of the ISTSS. In service of the honor of being elected, I interviewed as many of the founding members of the organization as I could access and subsequently wrote a history of the organization's first years. As had already been pointed out by others, one remarkable aspect of the organizational history was the extent to which the founding mothers and fathers had personal experience with trauma (van der Kolk, Weisaeth, & van der Hart, 1996). As I discovered,

> War crimes, war protests and war babies; child abuse, incest and women's liberation; burning monks, burning draft cards and burning crosses; murdered college kids and show trials of accused radicals; kidnappings, terrorism and bombings; a citizenry betrayed by its government and mass protests in front of the Capitol in Washington—all play a role in the backgrounds of the people who founded the organization and in the evolution of the organization itself. (Bloom, 2000, p. 28)

Among those who were pioneering this field of study there was no question that understanding and responding to the political and social context was vitally important, nor that struggle for human rights was at the core of the scientific field that was being developed. To be part of the solution instead of a part of the problem it was necessary to speak truth to power. Charles Figley, the original organizer and first ISTSS President, had served in Vietnam (Figley, 1985, 1986). Robert Lifton, psychiatrist in postwar Japan and in Korea and longtime human rights advocate, researcher, and activist, was one of the participants at the original organizing meeting, and his understanding of the sociological context for the traumas of combat, of totalitarianism, of the threat of nuclear annihilation, and of thought reform was embedded in traumatic stress studies from its inception (Lifton, 1961, 1963, 1967, 1973, 1986, 1987, 1993). The third President, Yael Danieli, served in the Israeli military before immigrating to the United States and was herself the child of Holocaust survivors (Danieli, 1997). She became very involved with the United Nations (UN) and was instrumental in bringing knowledge about traumatic stress studies to an international audience.

As the first person to call extensive attention to the plight of adult survivors of sexual abuse, Dr. Judith Herman (1992) wrote in her seminal book *Trauma and Recovery* that

To hold traumatic reality in consciousness requires a social context that affirms and protects the victim and that joins victim and witness in a common alliance. For the individual victim, the social context is created by relationships with friends, lovers and family. For the larger society, the social context is created by political movements that give voice to the disempowered. The systematic study of psychological trauma therefore depends on the support of a political movement. (p. 9)

In the 1980s and 1990s, I had the opportunity of learning about the impact of trauma from Dr. Judith Herman, Dr. Bessel van der Kolk, and several thousand adult survivors of child abuse and other forms of interpersonal trauma. I had the good fortune to be learning in an interdisciplinary environment where all of my colleagues were learning about these experiences at the same time (Bloom, 1997). As we saw the enormity of what we were uncovering in a psychiatric inpatient setting and in the relatively small community within which we were embedded, we recognized how little we had truly understood about the development of mental health problems in spite of good training. We also began to grasp the parallel impacts on us, our families, our workplaces, and our society. I began to conclude that traumatic experience has been so much a part of human evolution that it had been largely ignored as a central organizing principle of human thought, feeling, and behavior until there were sufficient numbers of the population to have *not* experienced the magnitude of trauma experienced by their predecessors. By 1991, we recognized that as an entire team, we had been experiencing a "paradigm shift," a fundamental change in the way we understood and responded to our patients and each other. At the time, we spoke of this shift as a change from asking the primary question of "What's wrong with you?" to "What's happened to you?" (Bloom, 1994).

I too went through a paradigm shift for myself when my prevailing and finally life-determining question became, "Why should those events have to happen to people in the first place?" The context of my patients' abusive and traumatic life experiences was critically important in understanding the impact those experiences had had on development of body, brain, and mind.

We were discovering what I have begun calling the science of suffering. The psychobiology of trauma, the emerging body of research and clinical wisdom about the multigenerational impact of traumatic experience and its impact on attachment behavior was offering us an underpinning for the practice of the therapeutic community. But it was also providing an integrative framework for multigenerational family therapy and the wide variety of therapeutic approaches that had evolved over the previous century to address widespread human suffering. I began thinking that the extreme fragmentation that had plagued the mental health world for so many years could be overcome through this scientifically grounded, integrative framework that would help all of us to come to grips with the complex biological, psychological, social, economic, political, and existential impacts of trauma (Bloom & Reichart, 1998).

Radical changes occurred in the patients when they were offered a different and coherent cognitive framework to understand their lives and their problems—a trauma-focused approach. This shift in our perspective that has now become known as *trauma-informed* (Harris & Fallot, 2001) allowed us to see our patients as survivors of life's torments who had adapted as best they could, as will any living creature, but who had in the process become derailed in a wide variety of ways. We came to see ourselves less as healers or fixers and more as educators, coaches, and mentors.

Throughout this period, the 1980s and 1990s were in full swing with all of the extreme emphases on materialism and denial of more fundamental social problems that characterized that era. Despite my previous political activism, little had prepared me for embracing the devastating magnitude of traumatic experience in my culture that we were learning about every day. As I wrote in another chapter,

> My job as an individual therapist, as the medical director for a psychiatric unit, and as the supervisor for several dozen other clinicians meant that over the course of two decades, I was compelled to bear witness to thousands – not hundreds, but thousands – of terrible stories. When it all began, we could not conceive that there could be so much evil in the world. Within a few years, we could not conceive of ever having not known there was so much evil in the world. (Bloom, 2017, p. 39)

By this time, the research arm of traumatic stress studies was launched and actively making the field of study more credible and academically acceptable. As research kept flooding in, supported by our own experience and observation, it also became evident that the vast majority of psychological and social pathology is related to a past history of trauma, that a substantial proportion of physical illness is likewise related, and that most of the clients in virtually every other social service system have a similar history. We began recognizing the mark of trauma everywhere, in ourselves, our systems, and the world around us, what we spoke of as the *parallel process* nature of reality, what in systems theory is known as *isomorphism*.

This was a wake-up call. At the time I was comfortably ensconced in suburbia with a lucrative and successful practice and a healthy management contract to operate our program designed to compassionately respond to the needs of the "mentally ill." My colleagues and I had never completely forgotten our roots in social psychiatry, but the mores of the 1980's did not lend themselves to philosophical speculation about the sources of oppression that constituted our psychiatric care. So when I began to grasp that the evolution of the psychiatric problems in the majority of our patients—and at the time these mostly middle-class Caucasians—had begun with exposure to violence in childhood, frequently exacerbated by exposure to more violence as adults, it was no longer possible to ignore the social and political forces around me.

This distress was paired with anger and righteous indignation as I grappled with a sense of betrayal by my profession (Freyd, 1996). I had been trained to believe that the illnesses of my patients were largely of indeterminate cause and recovery was not even discussed as a meaningful possibility. Our job, my job, was to reduce symptoms, and in doing so, alleviate suffering. As a physician, I was assigned the responsibility for diagnosis, for treatment planning, for medication management. For the most problematic symptoms, medications were both necessary and inevitable, despite the many side effects that accompanied them. Neurotic symptoms were to be addressed with psychotherapy and sometimes medication. Personality disorders were said to be largely untreatable without intensive, long-term forms of treatment that were becoming increasingly unavailable, so it was advised that we not even try to treat them. That I never had entirely swallowed all this I had attributed to my own quirkiness and relative ignorance, not to bad information.

But now the research in traumatic stress and later the Adverse Childhood Experiences work was demonstrating that the number of people exposed to overwhelmingly traumatic experiences either and/or as children represents a majority of the population. It became clear that people who have survived traumatic experiences are not just in psychiatric hospitals, prisons, or homeless shelters. They are doctors and lawyers, judges and teachers, mechanics and truck drivers. They campaign for human rights, and they resist the oppression of dictators. They are also the dictators. They serve in the military, and they serve in the Peace Corps. They run businesses and lead governments. As a consequence, it became obvious that one-to-one psychotherapy would never be able to reverse this situation and that most of the pathology we all have to address was at some point in time preventable.

That recognition produced a fault line in my psyche that is still unhealed, and it is a fault line in traumatic stress studies. As the field matured, and increasing numbers of clinicians and researchers became interested in what was being uncovered, and as traumatic incidents like the Oklahoma City bombing and 9/11 continued to unfold, most of the attention has gone to what those of us trained in the health care, mental health care, and social services fields know how to do—treatment. And that does make it appear that the field is being medicalized; meanwhile, the ability to rapidly and thoroughly bring about change even in the population of individuals who can be more effectively treated with trauma-specific methods has been severely limited and often curtailed by destructive changes in the funding of mental health services. Now reductionism, in the guise of a demand for "evidence-based practice," has come to dominate not only psychiatry but the other professions as well. Increasing numbers of clinicians are prohibited from providing services that are not manualized and evidence-based, meaning that they have been subjected to the rigors of randomized, controlled—and very expensive—studies. On its surface, developing conclusive evidence that a strategy is effective makes sense and should have been standard operating practice all along. Unfortunately, the standard for defining an intervention as "evidence-based" is so high that very few interventions can meet the criteria. Experienced clinicians who are confronted with the complexity of the problems related to prolonged suffering recognize that the evidence-based practices that exist are often "necessary but not sufficient."

In the early years, many of us thought that scientific discovery alone would be enough to change our systems. All of the progress has made a significant difference for individuals and their families, but little has happened to change the sources of the problems. We are still on the edges of the river, pulling babies threatened by drowning out of the water, but few are upstream figuring out how to keep the babies from being thrown in. That is where advocacy for human rights comes in. We must depend upon other people, with different available skills, who can change policy and change minds at every level and in every government, since we are now a global society. The trauma field has provided the scientific underpinning for the human rights movement, and somehow we have to bridge the gap between science and activism and offer our knowledge as an invaluable weapon in the war of ideas to those who can effectively use it. I have come to firmly believe that we live in a global culture that is organized around—and routinely reenacting—the unresolved traumatic experiences of the past. There is no more important goal than trying to figure out how everything we have learned from trauma survivors since that last World War can influence the current of events that is driving all of us toward a future that is unsustainable—to species suicide—and instead move us collectively toward a future worth surviving.

As a trauma specialist, I am certainly not alone in the frustration that affects everyone who works in helping trauma survivors. As a former President of the European Society for Traumatic Stress Studies (ESTSS) has put it,

> The ESTSS track record must involve raising awareness of trauma, its sequelae, and effective interventions. Yet, I still struggle with a question of what the core matter or crucial ingredient of psycho-traumatology really is. Two answers come to mind. The first is that all considerations of trauma interfaces with human rights as they pertain to individuals right through to global matters. It is this practical and legal perspective, not theories or models, that should furnish the foundation for our field. I would welcome a shift in ESTSS, so human rights becomes its explicit focus. (Ørner, 2013, p. 4)

And from the conclusion of two weighty tomes devoted to trauma psychology, the editors (Gold, Cook, & Dahlenberg, 2017) write,

> And yet with the waning connection of trauma studies to the consideration of the political structures that allow or actively promote the violent victimization of the powerless and disenfranchised – women, children, ethnic minorities, the poor, sexual minorities, the elderly, the disabled – trauma studies and trauma practice have been diminished by a certain level of detachment from the reality of human suffering and the political conditions that actively foster it. There is a limit to how much trauma psychology specialists can do to reduce trauma-related suffering if our work does not encompass the sociopolitical conditions that perpetuate

victimization through marginalization, disenfranchisement and disempowerment. (p. 573)

## THE CHALLENGE GOING FORWARD: INTEGRATION OR COLLAPSE

Humanity brings into the world of the twenty-first-century adaptations that belong to our ancestors and that helped us to survive but that now can be viewed as the major public health problem confronting us as an entire species. The overarching question that the authors of the chapters in this book ask is, "How can we integrate all of the advances in understanding and treating trauma-related dysfunction with an emphasis on monitoring, responding to, and ultimately preventing abuses of human rights?" If you watch current events, you may have noticed the strong human tendency to avoid or ignore highly complex problems such as this question asks while posing overly simplistic solutions to other complex problems such as climate change, worldwide shifts in populations, and nuclear disarmament.

In her book, *The Watchman's Rattle*, sociobiologist Rebecca Costa (2012) pulls headlines from today's news to demonstrate how accelerating complexity quickly outpaces the rate at which the human brain can develop new capabilities. She calls this the *cognitive threshold*, the point at which a society can no longer think its way out of its problems and instead passes the unresolved issues on to the next generation. With compelling evidence based on research in the rise and fall of Mayan, Khmer, and Roman empires, Costa shows how the tendency to find a quick solution to complex problems leads to frightening long-term consequence: a society's ability to solve its most challenging, intractable problems becomes gridlocked, progress slows, and collapse ensues. She raises the question about whether our knowledge of previous civilizations can help us avoid the same problems for our own. As the renowned sociobiologist, E. O. Wilson ("An Intellectual Entente," 2009, n.p.) has put it: "we have paleolithic emotions, medieval institutions, and god-like technology."

Visionary utopian ideas have always been criticized, but we need now not a vision of perfection but a vision of *survival* which can only happen through collective thought, feeling, action, and not just the survival of me, or my group or your group, or my country or your country, but the literal survival of life on Earth. We have never been here before. Behavior change is a result of changes in attitudes, while attitudes change as a result of changes in our systems that depend entirely on our deeply held mental models that only change when the scientific paradigm changes, and that can only change when the deepest systemic assumptions—our worldview—change. This level of change—a change in worldview—is the real power behind the integrated function of trauma studies and human rights advocacy.

Long ago, Adlai Stevenson, mid-twentieth century US Presidential candidate and Ambassador to the UN, observed:

> We travel together, passengers on a little space ship, dependent on its vulnerable reserves of air and soil; all committed for our safety to its security and peace; preserved from annihilation only by the care, the work, and, I will say, the love we give our fragile craft. We cannot maintain it half fortunate, half miserable, half confident, half despairing, half slave—to the ancient enemies of man—half free in a liberation of resources undreamed of until this day. No craft, no crew can travel safely with such vast contradictions. On their resolution depends the survival of us all... (quoted in Grinspoon, 2016, p. 405)

Until we collectively decide to stop promoting the conditions that allow children to be abused, neglected, and otherwise violated, and adults to be repeatedly exposed to interpersonal violence, we will continue to be confronted with the refugees of our own domestic warfare. Where does the study and treatment of trauma survivors and human rights advocacy come together? In a new global political principle and practice which is really our own hope of survival in this threatened world, Hannah Arendt (1979) summed it up:

> Antisemitism (not merely the hatred of Jews), imperialism (not merely conquest), totalitarianism (not merely dictatorship)—one after the other, one more brutally than the other, have demonstrated that human dignity needs a new guarantee which can be found only in a new political principle, in a new law on earth, whose validity this time must comprehend the whole of humanity while its power must remain strictly limited, rooted in and controlled by newly defined territorial entities. We can no longer afford to take that which was good in the past and simply call it our heritage, to discard the bad and simply think of it as a dead load which by itself time will bury in oblivion. The subterranean stream of Western history has finally come to the surface and usurped the dignity of our tradition. This is the reality in which we live. And this is why all efforts to escape from the grimness of the present into nostalgia for a still intact past, or into the anticipated oblivion of a better future, are vain. (p. ix)

We—meaning humanity—have taken a new evolutionary leap, and it is up for grabs whether we are going to fall into the chaos of destruction or leap into a new kind of species. We began as weak and vulnerable hunter-gatherers living in small groups only to become the dominant species now numbering in the billions. Our technological expertise gives us the capacity to destroy all life on the planet. We are now planetary stewards, and can we make that leap into the unknown, or will we create our own black hole of trauma? David Grinspoon (2016), an astrobiologist and senior scientist at the Planetary Science Institute and adjunct professor of Astrophysical and Planetary Science at the University of Colorado, has written that

> The scientific community is now converging on the idea that we have entered a new phase, or epoch, of Earth history—one in which the net activity of humans has become a powerful agent of geological change, equal to the other great forces of nature that build mountains and shape continents and species. The proposed name for this new epoch is the "Anthropocene" or the age of humanity. This concept challenges us to look at ourselves in the mirror of deep time, measured not just in decades or centuries or even in millennia, but over hundreds of millions and billions of years.... We are witnessing, and manifesting, something unprecedented and still completely unpredictable: the advent of self-aware geological change... Many species have changed the planet, to the benefit or detriment of others, but there has never before been a geological force aware of its own influence.... In seeing ourselves as a geological process, we also see the planet entering a phase where cognitive processes are becoming a major agent of global change.... We have, unconsciously, been making a new planet. Our challenge now is to awaken to this role and grow into it, becoming conscious shapers of our world. (pp. x–xiv)

## Note

1. American Psychiatric Association, *Diagnostic and Statistical Manual of Mental Disorders*, 1980, 1987, 1994, 2000, 2013, Washington, DC.

## References

Abuse of psychiatry in the Soviet Union: Hearing before the subcommittee on Human Rights and International Organizations of the committee on Foreign Affairs and the Commission on Security and Cooperation in Europe, House of Representatives, 98th Cong., 1st session. (1983). Retrieved from https://

www.csce.gov/sites/helsinkicommission.house.gov/files/Abuse%20of%20 Psychiatry%20in%20the%20Soviet%20Union.pdf.

Albee, G. W. (1981). Politics, power, prevention and social change. In J. M. Joffe & G. W. Albee (Eds.), *Prevention through political action and social change* (pp. 5–25). Hanover, NH: University Press of New England.

Albee, G. W. (2006). Historical overview of primary prevention of psychopathology: Address to the 3rd World Conference on the Promotion of Mental Health and Prevention of Mental and Behavioral Disorders September 15–17, 2004, Auckland, New Zealand. *Journal of Primary Prevention, 27*(5), 449–456.

Albee, G. W., Joffe, J. M., & Dusenbury, L. A. (Eds.). (1988). *Prevention, powerlessness and politics: Readings on social change*. Newbury Park, CA: Sage.

American Psychiatric Association. (1985). Report of the task force on human rights: Task force on human rights. *The American Journal of Psychiatry, 142*(11), 1393–1394.

An intellectual entente. (2009, September 10). *Harvard Magazine*. Retrieved from http://harvardmagazine.com/breaking-news/james-watson-edward-o-wilson-intellectual-entente.

Arendt, H. (1979). *The origins of totalitarianism: New edition with added prefaces*. New York, NY: Harcourt Brace Jovanovich Publishers.

Barber, C. (2008). *Comfortably numb: How psychiatry medicated a nation*. New York, NY: Random House.

Bell, N. W., & Spiegel, J. P. (1969). Social psychiatry: Vagaries of a term. In A. Kiev (Ed.), *Social psychiatry* (Vol. I, pp. 52–70). New York, NY: Science House.

Bentall, R. P. (2009). *Doctoring the mind: Is our current treatment of mental illness really any good?*. New York: NYU Press.

Bloom, S. L. (1994). The Sanctuary Model: Developing generic inpatient programs for the treatment of psychological trauma. In M. B. Williams & J. F. Sommer (Eds.), *Handbook of post-traumatic therapy, a practical guide to intervention, treatment, and research* (pp. 474–491). Santa Barbara, CA: Greenwood Publishing.

Bloom, S. L. (1997). *Creating sanctuary: Toward the evolution of sane societies*. New York, NY: Routledge.

Bloom, S. L. (2000). Our hearts and our hopes are turned to peace: Origins of the ISTSS. In A. Shalev, R. Yehuda, & A. S. McFarlane (Eds.), *International handbook of human response trauma* (pp. 27–50). New York, NY: Plenum Press.

Bloom, S. L. (2013). *Creating sanctuary: Toward the evolution of sane societies* (2nd ed.). New York, NY: Routledge.

Bloom, S. L. (2017). Encountering trauma, countertrauma, and countering trauma. In R. B. Gartner (Ed.), *Trauma and countertrauma, resilience and counterresilience* (pp. 28–44). London, UK: Routledge.

Bloom, S. L., Bennington-Davis, M., Farragher, B., McCorkle, D., Nice-Martini, K., & Wellbank, K. (2003). Multiple opportunities for creating sanctuary. *Psychiatric Quarterly, 74*(2), 173–190.

Bloom, S. L., & Reichert, M. (1998). *Bearing witness: Trauma and collective responsibility.* Binghamton, NY: Haworth Press.

Burrow, T. (1926). Insanity a social problem. *American Journal of Sociology, 32*(1), 80–87.

Burrow, T. (1927). *The social basis of consciousness: A study in organic psychology based upon a synthetic and societal concept of the neuroses.* New York, NY: Harcourt, Brace & Company.

Caplan, G. (Ed.). (1961). *Prevention of mental disorders in children.* New York, NY: Basic Books.

Caplan, G. (1964). *Principles of preventive psychiatry.* New York, NY: Basic Books.

Capra, F. (2002). *The hidden connection: A science for sustainable living.* New York, NY: HarperCollins.

Capra, F., & Luisi, P. L. (2014). *The systems view of life: A unifying vision.* New York, NY: Cambridge University Press.

Cooper, D. (2007). *Psychiatry and anti-psychiatry.* Abingdon, Oxon: Routledge.

Costa, R. (2012). *The watchman's rattle: A radical new theory of collapse.* New York, NY: Vanguard Press.

Danieli, Y. (1997). International handbook of multigenerational legacies of trauma. *PTSD Research Quarterly, 8*(1), 1–6.

Donnelly, J. (2013). *Universal human rights in theory and practice* (3rd ed.). Ithaca, NY: Cornell University Press.

Figley, C. (Ed.). (1985). *Trauma and its wake (Vol. I): The study and treatment of post-traumatic stress disorder.* New York, NY: Brunner/Mazel.

Figley, C. (Ed.). (1986). *Trauma and its wake (Vol. II): Traumatic stress theory, research, and treatment.* New York, NY: Brunner/Mazel.

Frances, A. (2014). *Saving normal: An insider's revolt against out-of-control psychiatric diagnosis, DSM-5, big pharma, and the medicalization of ordinary life.* New York, NY: William Morrow.

Freyd, J. J. (1996). *Betrayal trauma: The logic of forgetting childhood abuse.* Cambridge, MA: Harvard University Press.

Fromm, E. (1955). *The sane society.* Greenwich, CT: Fawcett Publications.

Goffman, E. (1961). *Asylums: Essays on the social situation of mental patients and other inmates.* New York, NY: Anchor Books.

Gold, S. N., Cook, J. M., & Dalenberg, C. J. (2017). Looking ahead: A vision for the future. In S. N. Gold (Ed.), *APA handbook of trauma psychology* (pp. 565–575). Washington, DC: American Psychological Association.

Greenberg, G. (2013). *The book of woe: The DSM and the unmaking of psychiatry.* New York, NY: Penguin.

Grinspoon, D. (2016). *Earth in human hands: Shaping our planet's future.* New York, NY: Grand Central Publishing.

Grob, G. N. (1991). *From asylum to community: Mental health policy in modern America.* Princeton, NJ: Princeton University Press.

Grob, G. N. (2005). The transformation of mental health policy in twentieth-century America. In M. Gijswijt-Hofstra, H. Oosterhuis, J. Vijselaar, & H. Freeman (Eds.), *Psychiatric cultures compared* (pp. 141–161). Amsterdam, The Netherlands: Amsterdam University Press.

Hari, J. (2018). *Lost connections: Uncovering the real causes of depression—And the unexpected solutions.* New York, NY: Bloomsbury.

Harris, M., & Fallot, R. D. (Eds.). (2001). *Using trauma theory to design service systems.* San Francisco, CA: Jossey-Bass.

Healy, D. (2012). *Pharmageddon.* Berkeley, CA: University of California Press.

Herman, J. L. (1992). *Trauma and recovery.* New York, NY: Basic Books.

Horney, K. (1966). *New ways in psychoanalysis.* New York, NY: W. W. Norton.

Hunt, L. (2007). *Inventing human rights: A history.* New York, NY: W. W. Norton.

Ishay, M. R. (2008). *The history of human rights: From ancient times to the globalization era.* Berkeley, CA: University of California Press.

Joffe, J. M., & Albee, G. W. (1981a). Powerlessness and psychopathology. In J. M. Joffe & G. W. Albee (Eds.), *Prevention through political action and social change* (pp. 321–325). Hanover, NH: University Press of New England.

Joffe, J. M., & Albee, G. W. (Eds.). (1981b). *Prevention through political action and social change.* Hanover, NH: University Press of New England.

Jones, M. (1953). *The therapeutic community: A new treatment method in psychiatry.* New York, NY: Basic Books.

Jones, M. (1962). *Social psychiatry: In the community, in hospitals, and in prisons.* Springfield, IL: Charles C. Thomas.

Jones, M. (1968a). *Beyond the therapeutic community: Social learning and social psychiatry.* New Haven, CT: Yale University Press.

Jones, M. (1968b). *Social psychiatry in practice.* Middlesex, UK: Penguin.

Kennard, D. (1983). *An introduction to therapeutic communities.* London, UK: Routledge & Kegan Paul.

Kennard, D. (1998). *An introduction to therapeutic communities.* London, UK: Jessica Kingsley Publishers.

Kennard, D. (2004). The therapeutic community as an adaptable treatment modality across different settings. *Psychiatric Quarterly, 75*(3), 295–307.

Kuhn, T. (1970). *The structure of scientific revolutions* (2nd ed.). Chicago, IL: University of Chicago Press.

Lamb, S. D. (2014). *Pathologist of the mind: Adolf Meyer and the origins of American psychiatry.* Baltimore, MD: Johns Hopkins Press.

Lamb, H. R., & Zusman, J. (1979). Primary prevention in perspective. *American Journal of Psychiatry, 136*(1), 12–17.

Lamb, H. R., & Zusman, J. (1982). The seductiveness of primary prevention. *New Directions for Mental Health Services, 1982*(13), 19–30.

Laszlo, E. (2008). *Quantum shift in the global brain: How the new scientific reality can change us and our world.* Rochester, VT: Inner Traditions.

Lief, A., & Meyer, A. (1948). A science of man. In A. Lief & A. Meyer (Eds.), *The commonsense psychiatry of Dr. Adolf Meyer: Fifty-two selected papers* (pp. 537–636). New York, NY: McGraw-Hill Book Company.

Lifton, R. J. (1961). *History and human survival: Essays on the young and old, survivors and the dead, peace and war, and on contemporary psychohistory.* New York, NY: Vintage Books.

Lifton, R. J. (1963). *Thought reform and the psychology of totalism: A study of brainwashing in China.* New York, NY: W.W. Norton.

Lifton, R. J. (1967). *Death in life: Survivors of Hiroshima.* New York, NY: Basic Books.

Lifton, R. J. (1973). *Home from the war: Vietnam veterans neither victims nor executioners.* New York, NY: Basic Books.

Lifton, R. J. (1986). *The Nazi doctors.* New York, NY: Basic Books.

Lifton, R. J. (1987). *The future of immortality and other essays for a nuclear age.* New York, NY: Basic Books.

Lifton, R. J. (1993). *The protean self: Human resilience in an age of fragmentation.* New York, NY: Basic Books.

Luhrmann, T. (2000). *Of two minds: The growing disorder in American psychiatry.* New York, NY: Alfred A. Knopf.

Marmor, J. (1983). Systems thinking in psychiatry: Some theoretical and clinical implications. *American Journal of Psychiatry, 140*(7), 833–838.

Moloney, J. C. (1949). *The magic cloak: A contribution to the psychology of authoritarianism.* Wakefield, MA: Montrose Press.

Moyn, S. (2012). *The last utopia.* Cambridge, MA: Harvard University Press.

Nightingale, E. O., & Stover, E. (1985). *The breaking of bodies and minds: Torture, psychiatric abuse, and the health professions.* New York, NY: Freeman.

Norton, K., & Bloom, S. L. (2004). The art and challenges of long-term and short-term democratic therapeutic communities. *Psychiatric Quarterly, 75*(3), 249–261.

Ørner, R. J. (2013). ESTSS at 20 years: "A phoenix gently rising from a lava flow of European trauma". *European Journal of Psychotraumatology, 4*(1), 1–4. https://doi.org/10.3402/ejpt.v4i0.21306.

Psychiatry and human rights abuses. (2004). *Psychiatric Times, 20*(11). Retrieved from http://www.psychiatrictimes.com/forensic-psychiatry/psychiatry-and-human-rights-abuses.

Sheth, H. C. (2009). Deinstitutionalization or disowning responsibility. *International Journal of Psychosocial Rehabilitation, 13*(2), 11–20.

Southard, E. E., & Jarrett, M. C. (1922). *The kingdom of evils.* New York, NY: Macmillan.

Sussman, R. W. (2014, November 8). There is no such thing as race. *Newsweek.* Retrieved from https://www.newsweek.com/there-no-such-thing-race-283123.

Szasz, T. S. (1974). *The myth of mental illness: Foundations of a theory of personal conduct.* New York, NY: Harper & Row.

Tucker, G., & Maxmen, J. (1973). The practice of hospital psychiatry: A formulation. *American Journal of Psychiatry, 130,* 887–891.

Ullman, M. (1969). A unifying concept linking therapeutic and community process. In W. Gray, R. J. Duhl, & N. D. Rizzo (Eds.), *General systems theory and psychiatry* (pp. 253–266). Boston, MA: Little, Brown.

United Nations. (1948). *Universal Declaration of Human Rights.* Retrieved from http://www.un.org/en/universal-declaration-human-rights/.

Van Cleef, J. L. (2008). *The palimpsest of human rights: A choral text-weaving comprised of simultaneously chanted paraphrases from Henry David Thoreau, Mohandas K. Gandhi, and Martin Luther King.* Madison, NJ: Spirit Song Text Publications.

van der Kolk, B. A., Weisaeth, L., & van der Hart, O. (1996). History of trauma in psychiatry. In B. A. van der Kolk, A. C. McFarlane, & L. Weisaeth (Eds.), *Traumatic stress: The effects of overwhelming experience on mind, body and society* (pp. 47–74). New York, NY: Guilford Press.

Von Bertalanffy, L. (1974). General systems theory and psychiatry. In S. Arieti (Ed.), *American handbook of psychiatry* (Vol. I, pp. 1095–1117). New York, NY: Basic Books.

Whitaker, R. (2010). *Anatomy of an epidemic: Magic bullets, psychiatric drugs, and the astonishing rise of mental illness in America.* New York, NY: Crown Publishing.

Whitaker, R., & Cosgrove, L. (2015). *Psychiatry under the influence: Institutional corruption, social injury, and prescriptions for reform.* New York, NY: Palgrave Macmillan.

Wilmer, H. (1958). *Social psychiatry in action: A therapeutic community.* Springfield, IL: Charles C. Thomas.

Wilmer, H. (1964). A living group experiment at San Quentin prison. *Corrective Psychiatry and Journal of Social Therapy, 10,* 6–15.

Witenberg, E. G. (1974). American neo-Freudian schools: A. The interpersonal and cultural approach. In S. Arieti (Ed.), *American handbook of psychiatry* (2nd ed., Vol. I, pp. 843–861). New York, NY: Basic Books.

# Index

CPI Antony Rowe
Eastbourne, UK
January 27, 2020